IC Op-Amp Cookbook

Second Edition

by
Walter G. Jung

Howard W. Sams & Co., Inc.
4300 WEST 62ND ST. INDIANAPOLIS, INDIANA 46268 USA

Preface

The preface to the first edition is generally totally applicable to the new edition as well. However, in addition to the basic intent of the first edition, the following changes highlight the second edition.

Retaining the basic style and format of the first edition, the second edition is greatly expanded in terms of device coverage, in keeping with state-of-the-art advancements. The introductory sections of the book reflect this, outlining a wide gamut of bipolar and FET op-amp devices, of various performance capabilities, in both single and multiple formats. Although the proliferation of devices prevents widespread detail, the numerous charts of this section facilitate selection of an appropriate device.

The applications section of the book is revised somewhat in chapter format, but expanded considerably in terms of the range of applications. Including Chapters 4 through 10, topical headings are voltage and current regulators, signal processing, log and multiplier techniques, amplifier techniques, comparators, integrators and differentiators, and signal generation. The applications discussed are updated both in terms of their range and scope, and also in terms of the appropriate applicable devices, reflecting the latest technology.

First edition sections on "Audio" and "Unique Devices" have been expanded into separate stand-alone texts so that greater emphasis might be placed on more general uses within this book.

The second edition concludes with an appendix that details part-number breakdowns for various manufacturers and source information and gives data sheets for a selected variety of devices.

WALTER G. JUNG

Preface to First Edition

At the time this book was conceived, several texts and handbooks concerning operational amplifiers had already been published. Indeed, many of them are well accepted, and the reader will find them referenced at appropriate points within this one. No attempt is made to detract from these previous efforts; however, it can be said that none addresses itself specifically and wholly to the IC op amp, with an in-depth discussion of applications for specific standard devices. Therein lies the philosophy behind this book and why it is intended to be an appropriate complement to the already existing literature.

Depending on one's particular background, working environment, etc., we each tend to take a slightly different approach to a design problem. There are, however, certain ground rules that the greatest percentage of people will follow in arriving at solutions to these problems. In the use of operational amplifiers, the trend has been toward the IC op amp, and among the numerous types available, there are definite standards that fulfill the greatest percentage of needs. Recognizing the inherent economy and widespread appeal of the IC op amp, this book attempts to address the considerations in applying it with maximum effectiveness in a wide variety of circuits. The name chosen, *IC Op-Amp Cookbook,* is intended to convey this concept. But, as will be seen, the book is more than just a "cookbook"; it involves general applications considerations as well as a substantial amount of theory to support the applications illustrated.

Some insight into the rationale behind the format of the book is helpful in assessing its value to the individual reader. If one is to undertake the task of discussing the uses of IC op amps, there are certain general requirements that must be met. Two of the biggest considerations are style and content—decide what to say and how best to say it. Before getting into the actual contents, a word about the style chosen is appropriate. "Style," as referred to here, is not style in a grammatical sense but is the level on which the book is written. The author firmly believes that practical writing is more useful than pure theory to greater numbers of people. Thus, while there is theory in this book, the main emphasis is on what the theory means in practical applications. The real world of the IC op amp is much more concerned with the details of making a device work as intended rather than making equations balance. So the format chosen is one of "down-to-earth" discussions as viewed from the *user's* standpoint. This is intended to appeal to users on various levels, from student to technician to design engineer, and hopefully to satisfy the needs of all. While a universally appealing book is perhaps somewhat unrealistic, the broadness of applicability can certainly be optimized by keeping everything as clear and understandable as possible while discussing problems meaningful to all users.

The "content" of this book also takes on the prerequisite of broad appeal. Thus, obvious inclusions are such op-amp standards as the 709, 101, and 741. But the scope of the book is not limited to general-purpose devices; it also encompasses other, more-specialized devices—those that are optimized for certain specific performance parameters. The specialized types chosen here are also standard type numbers, as evidenced by broad industry acceptance.

With the complement of devices chosen, a wide range of applications is thus possible, with optimized performance available in terms of virtually any specific criterion. This factor should be of interest to the designer seeking high performance by using op amps. Throughout the book, the discussions are directed to indicate the optimum device for a specific use, and considerations for its application, such as speed, accuracy, dc stability, power consumption, and other performance parameters, are covered.

Given this general format, there is one additional consideration that is generally applicable to circuitry discussions. An applications book may be used in various degrees by different owners. A person new to a particular technique may want to study circuits and theory in some detail. For this type of use, the supportive theoretical background is intended, and appropriate references are listed for further reading in most instances. Others may desire a circuit to fulfill a certain function, and will make minimal use of the text. For this type of use, well-annotated schematics are provided, replete with values and suggestions for modifications if desired. Wherever possible, the pertinent design equations, which summarize the function of the circuit, are also provided.

WALTER G. JUNG

Acknowledgments

No undertaking of this nature could be successful without aid from various sources. The author was most fortunate during the writing of both editions of this book to have the benefit of technical inputs from many industry sources. In the first edition, thanks were extended to Bob Dobkin, Carl Nelson, and Tom Frederiksen of National Semiconductor; to Bob Ricks of Fairchild Semiconductor; to Don Kesner and Don Aldridge of Motorola Semiconductor; to Don Jones of Harris Semiconductor; to Hal Wittlinger of RCA; to Werner Hoeft of Signetics; and to Bob Jones of AAI Corporation.

For this second edition, the author would like to reiterate those thanks, for much of the material which arose from those inputs still remains. In addition, thanks are now also extended to Lew Counts, Jeff Riskin, and Dan Sheingold of Analog Devices; Dennis Haynes of Burr-Brown; Dick Whitehead of Harris Semiconductor; Bob Pease, Nello Sevastopoulos, and Jim Solomon of National Semiconductor; George Erdi, Shelby Givens, and Donn Soderquist of Precision Monolithics; Harry Gill and Jim Schmoock of Raytheon Semiconductor; Guy Caputo of Signetics; and Dale Pippenger of Texas Instruments.

The author was also fortunate to obtain permission to use portions of manufacturers' technical literature. In this the assistance of the following companies is gratefully acknowledged: Analog Devices, Inc., Fairchild Semiconductor, Harris Semiconductor, Intersil, Inc., Motorola Semiconductor Products, Inc., National Semiconductor Corp., Precision Monolithics, Inc., Raytheon Semiconductor, RCA Solid State Division, Signetics Corp., and Texas Instruments, Inc.

Finally, and most certainly not least, my sincere thanks to an overworked wife, Anne, for enduring the punishment of literally thousands of pages of "hieroglyphics" and for transforming them into a manuscript. Thanks also go to research assistants, Jeannie and Mark.

W. G. J.

To Anne, with my love and appreciation

Contents

Part I—Introducing the IC Op Amp

CHAPTER 1

CHAPTER 2

CHAPTER 3

Part II—Op-Amp Applications

CHAPTER 4

CHAPTER 5

CHAPTER 6

CHAPTER 7

CHAPTER 8

CHAPTER 9

CHAPTER 10

Part III–Appendix

Introduction and
Historical Background

Before discussing modern operational amplifiers, we should first review the basics of what an operational amplifier (op amp) is. We will do this in two stages: (1) discuss what an op amp is in the *ideal* sense, and (2) discuss what an op amp *actually* is within the limitations of integrated circuits.

In many applications, the differences between ideal and actual (nonideal) operation will be so small that for all practical purposes they will be negligible. In other applications, the differences will be slight, yet still measurable. Often the overall performance can be enhanced by careful selection of the type of device and by optimizing the parameters that are under our control. This requires an understanding of both the basic concepts of op amps and the specific devices now available.

The original concept of the operational amplifier came from the field of analog computers, where operational techniques were used as early as the 1940s. The name *operational amplifier* derives from the concept of an extremely high gain, differential-input dc amplifier, the operating characteristics of which were determined by the feedback elements used with it. By changing the types and arrangement of the feedback elements, different analog *operations* could be implemented; to a large degree, the overall circuit characteristics were determined *only* by these feedback elements. Thus, the same amplifier was able to perform a variety of operations, and the gradual development of operational amplifiers grew into the beginning of a new era in circuit design concepts.

Early operational amplifiers used the basic hardware of that era—the vacuum tube. Significantly widespread use of op amps did not really begin until the 1960s, when solid-state techniques were applied to op-amp circuit design. This was first evidenced by solid-state op-amp modules, which realized the internal circuitry of the op amp in a discrete solid-state design. Then, in the mid 1960s, the first IC op amps were introduced. Within a few years, IC op amps became a standard design tool encompassing applications far beyond the original scope of analog computer circuits.

With the mass-production capabilities of IC manufacturing techniques, IC op amps became available in large volume, which, in turn, lowered their cost. Today, a general-purpose IC op amp having a gain of 100 dB, an input-offset voltage of 1.0 mV, an input current of 100 nA, and a bandwidth of 1.0 MHz can be purchased for less than a dollar. The amplifier, which was a system comprised of many discrete components in the early days, has evolved into a discrete component itself—a reality that has changed the entire picture of linear circuit design.

With this highly sophisticated parcel of gain available at passive-component prices, discrete active-component designs have become a waste of time and money for most dc and low-frequency applications. Clearly, the IC op amp has redefined the "ground rules" for electronic circuits by placing the emphasis of circuit design more on a systems basis. Intelligent application of these "components that are systems" is what we must now concern ourselves with in order to be ready for the challenges of the future.

I

Introducing the IC Op Amp

ONE

Op-Amp Basics

1.1 THE IDEAL OP AMP

The basic fundamentals of the ideal operational amplifier are relatively straightforward. Perhaps the best approach to understanding the ideal op amp is to forget any conventional thinking about amplifier components—transistors, tubes, or whatever. Instead, think only in general terms and consider the amplifier in block form with its input and output terminals. We will then discuss the amplifier in this *ideal* sense and disregard what is inside the block.

Such an idealized amplifier is shown in Fig. 1-1. This amplifier is a direct-coupled device with differential inputs and a single-ended output. The amplifier responds only to the difference voltage between the two input terminals, not to their common potential. A positive-going signal at the inverting (−) input produces a negative-going signal at the output, whereas the same signal at the noninverting (+) input produces a positive-going output. With a differential-input voltage, E_{in}, the output voltage, E_o, will be $A_{vo}E_{in}$, where A_{vo} is the gain of the amplifier. Both input terminals of the amplifier will always be used, regardless of the application. The output signal is single-ended and is referred to ground; thus, bipolar (±) power supplies are used.

With these functions of the input and the output in mind, we can now define the ideal properties of this amplifier, which are:

1. The voltage gain is infinite—$A_{vo} = \infty$.
2. The input resistance is infinite—$r_{in} = \infty$.
3. The output resistance is zero—$r_o = 0$.
4. The bandwidth is infinite—$BW = \infty$.
5. There is zero input offset voltage—$E_o = 0$ if $E_{in} = 0$.

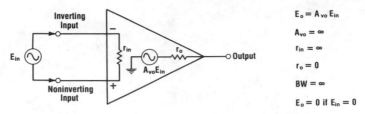

Fig. 1-1. Equivalent circuit for ideal operational amplifier.

From these ideal characteristics we can deduce two very important additional properties of the operational amplifier. Since the voltage gain is infinite, any output signal developed will be the result of an infinitesimally small input signal. Thus, in essence:

1. *The differential-input voltage is zero.*

Also, if the input resistance is infinite,

2. *There is no current flow into either input terminal.*

These two properties may be regarded as *axioms,* and they will be used repeatedly in op-amp circuit analysis and design. Once these properties are understood, the operation of virtually any op-amp circuit can be logically deduced. The following discussions of basic op-amp circuit configurations will serve to illustrate this point.

1.1.1 Basic Op-Amp Configurations

Operational amplifiers can be connected in two basic amplifying circuits: (1) the *inverting* and (2) the *noninverting* configurations. Virtually all other op-amp circuits are based in some manner on these two basic configurations. In addition, there are closely related variations on the two basic circuits, plus another basic circuit which is a combination of the first two—the *differential amplifier.*

The Inverting Amplifier

Fig. 1-2 illustrates the first basic op-amp configuration—the inverting amplifier. In this circuit, the $(+)$ input is grounded and the signal is applied to the $(-)$ input through R_{in}, with feedback returned from the output through R_f. By applying the ideal op-amp properties previously stated, the distinguishing features of this circuit may be analyzed as follows:

Since the amplifier has infinite gain, it will develop its output voltage, E_o, with zero input voltage. Since the differential input to A is E_s, $E_s = 0$. If E_s is zero, then the full input voltage, E_{in}, must appear across R_{in}, making the current in R_{in}

$$I_{in} = \frac{E_{in}}{R_{in}}$$

Summing Point (SP)

$I_s = 0$, $E_s = 0$, $\therefore$ SP is at zero potential or a virtual ground.

Then, $I_{in} = \dfrac{E_{in}}{R_{in}}$.

Since $I_s = 0$, $I_f = I_{in}$,

and $I_f = \dfrac{-E_o}{R_f}$ (due to inversion),

then $\dfrac{E_{in}}{R_{in}} = \dfrac{-E_o}{R_f}$.

Gain $= \dfrac{E_o}{E_{in}} = \dfrac{-R_f}{R_{in}}$.

Summary of Inverting Amplifier Characteristics:

(1) Gain $= \dfrac{-R_f}{R_{in}}$, unlimited in range (R_f may be 0 for 0 gain).

(2) Input Impedance $= R_{in}$.

(3) $I_f = I_{in}$, regardless of R_f.

(4) Summing point is a virtual ground at the same potential as (+) input.

Fig. 1-2. The op-amp inverting amplifier configuration.

Also, since $I_s = 0$ due to infinite input impedance, the input current, I_{in}, must also flow in R_f; thus,

$$I_f = I_{in}$$

The output voltage, E_o, appears across R_f and is negative due to a sign inversion in the amplifier. Stating I_f in terms of E_o and R_f, then,

$$I_f = \frac{-E_o}{R_f}$$

Since I_{in} and I_f are equal, we may state

$$\frac{E_{in}}{R_{in}} = \frac{-E_o}{R_f}$$

This equality may be restated in terms of gain as

$$\frac{E_o}{E_{in}} = \frac{-R_f}{R_{in}}$$

which is, in fact, the characteristic gain equation for the ideal inverting amplifier.

There are additional features of the inverting amplifier which should be noted. The gain can be varied by adjusting either R_f or R_{in}. If R_f is varied from zero to infinity, the gain will also vary from zero to infinity since it is directly proportional to R_f. The input impedance is equal to R_{in}, and E_{in} and R_{in} alone determine I_{in}. Thus, $I_f = I_{in}$ for any value of R_f.

The input to the amplifier, or junction of the input and feedback signals, is a node of zero voltage, regardless of the magnitude of I_{in}. Thus, the junction is a *virtual ground,* a point that will always be at the same potential as the (+) input. Since the input and output signals sum at this junction, it is also known as a *summing point.* This final characteristic leads to a third basic op-amp axiom, which applies to closed-loop operation:

3. *With the loop closed, the* (−) *input will be driven to the potential of the* (+) *or reference input.*

This property may or may not have been obvious already from the theory of zero differential input voltage. It is, however, very helpful in understanding op-amp circuitry to regard the (+) input as a reference terminal which will command the level that *both* inputs assume. Thus, this voltage may be ground (as shown) or any desired potential.

The Noninverting Amplifier

The second basic configuration of the ideal op amp is the noninverting amplifier, shown in Fig. 1-3. This circuit clearly illustrates the validity of Axiom 3. In this circuit, voltage E_{in} is applied to the (+) input, and a fraction of the output signal, E_o, is applied to the (−) input from the R_f-R_{in} voltage divider. Since no input current flows into either input terminal, and since $E_s = 0$, the voltage E_{in}' is equal to E_{in}. Inasmuch as

$$I_{in} = \frac{E_{in}}{R_{in}}$$

$E_s = 0$

$I_s = 0$

$I_R = 0$

$I_{in} = \dfrac{E_{in}'}{R_{in}}$

$E_{in}' = E_{in}$

then, $I_{in} = \dfrac{E_{in}}{R_{in}}$

$I_f = I_{in}$

$E_o = I_f (R_{in} + R_f)$

$E_o = I_{in}(R_{in} + R_f)$

and $E_o = \dfrac{E_{in}}{R_{in}} (R_{in} + R_f)$

then, Gain $= \dfrac{E_o}{E_{in}} = \dfrac{R_{in} + R_f}{R_{in}}$

Summary of Noninverting Amplifier Characteristics:

(1) Gain $= \dfrac{R_{in} + R_f}{R_{in}}$, lower limit of unity gain where $R_{in} = \infty$, or $R_f = 0$.

(2) Input Impedance $= \infty$.

(3) $I_f = I_{in}$, regardless of R_f.

Fig. 1-3. The op-amp noninverting amplifier configuration.

then it is also true that

$$I_{in} = \frac{E_{in}'}{R_{in}}$$

Also, since

$$I_f = I_{in}$$

then

$$E_o = I_f (R_{in} + R_f)$$

and

$$E_o = I_{in} (R_{in} + R_f)$$

Substituting,

$$E_o = \frac{E_{in}}{R_{in}} (R_{in} + R_f)$$

Then, in terms of gain

$$\frac{E_o}{E_{in}} = \frac{R_{in} + R_f}{R_{in}}$$

which is the characteristic gain equation for the ideal noninverting amplifier.

Additional characteristics of this configuration can also be deduced. The lower limit of gain occurs when $R_f = 0$, which yields a gain of unity. In the inverting amplifier, current I_{in} always determines I_f, which is independent of R_f. (This is also true in the noninverting amplifier.) Thus, R_f may be used as a linear gain control, capable of increasing gain from a minimum of unity to a maximum of infinity. The input impedance is infinite, since an ideal amplifier is assumed.

Configurations Based on the Inverting and Noninverting Circuits

The Differential Amplifier—A third op-amp configuration, known as the differential amplifier, is a combination of the two previous configurations. Although it is based on the other two circuits, the differential amplifier has unique characteristics of its own. This circuit, shown in Fig. 1-4, has signals applied to both input terminals and uses the natural differential amplification of the op amp.

The circuit may be understood by first considering the two signal inputs separately, then in combination. As before, $E_s = 0$, $I_s = 0$, and $I_R = 0$. In addition, $R_f' = R_f$ and $R_{in}' = R_{in}$.

The output voltage due to E_{in_1} may be termed E_{o_1}. Using the gain equation for the noninverting circuit, and adding the effect of divider R_{in}-R_f, the output, E_{o_1}, will be

$$E_{o_1} = E_{in_1}\left(\frac{R_f}{R_{in} + R_f}\right)\left(\frac{R_{in}' + R_f'}{R_{in}'}\right)$$

Cancelling equal terms and substituting

$$E_{o_1} = E_{in_1}\left(\frac{R_f}{R_{in}}\right)$$

which is the output due to E_{in_1}.

The output due to E_{in_2} is termed E_{o_2}. Using the gain equation for the inverting circuit, output E_{o_2} will be

$$E_{o_2} = -E_{in_2}\left(\frac{R_f'}{R_{in}'}\right)$$

$$= -E_{in_2}\left(\frac{R_f}{R_{in}}\right)$$

Since the combined output, E_o, will be equal to the sum of E_{o_1} and E_{o_2}, we may write

$$E_o = E_{in_1}\left(\frac{R_f}{R_{in}}\right) + \left[-E_{in_2}\left(\frac{R_f}{R_{in}}\right)\right]$$

By regrouping

$$E_o = \left(E_{in_1} - E_{in_2}\right)\left(\frac{R_f}{R_{in}}\right)$$

In terms of gain this is

$$\frac{E_o}{E_{in_1} - E_{in_2}} = \frac{R_f}{R_{in}}$$

which is the gain of the stage for differential-mode signals.

This configuration is unique because it can reject a signal common to both inputs. This is due to the property of zero differential input voltage, which is explained as follows:

In the case of identical signals at E_{in_1} and E_{in_2}, the analysis is straightforward. E_{in_1} will be divided by R_{in} and R_f to a smaller voltage, E_{cm_1}, across R_f. Because of infinite amplifier gain and zero differential input voltage, an equal voltage (E_{cm_2}) must appear at SP. Since the network R_{in}'-R_f' is identical to R_{in}-R_f, and since the same voltage is applied to both inputs, it follows that E_o must be at zero potential to maintain E_{cm_2} identical to E_{cm_1}; E_o will be at the same potential as the bottom of R_f, which is, in fact, ground potential. This very useful property of the differential amplifier can be used to discriminate against undesirable common-mode noise components while amplifying signals that appear differentially. If the ratio

$$\frac{R_f'}{R_{in}'}$$

is identical to

$$\frac{R_f}{R_{in}}$$

the gain for common-mode signals is zero since, by definition, the amplifier has no gain for equal signals applied to both inputs.

The two input impedances of the stage are unequal. For the $(+)$ input, the input impedance is $R_{in} + R_f$. The impedance at the $(-)$

Summary of Differential Amplifier Characteristics:

(1) Differential-Mode Gain $(E_{in_1} \neq E_{in_2})$:

$$\frac{E_o}{E_{in_1} - E_{in_2}} = \frac{R_f}{R_{in}}.$$

(2) Common-Mode Gain $(E_{in_1} \equiv E_{in_2})$:

When,

$$\frac{R_f}{R_{in}} \equiv \frac{R_f'}{R_{in}'}, \cdot = 0.$$

When,

$$\frac{R_f}{R_{in}} \neq \frac{R_f'}{R_{in}'}, = \frac{R_f R_{in}' - R_f' R_{in}}{R_{in}' R_{in} + R_{in}' R_f}.$$

In terms of resistor match (worst case),

$$= 4\delta \left(\frac{R_f}{R_{in} + R_f} \right),$$

where,

δ = fractional unbalance of resistors (1.0% = 0.01),

and,

R_{in} and R_f are the nominal values.

(3) Input Impedances:

$(-)$ input $= R_{in}'$
$(+)$ input $= R_{in} + R_f$
differential $= R_{in} + R_{in}'$

$E_s = 0, \ I_s = 0, \ I_R = 0$
$R_f = R_f', \ R_{in} = R_{in}'$

Let output due to $E_{in_1} = E_{o_1}$,

then $E_{o_1} = E_{in_1} \left(\frac{R_f}{R_{in} + R_f} \right) \left(\frac{R_{in}' + R_f'}{R_{in}'} \right)$

$$= E_{in_1} \left(\frac{R_f}{R_{in}} \right)$$

Let output due to $E_{in_2} = E_{o_2}$,

then $E_{o_2} = -E_{in_2} \left(\frac{R_f'}{R_{in}'} \right) = -E_{in_2} \left(\frac{R_f}{R_{in}} \right)$

Total output $= E_o = E_{o_1} + E_{o_2}$

$$E_o = E_{in_1} \left(\frac{R_f}{R_{in}} \right) + \left[-E_{in_2} \left(\frac{R_f}{R_{in}} \right) \right]$$

$$= \left(E_{in_1} - E_{in_2} \right) \frac{R_f}{R_{in}}$$

$$\text{Gain} = \frac{E_o}{E_{in_1} - E_{in_2}} = \frac{R_f}{R_{in}}$$

Fig. 1-4. The op-amp differential amplifier configuration.

input is R_{in}'. The differential-input impedance (for a floating source) is the impedance between the inputs, or $R_{in} + R_{in}'$.

The Summing Inverter—By utilizing the virtual-ground characteristic of the inverting amplifier's summing point, a useful modification is realized—the summing inverter (see Fig. 1-5). In this circuit, as in the inverting amplifier, $E_s = 0$, $I_s = 0$, and $I_f = I_{in}$. However, in the summing inverter I_{in} is the algebraic sum of a number of inputs such as I_{in_1}, I_{in_2}, I_{in_3}, etc. Thus,

$$I_{in_1} = \frac{E_{in_1}}{R_{in_1}}, \; I_{in_2} = \frac{E_{in_2}}{R_{in_2}}, \; I_{in_3} = \frac{E_{in_3}}{R_{in_3}}$$

and

$$I_{in} = I_{in_1} + I_{in_2} + I_{in_3}, \; I_f = \frac{-E_o}{R_f}$$

therefore,

$$\frac{-E_o}{R_f} = I_{in_1} + I_{in_2} + I_{in_3}$$

Finally, substituting and regrouping gives

$$E_o = - \left[E_{in_1}\left(\frac{R_f}{R_{in_1}}\right) + E_{in_2}\left(\frac{R_f}{R_{in_2}}\right) + E_{in_3}\left(\frac{R_f}{R_{in_3}}\right) \right]$$

Summary of Summing-Inverter Characteristics:

(1) Gain (per channel) = $\dfrac{-R_f}{R_{in_1}}$, $\dfrac{-R_f}{R_{in_2}}$, $\dfrac{-R_f}{R_{in_3}}$, etc.

(2) R_f varies gain of all inputs; R_{in_1}, R_{in_2}, R_{in_3}, etc., vary individual gains.

(3) Composite output = $E_o = - \left[E_{in_1}\left(\frac{R_f}{R_{in_1}}\right) + E_{in_2}\left(\frac{R_f}{R_{in_2}}\right) + E_{in_3}\left(\frac{R_f}{R_{in_3}}\right) \right]$.

(4) Input impedance = R_{in_1}, R_{in_2}, R_{in_3}, etc.

Fig. 1-5. The op-amp summing inverter.

which states that the output voltage is the inverted algebraic sum of the input voltages scaled by R_f. Thus, the circuit may be said to be a *scaling adder*.

The overall gain of the circuit is set by R_f, which in this respect behaves as in the basic inverting amplifier. The gains of the individual channels are scaled independently by R_{in_1}, R_{in_2}, R_{in_3}, etc. Similarly, R_{in_1}, R_{in_2}, and R_{in_3} are the input impedances of the respective channels.

Another interesting characteristic of this configuration is the fact that linear signal mixing takes place at the summing point without interaction between inputs, since all signal sources feed into a virtual ground. The circuit can accommodate any number of inputs by adding additional input resistors at the summing point, such as R_{in_4}, R_{in_5}, etc.

Although the preceding circuits have been described in terms of input and feedback resistances, the resistors may be replaced by complex elements, and the basic op-amp axioms will still hold true. Two circuits that demonstrate this are further modifications of the inverting amplifier.

The Integrator—It has been shown that both basic op-amp configurations act to maintain the feedback current, I_f, at all times equal to I_{in}. A modification of the inverting amplifier which takes advantage of this characteristic is the integrator, shown in Fig. 1-6. An input voltage, E_{in}, is applied to R_{in}, thus developing current I_{in}. As in the basic inverter, $E_s = 0$, $I_s = 0$, and $I_f = I_{in}$. The feedback element in the integrator is a capacitor, C_f. Therefore, the constant current, I_f, in C_f builds a linear voltage ramp across C_f. The output voltage is thus an integral of the input current, which is forced to charge C_f by the feedback loop. The change in voltage across C_f is

$$-\Delta E_o = \frac{I_{in}\Delta t}{C_f}$$

which makes the output change per unit of time

$$\frac{\Delta E_o}{\Delta t} = \frac{-E_{in}}{R_{in}C_f}$$

As with the other inverting-amplifier configurations, the input impedance is simply R_{in}.

The Differentiator—A second modification of the inverting amplifier, which also uses the current in a capacitor to advantage, is the differentiator, shown in Fig. 1-7. In this circuit, the positions of R and C are reversed from those in the integrator, placing the capacitive element in the input network. Thus, the input current is made to be proportional to the rate of change of the input voltage

$$E_s = 0, \ I_s = 0, \ I_{in} = \frac{E_{in}}{R_{in}}, \ I_f = I_{in}$$

$$-\Delta E_o = \frac{I_{in} \Delta t}{C_f}$$

$$\frac{\Delta E_o}{\Delta t} = \frac{-E_{in}}{R_{in} C_f}$$

Summary of Integrator Characteristics:

(1) Circuit integrates input current, thus

$$\frac{\Delta E_o}{\Delta t} = \frac{-E_{in}}{R_{in} C_f}.$$

(2) Input impedance $= R_{in}$.

Fig. 1-6. The op-amp integrator.

$$I_{in} = \frac{\Delta E_{in} C_{in}}{\Delta t}$$

Again

$$I_f = I_{in}$$

and since

$$-E_o = I_f R_f$$
$$E_o = -I_f R_f$$

Substitution gives

$$E_o = \frac{-\Delta E_{in} R_f C_{in}}{\Delta t}$$

$$E_s = 0, \ I_s = 0, I_{in} = \frac{\Delta E_{in} C_{in}}{\Delta t}, \ I_f = I_{in}$$

$$-E_o = I_f R_f, \ E_o = -I_f R_f$$

$$E_o = \frac{-\Delta E_{in} R_f C_{in}}{\Delta t}$$

Summary of Differentiator Characteristics:

(1) Circuit responds to the rate of change of input voltage E_{in}, thus

$$E_o = \frac{-\Delta E_{in} R_f C_{in}}{\Delta t}$$

Fig. 1-7. The op-amp differentiator.

$E_s = 0$, $I_s = 0$, $I_R = 0$

$\therefore E_o = E_{in}$

Summary of Voltage-Follower Characteristics:

(1) Gain = 1.

(2) Input impedance = ∞.

Fig. 1-8. The op-amp voltage follower.

The Voltage Follower—A special modification of the noninverting amplifier is the unity-gain stage shown in Fig. 1-8. In this circuit, R_{in} has increased to infinity, R_f is zero, and the feedback is 100%. E_o is then exactly equal to E_{in}, since $E_s = 0$. The circuit is known as a "voltage follower" since the output is a unity-gain, in-phase replica of the input voltage. The input impedance of this stage is also infinite.

Summary of the Basic Amplifier Configurations and Their Characteristics

All of the circuit characteristics that have been described are important because they are a basis for the entire foundation of op-amp circuit technology. The five basic criteria that describe the ideal amplifier are fundamental, and from these evolve the three main axioms of op-amp theory, which bear repeating:

1. *The differential-input voltage is zero.*
2. *There is no current flow into either input terminal.*
3. *With the loop closed, the (−) input will be driven to the potential of the (+) or reference input.*

These three axioms have been illustrated in all of the basic circuits and their variations. In the inverting configuration, the concepts of zero input current and zero differential input voltage give rise to the concepts of the summing point and the virtual ground, where the inverting input is held by feedback to the same potential as the grounded noninverting input. Using the concept of the noninverting input as a reference terminal, the noninverting amplifier and voltage follower illustrate how an input voltage is indirectly scaled through negative feedback to the inverting input, which is forced to follow at an identical potential. The full differential configuration combines these concepts, illustrating the ideal of simultaneous differential amplification and common-mode signal rejection. The variations of the inverter amplify its principles. In all these circuits, we have also seen how the performance is determined solely by components connected externally to the amplifier.

At this point, we have defined the op-amp in an ideal sense and have examined its basic circuit configurations. With one further definition—the symbology of the device—we will move to the real world of practical devices and examine their departures from the ideal and how to cope with them.

1.1.2 The Standard Op-Amp Schematic Symbol and Its Use

One additional basic tool of the op amp is its schematic symbol. This is fundamental, for a correctly drawn schematic transmits a great deal of knowledge about the workings of a circuit. The preferred op-amp symbol is illustrated with annotations in Fig. 1-9.

The basic symbol is the triangle, which is generally understood to imply amplification. The inputs are at the base of the triangle, with the output at the apex. In accordance with normal signal-flow convention, the symbol is drawn with the apex (output) to the right, but this may be altered if necessary for clarification of other circuit details.

The two inputs are usually drawn as shown with the noninverting (+) input the lower of the two. Exceptions to this rule occur in special circumstances where it would be awkward to retain the standard arrangement. Furthermore, the two inputs are always clearly identified by (+) and (−) symbols, which are adjacent to their respective leads and are drawn within the body of the triangle.

Supply-voltage leads are preferably drawn extending above and below the triangle as shown. These may not be shown in all cases (in the interest of simplicity), but they are always implied. Gener-

Fig. 1-9. The standard op-amp schematic symbol.

ally, in sketches it is sufficient to use the 3-lead symbol to convey an intent, with power connections understood.

Finally, the type or part number of the device used is centered within the body of the triangle. If the circuit is a general one indicating any op amp, the symbol used is A (or A_1, A_2, etc.).

1.2 THE NONIDEAL OP AMP

So far we have examined the op-amp concept only in a general sense, assuming idealized parameters. In a real-world situation, the ideal amplifier does not exist. However, it is important to stress the idealized line of thinking because in many applications, the differences between ideal and actual are close to negligible. Furthermore, we should always be aware of how closely we actually approach "idealized" performance. We will now examine the factors that determine how small these differences are and learn how to control performance so as to minimize them. As might be expected, these errors arise due to departures from the ideal characteristics set forth in Section 1.1.

1.2.1 Errors Due to Finite Open-Loop Gain

A principal source of error in op-amp applications is the factor contributed by finite open-loop gain. General-purpose IC op amps have a typical dc open-loop gain close to 100 dB, which, while large, is certainly a long way from being infinite. Also, the actual gain figure will vary from unit to unit because of the normal production tolerances associated with IC manufacturing processes. In a given device, the open-loop gain will also vary to some degree with temperature, loading, and supply voltage. In addition to this, the open-loop gain of an op amp decreases with frequency because of the necessity for correcting the overall phase response to ensure stability under closed-loop conditions. As a result, a typical open-loop gain-versus-frequency plot looks something like Fig. 1-10. Thus, in reality, the open-loop gain characteristics of practical IC op amps are nonideal in two of the basic criteria: (1) the dc gain is not infinite and (2) the bandwidth is not infinite.

To express the error factor due to a finite open-loop gain, we must again examine the closed-loop inverting and noninverting configurations and define a few more parameters associated with each. Assume all other characteristics of the amplifier are ideal (for the moment) except for the finite gain, A_{vo}.

Fig. 1-11A illustrates an inverting amplifier which has a finite gain, A_{vo}. R_f and R_{in} are the feedback and input resistors, and the E_{in} generator is assumed to have zero source impedance. If we examine the path of the feedback signal from E_o, we note that it undergoes an

Fig. 1-10. Typical op-amp open-loop gain response.

attenuation due to the presence of R_f and R_{in}. If we term the attenuated signal that appears at SP as E_e, then E_e is related to E_o by

$$\frac{E_e}{E_o} = \frac{R_{in}}{R_{in} + R_f}$$

This introduces a new term, β, which is defined as the *feedback attenuation factor* and is expressed as

$$\beta = \frac{R_{in}}{R_{in} + R_f}$$

By definition, β is the ratio of the feedback signal to the output signal. It can reach a maximum of unity (or zero attenuation) under the condition of 100% feedback. The feedback divider, which determines β, takes into account the total attenuation between the amplifier output and the summing point. This includes frequency-dependent effects due to reactive elements (if any) and, in general, all attenuation. Therefore, to be precise, R_f and R_{in} of Fig. 1-11A symbolize the total equivalent feedback attenuation network. (This will be more evident as we examine other error sources.) The signal, E_e, is amplified by the open-loop gain of the amplifier (A_{vo}) and produces output voltage E_o.

At this point, we have traversed the complete path around the feedback loop—through the feedback network, through the amplifier, and back to the output—for reasons which may not yet be obvious. However, if we can momentarily regard the feedback path from E_o

with the amplifier disconnected, an interesting observation will ensue. The signal fed back from E_o is attenuated by β, then amplified by A_{vo}. Thus, the total gain of the loop is $A_{vo} \times \beta$, and this expression is known as *loop gain*. Thus,

$$\text{Loop Gain} = A_{vo}\beta$$

Loop gain is a measure of how closely an amplifying configuration approaches the ideal. If A_{vo} were really infinite, we would not be

$$\beta = \frac{R_{in}}{R_{in} + R_f} \qquad \text{Loop Gain} = A_{vo}\beta$$

$$\text{Signal Gain} = \frac{-R_f}{R_{in}} \left(\frac{1}{1 + (1/A_{vo}\beta)} \right)$$

$$\text{Noise Gain} = \frac{1}{\beta} = \frac{R_{in} + R_f}{R_{in}}$$

(A) Inverting configuration.

$$\beta = \frac{R_{in}}{R_{in} + R_f}$$

$$\text{Loop Gain} = A_{vo}\beta$$

$$\text{Signal Gain} = \frac{R_{in} + R_f}{R_{in}} \left(\frac{1}{1 + (1/A_{vo}\beta)} \right)$$

$$\text{Noise Gain} = \frac{1}{\beta} = \frac{R_{in} + R_f}{R_{in}}$$

(B) Noninverting configuration.

Fig. 1-11. Gain errors in inverting and noninverting configurations.

concerned with the total gain around the feedback loop. This may be intuitively appreciated by visualizing the effects of variations in either A_{vo} or β on the error signal, E_e. Ideally, E_e is zero due to infinite amplifier gain. Any increase of E_e from zero represents a deviation from the ideal. In practice, this can result from either a low A_{vo} or a small β, either of which minimizes their product—loop gain. We have now reached a point where we can relate this to the original ideal gain expression and write a new expression that gives an error factor caused by the finite gain, A_{vo}

$$A_v = \left(\frac{-R_f}{R_{in}}\right) \underbrace{\left(\frac{1}{1 + (1/A_{vo}\beta)}\right)}_{\substack{\text{Error} \\ \text{Multiplier}}}$$

$\underbrace{\phantom{A_v = \left(\frac{-R_f}{R_{in}}\right)}}_{\substack{\text{Ideal} \\ \text{Expression}}}$

This equation is separated into two parts to illustrate the modification of the ideal by $A_{vo}\beta$. As the right-hand term of the denominator of the error multiplier approaches zero, the error multiplier approaches unity until $A_{vo} = \infty$, the point at which the equation reduces to the ideal. Thus, the greater $A_{vo}\beta$ is, the closer the amplifier is to ideal performance. In practice, this means that either a greater A_{vo} or a greater β (more feedback) maximizes $A_{vo}\beta$. From this it is obvious that high-gain stages (which require a small β) require more open-loop gain to approach ideal performance.

To examine the effects of loop gain on the noninverting amplifier, we refer to Fig. 1-11B. Although the method of signal amplification is different in this configuration, the feedback path is identical to that of the inverter. Therefore, β is determined in exactly the same manner, and the same general considerations apply concerning $A_{vo}\beta$. There is, however, an additional gain-error term in the noninverting amplifier, which is due to the presence of a common-mode voltage, E_{cm}. In the inverting amplifier, there is no common-mode input voltage, since both inputs are effectively grounded. In a noninverting stage, the inputs see a common-mode voltage equal to the input voltage, or

$$E_{cm} = E_{in}$$

Since a real amplifier responds to common-mode voltages, this error source must be taken into account. The relationship between the common-mode voltage of an op amp and its common-mode error voltage is expressed as a ratio, termed the *common-mode rejection ratio* (CMRR). The existence of a finite CMRR causes this input common-mode error voltage to be generated, which can be expressed as a fraction of the common-mode input voltage

$$E_{e_{cm}} = \frac{E_{cm}}{CMRR}$$

It is convenient to model this error voltage as a separate generator in series with an ideal amplifier and consider its effect on the gain. By expressing the error voltage as a fraction, we can include it with A_{vo} and generate a new expression which includes the effects of common-mode gain

$$\text{Common-Mode Error} = \frac{E_{e_{cm}}}{E_{cm}}$$

Since

$$E_{e_{cm}} = \frac{E_{cm}}{CMRR}$$

we may substitute, leaving

$$\text{Common-Mode Error} = \pm \frac{1}{CMRR}$$

We must add the qualifier of ($\pm$), since common-mode error can be an error in either direction; it can either add to or subtract from the input signal. This uncertainty prevents a simple cancellation of common-mode error by adjusting R_{in} or R_f.

We can now write the modified gain expression for the noninverting amplifier:

$$A_v = \underbrace{\left(\frac{R_{in} + R_f}{R_{in}}\right)}_{\substack{\text{Ideal} \\ \text{Expression}}} \underbrace{\left(\frac{1}{1 + (1/A_{vo}\beta)}\right)}_{\substack{\text{Error} \\ \text{Multiplier}}}$$

To summarize the gain error for both configurations due to finite or modified A_{vo}, we can express the error as a percentage

$$\% \text{ Error} = \frac{100}{A_{vo}\beta + 1}$$

Thus, a loop gain of 100 (40 dB), for example, will yield a gain error of approximately 1.0%.

As the reader may already have noted, there is a basic difference between the inverting and noninverting configurations in the method of signal amplification, but no difference in the method of calculating β. As a result, for equivalent *signal* gains, inverting and noninverting stages will have a different β, and thus will have different loop gains. This is also illustrated in Fig. 1-11.

If we examine a unity-gain condition for both configurations, it will be noted that for the inverting stage

$$\frac{R_f}{R_{in}} = 1, \text{ or } R_f = R_{in}$$

but for the noninverting stage

$$\frac{R_{in} + R_f}{R_{in}} = 1, \text{ or } R_{in} = \infty$$

The β equations for the two configurations are then

$$\beta \text{ (Inverting)} = \frac{R_{in}}{R_{in} + R_f} = \frac{R_{in}}{2R_{in}} = 0.5$$

and

$$\beta \text{ (Noninverting)} = \frac{\infty}{\infty + R_f} = 1$$

Thus, it can be seen that for equivalent signal gains, the two stages do not have the same β. This difference is most apparent at the lowest gain that both stages are capable of—unity, where the β of the inverting stage is half that of the noninverting stage. The point of this discussion is that for the two stages, signal gain and β do not have the same relationship. In order to compare the two stages directly in terms of β (and hence, loop gain), we must introduce a new term.

The parameter that is defined identically for both configurations is β. Therefore, a gain defined in terms of β would be a useful basis for comparing the two basic stages. This gain is the reciprocal of β and is termed *noise gain:*

$$\text{Noise Gain} = \frac{1}{\beta} = \frac{R_{in} + R_f}{R_{in}}$$

which is the ideal equation. The term that includes error factors due to nonideal gain is the *true noise gain* or *closed-loop gain*

$$\text{Closed-Loop Gain} = A_{cl} = \underbrace{\left(\frac{1}{\beta}\right)}_{\substack{\text{Ideal} \\ \text{Expression}}} \underbrace{\left(\frac{1}{1 + (1/A_{vo}\beta)}\right)}_{\substack{\text{Error} \\ \text{Multiplier}}}$$

Noise gain is the inverse of β. Thus, like β it takes into account all feedback resistance and includes frequency effects. Noise gain is the gain seen by amplifier input referred noise and error (offset and drift) parameters. It is often significantly different from signal gain. It is most important that this point be understood because noise gain —not signal gain—is the parameter used in calculations of closed-loop amplifier performance. To illustrate by means of the unity-gain example, the inverting stage has a noise gain of 2, whereas the noninverting stage has a noise gain of 1. In this example, then, the inverting stage would amplify input error components by a factor of 2.

At this point, it is appropriate to summarize the various gain definitions and bring them all into perspective by means of graphical illustration in Fig. 1-12. The definitions are:

Open-Loop Gain (A_{vo})—The open-loop voltage gain of the basic amplifier without feedback but with loading. This includes frequency dependence.

Signal Gain (A_v)—The closed-loop voltage gain of the amplifying circuit for signals applied, as appropriate to the configuration.

Feedback-Loop Attenuation (β)—The voltage attenuation of the feedback network including all impedances.

Noise Gain ($1/\beta$)—The voltage gain response given by the inverse of feedback-loop attenuation.

Loop Gain ($A_{vo}\beta$)—The net gain around the broken feedback loop as seen from the feedback network input terminal back to the amplifier output. This includes frequency dependence.

Closed-Loop Gain (A_{cl})—The noise gain including the effects of loop gain.

Fig. 1-12 illustrates these definitions on a Bode plot, the basic tool for graphing amplifier gain versus frequency. This is a log-log plot which pictures the entire amplifier response. Gain may be shown either numerically or in dB, but it is conventionally shown in dB; thus, this terminology is used in Fig. 1-12. With the various gains expressed in dB, they may be added and subtracted, which considerably simplifies the discussion.

The response, A_{vo}, of the basic amplifier is shown as equal to 100 dB at frequencies below 10 Hz. Above 10 Hz, A_{vo} becomes frequency-dependent and reduces 6 dB per octave (or 20 dB per decade) until at 1.0 MHz, $A_{vo} = 0$ dB, or unity. Such a response is typical of many of the general-purpose IC op amps that will be discussed in this book.

To illustrate β and $1/\beta$, a β of 0.01 or -40 dB will be assumed, with no reactive effects for simplicity. Therefore, β is drawn as a flat line (no frequency dependence) at -40 dB on the A_v scale. The reciprocal, $1/\beta$, is drawn as a flat line at $1/\beta = 1/0.01 = 100$, or $+40$ dB on the A_v scale.

Loop gain, or $A_{vo}\beta$, is the resultant of the combination of A_{vo} and β, including frequency dependence. Since A_{vo} is constant below 10 Hz, the product of $A_{vo}\beta$ will also be constant below this frequency. Working in dB, $A_{vo}\beta$ can be arrived at by simply adding A_{vo} and β. Thus, $A_{vo}\beta$ in dB is $+100$, -40, or $+60$ dB (below 10 Hz).

Rather than draw an additional curve referred to the zero-gain axis for $A_{vo}\beta$, we can make use of the information already implicit in the curves. Since $1/\beta$ is the inverse of β, subtracting $1/\beta$ in dB from A_{vo} (dB) will yield $A_{vo}\beta$ in dB. Thus, $A_{vo}\beta$ is that portion of the A_{vo} curve above the $1/\beta$ curve.

A careful study of Fig. 1-12 should make the foregoing discussion readily apparent.

With this technique, the loop gain of a configuration can be graphically determined at a glance. In the example shown, loop gain is $+60$ dB up to 10 Hz, but reduces at the rate of 6 dB per octave (due to decreasing A_{vo}) above this frequency, until at 10 kHz, $A_{vo}\beta$ has reduced to zero.

Although a flat β (and $1/\beta$) curve was used in this example, the general consideration regarding the resultant $A_{vo}\beta$ is true for any type of feedback and β. For example, if a slope (greater attenuation) were introduced into β at 100 Hz as indicated in Fig. 1-12 by the dotted-line response, the resultant $1/\beta$ curve would slope in the opposite direction as shown. Note that this reduces the loop gain, $A_{vo}\beta$, even faster at the higher frequencies, since $A_{vo}\beta$ is the difference in dB of A_{vo} and $1/\beta$.

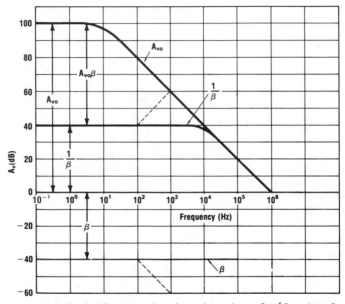

Fig. 1-12. Bode plot illustrating the relationships of A_{vo}, β, $1/\beta$, and $A_{vo}\beta$.

From these relatively limited examples, the reader may already have deduced a salient point: It is β *alone* that determines the overall response of the amplifier. This factor, coupled with $A_{vo}\beta$ (which determines how *closely* the $1/\beta$ curve is realized), is used to implement feedback configurations.

In an actual design example, the $1/\beta$ curve would be used as a starting point, since it is this curve that represents the final frequency response of the amplifier. Given $1/\beta$ as an objective, the required β may be drawn as its inverse, which defines the characteristics of the feedback network. In practice, a certain requirement for $1/\beta$ will dictate the choice of amplifier to yield a specified loop gain for the required accuracy. This explanation is somewhat simplified, but in sections to follow, we will discuss this and other points in greater detail.

34

The Curative Properties of Feedback

Operational feedback, as we have discussed, is a means by which the designer can exercise control over total circuit performance. Feedback has a general influence that can be called a "curative" property. This property generally improves such factors as linearity, gain stability, and input and output impedances. In all cases, the degree of improvement is related to loop gain, or the amount of working feedback the amplifier uses in any given situation. Expressions governing the extent of improvement will now be discussed.

Gain Stability—One reason for using a feedback amplifier is to develop a transfer gain that is relatively independent of amplifier characteristics—indeed, the entire reasoning behind the operational amplifier is to render variations in its open-loop characteristics negligible, and make the amplifier properties dependent only on the external components.

Variations in gain for a feedback amplifier may be calculated by

$$\Delta A_v = \frac{\Delta A_{vo}}{1 + A_{vo}\beta}$$

It can be seen that gain variation is controlled almost entirely by the loop gain if $A_{vo}\beta \gg 1$. This expression is a general one, applicable to any configuration. If A_{vo} and β are modified by other nonideal terms, the corrected A_{vo}' or β' should be used in calculations. This statement also applies, of course, for the remaining expressions.

Linearity—Feedback reduces open-loop distortion and nonlinearity to lower closed-loop levels according to

$$THD_{cl} = \frac{THD_{ol}}{1 + A_{vo}\beta}$$

where,
THD is the total harmonic distortion in percent.

Input and Output Impedances—Input and output impedances of op-amp configurations are also transformed (in the positive direction) by feedback. The output resistance (r_o) of any op amp is reduced by feedback to a new resistance, R_o

$$R_o = \frac{r_o}{1 + A_{vo}\beta}$$

The input impedance is transformed upward or downward, depending on the configuration. In the inverting configuration shown in Fig. 1-13A, the input impedance, R_{in}, seen at the summing point is

$$R_{in} = \frac{r_{in}\|R_f}{1 + A_{vo}\beta}$$

If $R_f \ll r_{in}$ (usually the case) and $A_{vo}\beta \gg 1$, a useful approximation is

$$R_{in} \cong \frac{R_f}{A_{vo}\beta}$$

This clearly demonstrates the virtual-ground properties of the inverting configuration, as R_f is "transformed" by feedback to a much lower value. This makes the inverting stage a natural one for processing the output from current generators.

The noninverting configuration is shown in Fig. 1-13B, and its property is to transform the input resistance to a higher value. Since the voltages across both ends of r_{in} are the same (due to zero input-voltage differential), r_{in} is effectively "bootstrapped" by the feedback. The two common-mode resistances, each of value $2r_{cm}$, are not bootstrapped, however, and they appear in parallel with the input terminal. Thus,

$$R_{in} = r_{in}(1 + A_{vo}\beta) \| r_{cm}$$

$$R_{in} = \frac{r_{in} \| R_f}{1 + A_{vo}\beta}$$

(A) Inverting configuration.

$$R_{in} = r_{in}(1 + A_{vo}\beta) \| r_{cm}$$
$$\left[r_{cm} \text{ will dominate at high } A_{vo}\beta \right.$$
$$\left. \text{if it is not} \gg r_{in}(1 + A_{vo}\beta) \right]$$

(B) Noninverting configuration.

Fig. 1-13. Effects of feedback on input resistance.

At high loop gains, such as with a voltage follower, the common-mode input resistance will usually be the upper limit on the input impedance of the noninverting stage.

From these few observations, it can be seen that loop gain is the primary determinant of feedback performance, and its effect is always positive. Thus, it should be kept in mind that in optimizing feedback, the parameter $A_{vo}\beta$ is the key performance parameter.

1.2.2 Errors Due to Finite Input Resistance

Another factor having definite effects on op-amp circuit performance, in both the inverting and noninverting configurations, is finite input resistance. In this section, we will examine these effects, with all other parameters assumed to be ideal.

Inverting Configuration

Fig. 1-14A illustrates the inverting amplifier connection with the addition of the input resistance, r_{in}. The effect of the input resistance, which appears in parallel with the summing point, is to modify β. R_{in} and r_{in} in parallel form a new β, β', which is lower than the ideal (unloaded) network. Thus,

$$\beta' = \frac{R_{in} \| r_{in}}{(R_{in} \| r_{in}) + R_f}$$

where,

β' is the β with finite input resistance r_{in}.

The net effect of finite input impedance is therefore a reduction in β and thus a reduction in loop gain.

In practice, the actual loading effects of r_{in} will depend on the feedback impedances and the input impedance of the amplifier used. Generally, as long as the amplifier input resistance is 10 or more times greater than the output impedance of the feedback network, the error due to input resistance loading will be negligible. General-purpose IC op amps provide input resistances of a few megohms, while FET-input devices achieve input resistances as high as 10^{12} ohms.

Noninverting Configuration

Similar to the inverting configuration, the noninverting configuration can also introduce a reduction in β. In this case, however, there are two potential contributions. This is illustrated in Fig. 1-14B. If the source resistance seen by the ($+$) input of A is low, then the error due to amplifier input resistance reduces to the same error as in the inverting stage. If the source resistance, R_s, is such that it subtracts significantly from the error voltage, E_e, then the modified equation for β is

$$\beta' = \left(\frac{R_{in} \parallel (r_{in} + R_s)}{[R_{in} \parallel (r_{in} + R_s)] + R_f} \right)\left(\frac{r_{in}}{r_{in} + R_s} \right)$$

Also, like the inverting configuration, sufficiently high input impedance in the noninverting configuration can render these error sources negligible and reduce the equation for β to that of the classic form. This is also the case when r_{in} is 10 or more times greater than the feedback source resistance, R_s.

$$\beta = \frac{R_{in}}{R_{in} + R_f}$$

$$\beta' = \frac{R_{in} \parallel r_{in}}{(R_{in} \parallel r_{in}) + R_f}$$

Note: If $r_{in} \gg R_{in} \parallel R_f$, $\beta' \cong \frac{R_{in}}{R_{in} + R_f}$.

(A) Inverting configuration.

$$\beta = \frac{R_{in}}{R_{in} + R_f}$$

$$\beta' = \left(\frac{R_{in} \parallel (r_{in} + R_s)}{[R_{in} \parallel (r_{in} + R_s)] + R_f} \right)\left(\frac{r_{in}}{r_{in} + R_s} \right)$$

Note:
If $r_{in} \gg R_{in} \parallel R_f$ and R_s, $\beta' \cong \frac{R_{in}}{R_{in} + R_f}$.

$$\beta'' = \left(\frac{(R_{in} \parallel 2r_{cm} \parallel r_{in}) + (R_s \parallel 2r_{cm})}{(R_{in} \parallel 2r_{cm} \parallel r_{in}) + (R_s \parallel 2r_{cm}) + R_f} \right) \left(\frac{r_{in}}{r_{in} + (R_s \parallel 2r_{cm})} \right)$$

Note: If $2r_{cm} \gg R_s$, r_{in}, $R_{in} \parallel R_f$, $\beta'' \cong \beta'$.

(B) Noninverting configuration.

Fig. 1-14. Effects of finite input resistance.

Unlike the inverting configuration, the noninverting configuration is subject to errors due to common-mode resistances. The common-mode input resistance is modeled in Fig. 1-14B as two resistances of $2r_{cm}$, one at each input terminal. Taking these resistances into account, the modified equation for β becomes extremely unwieldy

$$\beta'' = \left(\frac{(R_{in} \parallel 2r_{cm} \parallel r_{in}) + (R_s \parallel 2r_{cm})}{(R_{in} \parallel 2r_{cm} \parallel r_{in}) + (R_s \parallel 2r_{cm}) + R_f} \right)\left(\frac{r_{in}}{r_{in} + (R_s \parallel 2r_{cm})} \right)$$

In practice, this equation is of little more than academic interest, as typical common-mode input impedances of IC op amps are in the hundreds of megohms. Therefore, errors due to common-mode input resistance loading may be neglected in almost all cases; other effects are far more dominant.

1.2.3 Errors Due to Nonzero Output Resistance

The nonzero output resistance of practical op amps also contributes to gain error, having a common effect on either the inverting or non-inverting configurations, as illustrated in Fig. 1-15. A real amplifier with output resistance r_o can be modeled as an ideal amplifier with gain A_{vo} in series with output resistance r_o. From this it can be seen

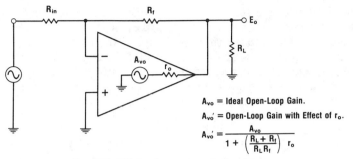

A_{vo} = Ideal Open-Loop Gain.
A_{vo}' = Open-Loop Gain with Effect of r_o.

$$A_{vo}' = \frac{A_{vo}}{1 + \left(\dfrac{R_L + R_f}{R_L R_f}\right) r_o}$$

Fig. 1-15. Effects of nonzero output resistance.

that the loading effects of R_L and R_f, combined with r_o, form a voltage divider that reduces the ideal gain to a new gain, A_{vo}'. Including the effects of the r_o-$R_f \parallel R_L$ divider yields a new open-loop gain equation

$$A_{vo}' = \frac{A_{vo}}{1 + [(R_L + R_f)/R_L R_f] r_o}$$

From this equation, the greater the open-loop output resistance, r_o, the greater the attenuation of A_{vo}. As a result, loop gain is also attenuated as r_o increases. The attenuation of open-loop gain due to loading can be a significant error in instances where r_o is high in relation to the load resistance. Since there are some IC op amps with output resistances as high as several thousand ohms, this is a factor to be considered when maximizing loop gain. Generally, as long as r_o is 1/10 or less of the total load resistance, it will not contribute excessive error.

Summary of Gain Errors

The nonideal properties of practical amplifiers discussed thus far all result in deviations from the ideal gain characteristic. This is due to a reduction in loop gain—either from a limited or reduced A_{vo}, or from a reduced β. Loop gain is the key parameter of feedback-amplifier configurations, since it determines the ultimate accuracy.

A complete gain equation that would include all sources of gain error is not given because it would not only be an extremely unwieldy expression but, in practice, the dominant sources of error may often be pinpointed by inspection. As a result, those error factors that warrant exact expression will usually be examined individually to generate modified figures for A_{vo} and β. Quite often the "rule-of-thumb" judgments previously mentioned for such parameters as input and output resistance will give values for $A_{vo}\beta$ to within a few percent, which in most cases is sufficient accuracy.

1.2.4 Effects of Input-Referred Errors

In addition to the static gain errors discussed in the previous sections, there are a number of error sources in practical op amps that are referred to the input terminals. These errors include input voltage and current offsets (with their associated drifts due to temperature changes), and self-generated and power-supply-induced input noise. These nonideal parameters, together with techniques for their minimization, will be covered in this section.

Input Offset Voltage

While the ideal op amp has the property of zero output voltage at zero input voltage, a real amplifier does not. Practical op amps have an input offset voltage, as illustrated in Fig. 1-16. This practical

Fig. 1-16. Input offset voltage errors.

$$V_o = V_{io}\left(\frac{R_{in} + R_f}{R_{in}}\right)$$

$$\Delta V_o = \Delta V_{io}\left(\frac{R_{in} + R_f}{R_{in}}\right)$$

amplifier is modeled as an ideal amplifier, A, with an offset voltage generator, V_{io}, in series with one of its inputs. It does not matter which input is used, since it can be shown that the net effect will be the same for either one. Also, the actual polarity of the offset voltage may be either positive or negative. The input offset voltage, V_{io}, is defined as the voltage applied between the input leads to obtain zero output voltage. Offset voltage is a characteristic independent of operating gain, and it is amplified by the noise gain of the stage. Thus, the output voltage due to V_{io} is

$$V_o = V_{io}\left(\frac{R_{in} + R_f}{R_{in}}\right)$$

Input offset voltage is due to imperfect matching in the input stage of the op amp. Different op-amp types will exhibit different degrees of matching and so will have better (or worse) input offset voltages. Offset voltage may be nulled by introducing an opposing voltage at one of the input terminals to cancel its effect, or by introducing an imbalance within the amplifier, resulting in an actual input offset of zero. In practice, control of offset voltage can be exercised either by selecting a device which yields an input offset below that required, or by nulling a device to achieve the required offset. Various methods of offset nulling will be discussed in detail in later sections.

Offset Voltage Drift

With input offset voltage adjusted to zero, the remaining voltage offset error is input offset voltage drift. Although input offset may be nulled at room temperature, temperature changes will alter the state of balance in the input stage, inducing an input offset voltage drift. Offset voltage drift, being a component of input offset voltage, is subject to the same considerations; i.e., it is independent of stage gain and is amplified by the noise gain. Thus, output drift is

$$\Delta V_o = \Delta V_{io}\left(\frac{R_{in} + R_f}{R_{in}}\right)$$

There is no technique for nulling or cancelling offset voltage drift per se, although methods do exist to minimize it. Offset voltage drift will be minimal when the amplifier used is adjusted internally for an input offset voltage of zero. Furthermore, for minimum total drift (after nulling), the amplifier used should have a low offset drift specification.

Input Bias Current

Another parameter of the ideal amplifier, not realized in practice, is zero input current. Real op amps have input currents which may range from as high as 1.0 μA to as low as 1.0 pA or less in FET-input units. Often the effects of these currents are not negligible and must be compensated. Fig. 1-17 illustrates the effects of input bias current.

The bias current flowing in the input terminals of an op amp can be modeled as a current source in parallel with each lead of an ideal op amp. In Fig. 1-17, these current sources are labeled I_{ib-} and I_{ib+}. Although shown as being returned to ground, in actuality these current sources (or sinks) may be referred to the positive or negative supply, depending on the design of the individual amplifier. The currents I_{ib-} and I_{ib+} are independent of the common-mode voltage and flow in a return path (provided externally) at each input.

External to the amplifier, the input currents flow in the source resistances seen at each input and thus develop voltage drops. Current I_{ib-} flows through R_{in} and R_f, thus dropping a voltage

$$V_{b-} = (I_{ib-}) (R_{in} \parallel R_f)$$

For the moment we will not consider R_{eq}, but we will assume the $(+)$ input to be grounded directly. Under these conditions, the voltage drop, V_{b-}, due to the $(-)$ input bias current is, in actuality, an input offset voltage (not to be confused with the input offset voltage of the amplifier, V_{io}, which is assumed to be ideal in this discussion).

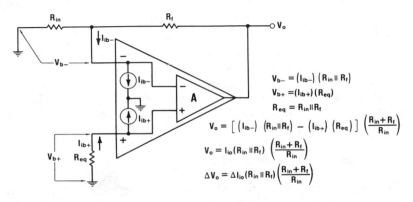

$$V_{b-} = (I_{ib-}) (R_{in} \parallel R_f)$$
$$V_{b+} = (I_{ib+}) (R_{eq})$$
$$R_{eq} = R_{in} \parallel R_f$$
$$V_o = [(I_{ib-}) (R_{in} \parallel R_f) - (I_{ib+}) (R_{eq})] \left(\frac{R_{in} + R_f}{R_{in}}\right)$$
$$V_o = I_{io}(R_{in} \parallel R_f) \left(\frac{R_{in} + R_f}{R_{in}}\right)$$
$$\Delta V_o = \Delta I_{io}(R_{in} \parallel R_f) \left(\frac{R_{in} + R_f}{R_{in}}\right)$$

Fig. 1-17. Input bias and input offset current errors.

As with V_{io}, V_{b-} is amplified by the noise gain of the stage. Whether or not V_{b-} is a significant error depends on two factors: (1) the magnitude of I_{ib-} and/or (2) the magnitude of $R_{in} \parallel R_f$. In general, to minimize V_{b-}, either $R_{in} \parallel R_f$ must be small or a very low (<1.0 nA) input current must be used. This latter condition is generally true for modern FET-input units, which allow high resistances to be used.

For bipolar-input op amps, such restrictions on feedback resistance can be lessened considerably by the use of an equivalent resistance, R_{eq}, to the $(+)$ input. R_{eq} is chosen to be equal to $R_{in} \parallel R_f$, then if $I_{ib+} = I_{ib-}$, R_{eq} will drop a voltage, V_{b+}, which will equal V_{b-}. In this manner, the input offset due to V_{b-} is balanced out, and the amplifier sees only the difference in V_{b-} and V_{b+} as an input voltage. If I_{ib-} and I_{ib+} are well matched, this input offset voltage can be quite low.

Input Offset Current

How well the input currents of an op amp match is described in another specification, the input offset current. Input offset current is defined as the difference in the currents into the two input terminals when the output is at zero. Thus, not only is a practical amplifier non-ideal from the standpoint that it requires input current, but it is also nonideal from the standpoint that the two input currents it does require are unequal, or offset.

In practice, the offset current is typically 10% or less of the bias current in a well-matched op-amp input, although this figure can vary with different devices. In terms of circuit considerations, the only compensation for bias-current-induced offset voltage that can be provided is a nominally matched set of resistances, such as $R_{eq} = R_{in} \parallel R_f$. Beyond this, an amplifier must be selected for a low and stable characteristic offset current. In general, to minimize bias and offset-current effects, the source resistances seen at both inputs should be matched and maintained as low as is practicable. If the use of high resistances is required, then a low-input-current amplifier should be used. FET-input amplifiers feature initial (room temperature) bias currents in the pA region; however, they also have large temperature coefficients.

Bias and Offset Current Drift

Bias current has a temperature dependence which is variable according to the type of input-stage design used in the op amp. Bipolar-input op amps tend to have relatively stable input bias currents, which also makes their input offset currents relatively stable. Input offset current drift is just as important a specification as input offset voltage drift, because it reduces to an equivalent offset voltage drift in a circuit. Also, like voltage drift, this source of error must be minimized by careful device selection as the final measure of control.

FET-input devices have the lowest bias currents, although on a percentage basis their *offset* currents are not as low as those of bipolar devices. Their input and offset currents are, however, low enough in absolute level that in many circuits they do not need offset-current compensation. A disadvantage of FET-input devices is the temperature dependence of bias (and offset) current, which roughly doubles for every 10°C of temperature rise. If very high operating temperatures are required, this characteristic tends to defeat their low-input-current superiority somewhat, although the degree to which this is true depends, of course, on the device and at how high a temperature one must operate it.

Summarizing the discussion on input offset voltage and currents, a combined model illustrating both is presented in Fig. 1-18.

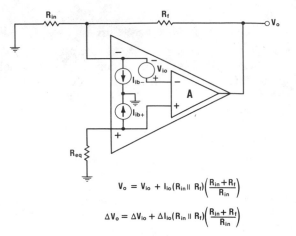

$$V_o = V_{io} + I_{io}(R_{in} \| R_f)\left(\frac{R_{in}+R_f}{R_{in}}\right)$$

$$\Delta V_o = \Delta V_{io} + \Delta I_{io}(R_{in} \| R_f)\left(\frac{R_{in}+R_f}{R_{in}}\right)$$

Fig. 1-18. Composite input offset voltage and current errors.

Power-Supply-Induced Input Offset Voltage

Due to an incomplete ability to reject power-supply voltage variations, practical op amps have another source of input offset voltage
change. This source is termed power-supply rejection or sometimes
supply-voltage sensitivity, and is a measure of how much variation
appears as an equivalent input offset change for a given amount of
variation in the power supplies. This parameter is illustrated in Fig.
1-19.

Inasmuch as this parameter is an input offset change, it may be
modeled as an input offset voltage generator in series with one input
lead (similar to Fig. 1-16). Since the source of this offset change is

$$\Delta V_o = \left(\frac{\Delta V_{io}}{\Delta V_s}\right)\left(\frac{R_{in}+R_f}{R_{in}}\right)$$

Fig. 1-19. Power-supply-induced errors.

either V+ or V−, the supply leads are also shown, labeled with the variations $\Delta V+$ and $\Delta V-$. Thus, the equivalent input offset change is

$$\frac{V_{io}}{\Delta V_s}$$

where ΔV_s implies both supplies varying symmetrically.

Like the previous input offset changes, this parameter is independent of stage gain but is amplified by the noise gain of the stage. Thus, the equivalent output change is

$$\Delta V_o = \left(\frac{\Delta V_{io}}{\Delta V_s}\right)\left(\frac{R_{in} + R_f}{R_{in}}\right)$$

Unlike the previous sources of input offset voltage change, power-supply-induced offset can contain ac components as well as dc. Thus, a complete evaluation of the effects of this error component, as it appears at the output, must include the frequency response of the coupling to the input as well as the frequency response of the amplifier configuration. In general, the power-supply rejection of an op amp will deteriorate at higher frequencies. This will vary according to the op-amp design and is usually given in the form of a graph. Also, the rejection for V+ and V− is not necessarily symmetrical, particularly with respect to frequency. This can be an important factor when operating from supplies having appreciable high-frequency noise components.

The minimization of power-supply noise sensitivity can take one of two general approaches: (1) selection of an op amp for inherently low noise sensitivity, or (2) selection of a standard (general-purpose) op amp and employment of local decoupling where necessary. The evaluation of a specific application to determine which approach is the most appropriate or economical is usually left up to the designer.

Input Noise

Although not specifically stated as one of the primary characteristics of an ideal op amp, it is desirable that noise-free operation be one of its virtues. However, practical amplifiers degrade the input signal by adding noise components. This noise is nearly random in nature and determines the ultimate lower limit of signal-handling capability. It is specified as equivalent input noise and, like the other input error factors, is increased by the noise gain of the stage. Unlike the other input parameters, however, input noise specification and control is by no means a straightforward process. It involves the interpretation of a number of involved specifications, as well as an understanding of the basic physics of its mechanism, to yield maximum performance. Disregarding the basic rules of noise-performance optimization, however, can result in signal-to-noise ratios that may be short of maximum by an order of magnitude or more.

A circuit model for the discussion of input-referred noise components is shown in Fig. 1-20. Similar to bias current and offset voltage, the noise generators of an amplifier are modeled as a series voltage-noise generator, e_n, and shunt current-noise generators i_{n+} and i_{n-}. These generators represent the mean values of voltage and current noise referred to the input of the amplifier. They are specified in terms of noise density in volts-squared or amperes-squared per hertz of bandwidth. To these generators must be added two other noise sources—the thermal noise of the source resistances seen by the amplifier, which is R_{eq} and $R_{in} \parallel R_f$.

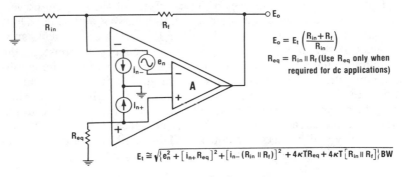

$$E_o = E_t \left(\frac{R_{in} + R_f}{R_{in}} \right)$$

$R_{eq} = R_{in} \parallel R_f$ (Use R_{eq} only when required for dc applications)

$$E_t \cong \sqrt{\{e_n^2 + [i_{n+} R_{eq}]^2 + [i_{n-}(R_{in} \parallel R_f)]^2 + 4\kappa T R_{eq} + 4\kappa T [R_{in} \parallel R_f]\} BW}$$

Fig. 1-20. Input current and voltage noise errors.

Thus, a real amplifier has five potential sources of noise to be considered for minimization. First, there is the thermal noise of (possibly) two source resistances seen by the inputs, which is an irreducible minimum, existing even with an ideal (noiseless) amplifier. For audio applications, where the lowest noise is of greater concern than lowest dc offset, a bias compensation resistor, such as R_{eq}, should *not* be used. This will reduce noise by the simple elimination of an unnecessary noise source. Next, there are the noise-current and noise-voltage generators. For low values of source resistance, the effect of i_n is often at a minimum. Under such conditions, which are usually typical for audio, e_n will dominate as the source of amplifier noise. As the source resistance is increased, the effect of i_n becomes larger until at high source resistances, $i_{n+} R_{eq}$ and $i_{n-}(R_{in} \parallel R_f)$ are the dominant components of amplifier input noise. Thus, in specifications these two parameters are detailed separately, with e_n specified at a low source resistance and i_n specified at a high source resistance. Both e_n and i_n are given in terms of spectral density, measured with a narrow-bandwidth filter at a series of points across the useful spectrum of the amplifier. Data are given either in terms of e_n (or e_n^2)

(A) Input noise voltage density.

(B) Input noise current density.

(C) Total input noise density.

(D) Broadband input noise voltage.

Courtesy Signetics Corp.

Fig. 1-21. Typical op-amp noise performance specifications—5534 amplifier.

or i_n (or i_n^2) versus frequency, with typical graphs shown in Figs. 1-21A and B. These particular curves are given in $e_n/\sqrt{Hz}$ and $i_n/\sqrt{Hz}$, but other manufacturers sometimes choose to display the same information in terms of e_n^2/Hz and i_n^2/Hz. Conversion between the two may be accomplished by simply squaring or extracting the square root as appropriate. When comparing such data in graphical form, however, it should be noted that variations in terms of e_n^2 will appear exaggerated over the same data expressed in terms of e_n. This clearly emphasizes the need for comparison of data on the same basis.

Although the spectral densities of both e_n and i_n are obviously not flat in the examples given (nor are they in general), it is not unreasonable to select a mean value for e_n and i_n if their total variation across the frequency range of the amplifier is within the same order of magnitude. An accurate calculation of total rms noise would involve integration across the bandwidth of the amplifier. The simplified approach given here will yield order-of-magnitude estimates of noise performance that are adequate for comparison purposes. Thus, given values of e_n, i_n, and bandwidth, the total noise of the circuit can be approximated as follows:

$$E_t \cong \sqrt{\{e_n{}^2 + [i_{n+}R_{eq}]^2 + [i_{n-}(R_{in} \parallel R_f)]^2 + 4\kappa TR_{eq} + 4\kappa T[R_{in} \parallel R_f]\}BW}$$

where,

E_t is the total circuit noise,

e_n is the amplifier noise voltage in $V/\sqrt{Hz}$,

i_n is the amplifier noise current in $A/\sqrt{Hz}$ (i_{n+} or i_{n-}),

R_{eq} and $R_{in} \parallel R_f$ are the source resistances ($R_{eq} = R_{in} \parallel R_f$),

κ is Boltzmann's constant ($1.38 \times 10^{-23} J/K$),

T is the absolute temperature (Kelvin),

BW is the noise bandwidth in Hz.

It is obvious from this expression that as e_n and i_n are reduced, the total noise approaches the thermal noise of R_s. A further point is that total noise is proportional to R_s and bandwidth. An illustration of this is given in Figs. 1-21C and D, with the individual noise components shown in Figs. 1-21A and B. Such performance curves are typically given for IC amplifiers and may, in fact, be adequate information for comparative evaluation.

In choosing an amplifier, the requirements will often dictate a certain source resistance from which the amplifier must work. This will dictate which noise generator is dominant and, therefore, which specification must be minimized—e_n or i_n. In general, low-input-current amplifiers, such as FET types or low-bias-current bipolar types, will have lower current noise, thus tending to be quieter with source impedances above 10,000 ohms. Below 10,000 ohms, the advantage swings to bipolar types, which have lower voltage noise. In any instance, absolute minimum values of feedback resistance should be used so that R_s is composed largely of generator resistance. This means that the feedback resistances used should be low in relation to the generator resistance. Another consideration is that the noninverting configuration has less noise gain than the inverting configuration for low signal gains; therefore, it offers a distinct advantage in signal-to-noise ratio (at high gains this advantage diminishes, however).

The equation for E_t also illustrates (indirectly) another property of noise behavior and calculations. This is the rms addition property of unrelated noise voltages, to arrive at a total noise voltage.

For instance, if there are two noise voltages whose sum is to be calculated, voltages E_1 and E_2, it is done as follows:

$$E_t{}^2 = E_1{}^2 + E_2{}^2 + \ldots E_n{}^2$$

or

$$E_t = \sqrt{E_1{}^2 + E_2{}^2 + \ldots E_n{}^2}$$

As an example, if $E_1 = 1\ \mu V$ and $E_2 = 1\ \mu V$, E_t will be 1.414 μV (not 2 μV!).

Likewise, taking a more practical example, suppose we had an amplifier circuit where there were three noise sources (expressed in $nV/\sqrt{Hz}$), which were 3 $nV/\sqrt{Hz}$, 1.25 $nV/\sqrt{Hz}$, and 4 $nV/\sqrt{Hz}$, respectively. Their sum would be

$$E_t = \sqrt{(3 \times 10^{-9})^2 + (1.25 \times 10^{-9})^2 + (4 \times 10^{-9})^2}$$
$$= 5.2 \ nV/\sqrt{Hz}$$

This is a realistic example, as it could represent a 5534 op amp (4 $nV/\sqrt{Hz}$), with a 100-ohm feedback resistance, fed from a 600-ohm source. The net noise of such a configuration would be 5.2 $nV/\sqrt{Hz}$.

It should always be borne in mind that the total noise of an amplifier working from a given source resistance will, therefore, be dictated by a number of factors, many of which are under the designer's control. Source resistance or feedback resistor noise can be readily determined and, obviously, such resistances should be minimized where possible.

To minimize total noise, it should be obvious from the equation for E_t that as many components within the radical as possible are to be either minimized or eliminated. In a case where it is desirable to characterize the noise performance of a given op amp, the source resistance should be held to an absolute minimum for measurement of e_n, or at a defined value for measurement of i_n.

In audio work, it is usually e_n that is the more important of the two, inasmuch as source resistances are always held to low values for low-noise amplifiers, and under such conditions only e_n will be significant. The noise characterization procedure described in reference 7 measures op amp e_n basically, and i_n optionally.

Noise of an op amp can be measured simply by placing the device in a high-gain configuration, with a defined source resistance, and measuring the output rms noise in a defined bandwidth. Of course, appropriate shielding, screening, and power-supply noise-isolation techniques must be used so as not to contaminate the reading with noise components external to the unit under test.

Two fundamental properties of noise behavior should be appreciated before noise measurements are attempted. First, bandwidth as related to the measurement of noise is not the same as 3-dB bandwidth, for fundamental reasons. Noise bandwidth is measured ideally by an infinitely fast rolloff filter, which rejects all noise components above the frequency of cutoff. A simple 6-dB/octave rolloff with a corner frequency will, of course, pass significant information above its cutoff frequency, as shown in Fig. 1-22. Therefore, if noise is to be measured by anything other than a "brick wall," or ideal noise filter, correction factors must be used.

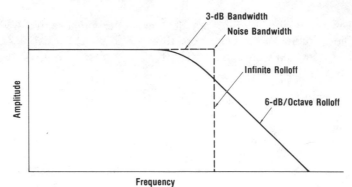

Fig. 1-22. Relationship between noise bandwidth and 3-db bandwidth.

For a single-pole, 6-dB/octave rolloff the relationship is

$$\text{Noise Bandwidth} = 1.57 \, f_c$$

where,

f_c is the 3-dB small-signal bandwidth.

Faster slope filters afford greater accuracy, as they approach the ideal noise bandwidth filter function.*

Another point is that noise should be measured by an *rms responding* voltmeter for best accuracy, because of the crest factor of noise voltages. Typical sine-wave-calibrated average responding meters will read 1 dB low on noise, compared to a true rms meter. They can still be used, however, if they have adequate bandwidth (10 times measurement or better) and a correction factor is used. The correction factor is +1 dB (or 113%). Mathematically, this is expressed as

$$E_{\text{rms (corrected)}} = 1.13 \, E_{\text{reading (average)}}$$

Crest factor errors can be minimized by avoiding near full scale readings, which can overload on noise peaks and cause errors.†

1.2.5 Errors Due to Dynamic Effects

As pointed out in Section 1.2.1, the predominant error factor in most op-amp applications is limited loop gain, due most often to finite open-loop gain. In this section, the Bode plot was introduced with a graphical example of the interrelationship of closed- and open-loop performance parameters. We will now examine some frequency-

---

* If a great number of high-accuracy, highly repeatable measurements are to be performed, a committed 20-kHz noise-bandwidth filter should be considered.

† For a discussion of noise measurement techniques applicable to IC op amps, see reference 7 at the end of the chapter. Also, reference 10 is an excellent general reference work on noise, its analysis and measurement.

response considerations of op amps to determine the closed-loop performance characteristics for wide bandwidths.

Gain and Bandwidth Relationships

As discussed previously, a real op amp does not have infinite gain; it also does not have infinite bandwidth. Open-loop bandwidth begins to roll off from the full dc value at some low frequency, generally between 10 Hz and 1.0 kHz, but most often between 10 Hz and 100 Hz in general-purpose op amps. As is noted in Fig. 1-23, from the open-loop −3-dB point (the point at which the gain is down 3 dB from the full dc value), the rolloff is 6 dB/octave (20 dB/decade)

$\frac{1}{\beta}$	BW @ −3-dB
0 dB (1)	1 MHz (10^6)
20 dB (10^1)	100 kHz (10^5)
40 dB (10^2)	10 kHz (10^4)
60 dB (10^3)	1 kHz (10^3)
80 dB (10^4)	100 Hz (10^2)
100 dB (10^5)	10 Hz (10^1)

Fig. 1-23. Illustration of gain and bandwidth interrelationship with constant GBP amplifier open-loop response.

with increasing frequency until the *unity-gain* frequency, f_t, is reached. In a curve such as this, the product of gain and frequency is constant at any point on the curve. Thus, the unity-gain frequency also defines the available gain at any point along the curve.

In Fig. 1-23, the example chosen is an amplifier with a unity-gain frequency of 1.0 MHz, typical of a large number of IC op amps. The product of gain and bandwidth (GBP) in an amplifier response such as this is constant; thus,

$$GBP = A_vBW$$

Graphically, the closed-loop −3-dB bandwidth point is defined as the point at which the ideal closed-loop gain curve $(1/\beta)$ intersects the open-loop gain curve. An entire family of $1/\beta$ curves is drawn on this plot to illustrate the point, and this relationship is also shown by the table of gains and bandwidths. Thus, for a gain of 10 (20 dB), the bandwidth is 100 kHz and the GBP is 1.0 MHz. Similarly, a gain of 1000 (60 dB) yields a bandwidth of 1.0 kHz, and the GBP is again 1.0 MHz. Although the curves shown are drawn in decade increments of gain and bandwidth for clarity, intermediate values of gain (or bandwidth) will likewise yield a constant gain-bandwidth product.

The conclusion to be drawn from this is a basic mechanism of the feedback process. More feedback (exemplified by the lower gains) allows greater bandwidth, up to the limit imposed by the open-loop response of the amplifier. As far as the amplifier open-loop response is concerned, it remains unchanged regardless of the amount of feedback. Thus, the rationing of gain and bandwidth is an exchange process—if more gain is necessary, reduced bandwidth is the by-product.

One final conclusion to be drawn from this is perhaps already obvious. With regard to loop gain, there is also an exchange process for various closed-loop gains. Loop gain, as stated previously, may be evaluated graphically as that portion of the response above a given closed-loop curve. For example, loop gain for $1/\beta = 20$ dB is 100 dB, −20 dB, or 80 dB at 1.0 Hz. The loop gain falls to zero at the $1/\beta$ −3-dB point, or 100 kHz. For the $1/\beta = 40$-dB curve, loop gain is 100 dB, −40 dB, or 60 dB at 1.0 Hz. The loop gain falls to zero at 10 kHz, the $1/\beta = 40$ dB, −3-dB point. Thus, the higher the closed-loop gain is, the lower the loop gain is and also (but just as important) the sooner the loop gain diminishes to zero, again due to the fixed gain-bandwidth product. It is sobering to consider these effects at high closed-loop gains—not only does the bandwidth shrink, but even before the −3-dB point is reached, loop gain is falling, diminishing the curative aspects of the feedback. We will now examine methods of optimizing loop gain with frequency, which at this point is obviously a nonideal property.

High GBP Amplifiers

Since the limitation on the available loop gain demonstrated in Fig. 1-23 is due to a limited gain-bandwidth product, it naturally follows that a greater gain-bandwidth product allows proportionally greater loop gain, or greater bandwidth. These factors are demonstrated in Fig. 1-24. For reference, this illustration includes the original 1.0-MHz GBP curve (curve A), as well as a 10-MHz GBP curve (curve B), and a 100-MHz GBP curve (curve C).

The evaluation of this new parameter can be approached from a number of viewpoints. For simplicity, a single $1/\beta$ curve is shown for a gain of 40 dB, but the same general considerations apply for any closed-loop gain. As an example, curve B extends the −3-dB point for the $1/\beta$ curve to 100 kHz, and curve C extends it to 1.0 MHz. This is also apparent from the 10-MHz and 100-MHz gain-bandwidth products, which when divided by a gain of 100 (40 dB), do in fact yield 100 kHz and 1.0 MHz. Moving the frame of reference lower in frequency to observe loop-gain differences, at 10 kHz the 10-MHz open-loop response (curve B) allows 20 dB of loop gain, while the 100-MHz response (curve C) allows 40 dB of loop gain. Moving even lower in frequency, it will also be noted that the higher open-loop −3-dB points allow the full low-frequency loop gain of 60 dB to be extended to 100 Hz and 1.0 kHz for curves B and C, respectively. Finally, if the new curves are viewed from the standpoint of a given bandwidth (or loop gain), the higher GBP curves allow more gain to be realized in a given bandwidth. The 10-MHz curve, for example, allows 60 dB of gain in a 10-kHz bandwidth, while the 100-MHz curve allows 80 dB of gain in a 10-kHz bandwidth.

Fig. 1-24. Gain and bandwidth interrelationships with extended gain-bandwidth products.

Figs. 1-23 and 1-24 should be instructive in the interrelationship of gain and bandwidth, and the necessity for a high GBP in achieving high loop gains and subsequent accuracy at high frequencies. The numerical evaluation of gain-bandwidth relationships may be done either mathematically or by using the Bode plot. It is suggested, however, that the reader become familiar with the Bode plot at the earliest opportunity as it yields a large amount of information very quickly, and it is a tool as fundamental to op-amp technology as the op-amp symbol itself.

So far, nothing has been said concerning the methods of achieving the higher gain-bandwidth products represented by curves B and C of Fig. 1-24. High GBP with stability in an op-amp circuit is one of the more "meaty" challenges with which the reader must become familiar, and this subject is discussed in the next section.

Frequency/Phase Compensation

The previous section stressed the characteristics of the 6-dB/octave open-loop rolloff rate which is typical of the greatest percentage of op amps. At this point, the reader might justifiably ask: "If more gain is needed at higher frequencies, why not just extend the open-loop bandwidth?" The answer to this question is basic and fundamental to stability in closed-loop feedback systems.

Stability Requirements—The 6-dB/octave rolloff rate is characteristic of a simple RC low-pass lag network such as that shown in Fig. 1-25A. In a network such as this, the maximum phase shift is $-90°$, as illustrated in Fig. 1-25B. At the -3-dB point of

$$f_1 = \frac{1}{2\pi RC}$$

the phase shift is $-45°$. As the frequency is increased, the phase shift reaches a maximum of $-90°$ at approximately

$$f_2 = \frac{10}{2\pi RC}$$

(A) Schematic.   (B) Amplitude and phase response.

Fig. 1-25. Response of a simple RC lag filter.

then remains at −90° for any further increase in frequency. This simple RC network has an important relationship to op-amp frequency response, as we shall see now in Fig. 1-26.

In all the discussions about feedback thus far, no mention of phase shift or its effect on closed-loop performance has been made. The fact is that phase shift and its control are of paramount importance in achieving closed-loop stability in a feedback system. We have been assuming a feedback loop with an inverting sign, which implies a phase shift of −180°. Consider now the effects of an additional phase shift. If, in addition to the −180°, we were to add more phase shift until we reached an additional −180°, we would have achieved 360° of phase shift, or an in-phase condition. If the loop gain is greater than unity at the frequency where this additional phase lag is −180°, we would also have succeeded in making an oscillator, for these are the two conditions which satisfy the criteria for oscillation. Thus, the control of phase shift and gain in feedback amplifiers is basic to achieving closed-loop stability. However, as there is a criterion for oscillation, there is also a corresponding stability criterion for feedback amplifiers. This fundamental rule can be applied to any feedback amplifier, and a stable system can be graphically determined with the aid of the Bode plot.

As may be deduced from the oscillation conditions just mentioned, the requirements for stability must reduce the total gain to less than unity before the additional 180° of phase shift is reached, in order to prevent oscillation. This means that the open-loop gain rolloff of the op amp must be done in such a manner as to prevent its phase from reaching −180° before the gain has dropped below unity. This characteristic is illustrated by the gain and phase plots of Fig. 1-26.

If the entire rolloff range of the amplifier can be made to act like the single RC lag element, then the maximum phase shift it can accumulate is −90°, which gives an additional 90° of phase margin before the −180° point of potential instability is reached. It is com-

Fig. 1-26. Open-loop gain and phase response for general-purpose op amp.

mon practice to provide a phase margin in feedback-loop design to allow for component tolerances, capacitive loading, and other effects that can further increase the total phase shift.

In Fig. 1-26, the amplifier open-loop rolloff appears as a single lag over most of the range. Such a response is typical of general-purpose op amps with a GBP of 1.0 MHz. At the -3-dB point of 10 Hz, the phase shift is $-45°$, increasing to $-90°$ at 100 Hz. It then remains at $-90°$ until the frequency nears the unity-gain crossover region, where additional internal phase shifts begin to accumulate, and the phase shifts further toward $-180°$. At the unity-gain frequency, however, the phase shift is appreciably less than $-180°$, usually by a phase margin of 60° or more. A phase margin of 45° is considered the minimum acceptable figure for conservative designs.

Such an amplifier as we have just described is said to be *unconditionally stable,* or *unity-gain stable,* because it can be used with any amount of feedback (including 100%) without oscillation or instability problems. The unity-gain condition is the "worst-case" feedback state for stability because under this condition, $\beta = 1$ and $A_{vo}\beta$ is a maximum. With no feedback attenuation, there is a maximum of available gain (the full open-loop gain of the op amp) attempting to satisfy the oscillation criterion. Therefore, control of phase shift is crucial to unity-gain feedback configurations. This is the impetus behind the use of a single, lag-element-type, open-loop response; it affords stable control of open-loop phase characteristics over many decades of gain rolloff, as seen in Fig. 1-26. It was the synthesis of just such a response as appeared in Fig. 1-26 that led to the general-purpose IC op amps we find so useful today.

General Stability Criterion—A more general examination of stability in IC op amps must include conditions other than the specific response shown in Fig. 1-26. These other conditions include multiple-slope rolloffs where the open-loop phase can become $-180°$ and greater, plus special cases of feedback where even the -6-dB/octave slope of Fig. 1-26 can be unstable in special cases.

For any feedback amplifier there exists a stability criterion, which can be stated as follows:

For unconditional stability, the ideal $1/\beta$ curve must intersect the open-loop response with a net slope of less than -12 dB/ octave.

Fig. 1-27 illustrates the open-loop response of a hypothetical op amp with a number of $1/\beta$ curves. The first significant difference to be noted about this open-loop curve is the fact that it has two slopes in its rolloff region. The first section rolls off at a rate of -6 dB/ octave, while the second section rolls off at -12 dB/octave, or twice the rate of the first section. A -12-dB/octave rolloff rate will ultimately reach −180° of phase shift; thus, it is potentially unstable if the loop is closed at or near the point where the phase is −180°. We will now examine the effects of different examples of loop closure (points of intersection shown in Fig. 1-27) on stability.

In the first example, the ideal gain curve, $1/\beta_1$, is a flat gain of 60 dB which clearly intersects the open-loop curve in a −6-dB/octave region. Thus, the net slope (slope between the two curves) is −6 dB/octave (since the $1/\beta_1$ curve has a slope of zero), and the loop is stable. An additional point which indicates stability of this loop closure is that the change in slope to −12 dB/octave is a full decade higher than the intersection of the $1/\beta_1$ curve with the open-loop curve. Thus, the phase changes that will be associated with this slope change have not yet begun, so the open-loop phase at this point will be −90°.

In the second example, the ideal gain curve, $1/\beta_2$, is also flat, but it is at a gain of 20 dB. This curve intersects the open-loop curve in the −12-dB/octave region, and since $1/\beta_2$ has zero slope, the net slope at the intersection is −12 dB/octave. Also, since this intersection point is beyond the point of slope change from −6 dB/octave to −12 dB/octave, the open-loop phase shift will have reached −180°. Thus, this loop closure will definitely be unstable and will result in oscillation, because there is still a 20-dB gain at the point where the curves intersect.

So far the examples considered have assumed a flat frequency response for the feedback characteristic, $1/\beta$. However, this is not always the case; $1/\beta$ may include reactive elements. Reactance in the feedback path changes the phase characteristic of $1/\beta$, just as reactance also changes the phase of the open-loop characteristic. For stable closed-loop operation, both reactance effects must be considered.

A reactive feedback characteristic can affect stability even when using the so-called "ideal" 6-dB/octave open-loop rolloff. Such a case is the $1/\beta_3$ curve in Fig. 1-27, which is a "peaked" open-loop response characteristic, typical of a differentiator. This curve intersects the open-loop characteristic with a +6-dB/octave slope, while the open-loop response is −6 dB/octave at the intersection. Therefore, the net slope is −12 dB/octave. The phase of the $1/\beta_3$ characteristic will be 90°, since it is two decades beyond the initial slope change at 100 Hz. The open-loop phase will be −90°, since it is one decade beyond the initial slope change. Thus, the net phase is −180° and the loop closure will be unstable. To restore stability to such a closed loop, the phase characteristic must be modified in order to reduce the net slope difference at the intersection. This may be done by modifying $1/\beta_3$ to the new curve, $1/\beta_3'$, which intersects the open-loop characteristic in a region where $1/\beta_3'$ is flat. Since this

Fig. 1-27. Stability considerations with various loop closures.

region of $1/\beta_3'$ is one decade beyond the last slope change, the phase will be close to zero, so the net phase is reduced to the $-90°$ of the open-loop curve; thus, the loop closure will be stable.

There are many other examples that could be used to demonstrate the working of the stability criterion, but they all reduce to control of the net phase between the ideal $1/\beta$ curve and the open-loop characteristic. With a given open-loop gain/phase characteristic, the feedback loop must be controlled in gain and phase so that the stability criterion is satisfied. Generally speaking, the -6-dB/octave slope characteristic of the general-purpose op amp allows freedom of feedback networks without much regard for stability considerations, except in certain special cases such as the $1/\beta_3$ curve in Fig. 1-27.

When gain-bandwidth is to be optimized, it may be more advantageous to exercise control over the open-loop characteristic of the op amp, in order to satisfy loop gain or stability requirements. The reason is that high **GBP** amplifiers with uniform rolloff rates of 6 dB/octave are rare. In fact, the 100-MHz, -6-dB/octave characteristic alluded to in Fig. 1-24 is not yet a reality in any IC op amp. Such a characteristic is quite difficult to realize because of inevitable high-frequency phase shifts and parasitic effects within the op-amp circuitry. However, over *portions* of the total response, a high gain-bandwidth product can be realized with controlled rolloff rates and controlled phase characteristics. Thus, high-gain, wideband amplifiers can be built using IC op amps with externally adjustable phase/frequency compensation, which allows some shaping of open-loop characteristics.

Effects of Phase/Frequency Compensation

A basic requirement of any op-amp frequency-compensation network is the control of open-loop rolloff so as to guarantee stability under closed-loop conditions. RC networks, placed at appropriate points in the op-amp circuit, cause the open-loop rolloff to assume the characteristic desired.

In general-purpose op amps, rolloff networks cause the open-loop response to assume a single rolloff slope of −6 dB/octave with an associated phase characteristic of −90° lag. This network can be self-contained within the amplifier; then, the amplifier is said to be *internally compensated*. Other op amps require external compensation networks to shape the open-loop response, either to a response similar to a general-purpose type or, with some amplifiers, to a response that may exhibit multiple slopes such as the open-loop characteristic of Fig. 1-27.

It is not the purpose of this discussion to describe the design of these networks, but to impart a useful appreciation of the value of their differences, the basics of what they accomplish, and, most importantly, how to interpret different open-loop responses so as to obtain maximum use of various IC amplifiers.

Basically, interpreting an open-loop response is evaluating the gain/phase characteristic in view of a particular application. With the previous background on gain-bandwidth, loop gain, stability requirements, and the general use of the Bode plot as a framework, the reader should now be developing an appreciation for the difference between the dc and ac performance of op amps. We will now examine what frequency-compensation networks accomplish in modifying open-loop response.

In Fig. 1-28, the uncompensated open-loop response of a hypothetical op amp is shown as curve A. This op amp has a number of internal phase shifts associated with it, as is evident from its three different rates of rolloff. The first rolloff begins at 10 kHz, where the open-loop response is 3 dB down and is at a rate of −6 dB/octave. The second rolloff occurs at 1.0 MHz and changes to a rate of −12 dB/octave. The third rolloff occurs at 10 MHz and changes to a final slope of −18 dB/octave. As it stands, this amplifier would be usable only with loop closures of 1.0 MHz or less (from point A2 upward on the curve), which limits it to gains of 60 dB or more. To make this amplifier usable at lower gains, from 60 dB down to unity, compensation must be introduced to synthesize a new rolloff slope of −6 dB/octave.

The most simple and direct method of doing this is to connect a capacitor at an appropriate point within the amplifier to introduce a lag. If the frequency at which this capacitance value reacts is low enough, its rolloff rate will become dominant, thus providing a single rolloff rate. To do this, the natural rolloff effects of the amplifier must be suppressed to a point where they occur at gains less than unity. Curve B demonstrates this effect, which is aptly called a "brute-force" technique. While this type of compensation will work, it ruins practically all the useful high-frequency response of the amplifier.

A much more desirable technique is to introduce the rolloff at a higher frequency as in curve C. A single capacitor lag introduced at this frequency will also result in a second rolloff due to the unsuppressed amplifier rolloff at 10 kHz. If left as such, curve C′ will result. This makes the amplifier usable with feedback down to 40 dB, but it is still not stable at unity gain because of the phase shift above 10 kHz. If, however, the rolloff due to C_C is removed at the first rolloff frequency (10 kHz), the composite curve can be made to approximate a single rolloff. It will then appear as the complete C curve, which extends to unity gain at 1.0 MHz. Now the amplifier will be stable at unity gain and will have an overall characteristic which resembles a 6-dB/octave rolloff.

Fig. 1-28. Phase compensation techniques.

Compensation is by nature a rolloff of gain, done in such a manner as to control the overall phase characteristic. Control of phase is the desired objective, and gain rolloff with frequency is the means to this end. As seen in Fig. 1-28, this is costly in terms of high-frequency gain. For example, if the unmodified response (curve A) and the compensated response (curve C) are compared at 10 kHz, the open-loop characteristic (curve A) has 100 dB of gain and can be stabilized at a gain of 60 dB, which will yield a gain accuracy of 1.0%. By contrast, the compensated response (curve C) can only achieve a gain of 40 dB at 10 kHz, the frequency where its loop gain is zero.

From this discussion it is hoped that the reader will be made aware of the tradeoff involved in frequency compensation. While the example chosen is not intended to portray an actual IC amplifier, it is close enough to be representative. Further study of manufacturers' data sheets will be more informative in terms of specific examples.

Slew Rate

The final source of error from dynamic effects is called the *slew rate*. Simply stated, slew rate is the maximum rate of change of the amplifier output voltage. In addition to the small-signal bandwidth discussed previously, it is another aspect of op-amp performance with frequency.

Slew-rate limiting is brought about by a limitation in the internal circuitry of an op amp to drive capacitive loads, either internal or external. The capacitance that limits this slewing ability with a given amplifier is most often the compensation capacitance, either internal or external, although in some instances it is the load capacitance. At high frequencies or high rates of signal change, the current available to charge and discharge the capacitance becomes exhausted,

(A) Response (dotted) to pulse or square-wave input.

(B) Response (dotted) to sine-wave input.

Fig. 1-29. Examples of amplifier output waveforms under conditions of slew-rate limiting.

and slew-rate limiting occurs. This is evidenced by distortion in the output, which will appear similar to the waveforms shown in Fig. 1-29. Under these conditions, the amplifier output will change at a maximum slew rate of

$$SR = \frac{\Delta E}{\Delta t}$$

Since slew rate is a large-signal performance parameter, a given rate also defines what is called the *power bandwidth,* which is

$$f_p = \frac{SR}{2\pi E_{op}}$$

where,

f_p is the full power frequency,
E_{op} is the peak amplifier output voltage.

Because slew rate is usually related to compensation capacitance, it follows that it is usually a variable for externally compensated amplifiers. One method used to minimize slew-rate problems is the selection of a device that can be optimized externally by adjusting the compensation (where stability requirements allow). If an amplifier is to be used at unity gain, however, a device must be chosen that will meet the slew-rate requirements under the conditions needed for stability.

Summary of Dynamic Effects

Bandwidth, compensation, and slew-rate considerations are some of the most important sources of error that will be encountered in op-amp circuitry. Where appropriate in the remainder of this book, special consideration will be given to optimum ac performance in the circuits discussed.

1.3 IC OP-AMP SPECIFICATIONS

IC op-amp specifications can be divided into two general categories: (1) maximum ratings and (2) electrical characteristics. These specifications provide two different kinds of information about an IC op amp, and both are important. Maximum ratings give the maximum operating conditions under which the manufacturer recommends that you operate his device. Exceeding the maximum ratings can lead to immediate destruction of the device at worst, and will almost always result in degradation of the general operating characteristics. Electrical characteristics tell a more detailed story of device performance under typical operating conditions of temperature, supply voltage, loading, etc. These specifications may be defined in terms of certain limits, either minimum or maximum, depending on the particular parameter. A typical value is also given in most cases. This serves as a nominal center for design guidance. In addition to these specification limits, supplementary data is provided in the form of graphs, curves, and test circuits under which specification measurements are made. Data given in the form of curves is not normally guaranteed, whereas "performance limits" are.

This section discusses IC op-amp specifications by first defining the term and identifying its symbol, then clarifying it in the light of practical examples wherever possible.

1.3.1 Maximum Ratings

Supply Voltage (V+ and V−)

The maximum allowable supply voltage that can safely be applied to the amplifier.

Although designed for ±15-volt supplies as standard, most IC op amps will operate over a wide range of potentials, some from as low as ±1.0 volt and some up to ±40 volts.

Power Dissipation (P_D)

The power that a particular device is capable of dissipating safely on a continuous basis while operating within a specified temperature range.

This rating will vary slightly according to the type of package used. Ceramic packages, for example, allow the highest power dissipation. Metal packages allow the next highest, while plastic-encapsulated packages generally allow the lowest. A typical power-dissipation capability for an IC op amp is about 500 milliwatts (up to a specified temperature); the exact figure will vary according to the manufacturer and the device.

Operating Temperature Range (T_{or})

The range of temperature over which the device will perform within the rated specification(s).

Military-grade devices operate from $-55°C$ to $+125°C$; industrial-grade devices operate from $-25°C$ to $+85°C$, and commercial-grade devices operate from $0°C$ to $+70°C$.

Differential-Input Voltage ($V_{id(max)}$)

The maximum voltage that can safely be applied between the differential-input terminals without excessive current flow.

Some amplifiers have clamping diodes connected back to back across the input terminals. These types are limited to a differential-input voltage of ±0.5 volt or less. Other types are limited to ±5.0 volts or less to prevent emitter-base breakdown in the input stage. The highest differential-input-voltage ratings are provided by devices using a combination pnp/npn cascode input, which provides a ±30-volt rating, or by FET-input devices with similar ratings.

Common-Mode Input Voltage ($V_{cm(max)}$)

The maximum voltage that can safely be applied between both input terminals together and circuit common.

There is both a positive and a negative limit to this rating, although typically they are equal.

Output Short-Circuit Duration

The length of time that the amplifier can withstand a direct short circuit from the output to ground or to either supply terminal.

Lead Temperature

The lead temperature that the device will withstand during the soldering process for a period of 60 seconds.

This rating is typically 300°C.

1.3.2 Electrical Characteristics

The electrical characteristics of an IC op amp provide a more detailed story of performance by defining the means and limits of behavior, usually in open-loop terms. A device is generally characterized by a range of performance limits, obtained from testing a large number of units on a production run. These limits are defined under standard conditions of room temperature and supply voltage (± 15 volts). Any further conditions are specified in detail with the individual measurements—for example, source resistance, frequency, load, temperature range, etc. Typical performance values are often accompanied by either a minimum or a maximum limit, although sometimes the typical values alone are given.

In the following discussion, the various parameters are grouped into categories such as input, output, dynamic, and general characteristics.

Input Characteristics

Input Offset Voltage (V_{io})—*The voltage that must be applied between the input terminals through two equal resistances to obtain zero output voltage.*

Ideally, an op amp will have zero input offset voltage. In practice, however, IC amplifiers have low but definite offset voltages. Offset voltage is lowest in bipolar-input op amps because bipolar transistors tend to match extremely well. It is unusual for a bipolar-input IC op amp to have an input offset greater than a few millivolts, and general-purpose types typically have offsets of ± 1.0 millivolt. Special selections of bipolar-input op amps have input offsets lower than ± 0.5 millivolt, with a number of actively trimmed devices offering offset voltages of ± 0.1 millivolt or less, some as low as 25 microvolts!

FET-input op amps are (comparatively speaking) poor in terms of input offset voltage because FETs do not tend to match nearly as well as do bipolar transistors; and the voltage being matched (V_P) is four to five times larger in a FET than the analogous voltage in a bipolar transistor (V_{BE}). Typical general-purpose FET-input amplifier offset voltages are in the 5- to 10-millivolt region, with some types having worst-case offsets that are greater. Actively trimmed FET units are available, however, with offsets to below ± 1.0 millivolt.

Most IC op amps have provisions for internal offset null adjustment, which allows the input offset to be adjusted to zero.

Depending on the input-bias-current characteristics of the particular device, the specified input offset voltage is guaranteed only up to a certain value of input resistance. In the case of general-purpose bipolar-input types, for example, this value is 10,000 ohms. Such a limitation is generally due to the offset current characteristics (difference in the two bias currents) of the device. With lower bias currents, offset current is also reduced; thus, higher source resistances may be used without offset voltage degradation.

Input Offset Voltage Temperature Coefficient ($\Delta V_{io}/\Delta T$)—*The ratio of change in input offset voltage to the change of circuit temperature for a constant output voltage.*

Input offset voltage temperature coefficient, or offset voltage drift, is specified in $\mu V/°C$ of offset voltage change and is an average value over the temperature range of the device. Again, due to the excellent matching characteristics of bipolar-input op amps, these types are best in terms of offset voltage drift. This is one of the more stringent operating parameters of IC op amps and is not specified for all devices. Premium IC op amps have offset voltage drifts of 1.0 $\mu V/°C$ or less.

Input Bias Current (I_{ib})—*The average of the two input currents.*

Input bias current is simply the current that is required at the input terminals of an op amp. It may flow either into or out of the input terminals, depending on the internal design used. In the balanced state, the two input currents are very nearly equal, but the parameter is usually specified as the average of the two input currents. In general, FET-input amplifiers will have lower bias currents, but bipolar amplifiers will have better-matched input currents (in terms of percent).

Input Bias Current Temperature Coefficient ($\Delta I_{ib}/\Delta T$)—*The ratio of the change in the input bias current to the change in circuit temperature.* This is an average value for a specified temperature range.

Input bias current temperature coefficient is a measure of how stable the input bias currents remain over the operating temperature range. It is most stable in bipolar-input op amps, usually rising at lower temperature extremes. On the other hand, FET-input op amps have a bias current that doubles (approximately) with every 10°C rise in temperature, because it is essentially a diode leakage current.

Input Offset Current (I_{io})—*The difference in the currents into the two input terminals when the output is at zero.*

Input offset current is a measure of the mismatch between the two bias currents. In general-purpose, bipolar-input op amps, the input offset current is typically 10% of the bias current, but it can be much lower in premium types. FET-input devices do not match as well because there is less control over the bias currents, but this may not be relevant due to their lower (absolute) bias currents.

Input Offset Current Temperature Coefficient ($\Delta I_{io}/\Delta T$)—*The ratio of the change in input offset current to the change in circuit temperature for a constant output voltage.* This is an average value for a specified temperature range.

Input offset current temperature coefficient is a measure of the change in offset voltage over the temperature range of the op amp. Like input offset voltage temperature coefficient, it is an average value. It is one of the more stringent parameters and is not specified for all IC op amps. Also, like input offset voltage temperature coefficient, it is better in bipolar-input devices due to better matching.

Input Resistance (r_{in})—*The resistance seen looking into either input terminal with the other input grounded.*

Input resistance in an IC op amp may be very high, as in the case of FET-input amplifiers; or it may be medium, as in the case of a bipolar-input amplifier. Input resistances for FET-input amplifiers can be as high as 10^{12} ohms at room temperature. General-purpose, bipolar-input op amps have input resistances around 1.0 megohm, but specialized types can be much higher. Ideally, of course, the input resistance is infinite, and this is very closely approximated by FET-input devices.

Input Capacitance (c_{in})—*The capacitance seen looking into either put terminal with the other input grounded.*

Input capacitance is important because of the reduction of input impedance it represents with increasing frequency. At higher frequencies, the input impedance can become limited due to the shunting effect of capacitive reactance. This must be considered when the source resistances seen by the input(s) of the amplifier are large enough to cause appreciable phase shift at the desired operating frequency.

Common-Mode Rejection Ratio (*CMRR*)—*The ratio of the input voltage range to the peak-to-peak change in input offset voltage over this range.*

An ideal op amp responds only to differential-input signals and ignores signals common to both inputs. In practice, this is only an approximation; real amplifiers have a small but definite common-mode error. The ratio of the common-mode voltage to the common-mode error voltage is the common-mode rejection ratio, CMRR. It is commonly expressed in dB.

Common-mode rejection is important to noninverting or differential amplifiers because these configurations see a common-mode voltage. It is specified at dc or a very low frequency, and it rolls off with a 6-dB/octave slope starting at the corner frequency. The corner frequency is about 100 Hz for general-purpose op amps, but it is greater in high-speed types. Dc rejection ratios can range from 90 dB to 120 dB, depending on the device. They are generally higher in bipolar-input amplifiers than in FET-input amplifiers, since FETs tend to have a poor common-mode rejection compared to bipolars.

Power-Supply Rejection Ratio (PSRR)—The ratio of change in input offset voltage to the change in supply voltages, with the supplies varied symmetrically.

The ability of an IC op amp to reject power-supply-induced noise and drift is an important parameter. Voltage changes on the supply lines can be coupled into the amplifier, and they appear as an equivalent input signal, regardless of the configuration used. For low-level, high-gain applications, this noise source must be considered. During measurement, the supply lines are varied equal amounts, and the measured changes are referred to the input. The measured value is noted as

$$PSRR = \frac{\Delta V_{io}}{\Delta V_S}$$

where ΔV_S is the increment of supply-voltage change.

Typical figures for power-supply rejection may be as low as 2.0 $\mu V/V$ or as high as 200 $\mu V/V$, the performance varying with different designs. In a given type of amplifier, there may also be different limits on the positive- and negative-supply rejection ratios; or, the manufacturer may specify the two measurements together, giving a typical value and a maximum limit. This parameter is also frequency-dependent, the exact degree varying with the type of amplifier.

Input Voltage Range (V_{icr})—The range of voltage on the input terminals for which the amplifier operates within specifications.

Input voltage range (also called the *operating common-mode range*) is the maximum range of voltage swing that the input stage can tolerate and still operate within the specification limits of the amplifier. It is applicable to either input since in an actual closed-loop situation, the two inputs will be at or near the same potential. In the case of a unity-gain voltage follower, the inputs are required to swing the full output range of the amplifier because the feedback is 100%. Therefore, it is necessary that the input stage be capable of operating with full specifications over the dynamic range of output swing. If it cannot, the possibility exists that the amplifier may saturate or "latch up" when its input range is exceeded.

Latch-up was a particular problem with early IC amplifiers because the maximum input range could be exceeded with normal output swings. This problem will be discussed in detail in a later section.

The 301, 741, and later amplifiers solved the input-voltage-range problem with typical specifications of ±13 volts or more. The input voltage range is directly related to the supply voltages used since it is the internal biasing potentials which set the input voltage range.

Thus, it is reduced for lower supply potentials and increased for higher supply potentials.

Output Characteristics

Output Voltage Swing (V_{op})—The peak output swing, referred to zero, that can be obtained without clipping.

Output voltage swing is the ability of an op amp to deliver its rated voltage across a specified value of load resistance. A symmetrical output swing is usually implied, although this is not necessarily true in all cases. The output swing can become limited due to loading effects, power supplies, frequency effects, and source resistance of the amplifier. Generally, IC op amps can supply peak voltage swings to within a few volts of the supply voltages used. There are normally two different load-resistance values into which the rated voltage swing is specified; these are typically 10,000 ohms and 2000 ohms.

With ±15-volt supplies, the 301 and 741 amplifiers are rated for ±14 volts typical swing into a 10,000-ohm load, ±12 volts minimum. Into a 2000-ohm load, the figures are ±13 volts typical and ±10 volts minimum. For supply voltages other than ±15 volts, the output-swing capability will change in proportion.

For load resistances below the rated value of 2000 ohms, the output begins to drop due to the effect of current limiting. This will not damage the amplifier as long as its power-dissipation limits are observed, but it will reduce the open-loop gain due to loading.

Output Short-Circuit Current (I_{osc})—The maximum output current available from the amplifier with the output shorted to ground or to either supply.

As a means of self-protection, IC op amps are usually provided with an internal current-limiting feature which prevents output current from rising above a level that would be destructive. This makes operation virtually foolproof from an accident standpoint, since situations will inevitably arise where an output will be short-circuited. Early op-amp types (such as the 709) were short-circuit proof only for brief durations and were subject to catastrophic failure if short-circuited for an appreciable length of time. Later op-amp types have incorporated full-time current limiting in the form of active devices which sense load-current flow and limit it to a maximum of 20 to 25 milliamperes in either direction. Since this is not a critical parameter, it is specified only as a typical value. The current is often sensed by a transistor junction voltage; thus, the current-limiting level is inversely proportional to temperature.

Output Resistance (r_o)—The resistance seen looking into the output terminal with the output nulled. This parameter is defined only under small-signal conditions at frequencies above a few hundred hertz, in order to eliminate the influence of drift and thermal feed-back.

IC amplifiers vary in output resistance, with resistances from below 100 ohms in general-purpose types up to some designs with output resistances approaching 10,000 ohms. Higher output resistances will result in a loss of gain when the load impedance becomes low in relation to the output resistance because part of the output signal is lost across the output resistance. This must be considered in cases where maximum gain is important. General-purpose op amps with output resistances less than 100 ohms are specified to operate into loads of 2000 ohms or higher, and they suffer little gain loss due to loading.

In all cases, the effective output resistance is reduced by feedback. The degree of reduction is in proportion to loop gain as discussed in the section on nonideal amplifier parameters.

Dynamic Characteristics

Open-Loop Voltage Gain (A_{vo})—*The ratio of the maximum output voltage swing with load to the change in input voltage required to drive the output from zero to this voltage.*

The open-loop voltage gain of an op amp is one of the most important specifications because it has the greatest effect on overall accuracy. General-purpose IC op amps have typical dc open-loop gains of 100 dB when operated with rated loads of 2000 ohms. This gain does not change excessively with operating temperature or variations in the supply voltage, although individual devices will vary in these regards. Special-purpose premium devices can achieve voltage gains of 130 dB.

Although the high gain available at dc is adequate to provide sufficient accuracy for most applications, the same is not true for ac. Because of the need for a 6-dB/octave rolloff to achieve closed-loop stability, internally compensated, general-purpose op amps typically have an open-loop −3-dB frequency of 10 Hz. Beyond this frequency, gain falls off at a 6-dB/octave (20-dB/decade) rate. An example of such an open-loop gain curve is the 741 response shown in Fig. 1-30A.

Small-Signal, Unity-Gain Frequency (f_t)—*The frequency at which the open-loop, small-signal voltage gain is unity with the amplifier compensated for unity-gain stability.*

The small-signal, unity-gain frequency is a very useful amplifier specification because it yields much information about the amplifier frequency response. In many applications, unity-gain stability is required of an op amp. Thus, the most meaningful frequency-response specification for such an amplifier is the unity-gain frequency, as this defines its gain-versus-frequency capability.

Courtesy Fairchild Semiconductor
(A) Open-loop response of 741 op amp.

Courtesy National Semiconductor Corp.
(B) Open-loop response of 301A op amp.

Fig. 1-30. Typical open-loop voltage-gain characteristics.

For example, with a 6-dB/octave rolloff such as shown in Fig. 1-30A, the frequency where this curve crosses the unity-gain axis defines the entire gain characteristic (since the slope is fixed). Once the f_t of a 6-dB/octave rolloff amplifier is known, its open-loop response can be drawn just by sketching a straight line with a -1 slope through the unity-gain frequency.

For the 741 example shown in Fig. 1-30A, the f_t is 1.0 MHz, which is typical of general-purpose amplifiers. High-speed IC op amps can achieve unity-gain frequencies of 10 to 15 MHz or more, which extends their high-frequency usefulness considerably.

Gain-Bandwidth Product (GBP)—The product of available open-loop gain and bandwidth at a specific frequency.

Gain-bandwidth product and unity-gain frequency are closely related, and in many instances they are actually the same thing. For example, the 741 gain-bandwidth product may also be stated as 1.0 MHz, since a gain of unity at 1.0 MHz yields a gain-bandwidth product of 1.0 MHz. It should also be noted that this product is constant regardless of frequency (or gain). Thus, a gain of 10^5 at 10 Hz yields a GBP of 10^6, or 1.0 MHz. In a 6-db/octave rolloff amplifier, the gain at any frequency can be found by dividing the GBP by the bandwidth, since

$$GBP = A_v BW$$

The difference between GBP and f_t becomes apparent with externally compensated amplifiers, which can achieve a higher GBP. This is illustrated in Fig. 1-30B, which shows the open-loop frequency response of a 301A amplifier compensated for two different closed-loop gains. The lower curve is identical to the 741 characteristic in Fig. 1-30A; it has an f_t of 1.0 MHz, which is also its GBP. However, the upper curve has a GBP ten times greater, or 10 MHz, as it yields a gain of 10 at 1.0 MHz. Note that this curve does not allow unity-gain stability as does the lower f_t curve. Therein lies the difference between f_t and GBP—f_t is actually a specific case of GBP, while GBP is a more general type of gain-frequency specification.

Unfortunately, **GBP** is not always implicit in numerical specifications, whereas f_t usually is. GBP is evident in the performance curves with various compensations, and the higher these curves extend in gain and frequency, the greater is the GBP for a given amplifier. It is true that with externally compensated amplifiers, extremely high GBPs can be achieved only at high gains, but it is also obvious that these are the conditions which require the high GBP for accuracy. Several IC op amps can yield GBPs of 100 MHz or more, in some instances.

Slew Rate (SR)—The maximum rate of change of output voltage under large-signal conditions.

Slew rate is the maximum rate of change of the output voltage of an amplifier under large-signal conditions, as opposed to the small-signal rise time. Unless otherwise specified, slew rate is measured and specified for closed-loop conditions, usually for a unity-gain voltage follower, which is the worst case for slew rate. The slewing rate of an amplifier will define a full-power bandwidth, the maximum frequency at which the amplifier will deliver full-rated output voltage with less than 1.0% distortion. The two are interrelated by

$$SR = 2\pi E_{op}f_p$$

where,

E_{op} is the peak output voltage and f_p is the full-power response frequency.

Slew rate is the parameter normally specified, although full-power response may also be specified. Slew rate is measured in a standard test circuit, using a full-scale input pulse with negligible rise time. The output will then change at a rate limited by the slewing ability of the amplifier.

The slewing rate of an externally compensated amplifier can be proportional to the closed-loop gain if the compensation is adjusted to optimize GBP. This is because more compensation is used at lower gains, and it is the compensation capacitance which determines slew rate. Slew-rate limitations are caused by the limited ability of the internal circuitry of the amplifier to charge and discharge this capacitance. When an operating frequency and output-voltage swing are reached which exceed the ability of the amplifier to charge and discharge the capacitance, the output no longer follows the input linearly but becomes "slew-rate-limited"; the output can then follow only at its rate limit.

In a given type of amplifier, reducing the capacitance that must be charged and discharged (the compensation capacitance) will raise the slewing rate in proportion to the capacitance reduction. Thus, higher-gain stages (which are compensated with less capacitance) have higher slew rates, which as we stated originally, makes slew rate proportional to closed-loop gain. This, of course, does not hold true for internally compensated amplifiers.

If a high slew rate is necessary concurrent with unity-gain stability, a FET-input device will most likely be suitable, as these devices are characterized by high slew rates.

Transient Response (TR)—The 10% to 90% closed-loop, step-function response of the amplifier under small-signal conditions.

Like slew rate, the transient response of IC op amps is specified under closed-loop conditions. With a small-signal pulse input, the output will be an exponential function, with a time constant inversely proportional to the bandwidth, according to

$$\text{bandwidth} = \frac{0.35}{\text{rise time}}$$

with bandwidth and rise time normally given in MHz and μs, respectively.

The test circuit used is typically a unity-gain voltage follower, with the amplifier driving its rated values of load resistance and capacitance. The signal level used is generally 0.5 volt or less, to ensure operation well below the slew-rate limits of the device.

Since bandwidth and rise time are interrelated, it follows that devices with high unity-gain frequencies will exhibit proportionally reduced rise times.

Settling Time (t_s)—The time it takes for the amplifier to reach (and to remain within) a specified accuracy band about some final voltage, after the application of a step input.

Settling time is a somewhat elusive op-amp performance specification inasmuch as it is not universally specified, and when it is, it will be for specific feedback and load conditions. Settling time is most important with regard to D/A and A/D conversion, where it is necessary to know how fast an amplifier can acquire and settle to a given accuracy after a pulse input. Typically, settling times are in terms of 0.01% to 0.1% for a 5- or 10-volt step, for either a follower or inverter configuration.

General Characteristics

Power Consumption (P_c)—The dc power required to operate the amplifier with the output at zero and with no load current.

The power consumption of an IC op amp is the power consumed for biasing purposes. It is not usable output power because none of it is delivered to the load. It should not be confused with power dissipation, which is a measure of the ability of the package to dissipate power.

Power consumption is normally specified numerically at supply voltages of ±15 volts. It may be given in the form of milliwatts of power, or milliamperes of supply current at these voltages from which power may be calculated. In addition, power consumption as a function of temperature and supply potential may be given.

With some IC op amps, power consumption may be controlled externally over an extremely wide range with a master bias terminal. This terminal may be used to switch the IC from completely "off" to "on" by removal or application of the bias current. In addition, the level of the current when "on" may be varied, which, in turn, varies the power consumption of the IC. These types are referred to as *programmable* types.

REFERENCES

1. *Applications Manual for Computing Amplifiers.* Philbrick Researches, Inc., Dedham, Mass., 1966.

2. Barna, A. *Operational Amplifiers.* John Wiley & Sons, Inc., New York, 1971.

3. Borlase, W. *An Introduction to Operational Amplifiers.* Analog Devices Application Note, September 1971. Analog Devices, Inc., Norwood, Mass.

4. Giles, J. N. *Fairchild Semiconductor LIC Handbook.* Fairchild Semiconductor, Mountain View, Calif., 1967.

5. Huehne, K. *Getting More Value Out of an Integrated Operational Amplifier Data Sheet.* Motorola Application Note AN-273A, February 1972. Motorola Semiconductor Products, Inc., Phoenix, Ariz.

6. JEDEC Engineering Bulletin No. 1-B, March 1971. *Glossary of Microelectronic Terms, Definitions, and Symbols.* EIA Engineering Dept., Washington, D.C.

7. Jung, W. G. *Audio IC Op-Amp Applications,* 2nd ed. Howard W. Sams & Co., Inc., Indianapolis, 1978.

8. Microsystems International Applications Bulletin 40001A, 1971. *Basic Principles and Applications of Operational Amplifiers.* Microsystems International Ltd., Ottawa, Ont., Canada.

9. Miler, G. G. *Equivalent Input Noise Measurements on High Gain Monolithic Operational Amplifiers.* Harris Semiconductor Application Note 506, October 1970. Harris Semiconductor, Melbourne, Fla.

10. Motchenbacker, C. D.; Fitchen, F. C. *Low Noise Electronic Design.* John Wiley & Sons, Inc., New York, 1973.

11. RCA Application Note ICAN-5290, March 1970. *Integrated Circuit Operational Amplifiers.* RCA Solid State Div., Somerville, N.J.

12. Roberge, J. K. *Operational Amplifiers—Theory and Practice.* John Wiley & Sons, Inc., New York, 1975.

13. Smith, J. I. *Modern Operational Circuit Design.* John Wiley & Sons, Inc., New York, 1971.

14. Smith, L.; Sheingold, D. "Noise and Operational Amplifier Circuits." *Analog Dialogue,* Vol. 3, No. 1, March 1969.

15. Solomon, J. E. "The Monolithic Op Amp: A Tutorial Study." *IEEE Journal of Solid State Circuits,* Vol. SC-9, No. 6, December 1974.

16. Stata, R. "Operational Amplifiers—Parts I and II." *Electromechanical Design,* September, November 1965. (Available as reprint from Analog Devices, Inc., Norwood, Mass.)

17. Tobey, G. E.; Graeme, J. G.; Huelsman, L. P. (eds.). *Operational Amplifiers—Design and Applications.* McGraw-Hill Book Co., New York, 1971.

18. Union Carbide Electronics AN-7, December 1966. *Operational Amplifier Static Gain Errors Analysis and Nomographs.*

19. Vander Kooi, M. K. *Predicting Op Amp Slew Rate Limited Response.* National Semiconductor Linear Brief LB-19, August 1972. National Semiconductor Corp., Santa Clara, Calif.

20. Widlar, R. J. *Drift Compensation Techniques for Integrated DC Amplifiers.* National Semiconductor Application Note AN-3, November 1967. National Semiconductor Corp., Santa Clara, Calif.

TWO

IC Op Amps:
The Evolution of General-Purpose
and Specialized Types

2.1 HISTORY AND DEVELOPMENT OF GENERAL-PURPOSE OP AMPS

No discussion of IC op amps would be complete without some historical background to place the different types in perspective. Due to the overwhelming proliferation of op-amp types, this is a challenging task; however, there are distinct evolutionary steps in the development of these devices. From this framework, we can at least lead up to the period of the late 1960s and middle 1970s when the diversity of types exploded, so to speak, into the broad spectrum of devices available today.

The foundation for IC op-amp design really began with the μA702, the first generally accepted IC op amp, which was introduced by Fairchild Semiconductor in 1963. For a number of reasons, the 702 was not a universally applicable op amp. It had a very limited common-mode input range, relatively low voltage gain (approximately 70 dB), used odd supply voltages (such as $+12$ and -6 volts), and was susceptible to burnout when the output was temporarily shorted. However, the 702 did set the stage for future trends in IC op-amp design by establishing the practice of using matched-component techniques. Although the 702 design is not covered in detail here, information is available through the references cited at the end of the chapter.

2.1.1 IC Design Philosophy

The design of monolithic integrated circuitry is entirely different from that of discrete-component circuitry, because of inherent limitations in the IC fabrication process. In fabricating ICs, resistors are limited to low values, have very poor tolerances, and exhibit poor performance with changes in temperature. Complementary transistors of equal performance are not feasible without additional processing steps; thus, designs must be either npn-only or worked around the poor-quality pnp transistors that are compatible with the npn process. Capacitors of more than a few picofarads in value are not desirable because they occupy excessive chip area and hence increase the cost per device.

Because conventional discrete-component design techniques were not compatible with monolithic IC processing, new methods had to be devised. The old "ground rules" were discarded in favor of ones which optimized designs based on inherent properties of the monolithic IC process. A brief review of these features is appropriate before we begin to discuss them in the context of actual IC op-amp circuits.

Because of the small size of the transistors used in integrated circuitry, it is possible to lay out and interconnect a large number of them in the space formerly occupied by a single conventional transistor. This is a big advantage, since for a given area (or "chip real estate" as it is termed in the IC world) it is just as economical to create a large number of the smaller IC transistors as it is to create only one discrete transistor. Active components are inexpensive in IC designs; therefore, a larger number of them may be used without materially affecting cost. This is in direct contrast to the reasoning behind discrete-component designs, where the object is to use the minimum number of components that will satisfy the circuit requirements. As a result, an IC schematic will invariably appear to have more transistors and diodes in it than are needed. From the standpoint of cost (which is directly proportional to chip area), it is advantageous to use as many of the smaller active components as possible to accomplish a given function. Since capacitors, resistors, and transistors occupy diminishing amounts of space in that order, designs will lean toward transistors first, resistors next, and capacitors last. Often a transistor may be biased to simulate a large value resistor, because if the resistor were used for the same function, it would occupy a much greater area. Transistors are used in many ways, a few of which are illustrated in Fig. 2-1.

In addition to the substantial use of transistors in various forms, another inherent advantage of the monolithic process is extensively utilized. Due to the very close physical proximity of IC components,

| (A) Transistor as a diode. | (B) Transistor as a zener diode. | (C) Transistors as constant-current sources. |

Fig. 2-1. Transistors are used to simulate other IC circuit elements.

and the fact that they are all made simultaneously on the same silicon chip (and thus are subject to identical conditions), all elements tend to match very well. Although the resistors are subject to tolerance variations of up to ±30%, the match between them is much better—within 3%. This matching characteristic not only holds true for resistors but also for transistors. Current gains and base-emitter potentials match up within a few percent, as do breakdown voltages. A pair of IC transistors laid down side by side can be matched to have base-emitter voltages (V_{BE}) within a millivolt of each other. This makes IC transistors naturally suited for balanced-gain stages such as differential amplifiers, which work on the symmetry principle. In addition, diode-connected transistors can be used readily as matched pairs. Since the components on an IC chip are all within a few thousandths of an inch of each other and are an integral part of the chip, these matching characteristics also track very well with temperature changes.

More recent technological advances are ion implantation and active trimming. Ion implantation first allowed high-quality JFET transistors to be fabricated along with bipolars in the 356 device series. Another FET-type amplifier family includes the 3130 and 3140 units. Active trimming, either by laser or zener shorting techniques, allowed very low (< 100 μV) input voltage offsets, as well as low drift, to be achieved.

To illustrate the preceding points and to give the discussion some perspective, we will now discuss several representative designs that are excellent examples of the optimum use of matched-component design.

2.1.2 The μA709

A major milestone in IC evolution came with the introduction of the Fairchild μA709 in 1965. The 709 improved upon the performance of the earlier 702 in a number of areas; notably, it had higher gain, a larger input and output voltage range, lower input currents, higher output currents, and operation from symmetrical power supplies of ±15 volts. The 709 became a standard type number and is still produced in volume by more sources than any other linear integrated circuit. So universal was the acceptance of the 709 that it must be regarded as a classic among IC op amps. Although many of its individual performance parameters have long since been eclipsed, the 709 remains a unique blend of performance, versatility, and economy —three ingredients that are a hard combination to beat. Therefore, it is fairly safe to assume that the 709 will not only be remembered for its historical value, but will remain valuable for many years to come. Proof of this fact is that it is still in vendor catalogs more than 15 years after its introduction.

709 Circuit Description

The design principles established with the 702 were exercised again in the 709, with some new advances also being introduced. In addition, many of the problems in applying the 702 were eliminated with the 709 design.

Fig. 2-2 is the schematic diagram of a 709 amplifier. Immediately you can see that a large number of transistors are used (15) and that the resistance values are chosen fairly low—R_{15} is the highest at 30,000 ohms. This is in keeping with the basic design philosophy set forth in the 702. Still, this entire circuit does not occupy an excessive chip area—the 709 is a 0.055-inch (1.4-millimeter) square chip of silicon. A photomicrograph of the layout is shown in Fig. 2-3.

Input Stage—In the 709, Q_1 and Q_2 form the input differential-amplifier pair. Each is operated at a collector current of 20 microamperes by the constant-current transistor, Q_{11}. This low current level establishes one important advantage—a big reduction in the input bias current to Q_1 and Q_2. With a typical β of 100 for Q_1-Q_2, this makes the input current 200 nanoamperes, or about 1/20 that of the 702. To obtain a 40-μA current by conventional means would require a very high resistance in the emitter of Q_{11}. In addition, to increase the negative common-mode input range of Q_1 and Q_2, Q_{11} must be biased close to the V− line, otherwise it would saturate as Q_1 and Q_2 swing negative. From this standpoint Q_{11} should swing to at least −10 volts peak. The solution to the biasing of Q_{11} at 40 μA was a new type of constant-current source made up of Q_{10} and Q_{11}.

In a pair of matched transistors, such as those that are readily available in a monolithic IC, the base-emitter voltages that are required for given collector currents form an extremely predictable parameter. Not only will these voltages be within 1 or 2 mV for equal collector currents, but the *difference* in the two base-emitter voltages for a *ratio* of currents is also very predictable. This is illustrated by Fig. 2-4A. With a current, I_1, flowing in diode-connected Q_1, Q_1

will develop a base-emitter voltage, V_{BE1}, which is proportional to this current. For an identical current to flow in Q_2, Q_2 is connected directly in parallel with the base-emitter junction of Q_1. Since the two transistors are matched, an identical current, I_2 will flow in Q_2 since the V_{BE} of Q_2 equals the V_{BE} of Q_1. This is a common IC circuit technique for generating a simple constant-current source. By

Courtesy Fairchild Semiconductor

Fig. 2-2. Schematic of μA709 op amp.

carrying this a step farther, advantage is taken of the fact that transistors Q_1 and Q_2 are well matched over their entire dynamic range of current flow. In this manner, the ratio of I_1 to I_2 is manipulated by subtracting a portion of the base-emitter voltage of Q_1 from that applied to Q_2, thus causing Q_2 to conduct a smaller current. Transistors are natural logarithmic elements—their base-emitter voltage is the logarithm of the collector current over many decades of current. Typically, for each 10-to-1 change in collector current in a pair of matched transistors, the base-emitter voltage will change by 60 mV.

Fig. 2-3. Photomicrograph of μA709 silicon chip.

Therefore, to scale I_2 to a level of $1/10$ of I_1, the base-emitter voltage of Q_2 must be reduced to 60 mV below that of Q_1. This is illustrated in Fig. 2-4B. For $I_2 = 1/100$ of I_1, the reduction would be 120 mV. This is accomplished by a simple emitter resistance, R_E, which drops the 60 mV or 120 mV, as the case may be. This allows microampere-level currents from Q_2 to be generated with very small values of resistance for R_E, as the drop across R_E will only be a few tens of millivolts.

Referring to Fig. 2-2, we can see how this is done in the 709 with Q_{10} and Q_{11}. Q_{10} is the reference transistor and R_{11} represents the V_{BE} scaling resistor, R_E (Fig. 2-4A). R_E subtracts a portion of the

(A) Basic current source.   (B) Logarithmic current source.

Fig. 2-4. Matched transistor current sources.

V_{BE} of Q_{10} from that of Q_{11}, forcing Q_{11} to conduct a much lower current. An additional advantage of this technique is the dynamic range of voltage it allows at the collector of Q_{11}. Since the base of Q_{11} is only 1 V_{BE} above the V− line, the emitters of Q_1 and Q_2 can drop very nearly to the V_{BE} of Q_{11} (or very close to −15 V) before Q_{11} saturates. This maximizes the negative input common-mode range of Q_1-Q_2.

Another interesting feature of the Q_1-Q_2 input stage is its performance with temperature changes. The output current from Q_{11} varies with temperature, but it does so in such a manner that it complements the transconductance variations of Q_1 and Q_2 with temperature changes. As a consequence, the resultant combination of these two opposite effects is a voltage-gain characteristic of the input stage, which stays constant within a few percent over the operating temperature range. In addition, the variations in the operating current of the Q_{11} current source with the supply voltage are reduced due to the relationship of the current in Q_{11} to the current in Q_{10}. The current in Q_{11} is related logarithmically rather than directly to the current in Q_{10}. Although the current in Q_{10} will vary with changes in the supply voltage, the resultant effect on the current in Q_{11} is very much reduced due to this logarithmic relation, so it is practically unaffected by supply-voltage changes.

Fig. 2-5. Simplified schematic of 709 second stage.

Second Stage—The second stage of the 709 is diagrammed in simplified fashion in Fig. 2-5. R_1 and R_2, the load resistors for the first stage, are high in value for high gain. The balanced-biasing feature possesses a property of immunity to supply-voltage changes. The full circuit is shown in the schematic of Fig. 2-2. Darlington connections are used for Q_5 and Q_6 to minimize loading on R_1 and R_2. An emitter follower, Q_7, is used to feed R_1 and R_2. This removes the input-stage currents flowing in R_1 and R_2 from Q_5 and improves the overall balance. The remaining element of the second stage is diode-connected Q_{15}, which stabilizes the Darlington pairs, Q_3-Q_5

and Q_4-Q_6, by removing excess leakage currents that occur at high temperatures.

In the 709, a high common-mode range is provided by second-stage transistors Q_5 and Q_6, which return to V− through bias resistors R_8 and R_{10}. In addition, the static voltage on R_1 and R_2 is made high enough so that Q_1 and Q_2 can swing typically to +10 volts with +15-volt supplies. The second-stage output is developed across R_6 and is buffered by emitter follower Q_8.

Output Stage—The output stage is composed of Q_9, Q_{12}, Q_{13}, and Q_{14}. For a wide range of voltage swing with moderate current output capability, a class-B output stage is highly desirable, as it provides the requisite power with low standby current. The 709 uses a class-B output stage consisting of complementary emitter followers Q_{13} and Q_{14}. This yields an inherently low output impedance with the advantage that both transistors cannot conduct simultaneously due to their direct base connection. A high voltage gain to drive the Q_{13}-Q_{14} pair is provided by common-emitter amplifier Q_{12} and is driven by common-base stage Q_9, which has no current gain. Its primary purpose is to shift the high dc level at Q_8 to a lower dc level compatible with the base-drive requirements of Q_{12}. The entire output stage is, in essence, a single-stage voltage amplifier (Q_{12}) with a buffered output. The voltage gain of the circuit would be essentially the ratio of R_{14}/R_{13}, or $20,000/75 = 267$, were it not for R_{15} and R_7. These resistors provide local feedback around the output stage. R_{15} is the feedback resistor, with R_7 serving as the input resistor. The gain of this local feedback loop from Q_8 to the output is R_{15}/R_7, or $30,000/1000 = 30$. The feedback is used mainly to correct for the "dead zone" of transistors Q_{13} and Q_{14} as the output circuit swings above and below ground level. In addition, it further lowers the output impedance of Q_{13}-Q_{14} by virtue of the negative feedback through R_{15}.

Two new components are introduced into the design in the output stage: Q_9 and Q_{13}, which are pnp transistors. Both of these transistors are made with the same process that is optimized for the remaining transistors, which are all npn. As pnp transistors go, Q_9 and Q_{13} are of poor quality, having current gains of 10 or less. However, this represents no great difficulty since the circuit is designed to allow for these compromises. Q_9 is used only as a level shifter, and thus low current gain does not present a problem since an excess of drive is available from emitter follower Q_8. Q_{13} also has relaxed performance requirements—in reality, it need function only as a diode, since an excess of drive is available from Q_{12}. The gain it may provide, however, can be regarded as a bonus.

A point not obvious from an examination of the circuit is the relative size of Q_{13} and Q_{14}. These transistors, like most of those used in linear ICs, are of small geometry and have a rapid falloff in gain when driven into high-current operation. As a result, the output stage protects itself against short circuits, at least for short durations, by the self-limiting current of the output transistors.

Frequency Compensation—As discussed in the section on basic theory, a prerequisite for stability in a feedback amplifier is the control of phase shift in the amplifier before feedback is applied. Amplifier phase shift must be less than 180° at the point where the open-loop and closed-loop gain curves intersect. In the 709, the control

(A) Frequency compensation circuit.

(B) Open-loop frequency response for various compensation values.

(C) Frequency response for various closed-loop gains.

Courtesy Fairchild Semiconductor

Fig. 2-6. Frequency compensation methods and responses for the 709 op amp.

of open-loop gain/phase characteristics is accomplished by three frequency-compensation components, as shown in Fig. 2-6A. R_1 and C_1 are called the input compensation, and C_2 is called the output compensation. These three components shape the open-loop response and, with the value noted, yield the family of open-loop responses shown in Fig. 2-6B. These are the networks necessary for stability in configurations of 0-, 20-, 40-, and 60-dB closed-loop gains (see Fig. 2-6C). The impedance at the 709 compensation terminals is high enough that full compensation can be realized with reasonably small capacitors (5000 pF maximum). These networks provide adequate stability with a 709 device under worst-case conditions of temperature, supply voltage, etc. A summary of the μA709 electrical characteristics is given in Table 2-1.

Table 2-1. Typical Electrical Characteristics of the μA709 Operational Amplifier (T_A = 25°C, V_S = ±15 V)

Parameter	Value	Unit
Input Offset Voltage	1.0	mV
Input Offset Current	50	nA
Input Bias Current	200	nA
Input Impedance	400	kΩ
Input Common-Mode Range	±10	V
Common-Mode Rejection Ratio	90	dB
Voltage Gain	45,000	
Output Voltage Swing		
R_L = 10 kΩ	±14	V
R_L = 2.0 kΩ	±13	V
Output Impedance	150	Ω
Power Consumption	80	mW
Power-Supply Rejection Ratio	25	μV/V

2.1.3 The 101 and 741 Families

The LM101*

Just as the improvements in the 709 over the 702 established a new level of performance and versatility, so also was the LM101 an improvement over the 709. Introduced in 1967 by National Semiconductor Corporation, the LM101 was the next evolutionary step in the history of IC op-amp technology. The 709 devices are regarded as the "first generation" of IC op amps; the arrival of the LM101 began the second generation of IC op amps.

For the same reasons that the 709 has historical and applicational importance, so also does the LM101. It is historically important because it represents the next level of technology. And it is also important conceptually, for it is still the basis for an entire range of general-purpose devices which are variations on its basic design. Like the 709, we will examine the 101 closely because once it is understood, the entire range of similar devices within the second generation can also be understood. This encompasses a large percentage of op amps now in general-purpose usage.

---

* The generic family is described here in terms of the "101" part number, which is the full (military) temperature range device. The applications (and later) sections of the book are in terms of commercial devices such as LM301A (vis-a-vis LM101A).

LM101 Circuit Description

The objectives of the 101 design were to eliminate the major problem areas associated with the 709. These were:

1. Inadequate short-circuit protection.
2. Complicated frequency-compensation networks.
3. Latch-up when common-mode range was exceeded.
4. Too low differential input voltage.
5. Excessive power dissipation.
6. Sensitivity to capacitive loading and susceptibility to oscillations.
7. Limited supply voltage range.

The 101 design solved all of these problems and also added some additional refinements. Gain was increased to 160,000 over the 45,000 of the 709, and the useful range of supply operation was increased from ±5 volts to ±20 volts. The device retained the 709 pin configuration for input, output, and power-supply leads. A simplified circuit of the 101 is shown in Fig. 2-7. Although this is a simplified schematic, one thing that is immediately obvious is the absolute minimum use of resistors and the use of a large number of active devices.

To accomplish the primary objective of simple frequency compensation, the 101 uses a two-stage amplifier design; the fewer the number of stages in a device, the fewer the phase shifts with which to contend. However, to meet the high gain required from the device, these two stages must provide the gain previously supplied by three stages in the 709. This means that the gain per stage must be highly optimized to achieve a total gain of 100 dB for the entire amplifier. In the 101, this is done by using active loads, which increase the

Courtesy National Semiconductor Corp.

Fig. 2-7. Simplified schematic of LM101 op amp.

available gain per stage to a maximum without resorting to undesirable high resistances.

An illustration of this is shown in Fig. 2-8A. A basic common-emitter amplifier will have a gain equal to the ratio of the load resistance (R_L) to the dynamic emitter impedance (R_e). Gain may be optimized by raising R_L to maximum, but a limitation is soon reached. Since high values of resistance are not desirable in an IC, operation with resistance loads at collector currents of 20 μA is prevented because the load resistance required for high gain would be over one megohm. However, with a transistor as a load as in Fig. 2-8B, the situation is different. The output impedance of a transistor biased for a constant collector current is extremely high and can easily achieve the required one-megohm level. An additional bonus of this technique is the fact that it requires a minimum of voltage drop across the transistor for operation (as opposed to a resistor), and this extends the dynamic range over which the stage can swing before reaching saturation.

(A) Achieving high gain with high R_L.

(B) Achieving high gain with active loading.

Fig. 2-8. Methods of achieving high single-stage gain in integrated circuitry.

First Stage—Referring to Fig. 2-7, we can see how active loading is utilized in the 101. Q_3 and Q_4 in this stage form an equivalent pnp differential pair. Since monolithic pnp transistors have low gains, their inputs in the 101 are buffered by high-gain emitter followers Q_1 and Q_2. The net equivalent is a composite, high-gain, pnp differential pair. The outputs of Q_3 and Q_4 are loaded by active loads Q_5 and Q_6. This stage also serves as a differential to single-ended converter, transforming the push-pull output from Q_3-Q_4 into an equivalent single-ended drive at the collector of Q_6. One may also note that the common-mode input range of this stage is quite high; Q_1 and Q_2 may swing positive to a limit equal to the V+ line; the negative limit is a level 3 V_{BE} above the V— line. This feature removes any tendencies toward latch-up due to input stage saturation.

The gain of this input stage is 60 dB. An additional feature is a very high differential input voltage rating, due to the high base-emitter breakdowns of the pnp transistors. The fact that the input can tolerate differential inputs of ±30 volts removes restrictions on differential input swings.

Second Stage—The second stage of the 101 is composed of a common-emitter amplifier, Q_9, loaded by an active transistor current source, Q_{13}. Again, this is an example of active loading to achieve high gain in a single stage. This high-gain voltage amplifier is buffered to a low impedance level by a class-AB emitter follower composed of Q_{11} and Q_{12}, Q_{14} and Q_{16}. At this point we are ready to consider the composite circuit as a whole, which is shown in Fig. 2-9B. Fig. 2-9A is a two-stage model of the 101.

Frequency compensation of the 101 is accomplished by a single external 30-pF capacitor connected between pins 1 and 8 as shown in Fig. 2-9A. This capacitor makes the second stage a Miller integrator and forces the gain to roll off from its open-loop value of 104 dB beginning at 10 Hz and continuing at a rate of 6 dB per octave down through the unity-gain frequency of 1.0 MHz. This single-capacitor compensation makes the device stable in any feedback configuration down to the worst-case, noninverting unity gain. This response is shown in Fig. 2-10 for both the unity-gain compensation (30 pF) and the lighter compensation (3.0 pF).

Some further details of the Fig. 2-9B circuit are also worthy of note. In the first stage, buffer transistor Q_7 has been incorporated to minimize the loading on Q_3 and to improve the balance of the input stage differential to single-ended connector. In a similar manner, Q_8 drives Q_9 in Darlington fashion to prevent loading of Q_4-Q_6, thus maximizing the gain of the input stage. In the output stage, Q_{11} and Q_{12} provide a slight forward bias to Q_{14} and Q_{16} to minimize crossover distortion. Current limiting is also added for both directions of output swing. Q_{14} is protected against overcurrent for positive outputs by R_8 and Q_{15}. When an excessive current (about 30 mA) through R_8 creates a drop which exceeds the V_{BE} of Q_{15}, Q_{15} conducts, removing drive from Q_{14} and thus limiting the output current. For negative outputs, overcurrent protection is provided by a combination of effects. When the voltage across R_7 equals 2 V_{BE}, the collector-base junction of Q_{15} conducts and pulls heavy current from Q_{11} through the two series junctions of Q_{15} and Q_{12}. Since Q_{11} is a low-gain pnp, Q_9 must also conduct heavily. This forces a large drop across R_5, which in turn trips Q_{10} on. Finally, Q_{10} limits the drive to Q_8-Q_9 to a safe level, and this limits the negative output current at 30 mA. This rather elaborate negative-swing current limiting not only limits the output current from Q_{16}, but also limits the output from Q_9. The limited output current from Q_9 allows external diodes

(A) Two-stage model of LM101.

(B) Complete schematic of LM101.

Courtesy National Semiconductor Corp.

Fig. 2-9. Two-stage model and actual schematic of LM101 op amp.

to be connected to the compensation terminal (pin 8) to clamp the voltage swing of the output stage to defined voltage limits, a valuable feature for comparator applications. The remaining transistors in the circuit (Q_{18}-Q_{22}) are used in providing a self-regulating input bias to the input stage and Q_{13}; they are not part of the signal-flow path.

The 101 again demonstrates the use of a large ratio of active to passive components, containing 22 transistors but only 9 resistors.

Fig. 2-10. Open-loop frequency response of LM101 for two compensation values.

Courtesy National Semiconductor Corp.

Performance and applicational ease are both improved from the 709. A summary of LM101 performance is given in Table 2-2. All the intended objectives were accomplished. And, in addition, more open-loop gain, a wider supply-voltage range, and a facility for use as a voltage comparator were realized.

The LH101

The first self-contained, internally compensated op amp—the LH101—was introduced by National Semiconductor in January of

Table 2-2. Typical Electrical Characteristics of the LM101 Operational Amplifier (T$_A$ = 25°C, V$_S$ = ±15 V)

Parameter	Value	Unit
Input Offset Voltage	1.0	mV
Input Offset Current	40	nA
Input Bias Current	120	nA
Input Resistance	0.8	MΩ
Voltage Gain	160,000	
Output Voltage Swing	±14	V
Input Voltage Range	±13	V
Common-Mode Rejection Ratio	90	dB
Power-Supply Rejection Ratio	90	dB
Temperature Range	−55 to +125	°C
Temperature Drift	3.0	μV/°C
Supply-Voltage Range	±5.0 to ±20	V
Power Consumption	50	mW

1968. The LH101 is a hybrid combination of an LM101 chip and a 30-pF capacitor in a single package. It has exactly the same specifications as the LM101 compensated externally with 30 pF. Pinout is the same except for the lack of internal offset null and the inaccessibility of the clamp point. A schematic of the LH101 is shown in Fig. 2-11.

Fig. 2-11. Schematic of LH101 op amp.

The μA741

In May of 1968, Fairchild Semiconductor introduced the μA741, an internally compensated IC op amp with ac and dc performance characteristics very similar to those of the LM101 compensated for unity gain. A schematic of the μA741 is shown in Fig. 2-12.

Although there are substantial differences in the internal circuitry of the 101 and the 741, these are associated mainly with biasing and the method of short-circuit protection. The 741 may also be modeled as a two-stage amplifier similar to the 101, as shown in Fig. 2-9A and as discussed in the previous section.

The main difference between the LM101 and the μA741 is that the 741 accomplishes frequency compensation by means of an on-chip capacitor. This marked the first time that frequency compensation had been accomplished by means of an on-chip capacitor in a monolithic IC op amp. An additional difference in the 741 is the method of offset null. Offset null is accomplished in the 741 by adjusting the differential currents in Q_5 and Q_6 at their emitters, as shown in Fig. 2-12 (pins 1 and 5 in Fig. 2-13A). In the 101, offset null is accomplished by adjusting the currents in Q_5 and Q_6 at their collectors (pins 1 and 5 of Figs. 2-9A and 2-13B). Both methods perform the same function with regard to dc—a slight imbalance of the collector currents of Q_3 and Q_4 to null the input offset voltage.

Fig. 2-12. Schematic of μA741 op amp.

(A) Offset null circuit for 741.

*See Chapter 3 for further considerations on offset nulling.

(B) Offset null circuit for 101.

Fig. 2-13. Offset null differences between the 741 and 101 op amps.

The differences in the actual external connections are shown in Fig. 2-13.

The LM101A

In December, 1968, National Semiconductor introduced the LM101A, an improved version of the LM101. The schematic of the LM101A is shown in Fig. 2-14. As will be noted, there is little difference in the appearance of the circuit from that of the 101. The portion changed is the biasing circuit for the input stage (Q_{18}-Q_{22}), which allows better control of input current characteristics over the operating temperature range. In addition, certain processing refinements for input transistors Q_1 and Q_2 resulted in much lower input and offset currents (typically 30 nA and 1.5 nA, respectively), or about a factor of 10 better than the 709. No changes were made in the other characteristics, and the LM101A is a pin-for-pin replacement for the LM101.

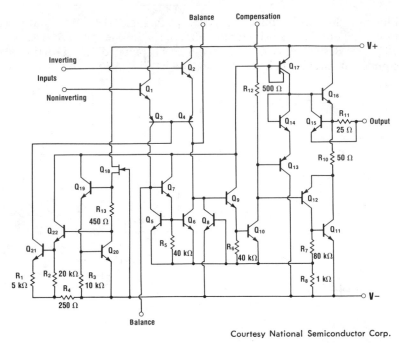

Courtesy National Semiconductor Corp.

Fig. 2-14. Schematic of LM101A op amp.

The LM107

National Semiconductor introduced the LM107 and the LM101A at approximately the same time. The LM107 featured the same improved dc performance as the LM101A, except that the 30-pF, frequency-compensation capacitor was built into the silicon chip. The LM107 schematic is shown in Fig. 2-15.

The μA748

In 1969, Fairchild Semiconductor introduced the μA748, an op amp with the dc performance of a 741 but with external frequency compensation. A schematic of the μA748 is shown in Fig. 2-16. The pinout for the 748 is functionally identical to the 101, although the circuit designs are different.

Comparison of 101 and 741 Families

At this point, it may already be obvious that there are many similarities between the basic 101 and 741 designs. In fact, if we were to redraw the simplified schematic of the 101, we would find that it applies equally well to all the general-purpose types. By assigning multiple reference designations to the transistors, we can further illustrate this basic similarity, as shown in Fig. 2-17. Note that even though there are considerable differences in the 101, 101A, and 741/748 designs, any one of them can be reduced to a functionally equivalent circuit such as that shown in Fig. 2-17. And, as stated

Fig. 2-15. Schematic of LM107 op amp.

previously, all of these amplifiers can be modeled as a basic two-stage design, with frequency compensation accomplished by an integrating capacitor connected around the second stage. This basic design concept is the principle behind the greatest percentage of op amps used today and virtually all of the modern bipolar general-purpose types. There are only a few subtleties that really separate the 101 and 741 families. Some important characteristics of the 101 and the 741 families should now be defined.

101 Family—Any "101-type" amplifier can be said to belong to the 101 family. This category includes the basic LM101, the LH101, the LM101A, and the LM107. It also includes corresponding devices of all temperature ranges. For example, LM101 op amps are supplied in three basic temperature ranges: (1) −55°C to +125°C (LM1— series), (2) −25°C to +85°C (LM2— series), and (3) 0°C to +70°C (LM3— series). Thus, an LM301A is the 0°C to +70°C temperature-range equivalent of an LM101A. Both are "101-type" devices, since they belong to the same family. Throughout the

Fig. 2-16. Schematic of μA748 op amp.

remainder of this book, the numbers used in referring to a device will be the commercial part number; e.g., a "301A" amplifier for 0°C to +70°C operation, such as an LM301A. The reader should be cautioned, however, that there are often specification differences between military- and commercial-grade devices such as supply voltages, gain, offset, etc. (the military-grade devices will almost always have superior ratings and, consequently, higher cost).

741 Family—As with the 101 family, any "741-type" amplifier can be said to belong to the 741 family. This includes the basic 741 device and also multiple versions such as the 747, 1558, 348, and MC4741. It also includes the 748, although the 748 may be said to be a "gray-area" device; it comes from the basic 741 design, but has the ac characteristics of a 101 type.

The same general considerations regarding temperature range and part numbers also apply for the 741 family (as well as for any of the other devices to be discussed). If a 741 is mentioned in a circuit, the specifications are assumed to be that of the commercial temperature-range (0°C to +70°C) device. The reader can make appropriate part number substitutions as his requirements dictate.

The salient features of these two general-purpose, op-amp families are summarized in Tables 2-3 and 2-4, and data sheets for the general-purpose types are included in the Appendix.

Fig. 2-17. Basic functional circuit diagram of the 101 and 741 op-amp families.

There are many other considerations involved in selecting one particular type over another. Ease of application and amount of necessary peripheral hardware are often considerations, not only from a convenience standpoint but also from the standpoint of board space, the number of parts to be stocked, etc. The 741 and its many derivatives will rate favorably in these regards if optimum compensation is not required. If the application requires optimizing speed or overcompensation, then the externally compensated 709 or 101 may be favored. In other situations, dc requirements may dictate a 101A. Although these three types will fulfill most general-purpose applications, no one type is overwhelmingly superior in all situations. Each situation should be evaluated on its own requirements. Where a multiplicity of devices is necessary, the multiple units will be found attractive (see tables).

For applications that are obviously out of the general-purpose area (high voltage, high speed, low input current, etc.), there are more specialized types from which to choose. These types cover a

Table 2-3. The 101 Op-Amp Family*

Military Temperature Range −55°C to + 125°C	Industrial Temperature Range −25°C to +85°C	Commercial Temperature Range 0°C to +70°C
LM101	LM201	
LH101	LH201	
LM101A	LM201A	LM301A
LM107	LM207	LM307
LH2101A	LH2201A	LH2301A

Comments

Basic device of family is the LM101. The LM101 is a general-purpose, externally compensated IC op amp. It is frequency-compensated with a single 30-pF capacitor. It features wide input and output voltage range with freedom from latch-up, output short-circuit protection, controlled power dissipation characteristics, operation from a wide range of supply voltages with little change, and relative immunity to oscillation tendencies.

The LH101 is an LM101 chip with a 30-pF capacitor added to form an internally compensated op amp in hybrid (2-chip) form.

The LM101A is similar to the LM101 but with better dc input characteristics.

The LM107 is an LM101A with internal compensation.

The LH2101A is a dual LM101A.

*The designations shown are not intended for ordering purposes. For complete ordering information (package styles, etc.) consult the manufacturer's catalog or individual data sheets.

broad range of remaining applications and will round out the devices to be discussed in this book.

2.1.4 Multiple Units

The RC4558

The RC4558 was introduced by Raytheon Semiconductor in 1974, and became a very popular device. Although the RC4558 is not a "true" 741 in the sense that it uses nonidentical circuit topology, it nevertheless is considered *functionally* so by many. It is a dual unit, offered in the same pinout as the MC1458 (this 8-pin dual-amplifier pinout has become standard).

The schematic diagram of one of the RC4558 circuits is shown in Fig. 2-18. As can be noted, the major difference from a 741 circuit is that the 4558 uses pnp input transistors, as opposed to the npn's in the 741. This, of course, reverses the direction of the bias current in the source resistance(s), which may affect the performance of some circuits. It is for this reason that the 4558 cannot be termed a "true" 741, but it equals or betters the performance of the 741 in other regards.

Table 2-4. The 741 Op-Amp Family*

Military Temperature Range −55°C to +125°C		Commercial Temperature Range 0°C to +70°C
Single	μA741 μA741A μA748	μA741C μA741E μA748C
Dual	μA747 μA747A MC1558	μA747C μA747E MC1458
Quad	LM148 MC4741	LM348 MC4741C

Comments

Basic device of family is the μA741. The μA741 is a general-purpose, internally compensated IC op amp. It features wide input and output voltage range with freedom from latch-up, output short-circuit protection, operation from a wide range of supply voltages, and relative immunity to oscillation tendencies.

The μA741A is similar to the μA741, but with tighter characteristics (to military specifications MIL-M-38510/10101).

The μA748 is a μA741 without internal compensation. Compensation and offset null are similar to the LM101. The dc specifications are identical to the μA741.

The μA747 is a pair of 741 op amps in a single 14-pin or 10-pin package.

The MC1558 is a pair of 741 op amps in a single 14-pin or 8-pin package.

The LM148 and MC4741 are quad 741 op amps in a single 14-pin package.

*The designations shown are not intended for ordering purposes. For complete ordering information (package styles, etc.) consult the manufacturer's catalogs or individual data sheets.

The RC4558 features improved performance over a standard 741 in terms of noise, slew rate, and bandwidth. A great many other op amps are patterned after the 4558 topology, and it appears in quad form as the RC4136. The RC4136 was the first quad op amp to appear on the market, and it enjoys wide popularity and multiple sourcing, as does the RC4558. An RC4558 data sheet is included in the Appendix. The RC4559 is an improved performance version of the RC4558.

The LM324

The LM324 quad op amp was introduced by National Semiconductor in 1974 and has become an extremely popular device. The 324 circuit is also not a "true" 741, as it uses pnp transistors; it also has a class-AB output stage. The LM324 is similar to a 741 in terms of speed and input currents, but there the resemblance ends. Designed with different objectives in mind, the 324 is useful for multidevice

Courtesy Raytheon Semiconductor

Fig. 2-18. Schematic of RC4558 op amp (½ shown).

applications which require very low power operation, operation from single (as opposed to split) power supplies, and high output currents.

A schematic of the LM324 circuit is shown in Fig. 2-19. A Darlington-connected pnp differential input allows linear operation of the input terminals at the V− supply level, or ground. Likewise, the output can swing to ground, and these two features optimize the utility of

Courtesy National Semiconductor Corp.

Fig. 2-19. Schematic of LM324/324A op amps (¼ shown).

the device for single-supply use. To minimize quiescent power, the output stage of the device is biased in a class-B mode. This results in a total quiescent current for the four amplifier circuits of less than 1.0 mA. The output stage can also source or sink substantially large currents, up to 40 mA.

The LM324 is available in a version with tightened dc parameters —the LM324A. A dual-amplifier version of the device is the LM358. Both of these units are widely second-sourced. An LM324 data sheet is included in the Appendix.

The LM324 established some basic performance features that have become standard on a number of devices, namely the input/output range, which includes V− (or ground). A related device that has these same features is the Motorola MC3403; however, the 3403 uses a class-AB output stage to eliminate the attendant crossover distortion of the 324's class-B design. Consequently, the 3403 consumes a greater quiescent current. The 3403-type circuit is available in dual form as the MC3458 or μA798, and in single form as the μA799.

The LM348 (LM349)

The LM348 and LM349 quad op amps were introduced by National Semiconductor as true 741 quad devices, with comparable input/output ranges and npn inputs. The 348 specifications are very similar to the 741 in ac terms, and meet or exceed the 741 in dc terms. The LM349 is a decompensated version of the LM348; that is, it is not a unity-gain-stable device. It is stable at a minimum closed-loop gain of 5.

The LM348 (LM349) circuit is shown in Fig. 2-20 and, as can be noted, it is very similar to the 741. The input stage employs a transconductance reduction technique to reduce the compensation capacitance and, thus, the overall chip area. This, however, has no external effect on performance, which is (as stated) equal to or better than a 741. The LM348 and LM349 are second-sourced by a number of manufacturers. A similarly performing device to the LM348 is the Motorola MC4741.

2.1.5 FET-Input Devices

Perhaps the greatest technological advance since the first edition of this book was published has been the maturation of the FET-input IC op amp. Prior to 1974, there were a number of monolithic FET op amps, such as the ICL8007, μA740, and NE536. However, these first-generation devices tended to be much less than ideal in dc characteristics, with typically high offset voltages and drift, and poor CMMR.

Today (circa 1980), there is literally a plethora of FET op amps, some with outstanding characteristics at very reasonable cost.

Inverting

Inputs

+ Noninverting

A2

A | A

+V_CC

25 Ω

Out

280 kΩ

40 kΩ

25 Ω

V_CC

A

A4   C_C

10 kΩ

5 pF*

A

A3

V_CC

1 kΩ

100 kΩ

75 kΩ

340 Ω

−V_EE

*1 pF on the LM349

Courtesy National Semiconductor Corp.

Fig. 2-20. Schematic of LM348/349 op amps (¼ shown).

The CA3130

The CA3130 was introduced by RCA in September 1974, and represents the first of a new wave of FET-input op amps. This group of devices is termed second generation, because it features many significant performance improvements.

A schematic of the CA3130 is shown in Fig. 2-21. As can be noted, the input stage uses a PMOS FET transistor pair, Q_6 and Q_7. These devices provide an extremely low input current, typically 5 pA. This factor is perhaps the single most outstanding performance attraction of the MOS devices. Input differential overvoltage protection is provided by diodes D_5 through D_8. Q_6 and Q_7 feed a differential-to-single-ended current mirror, Q_9-Q_{10}. The second-stage gain is provided by Q_{11}, with phase/frequency compensation provided by an external capacitor (pins 1 and 8). Q_{11} drives a CMOS drain-loaded complementary inverter pair, Q_8-Q_{12}. This stage provides 15-20 mA

Note: Diodes D_5 through D_8 provide gate-oxide
protection for MOSFET input stage.

Courtesy RCA Solid State Division

Fig. 2-21. Schematic of CA3130 op amp.

of output drive, and the unique property of a rail-to-rail output swing
(such as that found in CMOS logic devices).

The CA3130 is rated for a 5- to 15-volt supply voltage (16 volts
maximum) and is well suited to single-supply voltage systems. The
input stage can respond to common-mode voltages to V− (or ground
level), in fact to as low as 0.5 volt *below* the pin 4 potential. This
factor, coupled with the rail-to-rail output swing makes the 3130 useful in single-supply systems.

The CA3130 is a popular device and its characteristic performance
is also available in an internally compensated version, the CA3160.

The LF355/356/357 Series

In July of 1975, National Semiconductor introduced the LF355,
LF356, and LF357 series devices. This device family has had a major
impact on IC op-amp technology for a number of reasons. However,
the most basic reason for the importance of the LF355/356/357
series is that it marked the first use of ion implantation in an IC op
amp.

Ion implantation is a processing step which (in general) allows a greater degree of control over the *uniformity* of device characteristics. With regard to op-amp circuitry, the important thing it provides is the ability to simultaneously fabricate well-matched p-channel JFET transistors, as well as bipolars, as illustrated in Fig. 2-22. Not only is the matching improved, which results in better dc characteristics, but the JFET devices also are capable of much wider bandwidth than their counterpart device in all bipolar circuits, the lateral pnp. Therefore, in the LF355/356/357 series, a *combination* of very desirable op-amp parameters was achieved for the first time. This was a high-performance FET-input amplifier with good to excellent dc and ac performance, at a moderate cost. Ion implantation is now widely used in the industry in a number of op amps, as well as other ICs. (For further information, see the references at the end of the chapter.)

Fig. 2-22. Cross section of ion-implanted transistors.

The LF355/356/357 circuit also represents a substantial departure from the classical two-stage topology of the 741 designs (Fig. 2-9 or 2-17) and its many variations. This new circuit is shown in Fig. 2-23.

As can be noted, this basic circuit is used for all three devices of the series; the LF355 and LF356 (just as shown), and the LF357 with a 2-pF compensation capacitor. The 355 and 356 are unity-gain stable, while the 357 is stable at a minimum gain of 5.

The input stage of the circuit consists of a p-channel differential JFET pair, J_1-J_2, which are drain-loaded by current sources J_{10}-J_{11}. The amplified differential output of J_1-J_2 drives a second (bipolar) differential pair Q_7-Q_8, buffered by Q_6-Q_9.

The adjustment of the input offset voltage of J_1-J_2 is accomplished by current sources J_7-J_8 (via an external potentiometer). With no disturbance of the operating current in J_1-J_2, this offset trim technique results in little or no increase in drift, which was a serious disadvan-

Courtesy National Semiconductor Corp.

Fig. 2-23. Schematic of LF355/356/357 op amps.

Table 2-5. LF355/356/357 Specifications

Unit	Value
V_{Io}	2–10 mV(max)
I_{Ib}	50–200 pA(max)
$\Delta V_{Io}/\Delta T$	to 5 μV/°C(max)
f_t	4 MHz
SR	10 V/μs $\rbrace$LF356
t_s (0.01%)	1.5 μs
e_n	12 nV/$\sqrt{Hz}$ $\rbrace$LF356,
i_n	0.01 pA/$\sqrt{Hz}$ $\rbrace$ LF357
CMRR, PSRR	80 dB (min)

tage in some early FET amplifiers. A common-mode feedback loop is returned to J_1-J_2 for control of the operating point via Q_{13} and Q_{12}.

Compensation of the amplifier is accomplished by two capacitors; C_2, around Q_8-Q_9; and C_1, across Q_6. The output of Q_8, loaded by current source J_3, constitutes the fundamental output swing of the amplifier. Buffering and load drive is provided by Q_2-Q_3 for positive swings, and J_5-Q_{10}/Q_{11} for negative swings.

A summary of the specifications of this device series is given in Table 2-5. The dc specifications of all devices in the series are essentially similar; the major difference is in terms of speed; i.e., SR and f_t. The LF356 and LF357 devices are also capable of low-noise operation, particularly in terms of current noise, while the LF355 is a lower-power-consumption device.

The LF355/356/357 device series is well established as a standard FET-amplifier type and has multiple sources. A data sheet for the series is included in the Appendix.

The CA3140

The CA3140 was introduced by RCA in May of 1976, and, like its predecessor, the CA3130, features a low-bias-current (10 pA) MOSFET-input stage. The CA3140 has features more like a general-purpose op amp, however, in that it is capable of full-rated supply-voltage ranges of ±15 volts, and it also uses a bipolar output stage.

The schematic of Fig. 2-24 shows the circuit in detail. Q_9 and Q_{10} are PMOS FET-input devices, like the analogous units in the CA3130 (Fig. 2-21). Similar also to the CA3130 is the current mirror, Q_{11}-Q_{12}, and second stage, Q_{13}. Unlike the CA3130, however, the output stage of the CA3140 has no voltage gain and consists of emitter followers Q_{17}-Q_{18} for positive swings, and Q_{21}-Q_{16} for negative swings. The output stage swings very close to V− (or ground) potential for low currents, by virtue of current source Q_{15}.

Like the CA3130, the input of the CA3140 can respond to common-mode voltages which include V− (or ground). The device is characterized for operation over a range of supply voltages from +5 to +36 volts (or ±18 volts). The 3140 is second-sourced, and a device data sheet is included in the Appendix.

The TL081 Series

In October of 1976, Texas Instruments introduced the TL084, a quad JFET-input op amp, the first of a series consisting of single and

Courtesy RCA Solid State Division

Fig. 2-24. Schematic of CA3140 op amp.

dual, as well as quad devices. The circuit, shown in Fig. 2-25, is used in both multiple and single versions, the latter devices providing for offset null (shown dotted).

This circuit, as can be noted, is once again the classic differential-input two-stage amplifier similar to the basic 101 or 741 topology of Fig. 2-17, or the 4558 topology of Fig. 2-18. The essential difference is that the bipolar-input transistors have been replaced by an ion-implanted p-channel JFET pair, J_1-J_2.

In an op-amp circuit, the largest single improvement to be gained by the ion-implanted JFET is in the input stage, where lower bias currents and higher speed can be achieved (vis-a-vis the 741). Therefore, a topology such as this can be advantageous over the 355/356/

Courtesy Texas Instruments, Inc.

Fig. 2-25. Schematic of TL081/071 series op amps.

357 circuit, as it is basically more simple (requires less die area) and, consequently, will have potentially greater yields and lower ultimate cost. Also, the lower quiescent power drain of this circuit, compared to a 356 type, makes it feasible for multiple units, whereas a dual or quad 356 would be prohibitive in terms of dissipation.

The TL081 series consists of the TL080, an externally compensated unit pinned like the 301A, and internally compensated units consisting of the TL081 (single), the TL082/083 (dual), and the TL084 (quad).

Table 2-6. Typical Specifications for General-Purpose IC Op Amps*

	I_{ib}	I_{io}	V_{io} (mV)	$\Delta V_{io}/\Delta T$ ($\mu V/°C$)
Bipolar	50–100 nA	10–20 nA	2	10
FET	50–200 pA	5–20 pA	5	10–15

	CMRR (dB)	PSRR (dB)	A_{vo} (dB)	SR ($V/\mu s$)	f_t MHz
Bipolar	90	90	100	0.5–1	1–2
FET	85	85	100	10–15	3–5

* At 25°C, for commercial grade device with ±15-volt supplies and 2-kΩ load.

This device series could be called the general-purpose FET-input op amp, that is, a FET-input device with the utility and multiple device availability of the bipolar general-purpose units. Thus, a specification comparison can be made between the categories of devices by means of the hypothetical device specifications of Table 2-6.

The TL071 Series

Texas Instruments further improved and broadened their line of FET devices with the introduction of the TL071 series in July of 1977. These devices are numbered similar to the TL081 series; that is, TL071 (single), TL072 (dual), and TL074/075 (quad). The specifications of the devices are similar to the TL081 series, but feature lower noise and distortion for ac uses. A TL071 series data sheet is included in the Appendix.

The LF351/353/347 Series

In September of 1977, National Semiconductor introduced the LF351, a general-purpose, single-unit FET-input op amp. The LF351 also uses the classic two-stage amplifier topology with only a single JFET pair used at the input. This device is intended to be a more general-purpose unit than the LF356 to which it is comparable in speed. It has a lower supply current and, therefore, can be supplied in multiple device form as well. The LF356 is still the better choice, however, if dc input parameters are critical.

The schematic of the LF351 is shown in Fig. 2-26. This circuit achieves a performance that is very much like the general-purpose FET of Table 2-6. Device selections for offset voltage are available to maximums of 2 mV, as the LF351A. The LF353 is a similarly specified dual; the LF347 is a quad. A data sheet for the LF351 is included in the Appendix.

2.1.6 A Broad Overview of General-Purpose Op Amps

General-purpose IC op amps are used in the greatest percentage of applications. From Table 2-6 and the discussion thus far, such a unit would be loosely defined as having a unity gain bandwidth of 1 to 3 MHz, operation from power supplies of ±5 volts to ±20 volts without serious degradation of performance, and usually (but not always) internally compensated. This "loose" definition is fulfilled by a very great number of IC op amps, for example all of those just described, as well as many to follow. In fact, the range of devices available is so huge that is impossible to cover all of them in any degree of detail.

As has been noted, the definition given for a general-purpose op amp is perhaps too broad, as there are many distinctions that can be made among types that fit this general definition. The following dis-

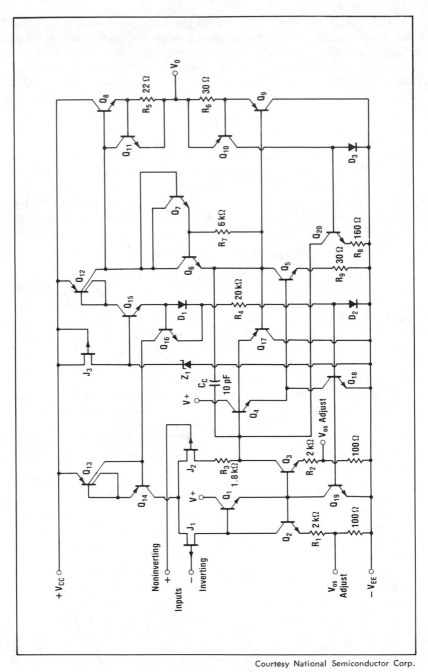

Courtesy National Semiconductor Corp.

Fig. 2-26. Schematic of LF351 (LF353, LF347) op amps.

cussion and classifying tables illustrate this point, by categorization of devices into groups by either FET or bipolar, and by single, dual, and quad pinout arrangements.

Table 2-7 illustrates standard pinout arrangements for single, dual, and quad devices. As can be noted, there is an almost overwhelming array of units from which to choose. And, it should be noted, this list of devices is not 100% complete, as that is beyond reason. It does, however, list representative devices in almost every performance category and type.

The units listed in these tables will plug into the pin arrangement as noted, and function as intended. In some cases, however, there may be subtle or secondary performance changes possible such as an optimum offset null with a 100-kΩ potentiometer (as opposed to 10 kΩ, as shown) for example. The manufacturer's literature will be your final guide in such cases. Data sheets are in the Appendix for devices previously mentioned.

The remarks columns of these tables are intended to give an "at-a-glance" assessment of the key feature of a device, beyond that of a pure general-purpose unit. The 1456 of Table 2-7, for example, will meet the general-purpose specifications of Table 2-6, but also (as noted) features a lower bias current and higher SR, compared to the general-purpose specifications for a bipolar device. As another example, the dual CA3240 of Table 2-8 has a lower bias current than the normal general-purpose FET, and is suitable for single-supply operation as well.

In the area of quad devices, there is a double standard in pinouts, namely the "324" and "4136" pinouts. The tables reflect this; that is,

Table 2-7. Single Amplifier Pinout Data

Type No.	Pinout No.	Remarks
Bipolar		
μA741	1	——
MC1456	1	Low I_{1b}, high SR.
MC1436	1	Low I_{1b}, high SR, high voltage.
LM343	1	Low I_{1b}, high SR, high voltage.
HA2645	1	Low I_{1b}, high SR, high voltage.
μA799	1	Single supply.
μA759	1	Single supply, high current.
MC1741S	1	High SR.
NE535	1	High SR, low I_{1b}.
NE530	1	High SR, low I_{1b}.
OP-01	1	High SR.
AD741	1	Improved dc performance.
OP-02	1	Improved dc performance.
3500	1	Improved dc performance.
RC4131	1	Medium speed.
RC4132	1	Low power.

Table 2-7 (cont). Single Amplifier Pinout Data

Type No.	Pinout No.	Remarks
FET		
TL081	1	—
TL071	1	—
TL061	1	Low power.
LF351	1	—
μA771	1	—
MC34001	1	—
CA3140	1	Single supply, low I_{ib}.
CA3160	1	Single supply, low I_{ib}.
AD515	1	Ultralow I_{ib}.
3528	1	Ultralow I_{ib}.
TL087	1	Low V_{io}.
AD542	1	Low V_{io}, low drift.
AD544	1	Low V_{io}, low drift, high SR.
AD503	1	
AD506	1	
AD540	1	First-generation FET devices—not all are recommended for new designs (consult the manufacturers).
ICL8007	1	
NE536	1	
3540	1	
Bipolar		
LM301A	2	$C_1 = 30$ pF, $R_1 = 5$ MΩ, $R_2 = 5$ MΩ.
μA748	2	$C_1 = 30$ pF, $R_1 = 5$ MΩ, $R_2 = 5$ MΩ.
LM344	2	$C_1 = 30$ pF, $R_1 = 5$ MΩ, $R_2 = 5$ MΩ, low I_{ib}, high SR, high voltage.
FET		
TL080, TL070	2	$C_1 = 30$ pF, $R_1 = 5$ MΩ, $R_2 = 5$ MΩ.
CA3130	2	$C_1 = 47$ pF, $R_1 = 100$ kΩ, $R_2 = 0$.
Bipolar		
LM310	3	Low I_{ib}, high SR (follower only); R_p 1–8 = 1 kΩ.
AD504*	3	Instrumentation grade; R_p 1–8 = 10 kΩ.
AD510	3	Instrumentation grade, ultralow V_{io}; R_p 1–8 = 10 kΩ.
AD517	3	Instrumentation grade, ultralow V_{io}; R_p 1–8 = 10 kΩ.
OP-05	3	Instrumentation grade; R_p 1–8 = 20 kΩ.
OP-07	3	Instrumentation grade, ultralow V_{io}; R_p 1–8 = 20 kΩ.
μA714	3	Instrumentation grade, ultralow V_{io}; R_p 1–8 = 20 kΩ.
HA2500 (Series)	3	High SR, fast settling; R_p 1–5 = 20 kΩ.
μA725/725A*	3	Instrumentation grade; R_p 1–8 = 100 kΩ.
LM312	3	Low I_{ib}; R_p 1–8 = 100 kΩ.
LM316(A)	3	Ultralow I_{ib}; R_p 1–8 = 100 kΩ.
HA2600 (Series)	3	High SR & GBP; R_p 1–5 = 100 kΩ
FET		
μA740	3	First-generation device; R_p 1–5 = 10 kΩ.
NE536	3	First-generation device; R_p 1–5 = 10 kΩ.
LF355	3	Low power; R_p 1–5 = 25 kΩ.
LF356	3	High performance overall; R_p 1–5 = 25 kΩ.
LF357	3	High SR & GBP; R_p 1–5 = 25 kΩ.
OP-15	3	Similar to 355 — Improved in dc & ac performance; R_p 1–5 = 100 kΩ.
OP-16	3	Similar to 356 — Improved in dc & ac performance; R_p 1–5 = 100 kΩ.
OP-17	3	Similar to 357 — Improved in dc & ac performance; R_p 1–5 = 100 kΩ.

* Compensation component(s) required.

Table 2-7 (cont). Single Amplifier Pinout Data

Pinout Diagrams

the TL075 is a "4136" pinout quad FET amplifier, with essentially general-purpose specifications (no remarks); the "324" equivalent of this device is the TL074.

There are many devices listed on these standard pinout charts that go far beyond general-purpose performance, insofar as their exact specifications are concerned. These types, covered in Section 2.2, may be optimized in terms of dc errors, speed, voltage, etc.

Table 2-8. Dual Amplifier Pinout Data

Type No.	Remarks	Diagram
Bipolar		
MC1458	——	
RC4558	Medium speed, low noise.	
RC4559	Medium speed, low noise.	
LM358	Single supply, low power.	
NE532	Single supply, low power.	
μA798	Single supply.	
MC3458	Single supply.	
MC1458S	High SR.	
NE5535	High SR.	
OP-04	Improved dc performance.	
OP-14	Improved dc performance.	
HA2655	High speed.	
NE5532	High speed, low noise.	
FET		
TL082	——	
TL072	——	
TL062	Low power.	
LF353	——	
μA772	——	
MC34002	——	
CA3240	Single supply, low I_{ib}.	

There are also, of course, a large number of pinouts that are different in some other detail, such as offset null and/or compensation. These cases are simply too numerous to document here. A number of such units are listed in the performance charts that follow.

High-Performance Op Amps

Some devices offer substantial improvement over the characteristic specification of the general-purpose amplifier, although they may be of a similar basic design in some instances. A case in point is the fact that the 741 design has now been refined to the point that several manufacturers offer devices with 30-nA input bias currents and 5 μV/°C maximum drift. These units can be very useful, either for a performance upgrade of an existing circuit or system, or new designs with good performance at moderate cost.

Tables 2-10 and 2-11 list a number of these devices, for both bipolar (Table 2-10) or FET units (Table 2-11). The tables themselves are generally self-explanatory; it should be noted that perform-

Table 2-9. Quad Amplifier Pinout Data

Type No.	Remarks	Diagram
Bipolar	**324 Pinout**	
LM324/324A	Single supply, low power.	
NE534	Single supply, low power.	
MC0400	Single supply.	
RC3403A	Single supply.	
LM348/349	––	
MC4741	––	
HA4741	Medium speed, low noise.	
RC4156	Medium speed, low noise.	
XR4212	Medium speed, low noise.	
OP-11	Medium speed, low noise.	
FET		
TL084	––	
TL074	––	
TL064	Low power.	
LF347	––	
μA774	––	
MC34004	––	
MC3471	High speed.	
Bipolar	**4136 Pinout**	
RC4136	Medium speed, low noise.	
OP-09	Medium speed, low noise.	
FET		
TL075	––	

Note: First number denotes "324" pinout. Number in ( ) denotes "4136" pinout.

Table 2-10. High Performance Bipolar Op-Amp Data

Type No.	I_{ib} (nA)	I_{io} (nA)	V_{io} (mV)	$\Delta V_{io}/\Delta T$ ($\mu V/°C$)	CMRR (dB)	PSRR (dB)	A_{vo} (dB)
AD741L	50	5	0.5	5	90	90	94
AD301AL*	30	5	0.5	5	90	90	98
OP-02E	30	2	0.5	8	90	90	100
OP-14E	50	2	0.75	8	90	90	100
3500E	50	30	0.5	1	88	100	100

Note: All specifications are worst-case values @ 25°C (minimum or maximum, as applicable).
* External compensation component(s) required.

Table 2-11. High Performance FET Op-Amp Data

Type No.	I_{Ib} (pA)	I_{Io} (pA)	V_{Io} (mV)	$\Delta V_{Io}/\Delta T$ ($\mu V/°C$)	CMRR (dB)	PSRR (dB)	A_{vo} (dB)	SR (V/μs)	f_t or GBP (MHz)	t_s† (μs to 0.01%, 10 V Step)
LF355	200	50	10	5†	80	80	88	5†	2.5†	4
LF355B	100	20	5	5†	85	85	94	5†	2.5†	4
LF355A	50	10	2	5	85	85	94	3	2.5†	4
OP-15G	200	50	3	15	82	82	94	5	50	2.4
OP-15F	100	20	1	10	86	86	98	7.5	3.5	2.3
OP-15E	50	10	0.5	5	86	86	100	10	4	2.2
LF356	200	50	10	5†	80	80	88	12†	5†	1.5
LF356B	100	20	5	5†	85	85	94	7.5	5†	1.5
LF356A	50	10	2	5	85	85	94	10	4	1.5
OP-16G	200	50	3	15	82	82	94	9	5.0	1.8
OP-16F	100	20	1	10	86	86	98	12	5.5	1.7
OP-16E	50	10	0.5	5	86	86	100	18	6.0	1.7
LF357	200	50	10	5†	80	80	88	50†	20†	1.5
LF357B	100	20	5	5†	85	85	94	30	20†	1.5
LF357A	50	10	2	5	85	85	94	40 *	15 *	1.5
OP-17G	200	50	3	15	82	82	94	25	26	1.6
OP-17F	100	20	1	10	86	86	98	35	28	1.5
OP-17E	50	10	0.5	5	86	86	100	45	30	1.5
AD542J	50	5	2	20	76	74	100	3	1.0†	—
AD542L	25	2	0.5	5	80	80	110	3	1.0†	—
AD544J	50	5	2	20	74	74	90	8	2†	3.0†
AD544K	25	2	1	10	80	80	94	8	2†	3.0†
AD544L	25	2	0.5	5	80	80	94	8	2†	3.0†

Note: All specifications are worst-case values @ 25°C (minimum or maximum, as applicable).
* A_V (minimum) = 5.
† Denotes typical specification.

ance specifications are given in terms of *worst-case limits,* either a minimum or a maximum. This guaranteed limit is, of course, the type of specification that is necessary to compile an error budget, or worst-case design to a given system specification.

These charts are arranged to highlight the general areas where a particular device type is notable. For example, the FET types are also capable of excellent speed; therefore, this is listed as well as the dc specifications. Note that Table 2-11 summarizes the major differences in the LF355/356/357 series of devices, the OP-15/16/17 units, and the AD542 and AD544 types.

2.2 SPECIALIZED GROUPS OF IC OP AMPS AND THEIR CHARACTERISTICS

There are many op-amp applications that cannot be met satisfactorily or optimally by general-purpose types. Special situations may demand very high speed (either wide bandwidth or high slew rate), very low input current, high input impedance, very low offset or offset drift, high voltage or high current output, or other confining characteristics. To complement the general-purpose op amps discussed in Section 2.1, this section discusses more special-purpose types. The array of types presented is broad, but there is a considerable amount of overlap. In fact, several of the ICs could even be categorized in both groups. Most of these types are also standards, representative of the popular version of a particular device. For reference, the key features that govern the selection of a particular op amp within its group are listed in the respective tables.

2.2.1 Instrumentation-Grade Op Amps

Table 2-12 lists amplifiers that are classified as "instrumentation grade." Generally, what this connotation implies is *precision;* that is, very high performance with regard to dc errors, low V_{io} (and drift), very high CMRR, PSRR, and A_{vo}. Such devices usually have low noise and low loading errors as well. In short, these devices are optimum for highly accurate dc amplification, such as may be found in instrumentation and control systems. Specifications are given in terms of worst-case limits, except as noted.

The first general instrumentation-grade op amp was the 725, an externally compensated type. As can be noted with this device (and many others as well), there are two offset-voltage-drift specifications given, one without null and one after null. With many units it should be noted that the condition of minimum drift is attained with the lowest (adjusted) offset voltage. In such cases, the manufacturer's recommended null procedure should be used, if nulling is to be used. (This is discussed further in Chapter 3).

Table 2-12. Instrumentation-Grade Op Amps

	Type No.	I_{Ib} (nA)	I_{Io} (nA)	V_{Io} (μV)	$\Delta V_{Io}/\Delta T$ (μV/°C) Unnulled	$\Delta V_{Io}/\Delta T$ (μV/°C) Nulled	CMRR (dB)	PSRR (dB)	A_{vo} (dB)
First Generation	μA725E*	75	5	500	2	1	120	106	120
	LM308A*	7	1	500	5	NA	96	96	98 ($R_L = 10$ kΩ)
	LM308A-1*	7	1	500	1	NA	96	96	98 ($R_L = 10$ kΩ)
Second Generation	AD504L*	80	10	500	2	1	110	100	120
	OP-05E	4	3.8	500	2	0.6	110	94	106
Actively Trimmed Devices	OP-07E	4	3.8	75	1.3	1.3	106	94	106
	μA714E	4	3.8	75	1.3	1.3	106	94	106
	AD OP-07E	4	3.8	75	1.3	1.3	106	94	126
	AD510L	10	2.5	25	2	0.5	110	100	120
	AD517L	1	0.25	25	0.5	0.5	110	110	120
	LH0044AC	15	2.5	50	0.5	0.5	120	120	120 ($R_L = 10$ kΩ)
	3510CM*	15	10	60	0.7	0.5	110	110	120
	OP-08E*	2	0.2	150	2.5	NA	104	104	94
	OP-12E	2	0.2	150	2.5	NA	104	104	94
Chopper Stabilized	SN72088*	10	0.6	150	1†	NA	80†	70†	100
	HA2905*	0.15†	0.05†	20†	0.2†	NA	120	120	174†
	TL089*	1	0.6	100	0.2†	NA	100	100	100
Electrometer Grade	AD515L	75 (fA)	—	1000	25	—	70	74	88
	3528CM	75(fA)	20(fA)	500	10	—	70	80	90

Note: All specifications are worst-case values @ 25°C (minimum or maximum, as applicable).
* External compensation component(s) required.
† Typical specification.

With the advent of the actively trimmed op amp, input offset voltage as a major source of error has become much less of a problem. The term *active trimming* means that at some point during processing, the manufacturer adjusts the internal circuitry of the op amp for a minimum input offset voltage condition. This is accomplished by either selectively shorting zener diode strings (popularly called "zener zapping") or burning resistor areas with a laser ("laser trimming"), The end result is the same—a device that reaches the user with an offset voltage of 100 μV or less. As can be noted from the listings, devices are available with offsets as low as 25 μV.

Such a device is the Precision Monolithics OP-07 device, shown in Fig. 2-27, which is trimmed for offset by adjustment of R_{2A} and R_{2B} on the chip. The OP-07 is essentially a trimmed version of the earlier OP-05. A comparison of their specifications reveals what the trimming achieves in terms of error reduction—nearly an order of magnitude reduction in V_{io}.

The advent of routine production-line trimming of circuits to extremely low errors has been a second major technological advance of recent years, as it has significantly advanced the op-amp state-of-the-art, at less than prohibitive cost. While any op amp can be nulled for zero offset *individually,* nulling often adversely alters (increases) drift. Also, an op amp with a potentiometer attached is *not* one that is field replaceable without recalibration and the attendant cost/complication. A specified low-offset device simply eliminates this problem.

Chopper-stabilized op amps attack the input voltage offset error in a different manner by using an on-chip modulation/demodulation process. This results in offset voltages on the order of 100 μV, or less, for the devices shown. The HA2905, for example, achieves a typical V_{io} of 20 μV, concurrent with a bias current of 150 pA, as well as other excellent specifications. The long-term drift of a chopper amplifier is, of course, an inherent minimum, as the device continually zeros itself.

Electrometer-grade amplifiers are, in general, devices that have bias currents of 1 pA or less—a very tall order for any op amp. The AD515 is a very high performer in this regard with its 75-fA bias current, as is the 3528.

2.2.2 High-Speed Op Amps

Table 2-13 lists a number of op amps that are generally classified as high-speed devices. Speed is a somewhat general parameter and can mean several things. However, these devices are characterized by exceptional performance with regard to f_t (or GBP), SR, and settling time (to a rated accuracy). They may or may not have good dc parameters as well.

Courtesy Precision Monolithics, Inc.

Fig. 2-27. Schematic of OP-07 op amp.

Since high performance in speed-related terms depends on a number of interrelated (and complex) factors, no single parameter will usually predict in a straightforward manner everything needed. The most complete and meaningful single specification in speed terms is settling time, as it indicates how quickly an amplifier will reproduce a changing step input to a rated accuracy. However, it is specified under

Table 2-13. High-Speed Op Amps

Device	Type No.	SR (V/μs)	f_t or GBP (MHz)	t_s (μs to 0.1%* 10 V Step)	V_{io} (mV)	I_{ib} (nA)
FET	CA3140	9	4.5	1.4	5	0.01
	TL071 (Series)	13	3	NS	3	0.03
	TL080*	$\geqq$12	$\geqq$3	NS	3–5	
	LF351,353,347	13	4	2 (0.01%)	1–5	0.05
	MC3471	20	10	NS	6 (max)	0.02
	LF356 (Series)	12	5	1.5 (0.01%)	†	†
	LF357 (Series)	50	20	1.5 (0.01%) ($A_v = 5$)	†	†
	OP-16 (Series)	23	7.2	1.8 (0.01%)	†	†
	OP-17 (Series)	62	26	1.6 (0.01%) ($A_v = 5$)	†	†
Bipolar	CA3100*	$\geqq$25	$\geqq$30	0.6 (0.5%)	1	700
	LM318	$\geqq$70	$\geqq$15	0.8	4	150
	NE5534*	$\geqq$7	$\geqq$10	NS	0.5	500
	MC1741S	12	1	3	2	200
	NE531*	$\geqq$30	$\geqq$1	2.5 (0.01%)	2	300
	NE535	15	1	3	2	65
	NE538	60	6	1.2	2	65
	HA2625*	$\geqq$7	$\geqq$12	NS	3	5
	HA2525*	100	20	0.2 ($A_v = 3$)	5	125
	AD509	120	20	0.2	5	125

Note: All specifications typical, except as noted.
* External compensation component(s) required.
† See Table 2-11.

closed-loop and specific conditions; therefore, a given specification may not match an intended use exactly. For applications such as data-conversion uses, settling time is the most meaningful parameter and may, in fact, be all that is needed.*

For ease of use, Table 2-13 is broken down into the subcategories of FET and bipolar amplifier types. Most of the data is self-explanatory and the specifications given are typical. The highest-performance FET types are the LF356/357 and OP-16/17 series; highest-performance bipolar types are the HA2525 and AD509.

---

* For a discussion of converter related uses for op amps, see the author's *IC Converter Cookbook*, Howard W. Sams & Co., Inc., 1978.

2.2.3 Other Op-Amp Devices

There are other considerations as to application category which may not have to be specifically addressed by the types discussed thus far. Generally, however, an op amp that does not fall into one of the categories discussed would be quite specialized. Examples of such categories would be:

- High-Voltage Op Amps
  MC1436
  LM343, LM344 (see Table 2-7)
  HA2645
  NE540, NE541
  3580, 3584

- High-Power Op Amps
  NE540, NE541
  μA759 (see Table 2-7)
  μA791

- Preamps
  MC1303
  μA739, μA749

- Programmable Op Amps
  4250
  μA776
  HA2725
  CA3078
  TL066

Of the categories mentioned, most are self-explanatory perhaps with the exception of the latter—programmable op amps. A programmable op amp is one that allows user adjustment of performance characteristics, via a programming input pin.

2.2.4 Parameter Optimization

When selecting an op amp for a particular application, very often one (or two) amplifier performance parameters will reduce to primary importance. The selection of an optimum device can then proceed, given a catalog of devices from which to choose.

As an aid to this process, the chart of Table 2-14 will be found helpful. This chart lists a number of basic op-amp performance parameters, and the category of the device that will be found to be optimum for that parameter. Then, a representative device and its specifications are listed. Although the specific device examples may change with the introduction of new types, the categories will not— thus the user generally will always know where to look.

Table 2-14. Op-Amp Parameter Optimization Chart

	Parameter	Category	Example	Specification
Input	V_{io}	Chopper stabilized or actively trimmed.	HA2905 AD510, AD517 OP-07	20–50 μV
	$\Delta V_{io}/\Delta T$	Chopper stabilized or actively trimmed.	HA2905 (See Table 2-12)	0.2 to 0.5 μV/°C
	I_{ib}	Electrometer.	AD515	75 fA
		MOSFET input.	CA3130	5 pA
	I_{io}	Same as I_{ib}.	Same	
	CMRR	Actively trimmed.	LH0044AC	120 dB
	PSRR	Actively trimmed.	LH0044AC	120 dB
	e_n	Bipolar.	NE5534	4nV/$\sqrt{Hz}$
	I_n	FET.	LF356 series	0.01 pA/$\sqrt{Hz}$
Output	V_{om}	Bipolar, high voltage.	HA2645	$\pm$35 V (@ $V_S = \pm$40 V)
		Single supply.	LM324(358)	$V_S = 1.5$ V
	I_{om}	Power (TO-3).	μA791	1.0 A
		Power (TO-99).	μA759	0.35 A
Dynamic	f_t	Bipolar.	HA2525	20 MHz
	GBP	FET (decompensated).	OP-17 (single)	30 MHz
		Bipolar (decompensated).	HA4625 (quad)	70 MHz
	SR	Bipolar.	HA2525	100 V/μs
	A_v	Chopper stabilized.	HA2905	174 dB

As has been mentioned, selected data sheets for individual devices are included in the Appendix. Also included in the Appendix is a complete list of devices and their manufacturers, for complete specification information.

Further background information on specific devices may be obtained by consulting the references listed at the end of the chapter.

REFERENCES

1. *Analog Data Manual*, 1977. Signetics Corp., Sunnyvale, Calif.

2. Borlase, W. H.; Maidique, M. A. "Precision IC's Challenge Chopper Amplifier Designs." *Electronic Products*, December 18, 1972.

3. Cave, D. L.; Davis, W. R. "A Quad JFET Wide-Band Op Amp IC Featuring Temperature Compensated Bandwidth." *IEEE Journal of Solid State Circuits*, Vol. SC-12, No. 4, August 1977.

4. Davis, S. "IC Op Amp Families," *EDN*, January 20, 1978.

5. *Designing With TL080 BIFET Op Amps*. Texas Instruments Bulletin CA-193, July 1977. Texas Instruments, Inc., Dallas, Texas.

6. Dobkin, R. C. *IC Preamp Challenges Choppers on Drift*. National Semiconductor Application Note AN-79, February 1973. National Semiconductor Corp., Santa Clara, Calif.

7. ———. *LM118 Op Amp Slews 70 V/μs.* National Semiconductor Linear Brief LB-17, September 1971. National Semiconductor Corp., Santa Clara, Calif.

8. Erdi, G. *A Low Drift, Low Noise Monolithic Operational Amplifier For Low Level Signal Processing.* Fairchild Semiconductor Application Bulletin APP-136, July 1969. Fairchild Semiconductor, Mountain View, Calif.

9. Fullagar, D. *A New High Performance Monolithic Operational Amplifier.* Fairchild Application Brief, May 1968. Fairchild Semiconductor, Mountain View, Calif.

10. ———. "Better Understanding of FET Operation Yields Viable Monolithic J-FET Op Amp." *Electronics,* November 6, 1972.

11. ———. *The 8007—A High-Performance FET-Input Operational Amplifier.* Intersil Application Bulletin A005, March 1972. Intersil, Inc., Cupertino, Calif.

12. Grant, D. "Low Drift Super Beta Op Amp." *Analog Dialogue,* Vol. 12, No. 1, 1978.

13. Gray, P. R. "A 15W Monolithic Power Amplifier." *ISSCC Digest,* February 1972, pp. 180–181.

14. Hearn, H. W. "Fast Slewing Monolithic Operational Amplifier." *IEEE Journal of Solid State Circuits,* Vol. SC-6, No. 1, February 1971.

15. Jung, W. G. "IC Op Amps For Audio," Parts I and II. *The Audio Amateur,* February 1973, January 1974, February 1974.

16. ———. "IC Op Amps Have Evolved." *Electronic Design,* January 9, 1978.

17. ———"An IC Op Amp Update." *Ham Radio,* March 1978.

18. Maidique, M. A. "A High Precision Super Beta Operational Amplifier." *ISSCC Digest,* February 1972, pp. 178–179.

19. ———. "Monolithic Operational Amplifier With 1 μV/°C Drift." *Analog Dialogue,* Vol. 5, No. 3, April–June 1971.

20. Metzger, J. "Bipolar and FET Op Amps." *Electronic Products,* June 1977.

21. Ochi, S.; Flink, J. *LM143 Monolithic High Voltage Operational Amplifier Applications.* National Semiconductor Application Note AN-127, April 1976. National Semiconductor Corp., Santa Clara, Calif.

22. Pippenger, D.; May, D. "Put BIFETs Into Your Linear Circuits." *Electronic Design,* January 4, 1978.

23. Roberge, J. K. *Operational Amplifiers—Theory and Practice.* John Wiley & Sons, Inc., New York, 1975.

24. Russell, R. W.; Culmer, D. D. "Ion-Implanted JFET-Bipolar Monolithic Analog Circuits." *ISSCC Digest,* February 1974.

25. ———; Frederiksen, T. M. "Automotive and Industrial Control Systems Building Blocks." *ISSCC Digest,* February 1972, pp. 116–117.

26. Schade, O. H. Jr. "CMOS/Bipolar Linear Integrated Circuits." *ISSCC Digest,* February 1974, pp. 136–137.

27. Sherwin, J. *Use the LM158/LM258/LM358 Dual, Single Supply Op Amp.* National Semiconductor Application Note AN-116, May 1974. National Semiconductor Corp., Santa Clara, Calif.

28. Soderquist, D; Erdi, G. *The OP-07 Ultra-Low Offset Voltage Op Amp.* Precision Monolithics Application Note AN-13, December 1975. Precision Monolithics, Inc., Santa Clara, Calif.

29. Solomon, J. E. "The Monolithic Op Amp: A Tutorial Study." *IEEE Journal of Solid State Circuits,* Vol. SC-9, No. 6, December 1974.

30. ———; Davis, W. R.; Lee, P. L. "A Self-Compensated Monolithic Operational Amplifier With Low Input Current and High Slew Rate." *ISSCC Digest of Technical Papers,* Vol. 12, February 1969, pp. 14–15.

31. ———; Russell, R. W. "A New Op Amp Is Born." *Motorola Monitor,* Vol. 18, No. 1, 1970.

32. Stout, D. F.; Kaufman, M. *Handbook of Operational Amplifier Design.* McGraw-Hill Book Co., New York, 1976.

33. Sullivan, D. R.; Maidique, M. A. "High Performance IC FET-Input Op Amp." *Analog Dialogue,* Vol. 4, No. 2, December 1970.

34. Tobey, G. E.; Graeme, J. G.; Huelsman, L. P. (eds.). *Operational Amplifiers—Design and Applications.* McGraw-Hill Book Co., New York, 1971.

35. Underwood, R. K. *New Design Techniques for FET Op Amps.* National Semiconductor Application Note AN-63, March 1972. National Semiconductor Corp., Santa Clara, Calif.

36. Widlar, R. J. *A Monolithic Operational Amplifier.* Fairchild Semiconductor Application Bulletin APP-105/2, July 1965. Fairchild Semiconductor, Mountain View, Calif.

37. ———. *A New Monolithic Operational Amplifier Design.* National Semiconductor TP-2, June 1967. National Semiconductor Corp., Santa Clara, Calif.

38. ———. "A Unique Circuit Design for a High Performance Operational Amplifier Especially Suited to Monolithic Construction." *Proceedings of the NEC,* Vol. XXI, October 1965, pp. 85–89. (Also available as Fairchild TP-32/2, November 1965. Fairchild Semiconductor, Mountain View, Calif.)

39. ———. *Design Techniques for Monolithic Operational Amplifiers.* National Semiconductor TP-12, August 1969. National Semiconductor Corp., Santa Clara, Calif.

40. ———. *Future Trends In DC Amplifiers.* National Semiconductor TP-4, January 1968. National Semiconductor Corp., Santa Clara, Calif.

41. ———. *IC Op Amp Beats FETs on Input Current.* National Semiconductor Application Note AN-29, December 1969. National Semiconductor Corp., Santa Clara, Calif.

42. ———. *IC Op Amps Close the Performance Gap on Discretes.* National Semiconductor TP-9, December 1968. National Semiconductor Corp., Santa Clara, Calif.

43. ———. "IC Op Amp With Improved Input-Current Characteristics." *EEE*, December 1968.

44. ———. *Super Gain Transistors for ICs.* National Semiconductor TP-11, March 1969. National Semiconductor Corp., Santa Clara, Calif.

45. ———. *The Improved μA702 Wideband DC Amplifier.* Fairchild Semiconductor Application Bulletin APP-111/2, July 1965. Fairchild Semiconductor, Mountain View, Calif.

46. ———. *The LM110—An Improved IC Voltage Follower.* National Semiconductor Linear Brief LB-11, March 1970. National Semiconductor Corp., Santa Clara, Calif.

47. Witten, S. *Designing Junction FET Input Op Amps.* Siliconix Application Note AN74-3, August 1974. Siliconix, Inc., Santa Clara, Calif.

THREE

General Operating Procedures and Precautions in Using IC Op Amps

In this final chapter of Part I, we are but one step removed from applying IC op amps in actual circuits. However, in a practical sense, this chapter may be the most important of all the introductory material because it deals with the actual problems involved in using the devices: offset adjustment methods, standard compensation methods, protection against abuses, failure mechanisms, and application pitfalls. It is recommended that this chapter be studied thoroughly before any attempts are made at building op-amp circuits, particularly if the reader has had little previous experience with ICs.

3.1 METHODS OF OFFSET ADJUSTMENT

In applications that require a high degree of dc accuracy, the residual input offset voltage of the op amp used may be a significant source of error, particularly when operating at high stage gains. These situations require that the input offset voltage be adjusted to zero (nulled) for best performance. Offset nulling can be accomplished either by using a technique recommended by the manufacturer for the particular device (termed *internal* nulling in these discussions), or by using a universally applicable *external* nulling procedure.

3.1.1 Internal Offset Nulling for Individual Devices

In general, the manufacturer's technique for nulling a particular device is usually optimum for that device. Unfortunately, as touched on previously, the exact method of nulling used varies widely from device to device, and there is no completely standard method of internal off-set adjustment (although the 741 technique shown in Table 2-7 enjoys a fair degree of usage). Other details necessary in the practical application of op amps are methods of frequency compensation and pin-out arrangements. In this section we will discuss alternate methods of internal offset nulling. Compensation techniques (when required) are by no means common and must be dealt with case-by-case due to the large number of devices involved.

Although most op amps are available in a variety of packages, the most popular are the 8-pin packages—the TO-99 metal can and the 8-pin, dual in-line package (MINI-DIP). For dual devices, the 8-pin MINI-DIP package is the most popular, although the limitation of eight pins sacrifices the null capability. Alternate pinout arrangements may be arrived at by consulting the manufacturers' data sheets for the particular device (see the Appendix).

Actually, the basic pinouts for single devices shown in Chapter 2 with offset null can be considered to be the "standard" forms of offset null—those most often seen. The discussions in this section supplement those basic modes and are for the remaining applications.

The information provided in this section will be sufficient to apply virtually any device in its basic circuit arrangement. Offset adjustments, and even compensation components, are not required in *all* circumstances and may be deleted where not necessary. Power-supply connections are obviously always required and are shown in this section for reference. Throughout the remainder of the book, however, the power connections are not shown as long as they involve standard supplies. In special circuits or nonstandard power-supply operation, the power connections will be shown in full detail.

Fig. 3-1 shows the standard op-amp pinout with dotted supply connections to illustrate this point. The V−, or ground, pin is pin 4 (for single devices) and is common for both *power and signal* in single-supply types. Typically, for example, a single-supply op amp might

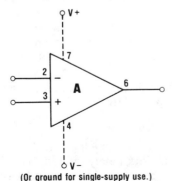

(Or ground for single-supply use.)

Fig. 3-1. Standard op-amp pinout for dual- or single-supply use.

operate from a +15-volt (only) power supply and handle a 0- to 10-volt signal range. In such a case, pin 4 would be grounded. It is assumed, by implication, that both input and output can operate over the 0- to +10-volt range.

For dual-supply op amps, the more general ±5- to ±15-volt (or other) supply ranges will be used.

3.1.2 Nulling Precision Op Amps

Although, in theory, virtually any op amp can be adjusted for a condition of zero input voltage, there are special techniques for accomplishing it when precision op amps are to be used.

A precision, instrumentation-grade op amp will most likely be a device with a low initial offset voltage and, consequently, a low offset voltage drift. This is because these amplifiers typically exhibit a drift change characteristic of 3.3 $\mu V/°C/mV$ of change in offset voltage. Thus, in theory, when $V_{io} = 0$, zero drift is attained. It is for this fundamental reason (as well as the low offset voltage itself) that a factory-trimmed, low-offset-voltage op amp is a desirable item—two major errors are minimized simultaneously. Obviously, for operation consistent with this high performance capability, it is desirable not to compromise the low drift/low offset voltage relationship.

In general, offset null of a precision op amp should be avoided, if at all possible. This is for the simple reason that if care is not taken, the nulling technique used may actually *increase* drift. However, where nulling of the last 50–100 μV offset of a precision op amp is necessary, one of two schemes should be used.

Fig. 3-2 illustrates a high-resolution null technique suitable for trimming 100–200 μV of offset to 1 or 2 μV. This magnitude of trim range is really about all that should be considered for null, and nulling of a precision op amp should *never* be used to compensate for other system errors.

Fig. 3-2. High-resolution null technique for precision op amps.

R_1-R_2 = 2–10 kΩ
1% film (see text)

Offset Adjust

*A = Low-offset-voltage actively trimmed op amp.

In this circuit, R_3 is a relatively high value multiturn cermet trimmer, which shunts the internal amplifier resistances of 1–10 kΩ (typically). Resistors R_1 and R_2 are 1% metal-film units, selected to yield the desired resolution and range, and will be in the range of 2–10 kΩ. (On some amplifier types, these resistors will not be necessary.) Trimmer R_3 should be placed as close to the amplifier as feasible for minimum noise pickup. The wiper arm of the trimmer (and R_1-R_2) should be connected directly to the V+ pin of the op amp.

Fig. 3-3. Offset null technique to preserve low drift of precision op amp.

Fig. 3-3 illustrates a method of offset null that will not alter the drift of a precision op amp. In this circuit, A_1 is a low-drift precision type and A_2 is a unity-gain summer. The variable current applied to A_2 from the offset network trims the amplified offset of A_1 (as well as that of A_2). Although the offset and drift of A_2 will appear at the output, as well as that of A_1, they will be negligible in proportion to those of A_1, for high A_1 gains. This allows a low-cost general-purpose unit to be used for A_2. Amplifier A_2 is also advantageous from the standpoint that it buffers A_1. This general concept is applicable to many other precision devices; not just the LH0044 shown.

3.1.3 More General Nulling Procedures

The generalized nulling technique shown in Fig. 3-4 allows almost any op amp to be nulled, using a voltage referred to ground. High value resistors R_1 and R_2 connect to the balance terminals, 1-8 (or 1-5), and sink (or source) a few microamperes of current. A variable voltage applied to R_2 unbalances the two currents and thereby changes the offset voltage.

This scheme will work with a degree of precision that depends somewhat on the specific op amp employed. This is because the circuitry seen at pins 1 and 8 (or 1 and 5) varies widely from type to type. Thus, R_1-R_2 may need to be optimized for individual cases.

Fig. 3-5 shows how this basic null technique can be used with an auto-null offset-correction scheme. Here, A_2 is a FET-input op-amp integrator which stores a dc offset voltage on capacitor C. The auto-null system timing periodically closes switch S and drives the output of A_1 to a low voltage, essentially the offset voltage of A_2.

Fig. 3-4. General-purpose null technique.

A final variation of this basic scheme is shown in Fig. 3-6, where digital control is used for offset changes. In this circuit, the DAC-08C is used as a 6-bit D/A converter, which develops a differential voltage across the 100-kΩ load resistors. The voltages are converted to currents by the 4.7-MΩ resistors, which control the offset voltage of the op amp.

Fig. 3-5. General-purpose auto-null technique.

This scheme is a useful one for large systems, as virtually any desired offset voltage can be stored in memory and applied to the amplifier when desired. The entire circuit can be made remote, of course, allowing correction at a transducer site, for example.

Fig. 3-6. General-purpose digitally controlled offset trim technique.

3.1.4 Universal External Offset Nulling Techniques

As pointed out in Section 3.1.1, the optimum method of offset adjustment for a particular op amp is the internal method provided for by the manufacturer. This method results in the condition of minimum input offset voltage drift, which occurs when the input offset voltage is zero. Unfortunately, the mechanism for accomplishing this is not available on all op amps, and *external* methods sometimes must be used. This section describes procedures for universal external offset adjustment at the *input* terminals, allowing any op amp to be nulled for an equivalent input offset voltage of zero. This allows types which do not provide an internal offset adjustment to be used with greater precision, or it preserves the low-drift operation of certain types. The exact method used varies slightly with the type of configuration, as detailed in the following discussion.

Inverting Configuration

There are actually two slightly different techniques that can be used with the inverting stage to adjust the input offset voltage. The simpler of the two is shown in Fig. 3-7A. This circuit uses the R_1 and R_2 input and feedback resistors as part of an attenuator network in conjunction with R_3 to generate a variable offset voltage at the inverting input. This voltage is scaled down from the ±15 volts available from R_4 by the R_3 and $R_1 \parallel R_2$ divider. In this case, the ratio is 1000/1, yielding an offset range of ±15 mV. For different supply voltages, greater range, or different R_1-R_2 values, R_3 may be rescaled by use of the equation given in Fig. 3-7A. Note that if more than one input is used, the offset range will be reduced because of the lower equivalent resistance. In this case, the more general equation for multiple inputs should be used to select R_3.

With just one additional resistor, the circuit of Fig. 3-7B accomplishes offset adjustment independent of the feedback elements. This circuit is generally more useful since it injects the offset voltage at

*A = any op amp.

Offset Adjustment Range $\cong \pm 15$ V $\left(\dfrac{R_1 \parallel R_2}{R_3} \right)$

$\cong \pm 15$ mV (as shown)

For Additional Inputs $\cong \pm 15$ V $\left(\dfrac{R_{1a} \parallel R_{1b} \parallel R_2}{R_3} \right)$
(as in a summer)

*A = any op amp.

**R₁ and R₂ are independent of the offset circuitry—may be any type of element(s).

Offset Adjustment Range

$\cong \pm 15$ V $\left(\dfrac{R_5}{R_3} \right)$

$\cong \pm 15$ mV (as shown)

(A) Offset voltage applied to the inverting input.

(B) Offset voltage applied to the noninverting input.

Fig. 3-7. Universal external offset null adjustment circuits—inverting amplifier.

the noninverting input terminal, away from the direct signal path. In this circuit, R_3 and R_5 form a simple 1000/1 divider, providing ± 15 mV of offset voltage across R_5 with the values shown. The exact values used for R_3 and R_5 are not critical, but it is good practice to keep R_5 below 1000 ohms.

Noninverting Configuration

A circuit for external null adjustment for low-gain, noninverting stages is shown in Fig. 3-8A. Here, a low resistance such as R_5 is inserted in the return leg for R_1. The offset voltage is thus developed by the R_3-R_5 high-ratio voltage divider at this point. Since gain-determining resistors R_1 and R_2 constitute a voltage divider for the voltage at R_5, the voltage appearing at the inverting input will be reduced by their ratio. This yields a slightly more complicated offset-voltage-range equation. Again, the values shown yield ±15 mV of adjustment voltage.

It should be understood that the gain and offset calculations for this stage are not independent. The presence of R_5 in series with R_1 alters the gain equation as shown; and, with the values shown, the error is 1.0% (ratio of R_1 to R_5).

*A = any op amp.

Offset Adjustment Range $\cong \pm15$ V $\left(\dfrac{R_5}{R_3}\right)\left(\dfrac{R_2}{R_1+R_2}\right)$

$\cong \pm15$ mV (as shown)

Precise gain of stage modified by presence of R_5 in series with R_1:

$$A_v = \frac{R_5 + R_1 + R_2}{R_5 + R_1}$$

(disregarding $R_3 \parallel R_5$, since $R_3 \gg R_5$)

(A) Circuit for low-gain noninverting amplifier.

*A = any op amp.

Offset Adjustment Range $\cong \pm15$ V $\left(\dfrac{R_1}{R_3}\right)$

$\cong \pm15$ mV (as shown)

(B) Circuit for high-gain noninverting amplifier.

Fig. 3-8. Universal external offset null adjustment circuits—noninverting amplifier.

At high gains, a null may be more simply achieved with what is basically a modification of Fig. 3-8A. This circuit is shown in Fig. 3-8B, which generates the offset voltage directly at the summing junction, using R_1 and R_3 as the offset divider. The reason this technique is not preferred at low gains is that the signal voltage across R_1 (equal to the input voltage by the theory of zero differential input) is larger at lower gains, which creates a change in the offset voltage generated as the input varies. At high gains, however, this is not as great a problem due to the lower input level.

Voltage Follower

The voltage follower, a special case of the noninverting amplifier, is externally nulled as shown in Fig. 3-9. This circuit introduces a small feedback resistor, R_2, across which the offset voltage is generated. R_1 and R_2 form a voltage divider from the arm of R_3, reducing the ±15 V to ±15 mV. The reader will note that the offset of ±15 mV will appear only when E_{in} is zero. As E_{in} changes from zero, the offset voltage generated will also change. This may not be a serious

Fig. 3-9. Universal external offset null adjustment circuit—voltage follower.

drawback because the error it does introduce is greater at full scale, where it is still a small percentage error.

It should be understood that R_1 introduces a small gain error, although the error is only 0.1% for the values shown. Both of the preceding points should be considered if absolute accuracy is important.

The Differential Amplifier

Fig. 3-10 illustrates a useful technique for balancing a differential-amplifier configuration. The main problem with introducing an offset voltage into a differential circuit is that it must be done without disturbing the differential signal balance.

In this circuit, high-ratio divider R_3-R_5 provides a variable potential at the common end of R_2', which is normally grounded. After being further divided by R_1' and R_2', this voltage serves to null the amplifier.

Fig. 3-10. Universal external offset null adjustment circuit—differential amplifier.

A small R_5 is chosen so that it will be a small percentage of R_2', thereby minimizing the deviation from the ideal bridge ratio. In demanding situations, R_2' may need trimming to ensure that

$$\frac{R_2}{R_1} = \frac{R_2' + R_5}{R_1'}$$

With the values shown, the offset voltage range is ±15 mV.

In all of the preceding discussions, it is assumed that the ±15-volt power supplies used to generate the offset voltages are stable potentials. If they are not, it should be obvious that they will introduce noise into the system in proportion to their deviation from perfection. A noisy or relatively unstable power supply may be dealt with by conventional decoupling techniques (see Chapter 4).

In the same light, the stability of the offset adjustment is also proportional to the quality of the components used. For best performance, stable multiturn trimming potentiometers and stable resistors are recommended.

3.2 PROTECTION AGAINST ABUSE AND FAILURE MODES

Monolithic IC op amps have a few idiosyncracies that can cause trouble under certain conditions of operation. Unfortunately, these troubles are not evident by abnormal operation alone; in certain instances a device may fail altogether, possibly causing damage to other components. For the most part, however, these failure modes are predictable, and if taken into account beforehand, there should be no problems in applying the devices. In this section, we will discuss such failure conditions and give positive treatment for their prevention.

3.2.1 Input Limitations

Failure in IC op amps can be induced in the input stage in two general ways: (1) by exceeding the differential input rating, or (2) by exceeding the common-mode rating. Of these two, the differential input rating is the parameter that is most susceptible to abuse; therefore, it will be discussed in some detail.

Differential Input Breakdown

One of the easiest methods of inducing failure in an unprotected op-amp input stage is to exceed its differential input voltage rating. When this happens, one or the other of the differential input transistors (depending on the relative polarity of the input voltage) will go into emitter-to-base zener breakdown. This is shown in Figs. 3-11A and B. An npn input differential pair is actually equivalent to a pair of back-to-back 7-volt zener diodes, as shown in Fig. 3-11B. The

(A) Unprotected differential input stage.

(B) Zener equivalent to differential input stage.

(C) Differential input voltage in a slew-rate-limited voltage follower.

(D) Differential input voltage in a slew-rate-limited inverter.

(E) Differential input voltage in a charged integrator at turnoff.

If C is charged to a high voltage, it can discharge into A at turnoff.

Fig. 3-11. Illustration of possible causes of differential input breakdown in unprotected op amps.

anodes of these two diodes are the (+) and (−) input terminals of the op amp.

Whenever the difference between the input terminals exceeds ±7.0 volts, these emitter-base diodes will break down (as will any zener) and conduct a current which will be limited only by the external source resistance. If the source impedance feeding both inputs is low, the current can rise to destructive levels very quickly. Currents greater than 50 mA will cause permanent failure—usually a junction short. Currents lower than this, while not causing junction damage, are still very undesirable because they can cause permanent changes in such dc input parameters as bias, offset current, gain, and noise.

Obviously, in order to prevent this type of breakdown, we must anticipate it beforehand. However, the possible sources of input breakdown can at times be somewhat subtle, as the following examples illustrate.

If a voltage follower (Fig. 3-11C) is driven with a fast step input of +10 volts, the op-amp output will be limited to a rate of rise determined by its slewing ability. During the slewing interval, the amplifier is not operating in a normal closed-loop mode where the differential input voltage is zero; rather, a large differential error voltage exists, as shown by the waveform sketches. These spikes are caused by the fast input rise which the amplifier cannot follow, so a ±10-volt peak differential exists during the slewing interval(s). In a voltage follower, both inputs can see low source impedance, so this can quickly ruin an input stage due to excessive zener current.

An inverter stage (Fig. 3-11D) can also go into zener breakdown due to slew-rate limiting. Here the problem is not nearly as bad because the resistances limit the zener current during breakdown.

Another problem configuration is the integrator, shown in Fig. 3-11E. In this circuit, input breakdown can result if the supply voltages are turned off while the capacitor is charged to a high potential.

The solution to all of the preceding is quite simple. It involves an input clamping network to limit the differential input voltage and some series resistance to limit the current during clamping. Two methods of accomplishing overvoltage protection are shown in Figs. 3-12A and B. Either method will suffice, but the reverse-connected parallel diodes (Fig. 3-12A) are less expensive. The resistances used with any op amp may range up to 10 kΩ with little degradation of offset voltage. In an actual working configuration, the input ends of the resistors may be considered the inputs of the op amp and used accordingly. Generally, for best dc accuracy, equal resistance will be desirable in each leg. However, in many instances it will be possible to eliminate one or possibly both resistors, as long as input or feedback resistances limit the clamping-diode current. Such an example would be the circuit of Fig. 3-11D, which could be protected just by the addition of the diodes, using the input and feedback resistances as current limiters.

The reader may wonder if perhaps these points on differential input protection are not belabored, since many IC op amps of newer design do not have restrictive input voltage limitations. This is certainly true for op amps such as the 101, 741, and the JFET-type families, but it is by no means a universal practice with other designs. The 725, for example, has an unprotected input stage. It is of prime importance, particularly in high-performance dc amplifiers, to prevent differential input breakdown because it can seriously degrade the dc characteristics.

Many instrumentation amplifiers now have the differential clamping diodes built into the device. In the absence of internal resistance, am-

(A) Preferred overvoltage protection for unprotected op amps.

*A = any op amp with an unprotected input stage; e.g., 709, 725, etc.

(B) Alternate overvoltage protection for unprotected op amps.

**A = any op amp with internal differential clamping diodes; e.g., 308,318,504, etc.

(C) Overcurrent protection for voltage-clamped op amps.

Fig. 3-12. Differential input overvoltage/overcurrent protection methods.

plifiers such as these must be used with external resistors to prevent possible excessive current in the diodes. This is illustrated in Fig. 3-12C.

Common-Mode Input Breakdown

Another cause of input stage failure is possible destructive input current flow due to exceeding the common-mode input voltage range of the device. Although the 101 and 741 families are notably free of differential input breakdown, they can under certain circumstances fail from common-mode voltage abuse.

This failure mechanism is illustrated by Fig. 3-13A, which shows the input stage of a 301-type op amp. In a 301A op amp, both inputs are the base terminals of npn transistors, the collectors of which go to V+. In normal operation, the input terminals will always be negative with respect to V+, so the collector-base junctions of these transistors are never forward biased. If, however, V+ is removed from the op amp with a positive potential remaining on pins 2 and 3, the transistors will then conduct through the collector-base junction into the V+ line. If the source impedance seen at either pin 2 or pin 3 is sufficiently low, the resulting current may be high enough to destroy the input transistors. Such a condition may occur when the input to a system is left connected and the power is removed. Another example is with a capacitive source charged to a high potential at the time of power turnoff. If the capacitance is greater than 0.1 μF, the discharge current from the capacitor can also destroy the input transistors.

The solution to the preceding is also rather simple. It involves series input resistors to limit the worst-case fault current to 10 mA or less (Fig. 3-13B). Since 301A input characteristics are relatively unaffected by input resistances up to 10 kΩ, the resistors may be this high with no side effects. For general use, however, 1000 ohms per side will be adequate. The resistors need only be connected to those inputs which see potentially low impedances or excessive voltage. If it can be guaranteed that neither of these conditions will occur under any combination of input and power, then the resistors can be deleted.

Before concluding, it should be noted that this type of failure mechanism is not peculiar to only 301-type op amps. The exact internal circuitry of 301A (and 741) types will vary from one manufacturer to another. It is best to check the particular devices you intend to use, either by a simple ohmmeter check (pins 2 and 3 to pin 7) or by measuring fault current in a series resistor under the stress conditions.

A more modern device type that must be protected against common-mode overvoltage is the LM324. This op amp (and its family members) must not be stressed with an overvoltage which can go below V− (or ground), or an internal diode will conduct. This can cause burnout, latch-up, or both. The cure is restriction of the input common-mode voltage for negative swings. A clamp diode with the anode

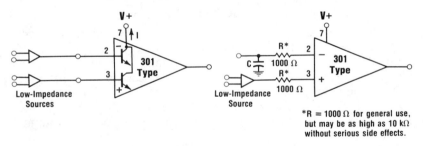

(A) Reason for common-mode input failure in 301-type op amps.

(B) Protection against common-mode input failure in 301-type op amps.

*R = 1000 Ω for general use, but may be as high as 10 kΩ without serious side effects.

$$^\dagger R = \frac{E_{source}(peak)}{10\ mA}$$
† See text.

(C) Protection against excessive source-voltage peaks for any op amp.

Fig. 3-13. Common-mode input protection methods.

connected to V− will restrict the voltage, and a series resistor (≅10 kΩ) between the diode and the (+) or (−) input will then protect the amplifier (see Fig. 3-13C).

Also, it is wise in general to be wary of possible power sequencing phenomena in any op-amp circuit, regardless of the device. When operating from sources of voltage which may have peaks in excess of the op-amp power supplies, the protection schemes of Fig. 3-13C can be used to protect any op amp. The 1N914 diodes clamp the inputs to a level such that the source-voltage peaks cannot exceed V+ and V− by more than the forward-biased voltage drops of the diodes. The series resistor limits the input current, either in the diode (R†) or the op amp (R‡). Schottky diode clamps are preferred for single-supply amplifiers, such as the LM324 discussed previously.

Latch-up

A phenomenon that sometimes occurs in op amps is called *latch-up*. Latch-up occurs most often in voltage-follower stages where the output swing is equal to the input and the op amp is driven to a high peak

| (A) General example illustrating latch-up source in an op-amp input stage. | (B) Elimination of latch-up (any op amp) by input limiting. |

Fig. 3-14. Illustration of latch-up in IC op amps, and method of elimination.

level. If the bias levels of the input stage are not well in excess of the maximum peak-to-peak voltage swing that the input terminals must undergo, the input stage can saturate on the peaks. When saturation occurs, a normally inverting stage no longer inverts; thus, what was negative feedback becomes positive feedback. With positive feedback the stage will then remain in saturation, and thus it is said to be *latched up*.

This is illustrated in Fig. 3-14A, an example of an op-amp input stage. To use a specific example, assume a minimum common-mode range of +8 volts, and an output swing as high as +14 volts. If a signal greater than +8 volts were applied to such an op amp connected as a follower, it is quite possible that it may latch up due to saturation of Q_2. Once latch-up occurs, the positive feedback can usually be broken only by removal of power.

Aside from the "nuisance" disadvantages of latch-up (the necessity of removing power to restore normal operation), there is a more serious potential hazard with the phenomenon. If the circuit of Fig. 3-14A uses an npn bipolar pair as shown, and is driven beyond its common-mode range, it will latch up on the positive peak. If an input signal from a low-impedance source is assumed, the input signal at pin 3 need go only 7 volts below the saturation level before Q_1 will go into emitter-base zener breakdown. This will almost surely ruin the device because both inputs are connected to low-impedance sources in this state. Latch-up may not even be triggered by the input signal. Any positive transient on the output line which is fed back to Q_2 can trigger it, and once in the latch-up condition the circuit will stay this way until power is removed.

There are remedies for the latch-up problem, which can be either specific to a given device, or general in nature. Perhaps general advice is best, as it can always be applied to any device.

Since latch-up will occur only at the extreme limits of input common-mode range, any method that reduces the common-mode input swing will eliminate (or lessen) the latch-up problem. Therefore, latch-up in an amplifier prone to it will have little likelihood of occurrence when the amplifier is operated at gains *higher* than unity or in cases when the input levels are safely *less* than that voltage which triggers latch-up. A circuit that takes advantage of this latter point can be used to prevent latch-up with any op amp, and is shown in Fig. 3-14B. Since latch-up will usually occur at only one common-mode limit, only one diode is (usually) needed. The $V_{cm(max)}$ can be a simple divider across the ±15-V supply.

Some general-purpose JFET-input op amps are subject to latch-up and/or state reversal, as are some single-supply bipolar types.

3.2.2 Output Short-Circuit Protection

Some early op amps (such as the 709) did not incorporate full-time current limiting in the output stage. Although a 709 will survive a short of a few seconds duration, a sustained short to ground, V+, or V− will result in destruction of the device.

Any amplifier type that does not incorporate current limiting may be protected against short circuits by a low value resistor in series with the output as shown in Fig. 3-15. If this resistor is connected within the feedback loop as shown, its presence will have little effect on performance, except for the obvious drop in output voltage it entails (10% with a 2000-ohm load).

A side benefit of this approach is the extra stability it provides with capacitive loads. For this reason, the series resistor may be helpful even if the amplifier used does have current limiting.

*A = any op amp with an unprotected output stage.

In addition to preventing destruction of the amplifier due to shorted loads, the series resistance will enhance stability by isolating capacitive loads.

Fig. 3-15. Output short-circuit protection.

3.2.3 Supply-Voltage Protection

Reversal of Polarity

Because of their internal construction, ICs must always be operated with the specified supply-voltage polarity. If the voltages ever become reversed, even momentarily, destructive currents will flow through the normally reverse-biased isolation diodes of the IC chip. This is a point to be wary of in any IC op amp, with no exceptions. Positive protection against this may be provided by connecting a rectifier diode in the negative supply lead as shown in Fig. 3-16A. Protection for a number of amplifiers in a system or on a printed-circuit card may be provided by connecting a single pair of power diodes in reverse across the supply leads as shown in Fig. 3-16B. The diodes used should have a current capacity greater than the fuse or short-circuit limit of the supplies used. When a supply reversal or transient condition attempts to force opposite polarity voltages on the amplifiers, D_1 and D_2 clamp the supplies into the limit mode (or blow the fuse) and nothing is damaged. This is a good feature to incorporate into any but the very smallest system.

Overvoltage

Commercial-grade IC op amps are generally specified for a total operating voltage of 36 volts (± 18 volts), while full-temperature-range devices can operate up to 44 volts (± 22 volts). These limits on supply voltage should not be exceeded even for brief durations. If there is a likelihood that the supply may exceed 36 volts (or 44 volts), a voltage clamp in the form of a zener diode should be used across the terminals as shown in Fig. 3-16C. This zener will be nonconducting

(A) Reverse-polarity protection for a single amplifier.

(B) Reverse-polarity protection for a number of amplifiers in a system.

(C) Overvoltage protection.

Fig. 3-16. Supply-voltage protection methods.

with normal ±15-volt (30-volt) potentials. For higher maximum-rated supplies, choose the zener voltage closest to but not more than the total maximum—for example, for ±22 volts use a 43-volt zener.

3.3 OPTIMUM STABILITY GROUND RULES

In using IC op amps, there are many operating conditions where stability becomes a significant problem. Stability, as discussed in this section, is intended to mean both ac and dc stability. Stabilizing a feedback amplifier is no easy task, and it can turn into an impossible situation if good, basic, high-frequency practices are not followed in the layout and circuit arrangement. Similarly, low-level dc amplifiers have unique considerations for stability also.

3.3.1 AC Stabilization Techniques
Layout and Bypassing

Of utmost importance to stability is a compact, minimum-lead-length layout. The leads to the input and compensation terminals (if used) of any op amp should be as direct as possible with a minimum of conductor length and proximity to other signal leads. Ground paths should have low resistance and low inductance. In wideband circuits, it is good practice (if possible) to use a ground plane on printed-circuit cards to obtain a high-quality ground.

Supply leads to amplifiers should be bypassed at least once for each PC card with good rf capacitors such as 0.1-μF disc ceramics or 1.0-μF tantalums, as shown in Fig. 3-17A. If the amplifiers used have a GBP above 10 MHz, more thorough bypassing will be necessary. In such cases, a set of local, rf-quality bypasses, such as 0.1-μF disc ceramics, for each amplifier is recommended. For good measure, a pair of tantalum bypasses for each PC card (or every five devices) should also be used. General-purpose devices are less critical as to bypassing, but they cannot be ignored. It is good practice, even with general-purpose devices, to include at least one set of bypasses for every five devices or at least one set per card, regardless of the number of ICs used.

*Low-inductance capacitors—0.1-μF ceramic or 1.0-μF tantalum. For high-speed op amps, connect C_1 and C_2 directly at supply pins, with low-inductance ground returns.

(A) Power-supply bypassing.

C_f** (3 - 10 pF typical)

**C_f may be larger if A is unity-gain compensated.

(B) Compensation of stray input capacitance.

C_f*** (3 - 10 pF typical)

***$X_{C_f} = \dfrac{R_f}{10}$ @ f_t of A

†A is compensated for unity gain.

†$R_o \cong 50$ - $200\ \Omega$

(C) Compensation of stray output capacitance.

Fig. 3-17. Stability enhancement techniques.

Input Capacitance Compensation

Stray input capacitance in feedback amplifiers can also lead to stability problems. Fig. 3-17B illustrates the nature of input-related capacitance problems. At the input of an op amp there will always be a few pF of stray capacitance, C_s, which consists of the amplifier input capacitance plus wiring capacitance. From the feedback path through R_f, this capacitance represents a potential phase shift at a corner frequency of

$$f = \frac{1}{2\pi R_f C_s}$$

The problem is particularly noticeable if R_f is large, since this moves the R_f-C_s frequency downward into a region where it can add to the amplifier phase shift. The result of these cumulative phase shifts may be enough to cause oscillation.

A simple solution is to keep R_f low, which forces the R_f-C_s frequency upward beyond the amplifier limit. But this is not always practical, since R_f may need to be high for gain reasons.

A more general solution is to use a compensation capacitor, C_f, across R_f, which in effect makes C_f-R_f and R_{in}-C_s a frequency-compensated divider. It may not be possible to readily determine the exact value of C_f to satisfy this relation, since C_s is not precisely known. C_f is best determined by experiment; or, if the amplifier used is compensated for unity gain, C_f may be greater than the formula relation to whatever degree desirable. In practice, values of 3–10 pF are typical with feedback resistors of 10 kΩ.

Output Capacitance Compensation

On many IC op amps, the phase shift caused by stray output load capacitance and the amplifier output resistance can be troublesome if the output capacitance is much more than 100 pF. By adding a series output resistance, R_o, the load capacitance is isolated from the amplifier (Fig. 3-17C). Feedback is taken after this resistor, thus compensating for its dc loss. The feedback capacitor, C_f, is then added to reduce the gain of the loop at high frequencies. C_f is chosen so that its reactance is 1/10 (or less) that of R_f at the unity-gain frequency of the amplifier used. The amplifier must be compensated for unity gain, since C_f reduces high-frequency gain to unity. Again, typical values for C_f fall in the 3–10-pF region.

Other Instability Sources

The preceding by no means represents all the sources of possible stability problems in IC op amps, just those that are most likely to occur. Other problem areas are more specific, either in terms of the devices themselves or in terms of circuits in which the devices are used. For example, source resistance may be a problem with some devices. In stubborn cases of instability when other alternatives have been exhausted, amplifier overcompensation may be the solution. If extra bandwidth or optimum slew rate are not necessary, it is usually wise to overcompensate an op amp. For example, this may be accomplished on 301A-type amplifiers by increasing the compensation capacitors by a factor of 10 (or by the ratio necessary to obtain stability).

High-current stages can cause instability by feedback through the power supplies. Such stages should be decoupled to localize their circulating currents. Similarly, ground-return paths for high-level and high-gain stages should be kept separate.

In general, many of the stability ground rules simply amount to good practices in layout and construction. These rules should obviously be followed for consistently stable results. Always consult the manufacturer's literature for specific recommendations and for more thorough background on specific op amps.

3.3.2 DC Stability Considerations

The stabilization of dc amplifiers can take on a number of meanings. Already discussed were considerations for minimizing offset voltage and its drift; in this section, some further considerations are undertaken.

Guarding

When very-low input currents are involved, such as with electrometer amplifiers, consideration of leakages on the order of a few picoamperes becomes part of the design process. Consequently, every low-level signal-path point must be carefully controlled for potential leakage and noise, which can easily contaminate the desired signals.

A technique that aids the control of excess leakage current is *guarding*. Guarding is simply the reduction of the potential difference between two conductors by bootstrap techniques. Its value can easily be assessed by the input current versus voltage graph of Fig. 3-18.

This curve is for the CA3130 op amp, which can operate with input pins 2 and 3 at a potential equal to pin 4. Clearly, when the difference between these pins is low (or zero), the leakage (bias) current falls to very low levels—below 1.0 pA. This illustrates, in principle, the concept of guarding, as the current flow is reduced when the potential difference is zero. This assumes, of course, that the amplifier has appropriately low bias currents to begin with.

With a standard 8-pin TO-99 op-amp package, leakage would normally be excessive because of large potentials at pins adjacent to pins 2 and 3 (pin 4 is at −15 volts, for example). Low-bias-current

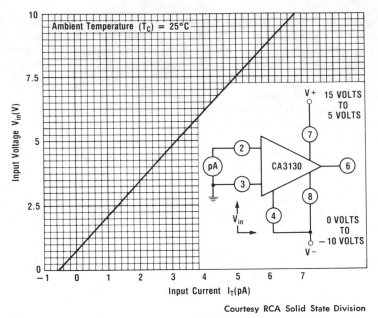

Courtesy RCA Solid State Division

Fig. 3-18. CA3130 input current change with common-mode voltage.

amplifiers usually employ the metal can as a shield, or guard, and bring it out to pin 8.

A printed-circuit layout for the IC must realize the full capability of guarding, and should be laid out as shown in Fig. 3-19. This bottom view of a guarded TO-99 IC shows how the guarding completely sur-

Fig. 3-19. Printed-circuit board guard techniques for low-input-current amplifiers.

rounds pins 2 and 3, preventing leakage. This is done on both sides of the PC board.

The signal is connected to pin 2 (or 3), as appropriate, by rigid, shielded guarding cable having low leakage. The signal path to the source should be minimized in length, and the cable should preferably have Teflon insulation.

The amplifier connection to be used will govern the connection of the guard ring, and will be similar to the circuits shown in Fig. 3-20 for the AD515 op amp.

In Fig. 3-20A for an inverting amplifier, the guard ring is connected to ground, since pin 3 is grounded for this mode of use. The series protection resistor is appropriate for sources that can supply currents of 0.5 mA or more (200 kΩ for a 100-volt overvoltage, for example). This circuit converts current to voltage with a 1.0-V/nA sensitivity (or, 1.0 mV/pA).

(A) Inverting mode.

(B) Noninverting mode.

Courtesy Analog Devices, Inc.

Fig. 3-20. Guarded input circuitry using AD515 op amp.

A noninverting connection is shown in Fig. 3-20B and, in this case, the guard is bootstrapped by the feedback voltage applied to pin 2 from R_s-R_f. To maintain low input capacitance, the signal cable can be bootstrapped as well, as indicated.

Just about all of the components associated with the input of an electrometer amplifier must be carefully chosen. PC boards must be cleaned carefully and sealed against humidity and dirt. Teflon or other comparable quality insulation is preferable, if not necessary.

Feedback resistors must be chosen for stability, low voltage coefficient, as well as tolerance; a difficult order for high-value types. Capacitors, if used, should be of Teflon, polystyrene, or polypropylene dielectrics, as few others will have the low leakage required.

The amplifier can be optimized also by minimizing self-heating, which will lower the bias currents. This can be realized by using only the lowest required supply voltages, heat-sinking the device package, and minimizing the load.

Further information on electrometers and low-current-level circuitry can be found in the references at the end of the chapter, and the circuit discussions in the applications section.

REFERENCES

1. Brokaw, A. P. "Analog Signal Handling for High Speed and Accuracy." *Analog Dialogue,* Vol. 11, No. 2, 1977.

2. ———. "An IC Amplifier User's Guide to Decoupling & Grounding." *Electronic Products,* December 1977.

3. ———. "Designing Sensitive Circuits? Don't Take Grounds for Granted." *EDN,* October 5, 1975.

4. Demrow, R. "Op Amps as Electrometers." *Analog Dialogue,* Vol. 5, No. 2, 1971.

5. Dobkin, R. C. *Universal Balancing Techniques.* National Semiconductor Linear Brief LB-9, August 1969. National Semiconductor Corp., Santa Clara, Calif.

6. Motchenbacker, C. D. "Protect Your Transistors Against Turn-on or Testing Transient Damage." *Electronics,* December 6, 1971.

7. Patstone, W. "Designing Femtoampere Circuits Requires Special Considerations." *EDN,* July 1, 1972.

8. Manufacturer's Data Sheets:

| Analog Devices | $\begin{cases} \text{AD515} \\ \\ \text{310/311} \end{cases}$ | Precision, Low-Power, FET-Input Electrometer Op Amp
Ultralow Bias Current Varactor Bridge Op Amps |

II

Op-Amp Applications

FOUR

Voltage Regulator and Reference Circuits

4.1 VOLTAGE REGULATORS

Voltage regulators using IC operational amplifiers as control elements make very attractive designs in some respects as compared to ICs designed specifically for the purpose of voltage regulation. The advantage of IC op amps is in their inherently high open-loop gain (100,000 typical) which, under closed-loop conditions, can provide regulation percentages as good as 0.01% if sufficient care is taken in layout and construction, and if consideration is given to the significant contributions to error. Compared to an integral IC regulator, an op-amp controlled version will have a larger number of parts, since the op amp is only one of the four basic elements of this type of voltage regulator.

4.1.1 Basic Elements of an Op-Amp Voltage Regulator

The four basic elements of a series-type, op-amp voltage regulator are shown in Fig. 4-1. In this functional diagram, a reference voltage source produces a constant output voltage, V_{ref}, under varying conditions of temperature and input voltage, $+V_{in}$. The reference voltage is applied to the noninverting input of op amp A_1. The output of A_1 drives the series pass transistor, Q_1. The output of Q_1 is the voltage, E_o, which is developed across the load resistance, R_L. Voltage E_o is also fed back through the feedback network, β, causing a fraction of E_o, or βE_o, to appear at the inverting input of A_1. Recalling one of the laws of ideal op-amp behavior, zero differential-input voltage will be present at the inputs of A_1; thus, voltage βE_o will be exactly equal to V_{ref}, since the infinite open-loop gain of A_1 will adjust E_o until this equality is satisfied. The feedback mechanism of the active components acts to generate an output voltage that is a multiple of the input voltage, V_{ref}. The relationship is simply

$$E_o = \frac{V_{ref}}{\beta}$$

where,
β is the attenuation of the feedback network.

The three active components may be thought of as reference, control, and power, represented by V_{ref}, A_1, and Q_1, respectively. The functions of V_{ref} and A_1 are obvious enough, and Q_1 is necessary to handle load currents beyond the basic output capability of the op amp.

Fig. 4-1. Functional diagram of a series-type voltage regulator.

Within the concept of this basic configuration, voltage regulators of practically any voltage and/or current capability can be constructed by using appropriate elements for V_{ref}, A_1, Q_1, and β. The concept can be extended to include negative voltages by using complementary devices to perform the functions of $+V_{ref}$, $-V_{ref}$, and Q_1. Therefore, to design a regulator using an op amp for A_1, we must have as a minimum the element for V_{ref} and a suitable feedback network, β. In most cases, we will also need a boost transistor, Q_1, to supply additional load current. To begin the discussion of op-amp voltage regulators, we will examine the first element, the reference voltage source.

4.1.2 Requirements of the Reference Voltage Source*

The prime requirement of the reference voltage source is that it must maintain a stable output voltage with time and temperature. A voltage regulator can only be as good as its reference source; therefore, it is desirable to make the temperature coefficient of the reference as close to zero as possible. Reference sources are commonly made up of a series string of reverse- and forward-biased diode junctions having equal and opposite temperature coefficients of voltage drift. In combination, the opposing effects cancel and the net zero temperature coefficient is usually found only at a specific value of current in the diodes. For a reference diode to maintain the temperature coefficient within its specified limits, a well-maintained current drive is required.

Reference diodes are specified to various degrees of accuracy and, depending on the number of series junctions used, are available in various terminal voltages. One example is the 1N821 series, a 6.2-V, 7.5-mA diode available with temperature coefficients from 0.01%/°C down to 0.0005%/°C. Another example is the 1N935 series, a 9.0-V, 7.5-mA diode available with a range of temperature coefficients comparable to the 1N821. The 1N4611 series is a 6.6-V, 2.0-mA diode available with temperature coefficients from 0.005%/°C down to 0.0005%/°C. The 2.0-mA operating current of this diode is compatible with the output current of a standard IC op amp.

Since the terminal voltage of a reference diode is sensitive to the current flowing in it, one usual function of the circuitry associated with the diode is to regulate this current against variations in temperature and input voltage. The latter is the more difficult consideration, since in a simple resistor-fed reference diode as shown in Fig. 4-1, the current in R_1 will vary as $+V_{in}$ varies. This will result in variations in the reference voltage, since reference diodes do have a finite impedance. The dynamic impedance of the 1N4611, for example, is 75 ohms. It is also undesirable to load a reference diode to any extent because a varying load will result in a change in the reference voltage due to the nonzero source impedance of the diode. For this reason, reference diodes are usually buffered to minimize loading or, if they are loaded directly, the load is carefully maintained constant.

Monolithic IC diodes have been developed that have extremely low dynamic impedances, low temperature coefficients, and close tolerances. A type representative of this class of diode is the LM329, which will be used in these discussions. Others available (but not discussed here) are the LM336, the AD584, the AD589, and the ICL8069.

---

* For a detailed discussion of references, see the author's *IC Converter Cookbook,* Howard W. Sams & Co., Inc., 1978.

4.1.3 A Basic Reference Voltage Source

The preceding considerations are illustrated in a simple but effective fashion in the +6.9-V reference voltage source of Fig. 4-2. This circuit uses a combination of negative and positive feedback to maintain the 1.0-mA current in D_1 constant, and it does this independent of variations in both the ambient temperature and the unregulated input. The circuit works as follows:

At the moment of turn-on, the circuit has heavy positive feedback due to the low resistance (R_1) from the output to the noninverting input of A_1, and the fact that D_1 is effectively an open circuit at voltages less than its breakdown voltage. This positive feedback forces the voltage across D_1 to rise in a positive-going direction until the breakdown voltage is reached. D_1 then clamps the noninverting input of A_1 at 6.9 volts, which, in turn, reduces the positive feedback due to the low dynamic impedance of D_1. At this point, the negative feedback through R_3 and R_2 predominates, and a stable condition is

Fig. 4-2. Basic reference voltage source—positive output.

$$E_{o2} = 6.9 \left(\frac{R_2 + R_3}{R_2} \right)$$

*Choose R_s for minimum required starting current at lowest V_{in} with diode used.

Sure-Fire Starting Circuit

established, with A_1 amplifying the 6.9 volts applied from D_1. The 6.9-V reference voltage is scaled upward to a more positive level at the output of A_1. Because a regulated voltage now exists at either end of R_1, a well-defined and stable voltage drop is created across R_1. Thus, the value of R_1 very effectively establishes the current in D_1. The values of R_2 and R_3 are chosen to set the output level of A_1, then R_1 is chosen for the desired current in D_1.

The unique feature of this circuit is that the reference diode regulates its own current. This current depends primarily on the reference voltage itself and thus will be stable, which lends further overall stability to the circuit. The reference voltage output can be taken directly from D_1 for high-impedance loads, or from the output of A_1 where it is scaled upward by the $(R_2 + R_3)/R_2$ ratio. This output appears at a low impedance and can supply appreciable current without the basic or scaled reference voltages being affected.

The circuit is capable of temperature performance consistent with the selection grade of the diode and op amp used. The temperature coefficient of the LM329 diode can be as good as 20 ppm/°C (maximum) for the higher-quality versions, such as the LM329B. These monolithic IC diodes are also available in heated substrate versions with temperature coefficients down to 1.0 ppm/°C in the same nominal voltage. These types are the LM399A series. When these premium diodes are used, a premium op amp should also be used. Also, for a very low overall temperature coefficient, the current-determining resistors used should be stable 1.0% film or, preferably, wirewound types. This circuit configuration provides exceptional performance in all respects except stability, even with the basic components shown. With a standard 741 op amp and virtually any zener diode in the 5- to 7-volt region, the rejection of line input variations is over 100 dB at 100 Hz.

A word of caution is appropriate at this point with regard to the *starting* of this circuit. The circuit is definitely *not* guaranteed to start properly if bipolar power supplies are used for A_1—a single-ended supply *must* be used. Although extensive testing with various amplifiers has not as yet revealed a case where the circuit failed to come up to the proper operating state, "Murphy's" law states that somewhere in the world such an amplifier exists and that someone will try to use it without success. Should this happen, the "sure-fire" starting circuit shown in the inset of Fig. 4-2 will make the most stubborn amplifier behave properly.

4.1.4 Error Sources in Op-Amp Voltage Regulators

When a specific degree of output voltage precision must be met in a reference source (or regulator), the various error sources that influence the total performance must be separated and analyzed. Among these error sources are the temperature coefficient of the reference diode, diode noise, wiring voltage drops, amplifier input offset voltage and current drift, amplifier noise, and rejection of power-supply and common-mode input changes. These error sources will be discussed briefly in this section, and the reader can apply the basic principles to any of the circuits covered in this chapter.

Input Offset Voltage Drift

Referring again to the basic regulator of Fig. 4-2, if we assume that a stable reference diode is used for D_1, another limitation on overall temperature performance is the input offset voltage drift of A_1. This parameter is not specified for the 741; therefore, it is not a good choice for applications where temperature drift is critical. The average temperature coefficient of input offset voltage ($\Delta V_{io}/°C$) for a 307 or a 301A is specified as 6.0 $\mu V/°C$ (typical), and 30 $\mu V/°C$ (maximum). We will now examine what this means to the overall circuit.

The input offset voltage will change by the average amount specified for each 1.0°C change in chip temperature. This chip temperature change can be due either to self-heating or to the effects of loading. For example, the thermal resistance (θ_{JA}) of a 307 or a 301A is 150°C/W for the TO-99 package, which means that for each watt of dissipation the chip temperature will rise 150°C above the ambient temperature. In the circuit of Fig. 4-2, if we assume a $+V_{in}$ of 30 volts and a V_{out} of 15 volts, then

$$V_{in} - V_{out} = 15 \text{ V}$$

Therefore, a 3.0-mA load represents a chip power dissipation (P_D) of 45 mW (15 V × 3.0 mA). We then divide the chip dissipation by the thermal resistance to determine the change in chip temperature ($\Delta°C$) due to chip dissipation:

$$\Delta°C = \frac{P_D}{\theta_{JA}}$$

Knowing in this example that

$$\theta_{JA} = 150°C/W = 6.7 \text{ mW}/°C$$

and

$$P_D = 45 \text{ mW}$$

then

$$\Delta°C = \frac{45 \text{ mW}}{6.7 \text{ mW}/°C} = 6.7°C$$

This 6.7°C change in chip temperature due to loading is added directly to the expected variation in ambient temperature to determine the total temperature change that the chip experiences. For example, an ambient temperature change of 40°C would result in a total chip temperature change of 46.7°C. The approximate change in input offset voltage caused by this temperature change would then be:

$$\Delta V_{io} = (\Delta V_{io}/°C)(\Delta°C)$$
$$= (6.0 \ \mu V/°C)(46.7°C)$$
$$= 280 \ \mu V$$

This figure of 280 μV is then multiplied by the working voltage gain of A_1 to determine the output drift figure.

An input offset voltage drift of 280 μV is reasonably good; however, it should be remembered that this was based on an average drift of 6.0 $\mu V/°C$ (typical) for the 307 and 301A. When the maximum figure of 30 $\mu V/°C$ for the 307 and 301A is considered, the total drift becomes five times greater, or slightly over 1.0 mV referred to the input. Since this is approaching the total drift of a high-quality reference, a better op amp may need to be considered. A good choice would be an instrumentation-grade device or one of the higher-performance general-purpose types. The simplest way to upgrade the circuit is to use a high-performance general-purpose unit such as an AD741L or an OP-02E (see Fig. 4-3).

Input Offset Current Drift

Another error source in op-amp voltage regulators that must be considered in applications where high stability is required is the input offset current drift of the amplifier. The type of op amp used has an important bearing on performance, as was also the case in the

Fig. 4-3. Op-amp types suitable as high-stability options in precision voltage-regulator circuits.

preceding discussion of input offset voltage drift. By itself, input offset current does not create much of a problem because this effect can usually be adjusted out. It is the change in input offset current with temperature that creates the major problem.

Referring to the basic regulator circuit of Fig. 4-2 once again, it will be noted that A_1 sees unequal dc input resistances at its two inputs. The noninverting input sees the nominally low impedance of D_1, while the inverting input sees the parallel equivalent resistance of R_2 and R_3, or about 1500 Ω. For best stability, these two resistances should be equalized by the addition of a compensating resistor in the lower-impedance input. For this example, a 1500-Ω resistor should be connected between D_1 and the noninverting input of A_1. This equalizes the input bias voltage drops due to source resistance and minimizes the input offset voltage generated by the bias current flowing through these source resistances. The remaining error voltage is due to the bias current offset, which cannot be directly eliminated, but only minimized by careful selection of amplifier type and by lowering the source resistances.

The real problem is due to the change in input offset current with temperature. In order to judge its total significance, offset current drift must be converted to an equivalent input offset voltage drift. Using the typical offset current drift of the AD741L (20 pA/°C) and a source resistance of 1500 Ω, an equivalent offset voltage drift can be calculated as follows:

$$\Delta V_{io}/°C = (\Delta I_{io}/°C)(R_s)$$
$$= (2.0 \times 10^{-11} A/°C)(1.5 \times 10^3 \Omega)$$
$$= 3.0 \times 10^{-8} V/°C$$
$$= 0.03 \ \mu V/°C$$

Thus, in this example, the input offset voltage drift due to input offset current drift is 0.03 $\mu V/°C$, which is much less than the pure input offset voltage drift of the AD741L (2.0 $\mu V/°C$ typical) and could be disregarded with little consequence.

If, however, the source resistances were on the order of 100 kΩ, the input offset voltage drift due to input offset current drift would be about 67 times higher (the ratio of the resistances), requiring a possible reevaluation of the situation.

Noise Filtering

It is an inherent characteristic of zener and reference diodes that they generate an appreciable amount of wideband noise. If a reference source is to be "clean" insofar as spurious ac outputs are concerned, this zener noise must be filtered by some means.

A simple method of filtering the reference source of Fig. 4-2 is to directly bypass D_1 with a capacitor, which lowers the ac shunt impedance and tends to minimize noise output. However, this is not a completely satisfactory solution because the capacitance required to adequately bypass the diode at low frequencies becomes prohibitively large. A much more effective solution is shown in Fig. 4-4. This illustration introduces amplifier A_2, which is used as a buffer to minimize loading on reference diode D_1. Since the input impedance of a voltage follower is very high, the point of interface between the reference diode and amplifier A_2 is an ideal place to insert a simple RC low-pass filter such as R_4-C_1. Resistor R_4 increases the output impedance of D_1 a thousandfold, which allows capacitor C_1 to be a small value. The values shown in Fig. 4-4 will provide at least 15 dB of noise attenuation at 100 Hz, and C_1 can be increased if desired.

Fig. 4-4. Noise filtering applied to the basic reference source.

Resistor R_5 is included to protect the input of A_2 against the discharge transients of capacitor C_1. If the small voltage drop caused by the bias current of A_2 flowing in R_4 and R_5 is objectionable, resistor R_6 is used and made equal to $R_4 + R_5$ to minimize the dc offset error due to bias current. This noise-filtering technique can be applied whenever required in any of the circuits to be discussed in this chapter.

Wiring Voltage Drops

One of the principal sources of error in a voltage regulator is the wire used between the regulation terminals and the actual circuit load resistance. One foot of No. 20 wire has a resistance of 0.01 Ω;

Fig. 4-5. Remote-sensing hookup to cancel the effects of wiring voltage drops.

therefore, a 100-mA load current flowing in this wire will create a voltage drop of 1.0 mV between the regulator and the load, which is the total allowable change for a 10-V, 0.01% regulator. Obviously, an actual circuit will have wire lengths much longer than one foot, which will considerably increase the voltage drop due to wire resistance. Wiring voltage drop is a factor that must be considered in any application requiring high currents and/or extremely close regulation tolerances.

To combat wire resistance, first of all use as heavy a wire gauge as is practical and minimize its length. Other than this, a technique known as *remote sensing* should be employed, as illustrated in simplified form in Fig. 4-5. In this illustration, the wiring resistances of the positive and negative regulator output leads are shown as R_W+ and R_W-, respectively. In a conventional hookup, R_3 and D_1-R_2 would be connected to the input (left-hand) side of R_W+ and R_W-, allowing the voltage drops in these resistances to subtract from the voltage across load resistance R_L. Using the technique of remote sensing, however, R_3 is connected *after* R_W+, or directly to the positive side of the load. Likewise, D_1 and R_2 are connected after R_W-, or directly to the negative side of the load. This allows feedback network R_3-R_2 and reference diode D_1 to develop the feedback voltage with respect to the voltage that is directly across load resistance R_L, rather than prior to wire resistances R_W+ and R_W-. In this manner, the feedback loop corrects for the voltage drops in the wiring resistances, and more precise regulation of the load voltage is maintained. In practice, the voltage-sensing leads to R_3 and D_1-R_2 can be relatively small, since the currents in them are small in comparison to the load currents in R_W+ and R_W-.

The effect of wiring voltage drops is the largest source of error that will be encountered in voltage regulator circuits; therefore, remote sensing should be employed in any application requiring close regulation tolerances ($\leq$0.1%) or large currents ($\geq$100 mA).

Power-Supply and Common-Mode Rejection

Another source of error in precision voltage-regulator applications is the change in op-amp input offset voltage due to changes in the unregulated input supply voltage. The degree of this error is dependent upon two electrical characteristics of the op amp itself. (1) power-supply rejection ratio (PSRR) and (2) common-mode rejection ratio (CMRR). The typical PSRR specification for a 741 is 30 μV/V, but the maximum can be as high as 150 μV/V. The typical PSRR specification for a 307 or a 301A is 16 μV/V. Any of these specifications may be adequate if the input supply-voltage changes are not excessive. Under conditions of widely varying input supply voltage, however, a better choice would be one of the precision types, which have a PSRR specification of 10 μV/V (maximum) or less.

Common-mode rejection is a factor because a single varying supply line is equivalent to a constant supply and a varying common-mode input voltage. A given amplifier will show an equivalent change in input offset voltage proportional to its CMRR. For example, the typical CMRR specification for a 741 is 90 dB, which is equivalent to a power-supply change of 31 μV/V. However, the minimum CMRR specification for a 741 is only 70 dB, which equates to a maximum power-supply change of 310 μV/V. The typical CMRR specification for a 307 or a 301A is 96 dB, which is equivalent to a power-supply change of 16 μV/V. Precision types are also excellent in this category; a minimum CMRR of 100 dB equates to a power-supply change of only 10 μV/V (maximum). Both the AD741L and the OP-02E are good choices here.

Summary

Voltage regulators using IC op amps make very attractive designs because of the inherently high open-loop gain of the op amp, which allows extremely low regulation impedances. However, there are several sources of error that can easily degrade a theoretical regulation tolerance of 0.005% to over 0.1% if attention is not paid to details. These error sources include temperature drifts, wiring voltage drops, power-supply induced noise and drift, and the quality of the reference source. These basic considerations apply to all subsequent applications in which op-amp regulator circuits are used. The reader will find sufficient information in this chapter to construct voltage regulators to virtually any degree of accuracy. In addition, a list of pertinent references is given at the end of the chapter.

Before proceeding into the discussion of the various regulator circuits, a few additional suggestions are offered which may prove

(A) Parasitic suppression.

(B) High-frequency output filter.

(C) Input filter.

†Use C_{in} close to amplifier if rectifier-filter is remote.

Fig. 4-6. Methods for improving power-supply stability.

helpful in achieving power-supply stability. These are illustrated in Fig. 4-6.

Boost or current-limiting transistors can create instability if they have very high gain-bandwidth products, as is true for types such as the 2N3904 and 2N3906. Instability can be prevented in these types by the use of a parasitic suppression resistor connected as shown in Fig. 4-6A. The resistance value of R_b is not critical, and examples are given in the circuits that follow.

The output filter capacitor of the power supply can also create stability problems if it is not a good high-frequency type. Instability can be prevented in these cases by connecting a 1.0-μF tantalum type across the output filter, as shown in Fig. 4-6B. Finally, an input capacitor may be needed, particularly if a number of amplifiers are used and the regulator is some distance away from the power-supply filter. This capacitor should also be a 1.0-μF tantalum type mounted close to the offending amplifier, as shown in Fig. 4-6C.

4.1.5 A Positive Reference Voltage Source With Buffered Output

The basic reference voltage source of Fig. 4-2 is useful as an integral part of larger circuits where the loading on D_1 is very light, such as the noninverting input in a voltage-follower configuration. A generally more useful reference source is the circuit shown in Fig. 4-7, which features a buffered output. (For simplicity, this circuit can use a dual op amp such as the 358 (or 1458) to accomplish the functions of both voltage reference and buffer within a single IC package.) The buffer stage raises the output current to 5.0 mA and lowers the output impedance to

$$Z_o = \frac{r_o(\text{op amp})}{1 + A\beta}$$

$$= \frac{7.5 \times 10^1}{1 + (2 \times 10^5)(1)}$$

$$\cong 3.75 \times 10^{-4}\ \Omega$$

For best overall temperature performance, low-drift op amps should be used, particularly for A_1. The 358 can supply 20–30 mA (maximum) from A_2. A 759 (single) for A_2 can supply over 300 mA.

Fig. 4-7. Positive reference source with buffered output (+6.9 V @ 5.0 mA).

4.1.6 A Negative Reference Voltage Source

For applications where a negative reference voltage is required, the basic circuit of Fig. 4-2 can be rearranged to operate from a negative supply, as illustrated in Fig. 4-8. The component values, theory of operation, and considerations for optimum performance are the same as for the circuit of Fig. 4-2. A buffered-output version of the basic negative reference source is illustrated in Fig. 4-9. This circuit is identical in performance to the positive buffered source of Fig. 4-7.

4.1.7 Reference Sources With Increased Voltage and Current Outputs

To increase the voltage output of a basic reference source, the R_2-R_3 voltage feedback loop can be designed to provide a specific voltage at the output of A_1, as shown in Fig. 4-10. Although this is still the same basic circuit as that of Fig. 4-2, an important difference is that the output voltage is now taken directly from the output of A_1. The voltage at this point must be more precisely maintained by

$$E_{o2} = -6.9\left(\frac{R_2 + R_3}{R_2}\right)$$

E_{o2} Scaled Reference Voltage

E_{o1} −6.9 V Reference Voltage

Fig. 4-8. Basic reference voltage source—negative output.

the use of close-tolerance resistances. In the example of Fig. 4-10, resistors R_2 and R_3 are chosen for a 15-V output, using the standard gain equation for a noninverting amplifier:

$$\frac{E_o}{E_{in}} = \frac{R_2 + R_3}{R_2}$$

Thus,

$$\frac{15}{6.9} = \frac{R_2 + R_3}{R_2}$$

and with R_2 set at 6.81 kΩ, then

$$2.17 = \frac{6.81 + R_3}{6.81}$$

Solving for R_3,

$$R_3 = (2.17 \times R_2) - R_2$$
$$= (2.17 \times 6.81) - 6.81$$
$$= 14.78 - 6.81$$
$$= 7.97 \ \text{kΩ}$$

Thus, the closest 1.0%-tolerance film or wirewound resistance value of 7.96 kΩ is used for R_3. The value for R_1 is chosen to drop the difference between the output voltage and the reference voltage with the reference current of 1.0 mA flowing. In this example,

$$R_1 = \frac{15 - 6.9}{1}$$

$$= \frac{8.1}{1}$$

$$= 8.1 \ \text{kΩ}$$

163

Fig. 4-9. Negative reference source with buffered output (−6.9 V @ 5.0 mA).

Thus, for R_1, an 8.25-kΩ film resistor is used for stability of the reference current (this value is not critical).

Due to the voltage feedback around A_1, this circuit can deliver a regulated output voltage of 15 volts at a low-impedance level. The current capability of the circuit is modest, however, because nearly 3.0 mA of the rated 5.0-mA output of the op amp is used to supply the biasing currents. A high-current type such as the 759, however, can allow up to 300 mA of output.

Fig. 4-10. Basic reference source with output voltage greater than reference voltage (+15 V @ 3.0 mA).

For applications that require appreciably more current, a booster transistor may be added inside the feedback loop, as shown in Fig. 4-11. In this circuit, Q_1 amplifies the output current of A_1 to a 1.0-A level. Q_1, an LM395, is a monolithic power IC with integral current limiting, thermal limiting, and overvoltage protection. It should be provided with adequate heat sinking for 1.0-A output currents.

Fig. 4-11. Basic reference source with output voltage greater than reference voltage, and with boost transistor added for increased output current (+15 V @ 1.0 A).

An example of a high-stability regulator that minimizes the error source discussed previously is shown in Fig. 4-12. A 308A op amp is used in this circuit because of its low offset drift and high common-mode/power-supply rejection capability. A low-drift version of the

Fig. 4-12. High-stability 15-V @ 1.0-A regulator circuit.

LM329 diode is chosen for D_1, and close-tolerance, low-temperature-coefficient film or wirewound resistors are used for R_1, R_2, and R_3. Remote sensing is used at the load to correct for wiring voltage drops.

There are many applications that do not require the precision capability of the circuit shown in Fig. 4-12. For such applications, a simplified version of this regulator (Fig. 4-13) can be used.

Fig. 4-13. Simplified 15-V regulator circuit.

4.1.8 Variable-Output Series Regulators

The examples presented thus far are useful as fixed-level regulators to furnish a precisely constant output voltage. It is often required, however, that a regulated output voltage be variable from zero up to the reference voltage, or from zero to some maximum voltage greater than the reference voltage. These requirements can be fulfilled with but slight modification of the circuits described thus far.

Positive Regulator—Zero to $+V_z$ (0 V to +6.9 V)

In order to vary the output of a positive reference source from zero up to the level of the reference diode voltage (V_z), the basic circuit of Fig. 4-2 is modified as shown in Fig. 4-14. Although it is generally undesirable to load a reference diode, this can be done if the loading is constant or if the loading is negligible, as was true with the buffered reference source of Fig. 4-7.

In the circuit of Fig. 4-14, potentiometer R_4 is connected across reference diode D_1, allowing output voltage adjustment from 0 V to +6.9 V. The loading on D_1 caused by R_4 is made negligible by voltage follower A_2. In order to maintain the current through the reference diode constant at 1.0 mA, the resistance value of R_1 must be lowered from 1.8 kΩ to 1.0 kΩ. This supplies the extra load current through R_4, making a total current through R_1 of about 2.0 mA.

A single-supply dual op amp can conveniently be used for A_1 and A_2 in this circuit because these devices allow linear input and output operation down to zero volts. The output of A_2 will supply 0 V to +6.9 V at 20 mA, with the level adjusted by R_4. If additional load current is required, an npn booster transistor can be used with A_2, as illustrated in the high-power regulator of Fig. 4-15 to be discussed next.

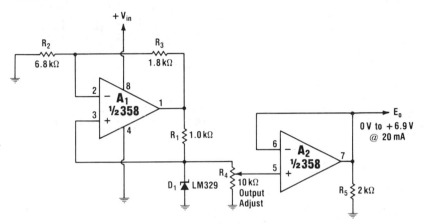

Fig. 4-14. Positive regulator with variable buffered output (0 V to +6.9 V @ 20 mA).

High-Power Positive Regulator—(0 V to +6.9 V)

A voltage regulator that is variable from 0 V to +6.9 V is very useful for powering low-voltage logic devices that require voltages in the range of +3.0 or +6.0 volts. However, the current demands of these systems can become appreciable; therefore, specific examples of 100-mA and 2.0-A regulators are given in Fig. 4-15. In this circuit, Q_1 is either a single transistor (2N3766) or a Darlington-pair device (2N6057), depending on the output current required. Or, for simplicity Q_1 can be an LM395 as shown previously.

In the circuit as shown, Q_2 provides short-circuit protection for Q_1 by sensing the current flowing in R_5. The output voltage is adjusted by R_4, as in the previous circuit of Fig. 4-14.

Since the circuit of Fig. 4-15 is usually adjusted to some specific level above zero, the negative supply lead of A_2 can be connected to common rather than to a $-V_{in}$ potential. Q_1 must have an adequate heat sink to safely dissipate the heat generated at high output currents and high-input/low-output voltages. Remote sensing is suggested for R_4-D_1 and for pin 6 (through R_8) of A_2 as shown. R_8 is included to protect A_2 from possible discharge of C_1 at turnoff. If desired, a dual op amp (as noted) can be used for A_1 and A_2.

**Change listed components to meet
required output current as follows:

	100 mA	2.0 A
Q_1	2N3766	2N6057 †
R_5	4.7 Ω	0.25 Ω
C_1	100 μF	1000 μF

†Heat sink required.

*A_1 and A_2 pin connections shown are for 1458 dual op amp.
If operation down to zero output is desired, use 358, 3458,
or other single-supply type.

Fig. 4-15. High-power positive regulator with variable buffered output (0 V to +6.9 V
@ 100 mA or 2.0 A).

Positive Regulator—Zero to $+KV_z$ (0 V to +15 V)

By adding an appropriate gain factor "K" to amplifier A_2, the basic regulator of Fig. 4-15 can be made to provide any output voltage from zero up to a level of $K \times V_z$, or $K \times 6.9$ V, within the range of A_2 and its power supplies. The circuit is shown in Fig. 4-16 and can be recognized as the basic reference source feeding a buffer stage that has gain due to feedback resistors R_5 and R_6. With an input voltage of E_{in}, the output of buffer stage A_2 will be:

$$E_o = E_{in} \left(\frac{R_5 + R_6}{R_5} \right)$$

Input voltage E_{in} is the variable potential of 0 V to +6.9 V from reference source A_1. The gain factor "K" is represented by $(R_5 + R_6)/R_5$.

For a specified output level such as +15 V, choose a value for K which sets the desired ratio of R_5 to R_6, using a worst-case reference voltage of 6.9 V −5%, or 6.5 V. Thus,

$$K = \frac{E_o}{E_{in}}$$
$$= \frac{15}{6.5}$$
$$= 2.3$$

then,

$$\frac{R_5 + R_6}{R_5} = 2.3$$

For resistor R_5, a 1.0%-tolerance, 6.81-kΩ value is chosen for stability, and to pass a current of approximately 1.0 mA at an E_{in} of 6.9 V. Then,

$$R_6 = (2.3 \times R_5) - R_5$$
$$= (2.3 \times 6.81) - 6.81$$
$$= 8.853 \text{ k}\Omega$$

Thus, for R_6, a 1.0%-tolerance, 9.53-kΩ (standard) value will allow E_o to be adjusted to $+15$ V with an E_{in} of 6.5 V.

The complete circuit for a 0-V to $+15$-V, 100-mA or 2-A regulator, which utilizes the foregoing principles, is shown in Fig. 4-16. As in the circuit of Fig. 4-15, the choice of transistor Q_1 determines the output current capability. Short-circuit protection is provided by transistor Q_2, which senses the load current flowing through R_7. A large output capacitor (C_1) is used to maintain a low output impedance at high frequencies, where the gain of A_2 falls off. Remote sensing is also suggested for this circuit, particularly for the higher-current version.

Negative Regulator—Zero to V_Z (0 V to 6.9 V)

The implementation of a variable-output negative regulator involves a simple modification of the variable-output positive regulator of Fig. 4-14. This is illustrated in Fig. 4-17.

The A_1 portion of this regulator circuit is similar to the negative reference source of Fig. 4-8, except that resistor R_1 is lowered in value to 1.0 kΩ in order to supply the extra load current through R_4. The output from R_4 is thus variable from 0 V to -6.9 V and is buffered by voltage follower A_2.

In this circuit, individual single 741-type op amps can be used for A_1 and A_2, which will allow linear input and output operation down to zero volts. The output of A_2 will thus supply 0 V to -6.9 V at 5.0 mA, with the level adjusted by R_4. If additional load current is required, a pnp booster transistor can be used with A_2, as illustrated in the high-power regulator of Fig. 4-18 to be discussed next.

Fig. 4-16. High-power variable positive regulator with increased output voltage
(0 V to +15 V @ 100 mA or 2.0 A).

High-Power Negative Regulator—Zero to $-KV_Z$ (0 V to -15 V)

The calculations involved in designing the circuit of Fig. 4-16 provided a variable-output positive regulator of 0-V to +15-V output at 100 mA or 2.0 A. The same circuit values can be applied to a design that is rearranged to operate from a negative supply. This will provide a circuit with an output variable from 0 V to -15 V with 100-mA

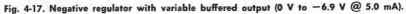

Fig. 4-17. Negative regulator with variable buffered output (0 V to -6.9 V @ 5.0 mA).

170

*A_1 and A_2 pin connections shown are for 1458 dual op amp. If operation down to zero output is desired, use two 741s and operate A_2 V+ at +3.0 V minimum.

+3.0 V (minimum)*

R_2 6.8 kΩ R_3 1.8 kΩ

A_1*

R_1 1.0 kΩ

Output Adjust

D_1 LM329

R_4 10 kΩ

R_5 6.81 kΩ 1.0%

R_6 9.53 kΩ 1.0%

A_2*

Q_2 2N3906

+E_o

C_1**

R_9 470 Ω

R_8 470 Ω

Q_1** R_7**

−E_o

V_in

**Change listed components to meet required output current as follows:

	100 mA	2.0 A
Q_1	2N3740	2N6050†
R_7	4.7 Ω	0.25 Ω
C_1	100 μF	1000 μF

†Heat sink required.

Fig. 4-18. High-power variable negative regulator with increased output voltage (0 V to −15 V @ 100 mA or 2.0 A).

or 2.0-A capability. This circuit is illustrated in Fig. 4-18, which is functionally identical to the circuit of Fig. 4-16, except that the supply potentials are reversed and pnp transistors are substituted for Q_1 and Q_2. Remote sensing is also suggested for this circuit, particularly for the higher-current version.

4.1.9 Tracking Regulators

A tracking regulator is a regulator that has two outputs, with one output "tracking" the other. This usually takes the form of a master/slave combination, wherein the output of one regulator can be varied from zero to some maximum level, and a second regulator creates a mirror image of the first. This is illustrated in Fig. 4-19.

In this circuit, amplifiers A_1 and A_2 constitute a variable-output positive regulator, similar to the circuit of Fig. 4-14. It supplies a 0-V to +6.9-V potential at the positive output terminal, +E_o. Amplifier

A₃ is connected as a unity-gain inverter, since R_5 and R_6 are equal in value. It produces a voltage that is always equal but opposite in polarity to the output of A₂. As A₂ varies from 0 V to +6.9 V, A₃ will vary from 0 V to −6.9 V. Therefore, potentiometer R_4 controls two outputs that are equal in magnitude but opposite in polarity. If desired, a dual op amp such as the 358 can be used for A₂ and A₃, since both amplifiers must be capable of operating down to zero volts and thus both require positive and negative supplies.

Fig. 4-19. Basic dual-output tracking regulator (0 V to ±6.9 V @ 5.0 mA).

The accuracy of tracking between A₂ (the master) and A₃ (the slave) is determined by the match between R_5 and R_6. Therefore, for accuracy and stability, 1.0% film or wirewound precision resistors should be used here. Resistor R_7 minimizes the effects of bias current in R_5 and R_6.

Dual-Output Tracking Regulator—Zero to ±KV$_Z$ (0 V to ±15 V)

A tracking regulator with a single adjustment is a very useful tool as a laboratory power supply. The basic tracking regulator of Fig. 4-19 can be extended to output voltages higher than the reference voltage, and with considerably higher current. Such a circuit is illustrated in Fig. 4-20. This circuit is a combination of previously described subcircuits. A positive 6.9-V reference source (A₁) is used

Fig. 4-20. High-power, dual-output tracking regulator (0 V to ±15 V @ 100 mA or 2.0 A).

to feed a 0-V to +15-V regulator consisting of A_2, Q_1, and Q_3. A_3, Q_2, and Q_4 comprise a slaved negative regulator, which tracks the voltage from the positive regulator. Both regulators have an output current capability of either 100 mA or 2.0 A, depending on the components used (see the table in Fig. 4-20).

Dual-Output, Independently Variable Regulators—Zero to +KV$_Z$ and Zero to −KV$_Z$ (0 V to +15 V and 0 V to −15 V)

A useful variation of the tracking regulator of Fig. 4-20 is illustrated in Fig. 4-21. This circuit features independently variable positive and negative outputs using a common reference source for both regulators. The reader may recognize this circuit as being a combination of the previously discussed circuits of Figs. 4-16 and 4-18 for the A_2 and A_3 portions. The main difference in this circuit is the method used to derive the positive and negative reference voltages. Buffer A_2 uses the positive reference voltage from R_4, while buffer A_3 uses a negative reference voltage developed from the positive voltage across D_1. To develop the negative reference voltage, amplifier A_4 is used to invert the +6.9 V across D_1 and produce −6.9 V across R_{11}. R_{12}, the input resistor for A_4, loads D_1 with an additional current of 0.69 mA; therefore, R_1 is decreased to 680 Ω in order to maintain the

** Change listed components to meet
required output current as follows:

	100 mA	2.0 A
Q_1	2N3766	2N6057†
Q_2	2N3740	2N6050†
R_7, R_{10}	4.7 Ω	0.25 Ω
C_1, C_2	100 μF	1000 μF

† Heat sink required.

Fig. 4-21. Dual-output, independently variable regulators (0 V to +15 V and 0 V to −15 V; 100 mA or 2.0 A at each output).

current in D_1. Potentiometer R_4 serves as the output adjustment for the positive regulator, while R_{11} serves the same purpose for the negative regulator. Both regulators have an output current capability of either 100 mA or 2.0 A, depending on the components used (see the table in Fig. 4-21). Note that amplifiers A_2-A_3 have common supply lines and can, therefore, be 324 or 348 types, if desired.

Fig. 4-22. Functional diagram of a shunt-type voltage regulator.

4.1.10 Shunt Regulators

A shunt voltage regulator is the direct opposite of a series voltage regulator. A shunt regulator controls the output voltage by controlling the conduction of a parallel- (or shunt-) connected transistor, while a series regulator does the same thing by controlling the conduction of a series-connected transistor. The basic configuration of a shunt regulator is shown in Fig. 4-22. In this circuit, the power transistor, Q_1, is the only element changed from the series configuration of Fig. 4-1. There is still a reference voltage, V_{ref}, an amplifier, A_1, and a feedback network, β. Power transistor Q_1 is now connected in parallel with load resistance R_L, rather than in series as in Fig. 4-1. The relationship between output voltage E_o and input voltage V_{ref} remains the same:

$$E_o = \frac{V_{ref}}{\beta}$$

The same requirements that exist for the series regulator also exist for the shunt regulator: a stable reference voltage, V_{ref}; a high-gain, stable op amp, A_1; a power control element, Q_1; and a feedback network, β, which determines the output voltage.

A shunt regulator is inherently inefficient because it achieves regulation by absorbing the current that is not required by the load. Since the maximum available load current is set by R_{in}, Q_1 must shunt this current away from R_L under conditions of small load-current demands. Therefore, the total current consumed in a shunt regulator is constant, since it will pass to either Q_1 or R_L, as required. The circuit can be thought of as an ideal zener diode because it uses the high-gain feedback loop and the variable conduction of Q_1 to simulate perfect zener action. This results in inefficiency because the circuit always consumes the total load current, whereas in a series regulator, only the current demanded by the load (plus unavoidable bias currents) is drawn from the source.

From the standpoint of total power consumption then, the shunt regulator is not as attractive as the series regulator. However, the same properties that make the power drain of a shunt regulator constant, also have positive side effects. Since the total power drain is constant, the use of a shunt regulator in a system reduces the effects of transient disturbances feeding back through the power supplies. Any transients due to load-current changes in R_L will be mostly absorbed by Q_1. Therefore, systems using shunt-regulated (or decoupled) stages tend to be "clean" and noise free.

Also, any changes in the unregulated $+V_{in}$ supply will automatically be smoothed by Q_1 and the feedback loop, and will not be transmitted to the output as changes in E_o. For example, should $+V_{in}$ become more positive and attempt to make E_o more positive, this voltage change will be fed back through β and will be amplified by A_1, thus increasing the conduction of Q_1 and opposing the original voltage change. A shunt-regulator system, therefore, resists any changes in operating level due either to changes in $+V_{in}$ or to changes in load current.

Shunt regulators are best used on a small-scale basis (as one might use zener diodes, for example). This keeps the basic inefficiency of the technique from becoming prohibitive, since a local shunt regulator might represent only a fraction of the total power of a system. Yet, the advantages of the active decoupling can be used to stabilize particularly critical stages where required.

Low-Power Shunt Regulator

IC op amps make just as effective shunt regulators as they do series regulators. The key to their effectiveness is in their class-B output stage, which can be either a current sink or a current source. In a shunt regulator, the usual requirement is to absorb the excess load current. An example of a low-power shunt regulator is shown in Fig. 4-23. In this circuit, the output voltage of A_1 is regulated at a value:

$$E_o = V_{ref}\left(\frac{R_2 + R_3}{R_2}\right)$$

where,

V_{ref} is the voltage of zener diode D_1.

The reference current in D_1 is established by R_1 as:

$$I_Z = \frac{E_o - V_{ref}}{R_1}$$

The total current in A_1 is determined by R_4 and output voltage E_o as:

$$I_t = \frac{V_{in} - E_o}{R_4}$$

Not all of the current in R_4 is available as load current, however, as part of this current is used to bias D_1, and part is consumed by R_2 and R_3. The reason that D_1 is fed from the output of A_1 rather than from $+V_{in}$ is that the output of A_1 is a regulated voltage, whereas $+V_{in}$ is unregulated. A large increase in the rejection of input-induced noise is gained by this "bootstrapping" technique of feeding the zener from the output of the op amp. The current drawn by D_1 can be compensated for by a small reduction in the value of R_4, with no sacrifice in the overall performance of the circuit.

To design the regulator of Fig. 4-23 for a specified output voltage, start by choosing a voltage for D_1. Since the primary purpose of a shunt regulator is the decoupling of noise from V_{in} to E_o, a nonzero temperature coefficient for D_1 is not a great disadvantage. Therefore, a standard, general-purpose 5.6-V zener such as the 1N5232 can be used, with a zener current (I_Z) of 1.0 mA. This smaller current will minimize the loading on R_4 and lower the diode voltage to approximately 5.1 V, which is closer to the low TC region of the 1N5232.

For a desired output voltage of 12 V, calculate a value for R_1 to produce 1.0 mA of current in D_1:

$$R_1 = \frac{E_o - V_Z}{1 \times 10^{-3}}$$

$$= \frac{12 - 5.1}{1 \times 10^{-3}}$$

$$= 6.9 \times 10^3$$

$$= 6.9 \text{ k}\Omega$$

The closest standard value of 6.8 kΩ is thus chosen for R_1. Next, select the R_2-R_3 relationship to provide the output voltage of 12 V:

$$12 = 5.1 \left(\frac{R_2 + R_3}{R_2} \right)$$

Since R_2 will have the same voltage across it as does D_1 due to zero differential input voltage, select a value for R_2 that will determine the R_2-R_3 current. This value should be high enough to maintain the R_2-R_3 current at 1.0 mA or less, but the resistance seen by the inverting input (pin 2) of A_1 should be 10 kΩ or less. A nominal value for R_2 would thus be 15 kΩ; then,

$$I_{R_2} = \frac{5.1}{15 \times 10^3}$$

$$= 0.3 \times 10^{-3}$$

$$= 0.3 \text{ mA}$$

Fig. 4-23. Low-power shunt regulator.

and,

$$R_3 = \frac{E_o - 5.1}{I_{R_2}}$$

$$= \frac{12 - 5.1}{3 \times 10^{-4}}$$

$$= \frac{6.9}{3 \times 10^{-4}}$$

$$= 2.3 \times 10^4$$

$$= 23 \text{ k}\Omega$$

The closest standard value of 22 kΩ is thus chosen for R_3. Next, select a value for R_4 that will provide the required total current of:

$$I_t = I_o + I_z + I_{R_2 - R_3}$$

Assume a +V_{in} of 20 V and an I_o of 5.0 mA, then

$$R_4 = \frac{V_{in} - E_o}{I_t}$$

$$= \frac{20 - 12}{6.3 \times 10^{-3}}$$

$$= \frac{8}{6.3} \times 10^3$$

$$= 1.27 \text{ k}\Omega$$

The lower closest standard value of 1.2 kΩ in thus chosen for R_4.

As a supply-voltage decoupler, the regulator of Fig. 4-23 has an effective output impedance of 0.01 Ω at 100 Hz. At the ripple frequency of 120 Hz, therefore, this regulator will have a filtering effect equivalent to a capacitor of 100,000 μF! Obviously, then, it offers an effective, low-cost alternative to bulky RC filters in low-current applications.

High-Power Shunt Regulators

The current-handling capability of a shunt regulator can be extended beyond the 5.0-mA output rating of the basic circuit of Fig. 4-23 by the use of booster transistors, as shown in the circuits of Figs. 4-24A and B. In these circuits, A_1 and its associated compo-

$$R_1 = \frac{E_o - V_{ref}}{I_z}$$

$$E_o = V_{ref} \left(\frac{R_2 + R_3}{R_2} \right)$$

$$R_{in} = \frac{V_{in(min)} - E_o}{I_o + I_z + I_{R2\text{-}R3} + I_{A1}}$$

*Q_1 = 2N3740 for 100 mA output current
= 2N6050 for 2.0 A output current

(A) Connections for positive regulation.

(B) Connections for negative regulation.

Fig. 4-24. High-power shunt regulators.

nents are used as a two-terminal regulator. The op amp regulates its supply (with assistance from Q_1) essentially the same as in the circuit of Fig. 4-23. The output voltage of the regulator is determined in the same manner as for the circuit of Fig. 4-23, and the current capacity is proportional to the gain and power rating of Q_1. For currents up to 100 mA, Q_1 can be a single transistor such as a 2N3740; for higher currents, Q_1 should be a Darlington-pair device such as a 2N6050 or similar equivalent devices.

Since this regulator is a two-terminal device, it can be applied in the same manner that an equivalent zener diode would be applied, using either terminal as common to regulate either positive or negative voltages. A high-power shunt regulator connected for a positive output voltage is shown in Fig. 4-24A, while the same circuit connected for a negative output voltage is shown in Fig. 4-24B.

Unlike a zener diode, the circuit cannot withstand a reversal of voltage (forward conduction in a zener), because this would reverse the supply polarity to A_1. If a transient condition exists which might reverse the voltage across A_1, a clamping diode (D_2) should be added as shown. A 1.0-μF tantalum capacitor (C_1) connected across the output terminals helps to maintain the output impedance low at high frequencies.

Single-to-Dual Power-Supply Converter

A very useful configuration in which a shunt regulator can be used is a single-to-dual power-supply converter, as illustrated in Fig. 4-25. This circuit is a special type of power supply—it is not really a series regulator and not really a shunt regulator but, rather, a hybrid type. It operates between the lines of a single supply, furnishing a floating output that is midway (or some fractional percent) between the two supply lines. This "derived" output terminal is regulated at the voltage set by R_2-R_3 and can either sink or source current, allowing the single supply to be used as two.

Fig. 4-25. Single-to-dual power-supply converter.

The circuit of Fig. 4-25 uses the 759, a power IC having a ±350-mA current output rating. Thus, it can regulate load imbalances of up to 100 mA. A_1 works essentially as a voltage follower in this circuit, with an input voltage set by R_2-R_3. R_1 provides unity-gain feedback from the output (the common terminal), so whatever voltage appears at the input from R_2-R_3 will also appear at the output at a very low impedance. When a load is connected from $+E_o$ to common, the common terminal would tend to rise toward the $+E_o$ potential. However, due to the low output impedance of A_1, the voltage is clamped at the R_2-R_3 potential. A load current from $+E_o$ to common, then, will return to the source through A_1 and the $-V_{in}$ line. A similar reasoning applies for loads from $-E_o$ to common.

In the circuit of Fig. 4-25, R_2 and R_3 are equal; therefore, the V_{in} potential will be equally split. Thus, for a 30-V input, ±15 V will appear at the output. Different output ratios can be selected by scaling R_2 and R_3 for unequal voltage drops. R_2 will drop the positive output voltage and R_3 will drop the negative output voltage since, by definition, their midpoint is at ground (output common). The 759 will require a heat sink; therefore, a power package is specified.

4.2 CURRENT REGULATORS

Current regulators are similar to voltage regulators in that they use the same basic elements of control to accomplish their function. The difference lies in their configuration.

The basic elements of a current regulator are illustrated in Fig. 4-26. There is a reference source, V_{ref}; an amplifier, A_1; and a feedback network, β, which consists in this circuit of R_{sense} and R_{load}. At this point, it appears that there is no difference between this circuit and the basic voltage regulator of Fig. 4-1. Actually, with a given value for R_{load}, there would be no difference. R_{load} and R_{sense} would form a feedback network to define some value of β, and the

$R_{in} = high$

$I_L = \dfrac{E_{in}}{R} = \dfrac{V_{ref}}{R_{sense}}$

I_L may be either polarity depending on the polarity of E_{in}.

$E_{o(max)}$ across $R_L = E_{o(max)}$ of $A_1 - I_L R_{sense}$

Fig. 4-26. Basic noninverting VCCS.

loop would generate an output voltage, E_o. However, the main difference in a current regulator is that it is the *current* rather than the voltage that we wish to maintain constant. In the circuit of Fig. 4-26, it will be noted that if V_{ref} is constant, if R_{sense} is a fixed value, and if A_1 is an ideal amplifier, the current, I_L, flowing in R_{sense} (and thus R_{load}) will remain constant at a value

$$I_L = \frac{V_{ref}}{R_{sense}}$$

This is true regardless of the value of R_{load}. The basic concept of a current regulator, then, is the maintenance of a definite value of current flowing in a variable load impedance, with independence from the load variations, temperature changes, and supply-voltage changes.

There are many different types of regulators, which attain various levels of performance. The performance attainable using IC op amps in current regulators can be nearly perfect if sufficient attention is paid to the significant sources of error.

Op-amp parameters which tend to be important to current regulators are offset voltage drift, bias current, CMRR, and PSRR. With modern amplifiers, virtually all of these factors can be made negligible in a wide range of applications.

4.2.1 Low-Power, General-Purpose Current Regulators
Basic Noninverting VCCS

With the assignment of component values, the circuit of Fig. 4-26 can serve as a highly useful, general-purpose, low-power current regulator. It can supply current of either polarity through R_{load} up to the rated output current and voltage of the amplifier used. The circuit has a high-impedance input, hence it presents a minimum of loading to the reference source.

If a variable voltage is used in place of V_{ref}, this circuit can be used as a voltage-controlled current source (VCCS). The sensitivity of the voltage-to-current conversion is inversely proportional to R_{sense}. For example, an R_{sense} value of 1.0 kΩ will yield a conversion sensitivity of 1.0 mA/V. It should be readily apparent that the overall stability of the circuit is directly proportional to the quality of the resistor used for R_{sense}. When high accuracy and constancy of load current is required, this resistor should obviously be a precision type.

Basic Inverting VCCS

The inverting op-amp configuration can also be used as a current regulator and a VCCS. This is illustrated in Fig. 4-27. In this circuit, input current I_{in} is equal to load current I_L; therefore,

$$I_L = \frac{E_{in}}{R_s}$$

Resistor R_s determines the sensitivity of the voltage-to-current conversion as in the previous circuit, but in this circuit it also determines the input resistance, which is equal to R_s. This circuit can also supply current of either polarity up to the rated output current and voltage of the amplifier. In addition, it has the advantage that more voltage is available to drive R_L because one end of R_L is at ground potential, whereas in the circuit of Fig. 4-26, one end of R_L is at the same potential as the input voltage, which subtracts from the voltage available to drive R_L.

I_L may be either polarity depending on the polarity of E_{in}.

$E_{o(max)}$ across $R_L = E_{o(max)}$ of A_1

Fig. 4-27. Basic inverting VCCS.

4.2.2 Boosted-Output Current Regulators

General-purpose op amps such as the 741 are limited to a maximum output current of ± 5.0 mA. Types such as the 759 and 791 can handle up to 300 mA, or 1.0 A. Low-current types can be boosted to higher currents, however, by adding current-gain transistors within the feedback loop.

Noninverting VCCS With Boosted Output

A circuit illustrating a boosted-output current regulator is shown in Fig. 4-28. This circuit is a 100-mA output, noninverting VCCS with bidirectional current capability in load resistance R_L. For positive input voltages, Q_1 conducts, Q_2 is turned off, and current flows from the $+15$-V supply through Q_1, R_L, and R_1, the 10-Ω sensing resistor. For negative input voltages, Q_2 conducts, Q_1 is turned off, and current flows from the -15-V supply through Q_2, R_L, and R_1. If only single-polarity current flow is required, the opposite polarity transistor can be eliminated. The conversion sensitivity of this circuit is 100 mA/V. Note that higher-current transistors will, of course, allow appreciably higher currents.

Fig. 4-28. Noninverting VCCS with boosted output.

Inverting VCCS With Boosted Output

An inverting VCCS with output boosted to 100 mA is illustrated in Fig. 4-29. One undesirable characteristic of the basic inverting configuration is the fact that the input current is equal to the load current, as diagrammed in Fig. 4-27. This is obviously a drawback for high-current use because the signal or reference might have to supply currents as high as 100 mA! However, there is a method of circumventing this problem known as *current scaling,* which provides an effective gain between the input current, I_{in}, and the load current, I_L.

The circuit of Fig. 4-29 utilizes the current-scaling technique, which works as follows: A voltage of -1.0 V at the input will create a current of 100 μA in R_1 and, because of feedback action, this same current must also flow through R_2. Therefore, the junction of R_2 and R_3 will be at a potential of $+1.0$ V, which means that R_3 will also have 1.0 V across it. Hence, the current in R_3 will be

Fig. 4-29. Inverting VCCS with boosted output.

$$I_{R_3} = \frac{1.0 \text{ V}}{10 \text{ } \Omega} = 100 \text{ mA}$$

Thus, I_{R_3} has been effectively scaled upward by the ratio of R_2/R_3, which in this case is 10,000/10, or 1000/1.

The total load current, I_L, flowing in R_L consists of the two currents, I_{in} and I_{R_3}, so the actual ratio of load current to input current will be

$$\frac{I_L}{I_{in}} = \frac{I_{R_3} + I_{in}}{I_{in}}$$

$$= \frac{100.1}{0.1}$$

$$= \frac{1001}{1}$$

which, to be precise, is 0.1% in error from the R_2/R_3 ratio, but the basic current-scaling technique is illustrated nonetheless. This circuit can also be made bidirectional by the use of complementary buffer transistors for Q_1 and Q_2. Note the practicality of controlling amperes of current in R_3 (given the appropriate booster transistor) for high ratios of R_2/R_3.

4.2.3 Unidirectional Current Sources With Single Output Terminals

The current sources discussed thus far have been capable of driving loads with both terminals available, or "floating." Often, however, both terminals of a load are not available for this type of connection. For various reasons, it may be necessary that one load terminal be connected to a fixed potential—either supply voltage, for example, or ground. In fact, these applications may be more commonplace than the two-terminal (floating) drives. Also, a large number of applications do not require a bidirectional output current—the current may always remain the same polarity, and even fixed in magnitude. There is a wide range of circuits that fall into these general categories, some with even more subtle options of their own, which will be discussed in this section.

Current Sources With Loads Referred to More-Positive Supply Potentials

Positive-Input VCCS—Fig. 4-30 illustrates a circuit that partially resembles the noninverting buffered VCCS of Fig. 4-28, but with one very important difference. In Fig. 4-30, load resistance R_L has been moved to the collector circuit of Q_1, which places R_L *outside* the feedback loop for A_1. In operation, this circuit maintains the Q_1

emitter current constant as it passes through R_1 by comparing it to input voltage E_{in}. In this respect, the circuit of Fig. 4-30 is the same as an npn buffered version of the Fig. 4-28 circuit. In Fig. 4-28, however, the total emitter current of Q_1 (collector current plus base current) passes through R_1 and R_L. The situation is slightly different in Fig. 4-30 since R_L is in the collector circuit, but the current that is regulated is the emitter current. Therefore, there is an error due to the base current of Q_1, which does not flow through R_L. This error is caused by the finite h_{FE} of Q_1. (In the example shown in Fig. 4-30, the h_{FE} of a 2N3904 is 100 minimum.) The difference between the current sampled and the current actually flowing in R_L will be $1/h_{FE}$ of the current in R_1, or typically less than 1.0% for currents in the region of 10 mA. The V+ supply to R_L and Q_1 can be either the +15-V line, or it can be as high as the V_{CB} rating of the transistor used, as long as the maximum power dissipation of the transistor is not exceeded. The V+ parameter is not limited by the op amp in this circuit. The circuit responds to positive voltages at E_{in}.

$$I_L = \frac{E_{in}}{R_1}, \; E_{in} > 0$$

Q$_1$	I_L
2N3904	1.0 μA - 1.0 mA
2N2219	1.0 mA - 100 mA
2N6057	100 mA - 10 A

*Use 741 for $I_L > 10$ μA; for $I_L < 10$ μA, use low-input-current type.

†Protection against input polarity reversal. Use 1N914 for general-purpose; use 1N458A for precision, low-current.

Fig. 4-30. Basic positive-input VCCS; load referred to V+.

Since this circuit does not load the reference source, E_{in}, it is a very useful type of current regulator. For the reference source, a circuit such as that of Fig. 4-2, or one of its variations, can be used. R_1 and Q_1 are selected for the desired operating current. Q_1 is selected primarily from the standpoint of power and voltage rating. Typical recommendations for Q_1, for different ranges of I_L, are listed in Fig. 4-30. Note that high h_{FE} transistors minimize error.

A 741 is generally adequate for A_1, since A_1 must be a unity-gain-compensated type due to the 100% feedback through Q_1. For very low values of I_L, the input bias current of A_1 (which subtracts from I_L) can become a significant percentage of I_L, thus causing a significant error. For I_L values below about 10 μA then, low-input-current FET types such as the 3140, TL071, 351, 356, or AD542 may be necessary for better accuracy.

One possible trouble with this circuit is failure of Q_1 if the input voltage is reversed from its normal operating polarity. Since Q_1 can conduct only a unidirectional current, a reversal of the input voltage to A_1 will result in an opposite-polarity, saturated output voltage from A_1. This may be sufficient to cause emitter-base breakdown and possible destruction of Q_1. This situation is easily prevented by diode D_1, which protects Q_1 by reverse clamping the output of A_1. Note that D_1 can cause an error due to leakage. At low current levels ($\leqslant 10$ μA), a low-leakage type such as a 1N458A is preferred. This comment applies to clamp diodes of other configurations as well.

**Q_1	I_L
2N3904	1.0 μA - 1.0 mA
2N2219	1.0 mA - 100 mA
2N6057	100 mA - 10 A

*Use 741 for I_L > 10 μA; for I_L < 10 μA, use low-input-current type.

†Protection against input polarity reversal.

Fig. 4-31. Basic negative-input VCCS; load referred to V+.

Negative-Input VCCS—For negative input voltages, the circuit of Fig. 4-31 can be used. This is essentially the same circuit as that of Fig. 4-30 converted to an inverting input. The same general considerations that were true for A_1 and Q_1 in Fig. 4-30 also apply in this circuit. Since Q_1 is biased at near ground potential, this circuit has a larger available output swing to drive R_L. The circuit has the same basic disadvantage as the circuit of Fig. 4-27, however, in that $I_{in} \cong I_L$, restricting operation to small input currents. This disadvantage can be overcome by using the current-scaling technique, as shown in Fig. 4-32. In this circuit, resistor R_3 forces Q_1 to conduct a much heavier current than the feedback current. The operation is similar to the circuit of Fig. 4-29, with the gain between I_{in} and I_L determined by the R_2/R_3 ratio.

Improving the Accuracy of the Output Current—The circuits discussed thus far are all somewhat imprecise, as was pointed out initially. There are several remedies that can be used to minimize the inaccuracies, and basically all are schemes to minimize that portion of the regulated current which does not reach the load. This problem can become rather severe, particularly at high currents where the gain of the transistor falls off, and inaccuracies can reach several percent.

The first remedy that can be used is to substitute a Darlington device for the single transistor used in Fig. 4-30. Such a circuit is shown in Fig. 4-33. In this circuit, Q_1 can be a single-package Darlington amplifier, such as the MPS-U45, or it can be two discrete transistors wired as a Darlington pair (shown as Q_1 and Q_2 in Fig. 4-33).

$$I_L = \frac{E_{in}\left(\frac{R_2}{R_1}\right)}{R_2 \parallel R_3}$$

*Use 741 for $I_L > 10\ \mu A$; for $I_L < 10\ \mu A$, use low-input-current type.

†Protection against input polarity reversal.

**Q_1	I_L
2N3904	1.0 μA - 1.0 mA
2N2219	1.0 mA - 100 mA
2N6057	100 mA - 10 A

Fig. 4-32. Negative-input VCCS with current gain.

The use of a Darlington amplifier will improve the accuracy by the additional gain, and it will suffice for all but the most stringent applications. For such applications, a FET can be used as shown in Fig. 4-34. This lowers the drive current to the FET (which is, in fact, the error component) to the reverse-bias gate leakage of the device used. At room temperature, a 2N4867 has a maximum leakage of 250 pA, but it rises to a maximum of 250 nA at 100°C. It should be remembered that the gate current of a JFET will double for every 10°C of temperature rise, so for high-temperature low-current use, a Darlington amplifier may still be the better answer.

$$I_L = \frac{E_{in}}{R_1}$$

*Use 741 for $I_L > 10\ \mu A$; for $I_L < 10\ \mu A$, use low-input-current type.

Fig. 4-33. Positive-input Darlington VCCS.

$$I_L = \frac{E_{in}}{R_1}$$

$$I_{L(max)} = I_{DSS} \text{ of } Q_1$$

*Use 741 for $I_L > 10 \ \mu A$; for $I_L < 10 \ \mu A$, use low-input-current type.

Fig. 4-34. Positive-input FET VCCS.

The FET used must have a minimum zero-bias drain current (I_{DSS}) that is equal to or higher than the desired load current, I_L. For a 2N4867, the minimum I_{DSS} is 0.4 mA, which is also, therefore, the maximum I_L for the device in the circuit of Fig. 4-34. As in previous circuits, the breakdown voltage and power dissipation ratings of Q_1 must be observed. Since this type of circuit will most likely be used at low currents, a FET amplifier will be a logical choice for A_1.

Some applications may require both a small bias-current error and a high I_L. Such requirements may be satisfied by a FET/power transistor combination, as shown in the circuit of Fig. 4-35. In this circuit, the FET drives the npn transistor as a source follower, and the combination is equivalent to a power FET. The breakdown voltage is limited to that of the device that has the lower rating, which in this circuit is the FET, Q_1. The power rating is determined primarily by Q_2, and the circuit can be used at any current level up to 50 mA with the devices shown.

For load currents above 10 mA, an LM395 transistor will allow excellent regulation and can directly replace Q_1-Q_2 in Fig. 4-35. For stability, a series base resistor of 5 kΩ should be used (see Fig. 4-12).

In all of the preceding VCCS circuits with improved accuracy, the general considerations regarding the op amp used should follow

$$I_L = \frac{E_{in}}{R_1}$$

*Use 741 for $I_L > 10 \ \mu A$; for $I_L < 10 \ \mu A$, use low-input-current type.

Fig. 4-35. Positive-input buffered-FET VCCS.

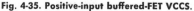

the points that were discussed for the circuit of Fig. 4-30, since they are modifications of this basic configuration. In all cases, R_1 is selected to provide the desired output current with a full-scale input voltage in accordance with the equation,

$$I_L = \frac{E_{in}}{R_1}$$

R_1 should, of course, be a precision type for high accuracy and stability.

If desired, the accuracy improvement techniques can also be applied to the inverting configurations of Figs. 4-31 and 4-32. This involves substitution of the appropriate control element (Darlington, FET, or buffered FET) for Q_1 of Figs. 4-31 and 4-32. The equations for I_L remain the same as stated in the respective illustrations.

Current Sources With Loads Referred to More-Negative Supply Potentials

So far, we have discussed a series of circuits which drive loads referred to a positive supply potential. Often, however, the load may be referred to a negative supply potential, with a constant-current source required to drive it, as described previously. In this section, we will discuss an equivalent series of circuits for negative referred loads, together with the types of devices used. Circuit operation is the same as described for the positive counterparts (except for voltage polarities), so a minimum of explanation accompanies these circuits.

Negative-Input VCCS—The basic circuit for a VCCS with a load referred to a more-negative supply potential is shown in Fig. 4-36. This circuit responds to negative voltage inputs to generate an output current,

$$I_L = \frac{E_{in}}{R_1}$$

which, in principle, is exactly the same as the circuit of Fig. 4-30. In the circuit of Fig. 4-36, however, Q_1 is a pnp transistor, which allows R_L to be returned to a V− potential. The same considerations for amplifier selection apply to this circuit as for the circuit of Fig. 4-30, and typical devices suitable for operation at different currents are also listed in Fig. 4-36. Input polarity reversal can be a problem in this circuit also; protection is provided by the reverse-clamping diode, D_1, if needed (with selection criteria as discussed previously).

Positive-Input VCCS—A VCCS which responds to positive input voltages to drive a load referred to V− is shown in Fig. 4-37. This circuit is the complement of the circuit of Fig. 4-31 and generates an output current equal to the input current,

$$I_L = \frac{E_{in}}{R_1}$$

*Use 741 for $I_L > 10\ \mu A$; for $I_L < 10\ \mu A$, use low-input-current type.

†Protection against input polarity reversal.

Q_i	I_L
2N3906	1.0 μA - 1.0 mA
2N2905	1.0 mA - 100 mA
2N6050	100 mA - 10 A

Fig. 4-36. Basic negative-input VCCS; load referred to V−.

$$I_L = \frac{E_{in}}{R_1}$$

This circuit can be modified to provide a current "gain," as shown in Fig. 4-38.

Improved Accuracy VCCSs for Negative Referred Loads—The three basic configurations of Figs. 4-36, 4-37, and 4-38 are subject to the same inaccuracies as those described for the circuits of Figs. 4-30, 4-31, and 4-32. This problem is solved for the circuits of Figs. 4-36, 4-37, and 4-38 in a similar manner as for the circuits of Figs. 4-30, 4-31, and 4-32—by the use of higher-current-gain control elements, such as Darlington pairs, FETs, and buffered FETs.

Three circuits that eliminate this problem for negative referred loads are shown in Figs. 4-39, 4-40, and 4-41. These circuits operate essentially the same as their counterparts in Figs. 4-33, 4-34, and 4-35, using devices that are complements to those described previously. All of these circuits respond to negative input voltages to develop an output current,

$$I_L = \frac{E_{in}}{R_1}$$

$$I_L = \frac{E_{in}}{R_1}$$

Q_1	I_L
2N3906	1.0 μA - 1.0 mA
2N2905	1.0 mA - 100 mA
2N6050	100 mA - 10 A

*Use 741 for $I_L > 10\ \mu A$; for $I_L < 10\ \mu A$, use low-input-current type.

†Protection against input polarity reversal.

Fig. 4-37. Basic positive-input VCCS; load referred to V−.

4.2.4 Bidirectional-Output VCCS

A very interesting category of VCCS is the most general-purpose type of all, and is known as a bidirectional-output VCCS, or Howland circuit.* This type of current source will drive a load referred to

* See references 30 and 37 at the end of the chapter.

$$I_L = \frac{E_{in}\left(\frac{R_2}{R_1}\right)}{R_2 \parallel R_3}$$

* Use 741 for $I_L > 10\ \mu A$; for $I_L < 10\ \mu A$, use low-input-current type.

† Protection against input polarity reversal.

Q₁	I_L
2N3906	1.0 μA - 1.0 mA
2N2905	1.0 mA - 100 mA
2N6050	100 mA - 10 A

Fig. 4-38. Positive-input VCCS with current gain.

$$I_L = \frac{E_{in}}{R_1}$$

*Use 741 for $I_L > 10\ \mu A$; for $I_L < 10\ \mu A$, use low-input-current type.

Fig. 4-39. Negative-input Darlington VCCS.

$$I_L = \frac{E_{in}}{R_1}$$

$$I_{L(max)} = I_{DSS}\ \text{of}\ Q_1$$

*Use 741 for $I_L > 10\ \mu A$; for $I_L < 10\ \mu A$, use low-input-current type.

Fig. 4-40. Negative-input FET VCCS.

ground (or any voltage within its linear output range) with either polarity of output current, and it can be operated from either polarity of input voltage. The general circuit is shown in Fig. 4-42. It uses a combination of positive and negative feedback, and consists only of an op amp and a set of performance-defining resistors.

The equation for the output current is deceiving in its simplicity, and there are actually a number of considerations for making this circuit work well.

*Use 741 for $I_L > 10$ μA; for $I_L < 10$ μA, use low-input-current type.

Fig. 4-41. Negative-input buffered-FET VCCS.

As noted, there are two scaling factors which govern operation. Resistor R_2 can be selected for the desired output current; then the scaling factor, K, can be used to set R_1, which essentially will determine the input impedance. Here, K is unity, but it could be higher if desired. Scaling factor M does not enter directly into the expression, but is nevertheless important. As M is lowered, the available output voltage at the R_2-R_4 node is maximized. With $M = 0.1$, 10-V (or more) output swings are available from most op amps.

$$*I_L = -\frac{E_{in}}{R_L}$$

$$K = \frac{R_2}{R_1} = \frac{R_4}{R_3}$$

$$M = \frac{R_3}{R_1} = \frac{R_4}{R_2}$$

As shown, $K = 1.0$, $M = 0.1$.
$I_L = -1.0$ mA with $E_{in} = +10$ V.

Fig. 4-42. General-purpose bidirectional-output VCCS.

The resistor ratios must be maintained as closely as possible if the circuit is to have a high output impedance, thus the close-tolerance types specified.

Since the circuit uses both positive and negative feedback, the user must provide assurance against latch-up or oscillation. A small value capacitor, C_f, will minimize oscillation tendencies, as will the load capacitance from R_2-R_4 to ground.

The example shown uses a 355 op amp and delivers a 1.0-mA load current (I_L) with a +10-V input. The sense of input polarity can be reversed if desired, by grounding R_1 and driving R_2. The signal source must be low impedance, to guarantee the correct ratio match (regardless of which input sense is used).

A useful form of VCCS is the buffered feedback circuit in Fig. 4-43. This circuit maintains the current, I_L, constant by sensing the voltage across resistor R_5.

As previously, the match of resistor ratios is critical to maintaining a high output impedance and constant current. Also, the scaling of R_4 to R_2 (and R_3 to R_1) can be used to minimize the voltage dropped across R_5, and thus maximize the output swing.

A FET-input amplifier is very useful in this circuit, as it allows operation down into the nanoampere (or less) region. Actually only A_2 needs to be a FET type for low output current while A_1 can be a conventional unit. Both amplifiers should have good CMRR for high performance, and A_1 can be selected for high output current, if desired.

Fig. 4-43. Bidirectional-output VCCS with buffered feedback.

The circuit can either sink or source current, according to the polarity of input voltage. If only a source of current to a ground-referred load is needed, the circuit can operate from a single positive supply using the 3240, 358, or other single-supply type.

4.2.5 Current Source With Integral Reference

An interesting and useful variation of current source is the type using an integral reference voltage source, as shown in Fig. 4-44. In this circuit, the reference voltage source "floats" and the output current drives a load referred to ground.

Fig. 4-44. Current source with integral reference.

Here, A_1 is a low-bias-current FET-input op amp with low offset voltage and drift. A_2 is a 2.5-V reference source IC which provides a stable 2.5 V between its COM and OUT terminals. R_1 and R_2 divide the output of A_2 to 0.25 V, the voltage labeled V_{ref}.

Because of the zero input differential of the op amp, the circuit will adjust so that 0.25 V also appears across R_{sense}. This stable voltage determines the output current, according to the relations shown.

The control of very low currents is a problem in op-amp circuits because it implies a very-low-bias-current op amp, and a high-value resistor. The 25-pA bias current of the AD542L simplifies the current aspect of the problem, and dividing the reference down to 0.25 V limits the size of R_{sense}.

The main errors of this circuit will be due to the PSRR and CMRR of A_1-A_2. For the units specified, this will be on the order of 80 dB, or 0.01%.

A list of references for further background on regulators for voltage and current circuitry is provided at the end of the chapter.

REFERENCES

1. Accardi, L. "Self-Stabilized Zener Insures Constant Current in Op-Amp Voltage Reference." *Electronic Design,* December 21, 1972.

2. ———. "Superstable Reference Voltage Source." *EDN, October* 1, 1971.

3. *Applications Manual for Computing Amplifiers.* Philbrick Researches, Inc. Dedham, Mass., 1966.

4. *Applications of OEI Products.* Optical Electronics, Inc., Tucson, Ariz., 1971.

5. Birman, P. *Power Supply Handbook.* Kepco, Inc., Flushing, N.Y.

6. Brokaw, A. P. "A Simple Three-Terminal IC Bandgap Reference." *IEEE Journal of Solid State Circuits,* Vol. SC-9, No. 6, December 1974.

7. Clayton, G. B. *Operational Amplifiers.* Butterworth, Inc., Toronto, Ont., Canada, 1971.

8. *DC Power Supply Handbook.* Hewlett-Packard Co., Palo Alto, Calif., 1970.

9. Dobkin, R. C. "Don't Forget A/D Reference Stability." *EDN, June* 20, 1977.

10. ———. *High Stability Regulators.* National Semiconductor Linear Brief LB-15, January 1971. National Semiconductor Corp., Santa Clara, Calif.

11. ———. *IC Voltage Reference Has 1 PPM Per Degree Drift.* National Semiconductor Application Note AN-161, June 1976. National Semiconductor Corp., Santa Clara, Calif.

12. ———. "On Chip Heater Helps To Stabilize Monolithic Reference Zener." *Electronics,* September 16, 1976.

13. Giles, J. N. *Fairchild Semiconductor LIC Handbook.* Fairchild Semiconductor, Mountain View, Calif., 1967.

14. Goldfarb, W. "Single-Supply Reference Source Uses Self-Regulated Zener." *Electronics,* June 7, 1973.

15. Gunn, J. "10 Volt ($\pm$1 mV) References." *Analog Dialogue,* Vol. 10, No. 1, 1976.

16. Henderson, B.; Glasser, S. "Constant Voltage Diodes Are Getting Sharper." *Electronic Products,* March 18, 1974.

17. Henry T. *Analysis and Design of the Op Amp Current Source.* Motorola Application Note AN-587, October 1972. Motorola Semiconductor Products, Inc., Phoenix, Ariz.

18. Jung, W. G. "Applications of the AD580." *Analog Dialogue,* Vol. 9, No. 2, June 1975.

19. ———. *IC Converter Cookbook.* Howard W. Sams & Co., Inc., Indianapolis, 1978.

20. ———. "IC Regulated Power." *The Audio Amateur,* April 1974.

21. ———. "Precision Reference Source Eliminates Power Supply Regulation Errors." *Electronic Design,* September 1, 1975.

22. ———. "Precision Reference Source Features Minimum Errors." *EDN,* August 5, 1976.

23. ———. "Programmable Voltage Reference Is Stable, Yet Simple." *EDN,* November 5, 1975.

24. ———. "Simple Regulator Circuits Provide Tracking Bipolar Reference Voltages." *Electronic Design,* July 5, 1976.

25. Kennedy, E. J. "Temperature Stable Supply Uses IC as Error Amplifier." *Electronic Design,* November 8, 1969.

26. Kesner, D. "Choose Regulator Op Amps With Care." *Electronic Design,* June 21, 1969.

27. ———. *Regulators Using Operational Amplifiers.* Motorola Application Note AN-480, October 1970. Motorola Semiconductor Products, Inc., Phoenix, Ariz.

28. Koep, K. "Solid State Voltage Standards." *Instruments and Control Systems,* October 1972.

29. Kuijk, K. E. "A Precision Reference Voltage Source." *IEEE Journal of Solid State Circuits,* Vol. SC-8, No. 3, June 1973.

30. Miller, W. "Single Amplifier Current Sources." *Analog Dialogue,* Vol. 1, No. 1, April 1967.

31. Nelson, C. *Monolithic Regulator Specifications.* Teletype Semiconductor Application Note, 1971. Teledyne Semiconductor, Mountain View, Calif.

32. Pouliot, D. "Build Precision Reference Sources." *Electronic Design,* July 5, 1976.

33. Ritmanich, W. "Bandgap Voltage Reference Applications." *Proceedings of EE Times IC Applications Seminar,* 1976.

34. Routh, W. S. *An Applications Guide for Operational Amplifiers.* National Semiconductor Application Note AN-20, February 1969. National Semiconductor Corp., Santa Clara, Calif.

35. Scott, M. *Circuit Building Blocks for Voltage Regulators.* Fairchild Application Note, 1968. Fairchild Semiconductor, Mountain View, Calif.

36. Shah, M. J. "Stable Voltage Reference Uses Single Power Supply." *Electronics,* March 13, 1972.

37. Sheingold, D. H. "Impedance and Admittance Transformations Using Operational Amplifiers." *The Lightning Empiricist,* Vol. 12, No. 1, January 1964. Philbrick Researches, Inc., Dedham, Mass.

38. Shirley, F. R.; Vanderlosk, L. "A Stable Voltage Reference Uses Only Six Components." *Electronic Design,* January 18, 1968.

39. Tobey, G. E.; Graeme, J. G.; Huelsman, L. P. (eds.). *Operational Amplifiers—Design and Applications.* McGraw-Hill Book Co., New York, 1971.

40. Widlar, R. J. "New Development in IC Voltage Regulators." *IEEE Journal of Solid State Circuits,* Vol. SC-6, No. 1, February 1971.

41. Williams, J. "Don't Bypass the Voltage Reference That Best Suits Your Needs." *EDN,* October 5, 1977.

42. Product Catalog, PRD Series Precision Reference Diodes; CODI Corp., Fairlawn, New Jersey.

FIVE

Signal-Processing Circuits

The broadest application area imaginable is one that is ideally suited to IC op amps. This is the general area of signal processing, where a circuit "operates" on an input signal to create a new form of output signal, altered in some manner from the original. Included in this area are such common functions as rectification, clipping, logarithmic or antilogarithmic conversions, phase shifting, filtering, and many others. The basic functions of dc and ac amplification are signal processing in a general sense, but since they are covered in a later chapter, they will not be detailed here except in special senses. Signal processing as treated in this chapter encompasses those "specialty" functions which, although common circuit techniques, do not fall into any other category.

5.1 THE PRECISION DIODE

A popular and useful signal-processing circuit is the precision diode circuit shown in Fig. 5-1A. This circuit is basically a voltage follower with a diode inside the feedback loop to confine its operation to half of the input signal swing, thus accomplishing half-wave rectification. D_1 is the rectifier diode, which conducts on input potentials higher than zero, forming a unity-gain replica of the input during the positive half cycle. During the negative half cycle, D_1 switches off and the output is zero.

The nonlinearity and temperature sensitivity of D_1 is not seen in the output waveform, because it is removed by feedback around the op amp. Furthermore, the circuit will not have a minimum forward threshold voltage, as does a conventional diode, because the high

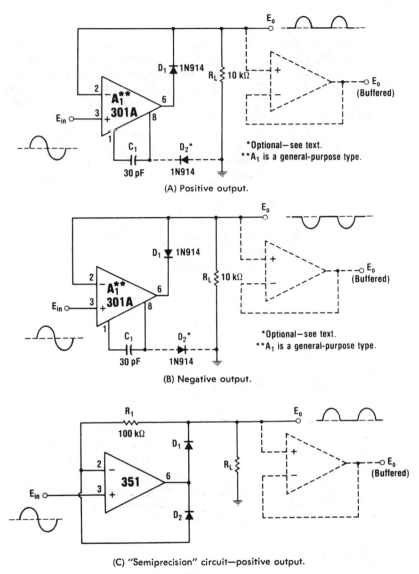

(A) Positive output.

(B) Negative output.

(C) "Semiprecision" circuit—positive output.

Fig. 5-1. Precision diode circuits.

amplifier gain will automatically adjust the voltage drive to the diode so that the rectified output is accurately maintained—even at millivolt input levels.

The limitations of the circuit are defined by the op amp used and are speed related. Since the feedback loop is broken when D_1 switches off, the amplifier alternates between half cycles of open- and closed-loop operation. The time it takes for A_1 to settle into a stable output condition after D_1 turns on is limited by the slewing rate and bandwidth of the amplifier, particularly since A_1 must be compensated for unity gain because it operates as a voltage follower when D_1 is on.

The 301A op amp is shown for this application because it can be clamped (optionally) at pin 8. This aids high-speed operation by eliminating internal saturation. Other unity-gain-stable op amps can also be used; FET types are generally preferred because of their high slew rates, which will allow operation to well beyond 10 kHz. General-purpose bipolar types such as the 301A or 741 will operate in this circuit up to about 1.0 kHz with full output. Beyond this, a faster-slewing type should be used, such as the AD544 or the 5105.

A lesser problem of the circuit is its high output impedance during the inactive period. The output and D_1 are floating during this time, so a resistive load to ground (R_L) is necessary if it is not provided by succeeding circuitry. A buffer can be added quite simply (as shown dotted), and is an attractive option for a dual device such as a TL082 or LF353.

The same general philosophy is also applicable to the sister circuit of Fig. 5-1B, arranged to rectify the negative-going portions of the input signal. This is accomplished merely by reversing D_1 (and D_2, if used).

A word of caution: Do not attempt to use this circuit with low differential-input-voltage op amps such as the 318 or 308, since the input voltage differential is high during the period when the loop is open. High-differential-input devices such as the 741 or FET-input families are necessary to prevent input breakdown.

An example of how the advantages of a modern, high-speed FET-input device can be married to this application is shown in Fig. 5-1C. Here, a 351 op amp is used as a "semiprecision" diode, operating the same as Fig. 5-1A. In this case, clamping for the off state is provided by D_2, and the output is isolated by R_1. Some signal is transmitted to R_L via R_1, which causes some loss of precision. This can be minimized by maintaining R_1 large in relation to R_L.

5.2 PRECISION CLIPPERS

Such a basically useful circuit as the precision rectifier, described in Section 5.1, naturally has variations. In this case they are numerous and all are very useful.

5.2.1 Simplified Series Clipper

One very slight variation of the circuits in Fig. 5-1 turns them into precision clippers. This is shown in Fig. 5-2. The circuit works by varying the output base line during the period when diode D_1 is off.

Since D_1 will conduct whenever the noninverting input is higher than the inverting input, it follows that the input threshold need not necessarily be ground (as in the circuits of Fig. 5-1). By varying the input reference, a clipper (biased rectifier) may be made. This is accomplished merely by returning R_L to a voltage other than ground. In the circuit of Fig. 5-2A, which is a positive-peak clipper, the output

(A) Positive-peak clipper.

(B) Negative-peak clipper.

Fig. 5-2. Precision clippers.

will be a replica of those portions *lower* than the reference voltage. The circuit requires a low-impedance source for reference, particularly if clamp D_2 is used. Note that one-half of a dual device can suffice as a buffer for V_{ref}, if desired. For example, high-speed clipping can be accomplished using a 353, TL072, or 772.

A negative-peak clipper can be implemented merely by reversing D_1 (and D_2, if used), as shown in Fig. 5-2B. Note that in both cases there is no restraint on the reference voltage as long as it is within the input range of A_1. The output will follow the input whenever the input exceeds V_{ref}. External loading on R_L has the effect of reducing the reference voltage due to voltage division, so the circuit may require an output buffer amplifier. General-purpose duals, such as the 1458, 4558, or 358, are useful here.

5.2.2 Self-Buffered Series Clipper (Linear OR Gate)

In situations where the output impedance of the simple series clip-per is a disadvantage, an alternate form of clipper is available (Fig. 5-3). In this circuit, the output is always in a low-impedance state because one feedback loop is always closed (around either A_1 or A_2). The two diodes perform a gating function for the input signals, allow-ing whichever input is greater to pass to the output; thus the terminol-ogy, "linear OR." If E_{in} is greater than V_{ref}, A_1-D_1 will be on and E_{in} falls below V_{ref}, A_1 turns D_1 off and A_2-D_2 provide the output signal, V_{ref}. The inputs are interchangeable, due to the complete symmetry of the circuit.

Because both amplifiers are switching as the input signal goes through threshold, the response time of this circuit is slowed consid-erably with general-purpose amplifiers, although they may be useful below 100 Hz. The faster-slewing FET units called for in Fig. 5-3, however, give good performance to above 10 kHz. A positive clipping action can be obtained by reversing D_1 and D_2, and returning R_1 to +15 V. This circuit is useful when the clipping potential must be pre-cise, when a low-impedance reference source is not available, or when a low output impedance is necessary. It is capable of very low offset errors if a precision dual such as the AD644 is used.

5.2.3 Shunt Clipper

A shunt clipper can be formed by yet another variation on the basic precision diode. This is diagrammed in Fig. 5-4. When E_{in} is above the reference voltage applied to the noninverting input of A_1, D_1 will be reverse biased and E_{in} will pass unaffected through R_1 to the output. When a negative peak of E_{in} exceeds V_{ref}, A_1 drives D_1 on and absorbs the input current from R_1, clamping the output at the V_{ref} level.

*$A_1 - A_2$ = TL072, 353, 772, AD644

Note: negative clipping shown. For positive clipping, reverse D_1, D_2, and return R_1 to +15 V. General-purpose op amps may be substituted at lower frequencies.

Fig. 5-3. Self-buffered series clipper.

Fig. 5-4. Shunt clipper.

The same considerations for speed apply to this circuit as to the basic one of Fig. 5-1A. An antisaturation clamp (D_2) is useful to minimize the clipper response time. If an antisaturation clamp is used, it requires a low source impedance from V_{ref}. A clipper of opposite polarity can be constructed by reversing D_1 (and D_2, if used).

Due to the high output impedance (essentially the value of R_1), this clipper will usually require a buffer amplifier. A 310 high-speed voltage follower will work well with no additional sacrifice in operating speed. One of the previously mentioned FET duals will also work well here and will allow much higher R_1 values, up to 1.0 MΩ.

5.3 DC RESTORER

Yet another useful variation of the ideal rectifier is the dc restorer or peak clamper of Fig. 5-5. This circuit charges C_1 to a voltage that clamps the input waveform peak at V_{ref}. When E_{in} swings negative (below V_{ref}), A_1 drives D_1 on, forming a low-impedance path to charge C_1. After the peak has passed and D_1 is turned off again, the charge on C_1 is retained, since the only bleed paths are the input currents of A_1 and A_2. This gives the circuit a fast-attack, slow-decay response to input level changes. Faster recovery between level changes is accomplished by a shunt resistance to ground (R_B), with some sacrifice in clamping precision. As with the precision diode, this

Fig. 5-5. Dc restorer (peak clamper).

circuit is responsive into the millivolt region, due to the high gain of A_1 driving D_1. The circuit as shown clamps negative peaks to V_{ref}, but positive-peak clamping is possible by reversing D_1. The value of C_1 may be changed to accommodate different input rates and pulse widths.

Note that since A_2 sees a high source impedance, it should be a low-bias-current type (1.0 nA or less). A FET dual type will work well in this circuit. Note also that E_{in} must be from a low source impedance to charge C_1.

5.4 HALF-WAVE RECTIFIER

Fig. 5-6 is a half-wave rectifier that produces an inverted half-wave replica of the input signal. For negative input signals at R_1, the output is positive, forward biasing D_1 and closing a negative feedback loop through R_2. This produces an inverted gain of almost exactly one, since R_1 and R_2 are closely matched. For positive input signals, the amplifier output is negative and D_1 is off. D_2 is on in this case, applying negative feedback to the summing point and clamping the op-amp output to -0.6 V. This clamped output swing aids in minimizing response time, because it prevents amplifier saturation.

With a 741 type, this circuit will be useful at frequencies up to approximately 1 kHz. Again, output impedance is nonuniform—low when D_1 is on and essentially 20 kΩ (or R_2) when D_1 is off. Negative rectified outputs are possible by reversing D_1 and D_2. Operation at higher frequencies is improved by using one of the faster amplifiers in terms of bandwidth and slew rate, such as were discussed in Section 5.1. R_3 is a bias compensation resistor and is not necessary for FET units (replace by a direct connection to ground).

With this circuit, and many of its derivatives that follow, the absolute values of R_1 and R_2 are not important, as only their ratio determines the accuracy of rectification. Therefore, they can be a pair from a resistor array with close *matching* tolerances, which is typically more economical than low absolute tolerances.

* See text.
** Reverse for negative output.
$R_1 = R_2$

Fig. 5-6. Basic half-wave rectifier.

Fig. 5-7. Fast half-wave rectifier.

5.4.1 High-Speed Rectifier

Many applications demand a rectifier having a good fidelity at frequencies far above a few kilohertz. This may be achieved with fast-slewing, wide-bandwidth amplifier configurations. The general-purpose 301A-type amplifier has an alternate form of compensation, termed *feedforward,* which is very useful in inverting applications; it allows rectification with low errors at frequencies up to 100 kHz. Since this circuit is an inverting configuration, feedforward compensation can be used as shown in Fig. 5-7. In this case, C_1 is the compensation capacitor. The circuit can be modified for a negative-going output by reversing D_1 and D_2. Due to the higher operating frequencies involved, oscillations are a potential problem. Therefore, a good layout and careful attention to power-supply bypassing are important considerations (see Chapter 3).

5.4.2 Rectifier With Buffered Output

Both of the previous rectifier circuits work in a similar fashion (except for response time), and they both have the slight problem of a nonuniform output impedance between alternations. For applications where this could be troublesome, the circuit of Fig. 5-8 can be used. This circuit contains a 310-type, high-speed voltage follower (A_2) within the feedback loop of A_1; the function of A_2 is to main-

Fig. 5-8. Fast buffered rectifier.

tain a low output impedance. During positive output alternations, D_1 and R_4 rectify the signal; A_2 "follows" this signal, returning feedback to the input through R_2. On opposite alternations, D_1 is off and the feedback loop of A_2 is closed through D_2. However, the output terminal is maintained at a low impedance by A_2, which sees a ground-level signal from R_4 during this period. As with previous circuits, opposite output polarity is obtainable by reversing D_1 and D_2. The buffering property of A_2 can be applied to either of the previous half-wave rectifier circuits—Fig. 5-6 or Fig. 5-7—with equally good results. Also, one of the previously mentioned wide-bandwidth, fast-slewing FET dual units will work well in this circuit.

5.5 ABSOLUTE-VALUE CIRCUITS
(FULL-WAVE PRECISION RECTIFIERS)

An absolute-value circuit, or full-wave precision rectifier, can be implemented by summing the output of a half-wave rectifier and its input with the proper phase and amplitude relations. Such a circuit in its basic form is shown in Fig. 5-9. This circuit will be the starting point for a number of other absolute-value circuits which have evolved from this basic form.

In this circuit, A_1 is an inverting rectifier similar to that of Fig. 5-6. The output from A_1 is added to the original input signal in A_2 (a summing mixer), with the signal amplitude and phase relations shown. Negative alternations of E_{in} result in no output at E_1 due to

Fig. 5-9. Basic absolute-value circuit (full-wave precision rectifier).

the rectification. E_{in} feeds A_2 through a 20-kΩ resistor, and E_1 feeds A_2 through a 10-kΩ resistor. The net effect of this scaling is that, for equal amplitudes of E_{in} and E_1, E_1 will produce twice as much current flow into the summing point. This fact is used to advantage here, as the negative alternation of E_1 produces twice the input current of that caused by the positive alternation of E_{in}. This causes a current of precisely half the amplitude which E_1 alone would generate due to the subtraction of E_{in}. It is the equivalent of having E_1 feed through a 20-kΩ input resistor and having E_{in} nonexistent during this half cycle, and it results in a positive-going output at A_2. During negative alternations of E_{in}, E_1 is absent and E_{in} produces the alternate positive output swing which, in summation, produces the desired full-wave rectified response. As before, operation with the opposite output polarity is possible by reversing D_1 and D_2.

The general-purpose dual 741 type indicated can be replaced with higher-speed units or FET types, as appropriate. The relationships between resistors for proper circuit operation are noted in the illustration, and may be satisfied best by a single network. Note that resistor R_6 can be used as an overall gain trim, or for scaling to net gains of (n) other than unity, as is shown.

5.5.1 Filtered Rectifiers

The previous full-wave rectifier can, with a minimum of complexity, be converted to a version having a dc-averaged output, as shown in Fig. 5-10.

This circuit is nearly identical to the full-wave circuit described before; any one of the half-wave circuits already described (Figs. 5-6, 5-7, and 5-8) can be used as the first stage. The addition of C_1 across R_3-R_5 converts A_1 to a low-pass filter that averages the input signals

*Adjust to calibrate dc output equal to rms value of E_{in}.
**Use R_6 ($\geq$ 1 kΩ) if $C_1 \geq 0.1\,\mu$F.

Fig. 5-10. Filtered full-wave rectifier.

from R_1 and R_2, thus developing a dc output voltage proportional to the full-wave rectified input. Resistor R_5 is added in series with R_3 to make the total feedback resistance greater by the difference between rms and average ac. This allows the output to be calibrated for a dc voltage equal to the rms value of the input. Capacitor C_1 and resistors R_3-R_5 establish the RC time constant of the low-pass filter. This time constant must be appreciably longer than the period of the lowest input frequency to be measured. The values shown give 1.0% accuracy down to 20 Hz, and if a feedforward circuit (Fig. 5-7) or other high-speed option is used for the half-wave rectifier, this accuracy is maintained up to 100 kHz.

The circuit can be used with either polarity of input rectifier, observing the appropriate polarity of C_1 (if it is an electrolytic type). Note that with a FET-input type for A_1, relatively high resistance values can be used without degradation, which allows C_1 to be proportionally smaller. This also allows C_1 to be a nonpolarized unit, with better relative results.

The remaining circuits of this section illustrate alternate means of achieving the absolute-value function, with emphasis on such areas as simplicity, number of precision components, accuracy, etc. In general, almost all of them provide an output of the form $n|E_{in}|$, where n is either positive or negative unity, but can also be a scaler in some cases. The circuits as shown will be in a form where n is positive, providing a positive-going rectified output. Unless stated otherwise, they can be arranged for negative outputs by reversing the diode(s) used.

Inasmuch as there has been considerable discussion in the literature on precision rectifiers, the reader will find the bibliographic references at the end of the chapter useful toward more insight on these techniques.

5.5.2 Equal-Value Resistance, Absolute-Value Circuit

The circuit of Fig. 5-11 is a form originated by Lloyd* to counter the unequal resistor values necessitated in the circuit of Fig. 5-9. In the Fig. 5-11 circuit, all resistor values are exactly equal, for an n of unity. Although there is no reduction in the number of values, they can be economically realized by a common array. Scaling is accomplished by adjustment of R_1; as shown here, n is 2.

Op-amp selection in this example is for maximum low-frequency and dc accuracy. The OP-07 devices have input offsets of 150 μV or less, depending on the grade used, which optimizes the dynamic range. The low bias currents of 2 nA (typical) minimize the requirement for matched dc source resistances; however, the compensation values are

---

* See reference 17 at the end of the chapter.

still shown. Low-leakage diodes must also be used (such as those shown), otherwise these advantages are lost.

With some sacrifice in dc performance, a single dual device, such as an OP-02, can be used. Speed is not a virtue of the circuit as shown, and it is only accurate to about 1.0 kHz. Better high-frequency performance can be obtained with high SR and GBP devices such as

Fig. 5-11. Equal-value resistance, absolute-value circuit.

the 356, AD544, or OP-16 FET devices, or duals such as the AD644, 3240, TL072, 353, or 772. These comments are basically true for all of the absolute-value circuits illustrated here, so it need not be repeated and the reader is encouraged to optimize them accordingly.

5.5.3 Improved Absolute-Value Circuit

Fig. 5-12 shows a circuit of a form described originally by Smither.* It is improved in the sense that it minimizes the number of precision resistors to only two, but still uses two op amps. It cannot be scaled for gain adjustment without additional complexity.

Basically, this circuit consists of a follower, A_1 and an inverter, A_2, whose outputs are ORed together through D_2 and D_3. For positive inputs, A_1 drives the load through D_2; for negative inputs, A_2 is active via D_3. In the off state of the amplifiers, they are clamped by D_1 and D_4.

In addition to the speed selection considerations mentioned previously, A_1 in this circuit should have good common-mode characteristics for best accuracy.

In the basic circuit shown, only R_1 and R_2 need to be precision types, since R_3 does not enter into the gain expression. An alternate form of the circuit trades one more precision resistor for increased input impedance.

---

* See reference 21 at the end of the chapter.

$$*E_o = n|E_{in}|$$
For $R_1 = R_2$, $n = 1$.

For $R_1 = \dfrac{R_2}{2} = R_3$, $n = 2$.

Fig. 5-12. Improved absolute-value circuit.

In the standard circuit as shown, the input impedance is set at a constant value by R_1, which may not be a problem if the source impedance is sufficiently low. However, for high-impedance sources, the circuit can be modified simply by connecting R_1 and D_1 and R_3, as shown dotted. This causes A_1, rather than the source, to drive R_1, and the source sees only the low bias current of A_1.

For this alternate form, the gain characteristics are no longer so simply defined. For positive inputs (A_1 active) the gain is $1 + R_3/R_1$. For negative inputs (A_2 active) the gain is R_2/R_1. To make these ratios the same, R_2 must be twice R_1, thus the 20-kΩ alternate value. All three resistors should be precision, or ratio-matched. Note that for this alternate form, $n = 2$, so the maximum input is ±5 V.

For either form of this circuit, a pulldown resistor (R_4) may be found useful at high frequencies. This is an option, however, and the necessity is governed to a large degree by the characteristics of the load.

5.5.4 Simplified Absolute-Value Circuit

The circuit of Fig. 5-13, similar to Wincentsen's,* is somewhat simplified from that of Fig. 5-12, and can employ fewer parts. It has a continuously buffered output at a low impedance, but its input impedance is nonuniform between positive and negative alternations.

---

* See reference 28 at the end of the chapter.

Fig. 5-13. Simplified absolute-value circuit.

For positive inputs, A_1 and D_2 are inactive, and A_2 operates as a simple follower to the output. For negative inputs, A_1 becomes active, driving A_2 through D_2, and with a gain defined by R_2/R_1. For positive inputs, the input impedance is R_1, while for negative inputs it becomes R_1 in parallel with $R_3/2$. For best accuracy, then, the driving source impedance should be low, to prevent nonuniform loading errors.

It should be noted that this circuit employs A_1 and A_2 in cascade, with overall feedback for negative inputs. Because of this factor, dynamic stability is a potential problem, and the circuit may oscillate with some op amps. C_1 is employed to control the effective circuit bandwidth to minimize this problem, and should be adjusted to suit the particular op amps used, if different than those indicated.

The 5535 and 5530 are high-slew-rate devices, which makes this circuit useful up to 100 kHz. For these (or other bipolar-input-stage) devices, bias compensation resistors R_4 and R_5 are used; they are not necessary for FET devices and can be replaced by shorts.

5.5.5 Single Amplifier Absolute-Value Circuits

A number of related circuits to achieve the absolute-value function can be realized with only a single op amp. Since, for economy, many will want to use only a single amplifier, three variations on this theme are shown in Fig. 5-14. It is interesting that these circuits, while very simple, are still capable of very high precision if certain operating conditions are met.

The first of the circuits is shown in Fig. 5-14A, and is called a T configuration because of the T arrangement of scaling resistors R_1, R_2, and R_3. In this circuit, R_2 and R_3 set the gain for positive inputs, and R_1-R_2 for negative inputs. Note that the load impedance *must* be high in regard to the resistances specified to preserve accuracy in the positive input range when R_2 and R_3 serve as a simple input attenuator and D_1 is off. During negative inputs, D_1 is on and the output is buffered.

As can be noted from the scaling relations, *n* must always be less than unity for this circuit (as well as those to follow). The problem of the unbuffered output and signal level loss can be optionally cor-

(A) T configuration.

$*E_0 = n|E_{in}|$
$R_1 = nR_2$
$R_2 = \dfrac{R_1}{n}$
$R_3 = \dfrac{R_1}{1-n}$
and $R_L \gg R_1 + R_2 \| R_3$
(As shown, n = 0.5.
For low-impedance output,
use buffer option; $R_5 = R_6$
yields overall n of unity.)

(B) Pi configuration.

$*E_0 = n|E_{in}|$
$R_1 = \dfrac{R_2}{n}$
$R_2 = nR_1$
$R_3 = R_1 (1-n)$
and $R_L \gg R_2 \| R_3$
(As shown, n = 0.5.)

Fig. 5-14. Single amplifier

rected by a buffer, as shown dotted. The other major constraint on the circuit is a nonuniform input impedance, which is R_2 for negative input swings and $R_2 + R_3$ for positive swings.

The version shown here is optimized for dc accuracy and uses the 308A, a low offset voltage and bias current op amp. It also uses low-leakage rectifier diodes. Other precision op amps useful here are the OP-07, the 714, and the AD542, a FET type.

The pi configuration circuit shown in Fig. 5-14B is very similar in operating principle, but arranges the scaling resistances in the form of a pi attenuator. In this form, R_3 and R_2 set the gain for positive inputs, while R_2 and R_1 do the same for negative inputs. A similar set of restraints on output impedance and input loading is true for this circuit, and n must be scaled less than unity. Of course, it can also be buffered at the output, at the cost of an additional amplifier. The circuit example for this version uses a general-purpose op amp and diodes, and has more modest dc performance.

The ladder configuration circuit of Fig. 5-14C uses the resistances in a series-connected ladder and develops the output across R_3. Note that R_3 may, in fact, be a *load* resistance; however, if this is to be the case, it should be a precise and stable type. This is simply because the scaling relations depend on this resistor, as well as on R_1-R_2.

Here, R_1-R_2-R_3 set the gain for positive inputs, while R_1 and R_2 do the same for negative inputs. Note that unlike the previous two circuits there is no feedback returned to the summing point for the input state when D_1 is off; therefore, A_1 operates open-loop. This would cause saturation of A_1 and subsequent recovery-time problems, were it not for D_2, a diode used to clamp the swing of A_1 in the off state. Also, because A_1 is allowed to see a large differential input swing during this period, it must have a high differential input rating.

$$*E_0 = n|E_{in}|$$
$$R_1 = R$$
$$R_2 = nR$$
$$R_3 = R\left(\frac{n(n+1)}{1-n}\right)$$

(As shown, $n = 0.5$.)

(C) Ladder configuration.

absolute-value circuits.

The circuit example shown is optimized for speed using the 2607, a high GBP and SR op amp. Also, Schottky diodes are used to help preserve speed. The resistance values are held low as well, to maintain low time constants. Loading can be less of a problem for this circuit because of the low resistance values used; however, it still has the same general constraints mentioned for the others (in terms of input loading and output impedance).

The circuit can, of course, use other op-amp devices, if speed is not a major requirement. The 301A, for example, will work well, as it can also be clamped at pin 8. Other examples are the 2645 and 344 units, which allow high-voltage operation.

5.5.6 Unity-Gain Self-Buffered Absolute-Value Circuit

In the circuit of Fig. 5-15, a form described by Graeme,* a very high input impedance is presented to the source, thus the name *self-buffered*. As can be noted from the circuit configuration, not only is the input self-buffered, but the output is also continuously buffered by A_2.

Four gain-scaling resistors are used, but they are only necessary in two values, with a binary relationship.

Gain switching between the negative and positive input ranges is accomplished by A_1 in this circuit. The complete gain expression for both ranges is quite complex; therefore, the circuit is most practical as shown here for unity gain ($n = 1$). Due to the common-mode voltages applied, the input dynamic range is limited to ± 5 V, for ± 10-V output range devices.

The op amps specified are very low input current FET units, and therefore present very low loading to the source—40 pA or less (at 25°C). Bipolar-input amplifiers that could also be used include the 3501 ($I_{ib} = 30$ nA maximum) or the 3500 ($I_{ib} = 100$ nA maximum). All the amplifiers mentioned are useful up to several kilohertz.

---

* See reference 10 at the end of the chapter.

Fig. 5-15. Unity-gain self-buffered absolute-value circuit.

5.5.7 Programmable-Gain Self-Buffered Absolute-Value Circuit

The circuit of Fig. 5-16 is also a self-buffered type, of a form also attributed to Graeme.* This circuit requires only three precision resistors, and has the virtue that its gain can be easily programmed by a suitable choice of values.

Here, A_1 performs the function of input buffering and, in conjunction with D_1 and D_2, gain switching. For positive signal inputs, D_2 is on and a follower-with-gain loop is closed around A_2 and A_1. For negative inputs, D_1 is on and A_1 drives A_2 as an inverting amplifier.

The gain, n, may be set up for various values greater than unity, with a relative degree of freedom. In the example shown, n is set equal to 2, a scaler which results in convenient ratios of resistances, realizable from a single common array.

Fig. 5-16. Programmable-gain self-buffered absolute-value circuit.

In the example shown, a FET-input amplifier is specified for A_1, which reduces the input bias current to 20 pA or less. A_2 need not have such low bias currents, as it is driven from A_1; thus, a bipolar unit can be employed—the 3500. Of course, if ultralow bias current is not a major criterion, a bipolar type can be used for A_1 as well.

Since A_1 and A_2 operate in cascade for positive inputs, capacitance C_1 is suggested to control potential oscillations. It should be optimized in accordance with the specific gain and amplifier types used.

5.5.8 Simplified Unity-Gain Self-Buffered Absolute-Value Circuit

The circuit of Fig. 5-17† has the same self-buffered properties as the previous two examples, but trades circuit flexibility for simplicity. It is limited to gains of only unity, but as such requires only two precision resistors, R_1 and R_2.

---

* See reference 8 at the end of the chapter.
† See reference 11 at the end of the chapter.

Fig. 5-17. Simplified unity-gain self-buffered absolute-value circuit.

A general-purpose dual amplifier type is illustrated, the 4558. This unit will suffice up to several kilohertz for 10-V outputs, and has reasonable dc accuracy also. Other suitable duals are the 4559, OP-14, and 358, or one of the dual FET types such as the AD644, 3240, TL072, 353, or 772. The FET units will extend the frequency range to nearly 100 kHz.

5.5.9 "Diodeless" Absolute-Value Circuit

The circuit of Fig. 5-18 is a type illustrated by Dobkin,* and is unique in that it requires no rectifier diodes for its operation, and uses a pair of general-purpose op amps.

---

* See reference 3 at the end of the chapter.

Fig. 5-18. "Diodeless" absolute-value circuit.

This circuit takes advantage of the fact that internally the 301A op amp can sink larger currents at the pin 8 node than it can source. Thus, when two devices such as A_1-A_2 have these pins wired together, the device in which pin 8 is the lower of the two will command control.

In this circuit, A_1 is connected as a follower and A_2 as a unity-gain inverter, and feedback is taken from the output of *one* device. For negative inputs, A_1 is active; for positive inputs, A_2 is active, and the output is equal to $-|E_{in}|$.

Note that due to the unique nature of this type of rectification, it is not possible to obtain positive range outputs (unless an inverting buffer is added, of course). It should also be noted that the input impedance is nonuniform; it is R_1 for positive inputs and a very high value for negative inputs.

5.5.10 Single-Supply Absolute-Value Circuits

It is a somewhat surprising, yet very useful, fact that a variety of absolute-value/precision-rectifier circuits can be implemented with certain op amps, using only a single power supply. Obviously, such circuits have great value to battery-powered or other simply powered instruments, so a few of them are presented here.

Fig. 5-19. Simple single-supply absolute-value circuit.

A very simple single-supply absolute-value circuit is shown in Fig. 5-19. This circuit was derived from one the earliest absolute-value circuits, which was designed well back into the era of vacuum-tube op amps.*

In this circuit, A_1 is an inverting unity-gain amplifier for negative inputs when D_1 is off. For positive inputs, D_1 turns on and couples the input to the noninverting ($+$) input of A_1, and the circuit acts as

---

* See reference 15 at the end of the chapter.

a follower. A flaw in the operation of the circuit is the voltage drop across D_1. When on, D_1 introduces an error for positive input signals. This error can be minimized somewhat by maintaining R_3 at a large value and trimming it out for near full-scale inputs with R_4. However, because D_1 is *not* an ideal rectifier, the circuit does have appreciable error at low levels and should best be used at high input levels (± 5 V to ± 10 V).

The key to single-supply operation is the fact that A_1 can operate with the $(+)$ and $(-)$ inputs at ground potential ($V-$, or pin 4 potential). The 3140, 3160, and 3130 are FET-input devices which can accomplish this feat. Bipolar-input types are the 358 and 324 families, the 759, the LM10, and the OP-20.

Fig. 5-20. Battery-powered absolute-value circuit.

A circuit that is very well suited to battery operation is shown in Fig. 5-20. This circuit takes advantage of the very low (1.0 mA) supply current of the 358 op amp.

In this circuit, A_1 performs as an inverter for negative inputs, as before. However, in this circuit, D_1 and A_2 clamp the noninverting $(+)$ input of A_1 to ground for negative inputs, by virtue of the current in R_3. For positive inputs, D_1 is off, and A_1 operates as a follower with low errors, achieving the absolute-value function.*

With the 358 (or 324) op amp, the circuit will be useful up to several kilohertz. But in terms of amplitude range, its performance ex-

---

* See reference 23 at the end of the chapter.

tends down to the tens of millivolts, when the bias errors of the op amps begin to reduce accuracy. If very fast or high-amplitude inputs are expected, a Schottky diode clamp (D_2) is suggested to prevent common-mode problems.

The circuit of Fig. 5-21 is capable of even greater accuracy than the two previous ones, if certain conditions are fulfilled. It employs a dual FET amplifier, the 3240, and has several features which can enhance its usefulness.

The A_1 stage of this circuit can be recognized as a ladder-type single amplifier absolute-value circuit (Fig. 5-14C) arranged to employ a single-supply op amp, similar to the operation described by H. A. Wittlinger in the RCA CA3140 data sheet ("Applications"). In this section of the circuit, n is 0.5, thus an absolute value of $+5$ V peak is developed across R_3 for a $\pm$ 10-V input to R_1.

Fig. 5-21. Single-supply absolute-value circuit with filter and buffer.

The second section is a filter and buffer amplifier, where R_6-C_1 provide low-pass filter averaging, and R_4-R_5 set the gain of A_2 to 2. This provides an overall scale factor of unity (n times m equals 1). Although it is not shown in this particular example, the 3240 can be offset-nulled for optimum accuracy (using the 14-pin package with offset null provision).

5.6 PEAK DETECTORS

Peak detectors measure the maximum value of a fluctuating voltage. In this section we will examine op-amp circuits for accomplishing this function.

5.6.1 Basic Peak Detector

The basic peak detector using an op amp is shown in Fig. 5-22. This circuit operates like an ideal diode, but with the addition of C_1 to store a dc voltage equal to the peak input voltage value. As the input signal crosses zero, A_1 will drive D_1 on and the circuit output will follow the rising signal slope. When the input signal reaches a peak and reverses its slope, C_1 is left in a charged state. In the absence of any bleed resistor to discharge C_1, the only means of discharge is the bias current at the inverting $(-)$ input of A_1.

*To optimize stability of A_1, according to
the load effect of C_1, adjust C_2 for
minimum settling time.
**Reverse for negative output.

Fig. 5-22. Basic peak detector.

Since the circuit operates with 100% feedback when the loop is closed, unity-gain compensation is necessary for A_1. The rate of voltage rise across C_1 is either I_{max}/C_1 (volts/second, where I_{max} is the short-circuit current of A_1), or the slewing rate of A_1 (volts/second), whichever is smaller.

Amplifiers appropriate for use in a peak detector should be types that are relatively immune to instability due to capacitive loading, with high output drive and slew rate. They should also have a high differential input voltage rating and low input currents. One type that fits these requirements quite well is the 356, which is shown in the circuit of Fig. 5-22.

The capacitor used for C_1 should be a type that has low leakage and low dielectric absorption. The diode used for D_1 should also be a low-leakage type.

Capacitor C_2 can be adjusted to minimize settling time, and the optimum value will vary somewhat according to the value of C_1. In the circuit as shown, settling to within 0.1% of a 10-V peak is accomplished in 10 μs or less.

Resistor R_2 is used to protect the input of A_1 against dangerously large discharge currents from C_1 when the power supply is switched off; R_2 is particularly necessary if C_1 is 0.1 μF or greater. R_3 is included to balance the effect of R_2 for bipolar amplifier types.

C_1 can be reset with a switch, either manually or electronically via a normally off transistor. Alternately, if a fast-attack, slow-decay response is tolerable, connecting a bleed resistance (R_B) across C_1 will also deplete the charge. Peak reading of negative-polarity signals is possible by reversing D_1. A post amplifier in the form of a second FET-input voltage follower will usually be necessary for this circuit.

5.6.2 Buffered Peak Detector

When extremely long holding times are required of a peak detector, the bleedoff leakage of C_1 becomes important. Therefore, to minimize this discharge current, C_1 is usually buffered (Fig. 5-23) by a low-input-current voltage follower, A_2. The 356 type used here will require an input current of only about 200 pA (leakage drain current from C_1), so the voltage discharge rate for C_1 will be

$$\frac{\Delta V}{\Delta t} = \frac{I}{C} = \frac{2 \times 10^{-10} \text{ A}}{1 \times 10^{-8} \text{ F}} = 0.02 \text{ V/s} = 20 \text{ } \mu\text{V/ms}$$

In practice, diode leakage will most likely be greater than 200 pA, and so will be dominant. If very-low-leakage operation is critical, the optional clamp diode, D_3, can be used, which limits the bias across D_1 to just over 1.0 V. This will lower the leakage current substantially. Note that only D_1 is required to be a low-leakage diode.

Amplifier A_2 in this circuit provides the input bias current for A_1 as well as the output current. R_2 is included here to allow A_1 to be clamped in the off state by D_2, resulting in faster recovery. R_2, R_3, and C_2 perform functions here similar to those described for Fig. 5-22. This circuit will acquire a 10-V peak signal to an accuracy of 0.1% or less in 10 μs.

Fig. 5-23. Buffered peak detector.

5.6.3 Bootstrapped-Diode Peak Detector

The circuit of Fig. 5-24 obviates the need for ultralow-leakage diodes for the peak detection.* This is accomplished by reducing the reverse bias on the diode in the off state, and thus reducing its leakage.

In this circuit, A_1 and A_2 operate somewhat similarly to the circuit of Fig. 5-23, the main difference being in the detector circuit. D_1 charges the storage capacitor, in series with D_2, both being ordinary diodes. In the off state of D_1 and D_2 (input below the peak level), D_2 sees a large reverse bias, but D_1 sees only the voltage drop across R_f, developed from the leakage of D_2. This reduces the reverse bias on D_1 by as much as two orders of magnitude, and allows it to function effectively as a low-leakage unit.

- By adding D1 and R_f, $V_{D1} = 0$ during hold mode. Leakage of D2 provided by feedback path through R_f.
- Leakage of circuit is essentially I_b (LF155, LF156) plus capacitor leakage of Cp.
- Diode D3 clamps V_{OUT} (A1) to $V_{IN} - V_{D3}$ to improve speed and to limit reverse bias of D2.
- Maximum input frequency should be $\ll 1/2\pi R_f C_{D2}$ where C_{D2} is the shunt capacitance of D2.

Courtesy National Semiconductor Corp.

Fig. 5-24. Bootstrapped-diode peak detector.

To take advantage of this low leakage, A_2 should be a FET-input device such as the 355 or 356, and the storage capacitor should be a plastic-film type, such as polystyrene, polypropylene, or Teflon.

5.6.4 Peak-to-Peak Detector

The circuit of Fig. 5-25 detects both positive and negative peaks and, in so doing, accomplishes peak-to-peak detection.†

---

* See reference 4 at the end of the chapter.
† See reference 24 at the end of the chapter.

In this circuit, A_1 is a dc restorer which clamps the most-negative peak of the input to the potential, V_{ref}. A_2 then detects the most-positive peak of the voltage across R_2 and stores it on C_2. The voltage on C_2 is then equal to $V_{ref} + V_{p-p}$, where V_{p-p} is the peak-to-peak input voltage.

Note that with the 3240 single-supply op amp, V_{ref} can range all the way to ground, enhancing the versatility of the circuit. Other single-supply op amps can be used, but the low input currents of the 3240 (or two 3140s) allow long time constants to be most easily realized.

Fig. 5-25. Peak-to-peak detector.

5.7 SAMPLE-AND-HOLD CIRCUITS

A sample-and-hold circuit is one having two basic operational states; one in which an input signal is sampled and thus transmitted to the output, and a second in which the last value sampled is held until the input is sampled again.

5.7.1 Basic Operation

The basic circuit operation is diagrammed in Fig. 5-26. In Fig. 5-26A, an input signal (E_{in}) is applied to electronic switch S_1 and, depending on the state of S_1, will be either transmitted to C_1 or blocked. The state of switch S_1 is controlled by the sample/hold control line. When S_1 is closed, the input signal appears across C_1, is buffered by A_1, and also appears at the output. If S_1 is connected for a period of time while E_{in} is varying, as with an ac waveform, the operation may also be said to be *tracking* E_{in}; any input changes are transmitted to the output. When S_1 is opened, the latest value of E_{in} is retained on C_i as a charge, and A_1 continues to read this voltage until the next sample period. This is illustrated by the waveforms in Fig. 5-26B. Sample/hold circuits are used for a wide variety of

(A) Basic circuit.

(B) Input/output waveforms.

Fig. 5-26. Sample/hold operation.

signal-processing functions, such as data-handling systems, analog/digital interfaces, etc.

5.7.2 Fast Sample/Hold Circuit

The circuit of Fig. 5-27 almost directly follows that of Fig. 5-26A. The JFET switches provide the sample/hold control function, A_1 serves as an input buffer to drive the hold capacitor, and A_2 serves as an output buffer to isolate the capacitor from external loads.

Courtesy National Semiconductor Corp.

Fig. 5-27. Fast sample/hold circuit.

In this circuit, the dc errors will be a sum of the errors of A_1, the switches and capacitors, and A_2. Individual offset adjustments are necessary for both A_1 and A_2 to minimize the accumulation of these errors.

The circuit is a relatively fast sample/hold type, because the settling dynamics of A_1 and A_2 are kept separate, and are thus not complicated. Also, the low output impedance and high slew rate of the 356 is very useful in driving capacitive loads. With a 1000-pF capacitor for C_h, this circuit can achieve settling times of under 1.0 μs, to within an accuracy band of 0.01%, for a 10-V step change.

5.7.3 High-Accuracy Sample/Hold Circuit

The circuit of Fig. 5-28 is arranged slightly different from that of Fig. 5-27, and closes the control loop around both A_1 and A_2 during sample. During hold, A_2 reads out the voltage held on C_h, while A_1 continues to track the input via the closed switch, SW_2.

Because the loop closure around two amplifiers necessarily compromises the dynamics of this circuit, settling time is lengthened (to the same 0.01% level). However, only the errors of A_1 are seen in the sample state, and only those of A_2 are seen in the hold state. Thus, no offset adjustment is necessary for A_2.

Courtesy National Semiconductor Corp.

Fig. 5-28. High-accuracy sample/hold circuit.

5.8 LIMITERS

In a signal chain, it is often necessary to symmetrically limit or "bound" the peak amplifier output. It is usually desirable to do this before the amplifier reaches saturation voltage, because saturation almost always involves a long recovery time before the amplifier can operate linearly once again. Many applications require peak limiting for other reasons—such as, for example, to interface the op-amp output to digital logic circuits. The positive or negative limit required for

*Or substitute any op amp consistent with speed requirements and compensated for unity gain.
**Chosen to suit desired output swing — e.g., for 3.6 to 5.0-V logic, use 1N746 (3.3 V).

Fig. 5-29. Unipolar feedback limiter.

digital logic is usually much lower than the typical op-amp voltage swing.

5.8.1 General-Purpose Unipolar Limiter

Fig. 5-29 shows a feedback limiter that is very useful in converting linear input signals to logic levels. This circuit uses a zener diode in the feedback loop of an inverter, establishing the limits of the output voltage as equal to the zener forward and reverse voltages. If the input is more positive than ground, the output of A_1 swings negative and forward biases D_1, causing feedback current in D_1 to the summing point. This sets the negative output limit as 0.6 V, equal to the forward voltage drop of D_1. When E_{in} swings negative, the output of A_1 goes positive and the current through D_1 reverses, driving it into the breakdown region and clamping the positive output at the zener voltage, V_Z.

Note that the circuit will have a high gain at low input levels, because D_1 will have a high reverse impedance below the breakdown voltage. This tends to amplify low-level inputs, but only up to the level of V_Z, where the output is clamped by the breakdown of D_1. As a result, the circuit maintains the output swing at the limit of the diode over a rather wide range of input amplitudes.

The output voltage is equal to that of the diode used and may be reversed by reversing D_1. Due to the essentially 100% feedback through the low impedance of D_1, the op amp used must be compensated for unity gain.

5.8.2 Bipolar Zener Limiter

The unipolar limiter of Fig. 5-29 is actually a special case; the more general form of zener limiter is shown in Fig. 5-30.

This circuit limits the op-amp output swing in either direction to the value of $V_Z + V_f$, where V_Z and V_f are the zener- and forward-breakdown voltages of D_1 and D_2. With matched zener voltages, the positive and negative limiting levels will be symmetrical. For example, using 10-V zeners for D_1 and D_2, the output swing of A_1 will be limited at slightly over 10 volts $(10.0 + 0.6$ volts$)$; this allows a

Fig. 5-30. Bipolar zener limiter.

linear ± 10-V swing, but still avoids saturation of A_1. Below the break-down potentials of D_1 and D_2, the amplifier operates as if they were not there, with gain determined by R_1 and R_2 in the conventional fashion. The degree of limiting, or "hardness," is determined by the ratio of the zener network impedance to the resistance of R_2. If the value of R_2 is high in relation to the combined impedances of D_1 and D_2, the limiting will be sharp with little rounding; typical R_2 values of 10 kΩ or above give very sharp limiting.

5.8.3 Bipolar Limiter With Adjustable Level

One drawback in designing symmetrical zener limiters is that zener diodes generally have imprecise breakdown voltages, and hence are difficult to match. If accurate symmetry is desired, one solution is the circuit of Fig. 5-31, which uses a matched pair of monolithic diodes and has an adjustable limit voltage.

A typical pair of monolithic IC transistors will have emitter-base breakdown voltages that match within a few percent or less. Also, the temperature coefficient (TC) of the matched pair will be small, typi-cally less than 1 mV/°C. In Fig. 5-31A, a small fraction (β) of the op-amp output voltage (E_o) is fed to D_1-D_2 through R_4. Resistor R_4 is adjusted to set the limit voltage, which can range from zero to about 10 volts. R_4 should have a relatively low impedance (typically 5 kΩ), so that this resistance will not appreciably affect the output voltage as the output current changes. Fig. 5-31B shows how the matched zener pair can be generated from a CA3093 chip. With the values shown, $V_L \cong \pm 8.4$ V, and the zeners track very well with temperature. Other possible units are the CA3046 and CA3086.

5.8.4 Transistor Junction Limiter

For very high speed in a general-purpose limiter, transistor emitter-base junctions can be used effectively, because they have a low capacitance. Such a limiter configuration is illustrated in Fig. 5-32. The 2N3906 transistors provide a limit voltage, V_L, of about ± 7 V; again, this value can be varied by adjusting R_4.

5.8.5 Zener Bridge Limiter

A single zener diode is sometimes used for symmetrical limiting by placing it in a diode bridge so that it conducts on both polarities

(A) Basic circuit.

$V_L = (V_z + V_t)/\beta$

* This configuration produces a symmetrical ± 8.4-V zener with very little temperature dependence.

(B) Synthesizing matched zeners.

Fig. 5-31. Adjustable bipolar limiter.

of the output swing. This is illustrated in Fig. 5-33. The diodes can be ordinary general-purpose types such as the 1N914, unless very precise symmetry is required; monolithic diode bridges will provide more accurate symmetry, if needed. A very hard limit characteristic can be obtained by using a synthesized zener such as the LM329 (6.9 V), but more general-purpose types such as the 1N4728 series allow flexibility in voltage selection. Speed can be enhanced by pre-biasing the zener with R_4 and R_5, but this is not essential.

Fig. 5-32. High-speed limiter using transistor junctions.

5.8.6 Dual Zener Diode Limiter

The circuit of Fig. 5-34 is useful when the limiting is to be asymmetric, but still predictable; or when it must be sharp with reasonably high speed.

In this circuit, D_1 and D_2 are zener diodes that are biased on by resistors R_4 and R_5, respectively. These diodes conduct continuously, and thus need not be particularly fast.

$$V_L = V_z + 2V_f$$
$$D_1 - D_4 = 1N914 \text{ (see text)}$$
*Selected according to limit voltage:
LM329 = 6.9 V.

Fig. 5-33. Diode bridge limiter using one zener.

The output is limited in its negative swing when D_3 conducts at a level of V_Z (D_1) + V_f (D_3). It is limited in the positive direction when D_4 conducts at a level of V_Z (D_2) + $V_f(D_4)$. Note that if R_1 and R_2 are relatively large resistances it will be advisable to make D_3 and D_4 low-leakage units, such as 1N458As.

Fig. 5-34. Dual zener diode limiter.

5.8.7 T Feedback Limiter

In very-high-impedance applications, such as when using electrometer-type op amps, it will be necessary to use special means to control leakages when limiting is employed. The circuit of Fig. 5-35 is useful for this task.

*Bridge diodes = 1N914s (see text).

Fig. 5-35. T feedback limiter to decouple leakage.

$$V_L = V_f \left(\frac{R_1}{R_1 + R_2} \right)$$

(As shown, $V_L \cong 0.2$ V.)

Fig. 5-36. Low-voltage shunt limiter.

This limiter is in T form, in order to decouple the leakage of bridge diodes D_1–D_4 to ground through R_3. R_3, being a relatively low resistance, allows only a few millivolts of bias to be applied to low-leakage types D_6 and D_7, greatly enhancing their usefulness. Although two ultralow-leakage types are listed ($I_L = 1.0$ pA), their actual necessity will depend on the temperature range of the circuit, and relative impedances seen at R_1-R_2. For example, using 1N458As for D_6-D_7 and 1N914s (or 1N458s) for D_1–D_4 may suffice for many uses, and should be checked first. Note also that the value of R_3 can be minimized to bleed off leakage from D_1–D_4.

The T decoupling technique for leakage is not limited to bridge-type feedback circuits, and any of the previously described circuits can be modified to use it. In the example shown, a 10-V zener provides limiting at just under ±12-V output.

5.8.8 Low-Voltage Shunt Limiter

The circuit of Fig. 5-36 is a useful one when the signal level must be limited at a very low level, such as several hundred millivolts. Such levels are, of course, below the range of conventional diodes, so alternate means are necessary to accomplish this trick.

In this circuit, a variation of a form by Schlesinger,* the op amp is used to amplify and level shift the threshold of a conventional diode. The limit voltage is of the form shown, and can be adjusted to be any fraction of the diode voltage. Although a conventional diode is shown for D_1, low-drift zeners (such as the LM113 or AD589 types) can be used if temperature stability is required.

D_1 can be back-to-back connected diodes for symmetrical clipping, in which case the shunt antisaturation clamp, D_2, will not be necessary. Note that this circuit divides down the signal level, even when below the threshold, because of the feedback through R_2.

---

* See reference 18 at the end of the chapter.

5.9 DIODE BRIDGE CIRCUITS

5.9.1 Input Current Limiter

One of the more precise types of signal limiters is formed by passing the signal through a diode bridge, as shown in Fig. 5-37. Here, diodes D_1 through D_4 are biased at a continuous current by R_4 and R_5, which are equal-value resistors connected to equal voltages. If D_1 through D_4 are all closely matched in characteristics, the dc potential at the bridge output (D_1-D_3 junction) can be connected directly to the summing point of A_1.

Fig. 5-37. Input current limiter.

Note that there is no direct path for the signal to take through the bridge to the summing point; instead, signal variations are transmitted to A_1 as variations in the currents supplied by R_4 and R_5. Limiting occurs when the input current in R_1 exceeds that capable of being transmitted by the bridge assembly. The bridge "opens," with D_2 and D_3 reverse biased on positive swings and D_1 and D_4 reverse biased on negative swings.

In this state, the entire current available from R_4 or R_5 is diverted through D_1 and D_3 on signal peaks, and the current from the opposite member (R_5 or R_4) is then passed through D_1 or D_3 to the summing point. In this manner, the bridge "peak limits" the input current to A_1 and so controls the output voltage of A_1.

The operation of a current-mode limiter such as this is very smooth and fast, with no "glitches" or overshoots as in voltage-switching limiters. This type is a good choice when the most abrupt limiting possible is desired. Diode nonlinearities do, however, introduce some distortion in the input signal, and this effect can be minimized by making R_1 large in relation to the diode impedance. As an example, the values shown give less than 0.5% distortion. The op amp used should be compensated for unity gain, because when the bridge opens, the feedback is nearly 100%.

The limiting current threshold of the circuit is set by the current in the bridge. With a given value of current flowing in R_4-R_5, the input and output voltages are set by the choices of R_1 and R_2, with the usual considerations for gain. The values shown are for clipping at ±11 volts of output and can, of course, be rescaled if desired. Higher-speed op amps in place of the 741 (e.g., a FET unit such as the 356) will take greater advantage of the inherently fast bridge switching capability.

5.9.2 Feedback Circuit With Dead-Band Response

Advantage may be taken of the "current depletion" property of a diode bridge in other unusual circuits. For instance, in Fig. 5-38, the bridge is placed in the feedback loop such that for low-level input signals there is essentially 100% feedback around A_1, and very little voltage output. The only voltage appearing at the output is the relatively small swing required to modulate the current in the bridge as it passes the feedback current.

Fig. 5-38. Dead-band circuit.

*Or other op amp compensated for unity gain.

**D_1 - D_4 are matched monolithic diodes, such as the CA3019. For peak voltages higher than ±7 V, use 1N914s.

Fig. 5-39. Variable dead-band circuit.

When the input current in R_1 becomes greater than the allowable current, however, the bridge opens and the output voltage "jumps" to a new level determined by R_2, and the input is amplified by the ratio of R_2/R_1 in a linear manner.

This feature gives the circuit a *dead-band* property for low levels, but when the bridge current is exceeded, the circuit amplifies normally. The current and voltage threshold at the input are determined

Fig. 5-40. Variable-offset voltage follower.

as before, by selecting R_1 for an input current equal to the bridge current at the threshold level.

5.9.3 Variable Dead-Band Circuit

The previous circuit is easily modified to provide a controlled amount of dead-band response, as shown in Fig. 5-39. With R_2 shorted, this circuit is the same as Fig. 5-38. For low-level input signals, increasing the value of R_2 raises the voltage developed across it, which raises the dead-band level. The circuit gain for small signals is then $(R_2 \parallel R_3)/R_1$. For large signals, the bridge opens and R_2 is effectively removed from the circuit; therefore, the gain becomes R_3/R_1. Note that if R_2 is greater than R_3, the adjustment of R_2 will vary the dead-band level from minimum to nearly the full gain of the circuit. One use for such a circuit is in generating a variable and controlled amount of distortion.

5.10 VOLTAGE FOLLOWER WITH VARIABLE OFFSET (PRECISION LEVEL SHIFTER)

In some circuits it is necessary to shift the dc operating point between stages without losing signal level or loading the source. A circuit which accomplishes this is the variable-offset voltage follower of Fig. 5-40.

Diodes D_1 and D_2 provide a bias of ± 2.5 V about the output potential of A_1. Since the tap of R_1 is at the same potential as E_{in}, adjustment of R_1 allows the output to be varied by the diode drop of D_1 or D_2 (about ± 2.5 V). D_1 and D_2 have negligibly small impedances by comparison with R_2 and R_3, so there is little dynamic signal loss across this network and the gain is very close to unity. Furthermore, the LM336 diode is a reference type with low temperature coefficient. Thus, the temperature drift will be low (less than 100 $\mu V/$°C). An alternate, lower-input-current form of this circuit uses an AD542 op amp and AD589 (1.2-V) reference diodes.

5.11 SINGLE-SUPPLY VOLTAGE FOLLOWERS

Some currently available op amps have the unique ability to operate from single power supplies while processing wide-range analog signals. Two good examples of this capability are the single-supply followers of Fig. 5-41.

In Fig. 5-41A, the op amp is a 3130, which can accept inputs in the range of 0 to approximately +12 V while operating as a precision voltage follower. Offset null is accomplished by the potentiometer, as shown, for applications requiring the lowest dc errors. Unity-gain compensation is provided by the 56-pF capacitor. Pin-for-pin amplifiers which also work in this circuit are the 3160 and 3140 (no compensation required), and the 3240 functions similarly. All of these types have low bias currents due to their MOSFET input stages.

In Fig. 5-41B, a bipolar-input-stage device is shown used as a single-supply voltage follower—the LM10. Although the input current

Courtesy RCA Solid State Division

(A) Using MOSFET-input device.

(B) Using bipolar-input device.

Fig. 5-41. Single-supply voltage followers.

is higher than that of a FET device (10 nA), it will generally have lower offset voltage and offset voltage drift. Also, the LM10 device is unique because of its extremely broad power-supply range, even down to 1.1 V, suitable for a single cell.

The input range of this circuit is from ground to 1.0 V less than the supply voltage, and the output range is comparable. Offset null is optional (R_1), but the output pulldown resistance, R_2, should be used to enhance the voltage swing. The load for this circuit must be referred to ground for it to work properly.

Other compatible single-supply follower op amps are the 358 and 324 series, the 3403 and 3458 types, the OP-20, and the 759.

5.12 SIGN CHANGER

An interesting op-amp configuration is one that allows the choice of 0° or 180° phase reversal. This is the sign changer of Fig. 5-42.

*Linear taper, if calibration desired.

Fig. 5-42. Sign changer with variable output.

The circuit can be best understood by visualizing the operational state at various positions of R_3. If the arm of R_3 is at ground, the circuit is an inverter, providing a 180° phase shift. If the arm is at E_{in}, E_{in} will appear at both inputs of A_1; therefore, both ends of R_1 are at the same potential, which implies no current in R_1. If this is true for R_1, it must also be true of R_2; therefore, R_2 will have a potential of E_{in} on both ends, which makes $E_o = E_{in}$. Positions of R_3 at intermediate settings provide gains reduced from these two extremes. For instance, at the midpoint of R_3, the circuit will be recognized as a differential amplifier with a voltage of $E_{in}/2$ at each input. In this case, the output will be zero, because the circuit rejects the common-mode input signal (in proportion to the CMRR of A_1). R_3 may be calibrated for a linear variation from $+1$ through zero to -1, if desired. The best common-mode error will generally be found in bipolar-input types—for example, the 312 shown in Fig. 5-42. The 312 is an internally compensated 308 (with offset null). Other suitable bipolars are the OP-07 and AD517; FETs include the AD542, 5105, OP-16, and 356.

The circuit can be used with a switch to select the choice of phase, as shown in Fig. 5-43, which allows remote programming. The basic operation of this circuit can be understood by referring to Fig. 5-43A.

$$E_o+ = E_{in}$$
$$E_o- = -E_{in}\left(\frac{R_2}{R_1}\right)$$

Control Table

Sign Bit	Output Voltage
0	0 to +10 V
1	0 to −10 V

**R₁ = R₂

(A) Unipolar input range (0 to +10 V).

*R₁ = R₂ (Match to required accuracy.)

(B) Bipolar input range (±10 V).

Fig. 5-43. Switch-selectable sign changers.

Here, logic-programmable switch A_2 connects the $(+)$ input of A_1 to either ground or the input voltage. A_2 is a CMOS array analog switch, the CD4007.* The analog input range is 0 to $+10$ V and the output is either 0 to $+10$ V or 0 to -10 V, with logic as indicated.

The circuit of Fig. 5-43B is similar, but allows full ±10-V input ranges using a DG305 analog switch. Best accuracy is achieved with a 356A amplifier, with R_1 and R_2 well matched (to 0.01% or better).

---

* For a comprehensive discussion of analog switches, see Chapter 5 of the author's *IC Converter Cookbook,* Howard W. Sams & Co., Inc., 1978.

REFERENCES

1. *Applications Manual for Computing Amplifiers.* Philbrick Researches, Inc., Dedham, Mass., 1966.

2. Dobkin, R. C. *Feedforward Compensation Speeds Op Amp.* National Semiconductor Linear Brief LB-2, March 1969. National Semiconductor Corp., Santa Clara, Calif.

3. ———. *Op Amp Circuit Collection.* National Semiconductor Application Note AN-31, February 1970. National Semiconductor Corp., Santa Clara, Calif.

4. ———. "Peak Detectors." *Electronic Engineering Times,* June 17, 1974.

5. ———. *Precision AC/DC Converters.* National Semiconductor Linear Brief LB-8, August 1969. National Semiconductor Corp., Santa Clara, Calif.

6. Dudley, R. L.; Laing, V. L. "A Self-Contained, Hand-Held Digital Multimeter—A New Concept in Instrument Utility." *Hewlett-Packard Journal,* November 1973.

7. Frederiksen, T. M. "Multiple-Function LICs." *Proceedings of Electronic Products Magazine LIC Seminar,* March 1973.

8. Graeme, J. G. "Full-Wave Rectifier Needs Only 3 Matched Resistors." *Electronics,* August 8, 1974.

9. ———. "Measure Differential AC Signals Easily With Precision Rectifiers." *EDN,* January 20, 1975.

10. ———. "Op Amps Form Self-Buffered Rectifier." *Electronics,* October 12, 1970.

11. Jung, W. G. "Get Accurate Absolute Value Outputs With Only One Matched Resistor Pair." *Electronic Design,* December 20, 1978.

12. ———. *IC Converter Cookbook.* Howard W. Sams & Co., Inc., Indianapolis, 1978.

13. ———. "IC Differential Amplifiers Yield Matched Zener Pairs." *Electronic Design,* April 26, 1969.

14. Korn, G. A.; Korn, T. M. *Electronic Analog and Hybrid Computers,* 2nd ed. McGraw-Hill Book Co., New York, 1972.

15. *K2 Amplifier Series Applications Manual.* G. A. Philbrick Researches, Dedham, Mass., 1956.

16. Lloyd, A. G. "Ideal Rectifiers." (Letters) *Electronic Design,* December 20, 1967.

17. ———. "Ideal Rectifier Uses Equal Value Resistors." *Electronic Design,* June 21, 1967.

18. Schlesinger, E. R. "Active Zener Circuit Provides Clipping Adjustable Down to Almost Zero." *Electronic Design,* April 26, 1977.

19. Sheingold, D. H. (ed.). *Non-Linear Circuits Handbook.* Analog Devices, Inc., Norwood, Mass., 1974.

20. Smith, J. I. *Modern Operational Circuit Design.* John Wiley & Sons, Inc., New York, 1971.

21. Smither, M. A. "Improved Absolute Value Circuit." *EEE,* March 1969.

22. Tobey, G. E.; Graeme, J. G.; Huelsman, L. P. (eds.). *Operational Amplifiers—Design and Applications.* McGraw-Hill Book Co., New York, 1971.

23. Vogler, D. L. "BI-FET Devices Improve Absolute Value Amplifier." *Electronics,* May 12, 1977.

24. ———. "Precision Peak-to-Peak AC-DC Converter Built With Single-Supply Op Amp Circuit." *Electronic Design,* November 22, 1977.

25. Widlar, R. J. "Designing With Super-Beta Transistor Op-Amp ICs." *EEE,* December 1969, February and March 1970.

26. ———. *IC Op Amp Beats FETs on Input Current.* National Semiconductor Application Note AN-29, December 1969. National Semiconductor Corp., Santa Clara, Calif.

27. ———. *Monolithic Operational Amplifiers—The Universal Linear Component.* National Semiconductor Application Note AN-4, April 1968. National Semiconductor Corp., Santa Clara, Calif.

28. Wincentsen, R. J. "Absolute Value Circuit Uses Only 5 Parts." *EDN,* November 1, 1972.

29. Manufacturers' Data Sheets:

Fairchild	FD300	Diode
Semiconductor	FJT1100	Diode
National	LM10	Operational Amplifier
Semiconductor	LM329	Reference Diode
	LM336	Reference Diode
	CA3019	Diode Array
	CA3046	IC Array
	CA3086	IC Array
RCA	CA3093	IC Array
	CA3130	Operational Amplifier
	CA3140	Operational Amplifier
	CD4007	CMOS Inverter
Siliconix	DG305	Analog Switch
	PAD-1	Diode

SIX

Logarithmic and Multiplier Circuit Techniques

6.1 LOGARITHMIC CONVERTERS

Some of the most useful circuit techniques with op amps are related to the use of logarithms: dynamic range compression, raising to powers or taking roots, rms conversion, and multiplier/divider circuits are only a few examples. Virtually all of these operations depend on the conversion of a linear voltage or current into a corresponding logarithmic value.

The heart of the analog logarithmic converter is the simple bipolar transistor. It is a highly useful fact that the base-emitter voltage, V_{BE}, of a silicon transistor is logarithmically related to the collector current over an extremely wide range. Using well-matched, monolithic transistors and IC op amps, it is possible to build log converters with a typical dynamic range of 5 decades (10^5 or 100 dB).

6.1.1 Transistor Logarithmic Characteristics

Since the pn junction is the basis of all the log converters to be discussed, some review of the basic mechanism is in order. The V_{BE} of a silicon planar transistor for a V_{CB} of 0 V can be expressed as

$$V_{BE} = \frac{\kappa T}{q} \log_e \left(\frac{I_C}{I_o} \right)$$

where,

κ = Boltzman's constant (1.38×10^{-23} J/K),
T = absolute temperature (Kelvin),
q = charge on an electron (1.6×10^{-19} coulomb),
I_C = collector current,
I_o = theoretical reverse saturation current (10^{-13} A @ 27°C).

Stating the equation in terms of $\log_{10}$, it becomes

$$V_{BE} = \frac{2.3\,\kappa\,T}{q} \log_{10}\left(\frac{I_C}{I_o}\right)$$

At $T = 27°C$, the $\kappa T/q$ term is 26 mV, which yields

$$V_{BE} = 60\ \text{mV}\ \log_{10}\left(\frac{I_C}{I_o}\right)$$

This reduced expression may be stated quite simply: At 27°C, the V_{BE} of a silicon transistor will increase about 60 mV for each decade increase in I_C.

As stated previously, this relationship holds true over a wide range of voltages for low-leakage, high-gain transistors. The lower end of the dynamic range is limited (practically) by the op amp, while the upper end departs from logarithmic operation due to logging element ohmic resistance drops above 10^{-2} to 10^{-3} A; exact figures depend on the specific device.

6.1.2 Basic Transistor Logger

The circuit of Fig. 6-1, called a *transdiode* configuration, is one of the basic logarithmic converters. The collector current of transistor Q_1 is equal to the op-amp input current and, since the base of Q_1 is grounded, the output of A_1 is the V_{BE} of Q_1.

This circuit maintains the collector and base voltages of Q_1 equal through the virtual ground at the input of A_1; thus, the effects of collector-voltage changes on the logging operation are eliminated. Performance limits are governed by the transistor used and, more often, by the op amp; at very low log currents, the input current of A_1 becomes an appreciable error factor.

The circuit of Fig. 6-1 provides the closest approximation to actual logarithmic operation. In this simple form, however, it has two important drawbacks: first, there are temperature-dependent components that can introduce error. Second, the relatively small (60 mV) output change per decade is inconvenient—some value such as 1.0 V/decade is usually preferred. From the equations of Section

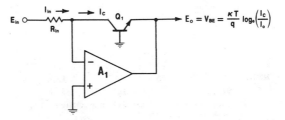

Fig. 6-1. Transdiode logarithmic converter.

**Fig. 6-2. Log converter with tempera-
ture compensation of $\kappa T/q$.**

6.1.1, the temperature-affected parameters are seen to be $\kappa T/q$, which is a scaling factor, and I_o, which is an offset factor; both of these may be compensated by additional circuit elements.

The temperature coefficient of $\kappa T/q$ amounts to $+0.3\%/°C$. This can be compensated as shown in Fig. 6-2 by using a thermistor (R_2) to track the changes in output voltage. Resistor R_1 determines the logarithmic scale; with the values shown, the scale factor is about 1.0 V/decade. Thermistor R_2 should be selected to have a temperature coefficient of $+0.3\%/°C$, to compensate the $\kappa T/q$ factor.

The I_o factor in the equations also changes with temperature. This is compensated by an identical transistor operating at the same temperature and having a constant collector current. The circuit of Fig. 6-3 illustrates this principle, which will be detailed further in actual circuits.

6.1.3 Other Logger Configurations

The transdiode connection is by no means the only transistor circuit useful in log converters. Two alternate feedback configurations are shown in Fig. 6-4. The feedback element can be connected either as a diode (Fig. 6-4A) or as a transistor (Fig. 6-4B).

The diode-connected transistor configuration of Fig. 6-4A is useful from the standpoint that it is a two-terminal device and is, therefore, easily reversible to accommodate input signals of negative polarity.

* Matched to track with temperature.

** Current source, typically connected so as to maintain a
constant collector current for Q_2.

Fig. 6-3. Log converter with temperature compensation of $\kappa T/q$ and V_{BE}.

It becomes limited in accuracy at lower input currents, however. The falloff in transistor gain (β or h_{FE}) creates an increasing error since all of the input current does not flow through the collector as it does in the transdiode. This circuit is useful over about 5 decades of input current, from approximately 10 nA to 1.0 mA, using high-performance transistors as diodes. Examples are monolithics such as the AD810 series, or discretes such as the 2N5067 (pnp) or 2N5089 (npn).

$$E_o = V_{BE} = \frac{KT}{q} \log_e \left[\frac{I_{in}}{I_o} \left(1 - \frac{1}{\beta} \right) \right]$$

where,

β = transistor current gain.

(A) Diode feedback.　　　　(B) Transistor feedback.

Fig. 6-4. Alternate log configurations.

The transistor connection of Fig. 6-4B is similar in performance to the diode connection. It does reduce loading on the op amp by virtue of the transistor current gain, but it also introduces some additional bias error due to the higher collector-base voltage. The dynamic range of this circuit is comparable to that of the diode connection, and it has similar errors due to gain falloff. These types of logging elements will not be covered here in great detail; interested readers should consult the references cited at the end of the chapter for further information.

Log generators using transdiode connections are notoriously difficult to stabilize, because the feedback network can actually contribute gain, rather than a loss which is usually the case. The gain is in excess of the open-loop gain of the op amp and must be considered in the overall loop. Further complicating matters is the fact that the gain of the transdiode changes with I_C. As a result, circuit stability requires either heavy frequency compensation of the amplifier or a gain reduction within the loop. Both techniques are commonly utilized, as will subsequently be seen.

6.1.4 Log Generator With 120-dB Dynamic Range

A circuit employing many of the design principles set down earlier is the log generator of Fig. 6-5. In this circuit, A_2 supplies a constant reference current (I_{C_2}) to Q_2, which will have a value of V_{ref}/R_3, since the collector of Q_2 is held at virtual ground by the noninverting input of A_2. A_1 supplies a current (I_{C_1}) through Q_1, which will have a value of E_{in}/R_{in}, since the collector of Q_1 is also maintained at ground potential, in this case by the noninverting input of A_1. For best stability of reference current, a stable voltage should be employed such as with the LM329 reference diode (D_2) shown. R_3 is trimmed about its nominal value for calibration of I_{C_2}.

Q_1 is being operated here as a transdiode connection, with Q_2 supplying temperature compensation of the offset voltage. The logged output of A_1 is temperature compensated by divider R_1-R_2 and scaled to 1.0 V/decade, as explained in Section 6.1.2. Using either of the thermistor options specified for R_2, temperature compensation is within 1.0% over the respective ranges given. Feedback capacitor C_3 helps to stabilize the loop gain, as does the loss across divider R_1-R_2. Similarly, R_4 and C_4 stabilize A_2.

(A) Circuit schematic.

*Type Q81 (Tel Labs, Londonderry, N.H.)
or equivalent; TC = +0.3%/°C,
accurate from −25°C to +100°C.

(B) Alternate compensation network.

**470 Ω Sensistor (Texas Instruments);
TC = +0.7%/°C. (From 0°C to +50°C.)

Fig. 6-5. Log generator with 120-dB dynamic range.

245

This circuit actually generates the log ratio of two currents, I_{C_1} and I_{C_2}. Normally I_{C_2} is fixed at some reference value, which in this case is 10 μA. This reference current determines the value of I_{C_1} for which the log output will be zero, since log $(I_{C_1}/I_{C_2}) = 0$ when $I_{C_1} = I_{C_2}$.

The actual dynamic range that can be achieved with this circuit is largely due to the care used in its construction. When logging voltages over a wide range, the lowest offset voltage and lowest drift amplifier should be used for A_1. In bipolar types, such low-bias-current units as the OP-07, LM11, or 308A are suggested. Either a very low trimmed selection should be used, or offset null should be employed to minimize offset voltage error.

If a true current source is the signal, offset voltage becomes less of an error factor, and many more amplifiers can be used. Such FET devices as the AD542, AD545, OP-15, or 355 are good choices, and low-offset-voltage FET units are perhaps the best all-around choice, except for high temperature extremes.

For any low current (10 nA or less) logging use, *very* careful construction techniques should be used. This includes guarding around pins 2 and 3 of A_1 (and all connected common points), good PC layout (including guards on top and bottom), careful cleaning and preservation of the board, heat sinking of a FET device for A_1, and low-leakage components (C_3, a polystyrene type, for example). If these precautions are not taken, the ultimate performance of the better ICs will not be realized. Q_1 and Q_2 are a well-matched high-gain pair, such as the LM394, AD818, MAT-01; or, alternatively, matched discretes such as 2N5089s. D_3 and D_4 are protective clamps.

If the preceding precautions are taken, it is possible to achieve dynamic ranges of over 120 dB for this circuit, using an AD542 for A_1, over a 1.0-mA to below 1.0-nA range. These application considerations are also generally applicable to the circuits that follow.

6.1.5 Fast Log Generator

Fig. 6-6A is a log converter similar in concept to Fig. 6-5, except that the major design criterion here is speed rather than dynamic range. This circuit has a dynamic range of 80 dB, but a settling time of 10 μs. A type 310 voltage follower buffers the base current of Q_1 and the input current to A_1, allowing Q_1 to operate in a diode connection while demanding a minimal input current to A_3. Again, the scale factor of this circuit is 1.0 V/decade, and the zero-crossover point of the output swing is controlled by R_3 as before. The logging range is nominally from 100 nA to 1.0 mA with 1.0% accuracy.

The circuit of Fig. 6-6B is similar, but employs a FET amplifier for the input device and is, therefore, more simple.

(A) With bipolar-input devices.

$$|V_{OUT}| = \left[1 + \frac{R2}{R_T}\right] \frac{kT}{q} \ln V_i \left[\frac{R_r}{V_{REF} R_i}\right] = \log V_i \frac{1}{R_i I_r}$$

R2 = 15.7k, R_T = 1k, 0.3%/°C (for temperature compensation)

Courtesy National Semiconductor Corp.

(B) With FET-input device.

Fig. 6-6. Fast log generators.

With the 356 used in the input stage and an LM394 logging transistor pair, this circuit is capable of a 5-decade (100-dB) dynamic range from 1.0 mA down to 10 nA. The 356 should be offset nulled as shown (with voltage source inputs) for best accuracy.

The scale factor is 1.0 V/decade, as in Fig. 6-6A, and the output zero-crossover point occurs at 100 μA input current. The step response time of this circuit is 3 μs for a 1-decade current-level change near a full scale of 1.0 mA. Protective clamp diodes may be desirable with some matched pairs for Q_1-Q_2, as in Fig. 6-5, although the 394 is protected internally.

6.1.6 Antilog (Exponential) Generator

The generation of an antilog response is a straightforward matter of rearranging the basic log circuitry to perform the inverse operation. An example is the antilog circuit of Fig. 6-7.

In this circuit, Q_2 generates the exponential current, and its output current is summed at the current-to-voltage converter, A_2. Q_1 provides voltage drive to Q_2 such that the collector current of Q_2 is exponentially related to the voltage at the base of Q_1. A temperature-compensating divider scales the input sensitivity to 1.0 V/decade as previously. The feedback of A_1 maintains the collector current of Q_1 constant at 100 μA. This circuit is optimized for speed, using feedforward connections at both A_1 and A_2.

So far, log and antilog generators have been discussed as separate entities. They may be used together, however, with considerable simplification. In cases where the antilog function is derived immediately, the log/antilog transistors can be matched for thermal tracking, which eliminates the need for a temperature-compensated scaling divider. An example is the multiplier/divider circuit of Fig. 6-8.

Fig. 6-7. Antilog generator.

Fig. 6-8. Multiplier/divider circuit.

249

6.1.7 Logarithmic Multiplier/Divider

Multiplication by the use of logarithms is a simple process of addition. Thus, given two numbers in log form, their addition yields the product in log form, and taking the antilog gives the product in conventional form. Similarly, division involves a subtraction of logs and then taking the antilog of this difference to obtain the quotient.

Fig. 6-8 may be recognized as a combination of two previous circuits. The upper half is similar to the log converter of Fig. 6-5, where the output at A_1 is the log ratio of E_1 and E_2. A_3 and Q_3 form another log converter for the E_3 input, and the log output of this converter is added to that of the E_1/E_2 circuit, producing log (E_1E_3/E_2) at the emitter of Q_4. Q_4 and A_4 take the antilog; this output is $E_1E_3/10E_2$. If just the multiplication process is desired, E_2 can be a reference voltage as in Fig. 6-5, and R_4 will establish the reference current. Matching of transistor pairs should be as shown, and LM394 units are recommended for best results. Note that a quad amplifier, such as the 348 or 324, can work well here. Use clamp diodes as appropriate.

6.1.8 Power Functions of an Input

Just as multiplication and division become processes of addition and subtraction using logarithms, the generation of power functions becomes a process of scaling (multiplying) logarithms. Raising to powers greater than unity (x^2, x^3, etc.) is the scaling upward of the number in log form; taking a root ($x^{1/2}$, $x^{1/3}$, etc.) is the scaling downward of the number in log form. A circuit that will raise the input to a power or take roots is shown in Fig. 6-9.

This circuit is a combination log converter and antilog generator, with a variable scale adjustment between the log/antilog interface. The variable scaling modifies the exponent of the logged input to a value other than unity; therefore, $E_o = (E_{in})^x$ where x is variable.

In this circuit, the divider networks of R_4-R_5 and R_3-R_5 alter the percentage of A_1's output signal fed to Q_2 and Q_3. If the attenuation in the two legs from A_1 is equal, both Q_2 and Q_3 see the same signal and the circuit operates as a straight log/antilog converter. If Q_3 receives a greater percentage of signal than Q_2, this is equivalent to a gain in the exponent, and the output is raised to a power. If Q_3 receives less signal than Q_2, there is a loss in the conversion process, equivalent to the taking of a root. With the values shown, the exponent of E_{in} is variable from $\frac{1}{2}$ to 2. Greater powers or smaller roots are possible by adjusting the R_3-R_4-R_5 values appropriately, although the span of exponents available will be limited by the dynamic range of the output amplifier, A_4. Clamp diodes are not shown, but will be necessary for unprotected pairs.

Fig. 6-9. Power-function generator.

6.2 ANALOG MULTIPLIERS

In Section 6.1 it was seen how the multiplication of two dc voltages (or currents) is accomplished using logarithmic modules. Generally, logarithmic multiplication is confined to unipolar dc signals rather than bipolar dc or ac signals. When ac signals are to be multiplied, either by a unipolar dc signal or by a bipolar signal, the need arises for a different type of multiplier. This type is what is generally termed an *analog multiplier,* since it processes two analog signals to arrive at their product in analog form. Analog multipliers come in two basic types—two-quadrant and four-quadrant. The difference between these two types is in the response to different input signal polarities.

6.2.1 Two-Quadrant Analog Multiplier

Fig. 6-10 depicts the output response of a two-quadrant multiplier to inputs E_x and E_y. From this may be noted several key features of operation. First, and perhaps most important, is the fact that if either E_x or E_y is zero, the output is zero. This satisfies the mathematical definition of multiplication by zero. Several curves of $E_o = E_x E_y$ are

Fig. 6-10. Two-quadrant multiplier characteristic.

drawn for different values of E_x; E_y ranges continuously from 0 V to +10 V. The output resulting for a given E_x and E_y can be determined graphically by locating the intersection of the E_x and E_y curves. For example, if $E_x = +5$ V and $E_y = +6$ V, then $E_o = +30$ V. A second example is $E_x = -10$ V and $E_y = +8$ V; in this case $E_o = -80$ V. These two examples illustrate two-quadrant operation—that is, the output responds to both polarities of E_x but to only one polarity of E_y. The output will follow the sign of E_x, but E_y must always remain in the range of 0 V to +10 V. In circuit terms, this means that E_x can be either a bipolar dc signal or ac signal, but E_y must be a single polarity of dc. This type of multiplier is often used as a linear gain control. Its usefulness can be appreciated by considering a fixed value of E_x as E_y ranges from zero to maximum. With E_x a constant dc value (or steady ac level), the output will be directly and linearly controlled (multiplied) by E_y. Conversely, if operation is viewed from the standpoint of E_y as a signal controlled by E_x, the output will be a varying level as E_x varies, but with the additional capability of sign reversal as E_x goes through zero.

6.2.2 Four-Quadrant Analog Multiplier

Going a step further, the four-quadrant multiplier extends operation of the E_y input into the opposite polarity (Fig. 6-11), allowing unrestricted operation with either E_x or E_y in the range of ±10 V. For operation with E_y from 0 V to +10 V, operation of a four-quadrant multiplier is completely like that of a two-quadrant type. This is shown by the right half of Fig. 6-11. However, for operation with E_y

from 0 V to −10 V, the outputs from a four-quadrant type are as shown in the left half of Fig. 6-11.

To illustrate four-quadrant operation in E_x and E_y, let $E_x = +5$ V and $E_y = -6$ V. The output is read from the curve of E_o for $E_x = +5$ V in the lower left quadrant. For this example, $E_o = -30$ V. Note that any product obtained in the lower two quadrants will be negative. As a second example, let $E_x = -10$ V and $E_y = -8$ V. The output is in the upper left quadrant on the $E_x = -10$-V line; $E_o = 80$ V.

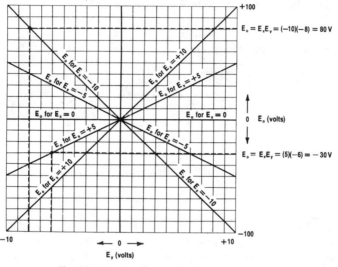

Fig. 6-11. Four-quadrant multiplier characteristic.

This is the correct mathematical expression for the product of two negative numbers—a positive result. The output of a four-quadrant multiplier will be the product of the two inputs, always with the correct sign. Finally, as with the two-quadrant type, the output will always be zero if either E_x or E_y is zero. In operation, a four-quadrant multiplier may be considered fully symmetrical. Either input offers control of amplitude and sign, and the output is always correct for instantaneous sign(s) and magnitude(s) of E_x and E_y.

So far we have spoken of multipliers in general terms only. To move into practical considerations requires some further definition of multiplier considerations and an understanding of the operation of typical devices. There are a number of circuit techniques for performing analog multiplication. Among these are the logarithmic technique mentioned earlier, the quarter-square technique (piece-wise approximation), pulse-width and/or pulse-height modulation techniques, and variable transconductance methods. Of these the variable transconductance multiplier is the simplest and most economical, and it is realizable in a number of IC configurations. This technique is chosen as the foundation for discussion in this section. In the references provided, the interested reader can find material covering other approaches.

The symbolic representation for analog multipliers used in this book is shown in Fig. 6-12. The symbol is largely self-explanatory—like the op-amp symbol, it is not intended to denote circuit details, but simply indicates the function of the device. As will be seen shortly, the inputs may be differential for E_x and E_y, allowing a great deal of sign and scale-factor flexibility. Also, the output signal from a multiplier is normally scaled to a range of ± 10 V to provide compatibility with standard op-amp signal levels. Typically, the output

All voltages (E_x, E_y, and E_o) may be single-ended or differential.

Fig. 6-12. Symbolic multiplier representation.

is scaled by a factor of $K = 0.1$, to allow two full-scale inputs of ± 10 V. This in no way alters the basic multiplication principles; it is a provision for setting the output dynamic range at a practical level. Were this not done, the required output with $E_x = E_y = 10$ V would be ± 100 V, as shown in the theoretical graphs of Figs. 6-10 and 6-11.

6.2.3 Basic Arithmetic Functions Using Multipliers
Division

The process of multiplication is a function upon which many other operations are based. Division can be regarded as multiplication by the reciprocal of the divisor; thus $E_o = E_x/E_y$ can also be written $E_o = (E_x) (1/E_y)$. Since we can generate the reciprocal of a transfer function by placing it within a feedback loop, division is accomplished as shown in Fig. 6-13.

The output of a multiplier is the scaled product of its two inputs (E_x and E_y). In this case, $E_o' = K(E_x E_y) = 0.1 (E_o E_y)$. Since the E_o' voltage also feeds the summing point of A_1 through resistor R_1, it must also be true that $E_o' = -E_z$, since both these voltages must sum to zero at the summing point of A_1. Substituting,

$$E_o' = 0.1 (E_o E_y) = -E_z$$

which yields for E_o

$$E_o = \frac{-10E_z}{E_y}$$

It should be noted that for this circuit to function correctly, E_y must always be a positive voltage. If E_y goes negative, the multiplier feedback becomes positive and a latch-up condition of A_1 occurs.

$E_o = E_x = \dfrac{-10E_z}{E_y}$

$E_o' = K(E_xE_y) = \dfrac{E_o E_y}{10}$

Also, $E_o' = -E_z$, since $R_1 = R_2$ and $E_{in\ (diff)}$ of $A_1 = 0$.

$\therefore \dfrac{E_o E_y}{10} = -E_z$, or $E_o = \dfrac{-10E_z}{E_y}$

$^*E_y$ must be positive to maintain negative feedback around A_1.

Fig. 6-13. Division using a multiplier.

Squaring and Higher Powers

An obvious use for a multiplier is the multiplication of a signal by itself, or the square function, illustrated in Fig. 6-14A. Since $E_o =$

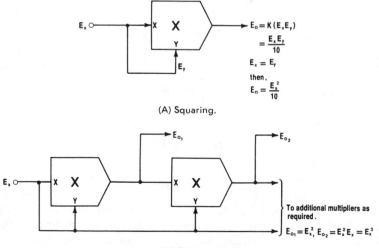

$E_o = K(E_xE_y)$

$= \dfrac{E_xE_y}{10}$

$E_x = E_y$

then,

$E_o = \dfrac{E_x^2}{10}$

(A) Squaring.

To additional multipliers as required.

$E_{o_1} = E_x^2,\ E_{o_2} = E_x^2E_x = E_x^3$

(B) Cubing.

Fig. 6-14. Generating powers with a multiplier.

$E_x E_y/10$, and E_x and E_y are identical signals, the output is then $E_o = E_x^2/10$. In similar fashion, the output of a squaring circuit may be fed into a second multiplier (Fig. 6-14B) along with the original signal to obtain a cube function: $E_o = E_x^2 E_x = E_x^3$. This concept can be extended to generate high-order functions to whatever degree necessary.

Square Root

A square-root function can be realized by placing a squarer within the feedback loop of an op amp, as in Fig. 6-15. Since the output of the multiplier is $E_o^2/10$, which will always be positive, the equal values of R_1 and R_2 will cause this value to be equal to $-E_z$. Thus, input E_z must be *negative* to produce a positive output at the amplifier.

Fig. 6-15. Square-root generator using a multiplier.

Finally,

$$\frac{E_o^2}{10} = -E_z$$

and if $E_z < 0$,

$$E_o^2 = 10\, E_z$$

so,

$$E_o = \sqrt{\,|\,10E_z\,|\,}$$

These are the basic arithmetic functions that can be generated using multipliers. There are elaborate variations and combinations of basic arithmetic functions, but they will not be detailed here. The interested reader should consult the references for further information.

6.2.4 Transconductance Multipliers

Virtually all popular IC multipliers operate on the principle of variable transconductance. A very rudimentary circuit that performs two-quadrant multiplication using this technique is shown in Fig. 6-16; it will be used as a developmental model for the more detailed structures to follow.

The circuit works by varying the emitter current of a matched pair of bipolar transistors. If the differential voltage, E_x, applied to Q_1-Q_2 is zero, the output is zero. As E_x varies, the output signal (I_o) from Q_1-Q_2 will be

$$I_o = \frac{q}{2\kappa T} I_E E_x$$

This differential output is applied to A_1, a differential current-to-voltage converter. The output from A_1 will be

$$E_o = I_o R_o = \left(\frac{q}{2\kappa T} I_E E_x\right) 2R_{10}$$

Finally, if we vary the emitter currents of Q_1 and Q_2 with a second input, E_y, the value of I_E will be approximately $I_E = E_y/R_3$. This can be substituted into the equation for E_o and, with some rearrangement,

$$E_o = E_x E_y \left(\frac{q}{2\kappa T}\right)\left(\frac{2R_{10}}{R_3}\right)\left(\frac{R_2}{R_1 + R_2}\right)$$

From this it can be seen that the circuit accomplishes multiplication of E_x and E_y if the other terms of the equation are considered constant. Note that this expression includes the attenuation of the R_1-R_2 divider.

An examination of Fig. 6-16 will reveal that this circuit responds only to single polarities of E_y (negative in this example), but to bipolar signals at E_x. This is (by definition) two-quadrant multiplication. As E_y is varied to change I_E, the collector voltages of both Q_1 and Q_2 rise and fall with the change in common-mode signal. A_1 and the differential bridge resistors (R_9 through R_{12}) reject this common-mode signal while amplifying the desired differential signal (I_o) from E_x. Balance of the bridge is critical to good rejection of the E_y signal at the output; therefore, the bridge should either use close-tolerance (0.1%) resistors or be nulled, as shown, with R_8. R_7 zeros the offset voltage of Q_1-Q_2.

An inherent property of this circuit is that linearity holds only for relatively small signal amplitudes of E_x. Directly at Q_1, this limit is ±10 mV for 1.0% linearity; thus, an attenuator network such as R_1-R_2 is necessary to scale the input range up to the standard ±10-V

Fig. 6-16. Basic two-quadrant transconductance multiplier.

levels. Also, to compensate the TC of gain due to the $\kappa T/q$ factor, R_2 can be made a thermistor with a TC of $+0.3\%/°C$, as in Fig. 6-5.

6.2.5 Improving the Basic Two-Quadrant Multiplier

The circuit of Fig. 6-17 is an improvement on the basic multiplier circuit in two major respects. First, the nonlinearity displayed by Q_1-Q_2 at the E_x input has been compensated by developing a pre-distorted voltage drive with the feedback loop around A_2 and Q_3-Q_4. Q_3 and Q_4 are a differential transistor pair, operated at a fixed emitter current. They are connected so that the current swing in Q_3 must equal the current swing in R_1. A_2 will force this current to be linear, even though the voltage drive at the input to Q_4 (and Q_1) will be nonlinear. This method ensures a linear current output from the differential pair, Q_3-Q_4; therefore, an identical pair (Q_1-Q_2) can also be driven in parallel, with a similar linear output. R_1 is selected for the desired full-scale input current, I_x; in this case $I_x = \pm 250$ μA at ± 10 V.

The other improvement is the method of current drive for the controlled pair, Q_1-Q_2. The simple resistive current drive (R_3) used in Fig. 6-16 is not entirely satisfactory in providing a linear variation of I_E as E_y approaches zero. A feedback configuration improves linearity, and this is accomplished by a bilateral VCCS (see Chapter 4), consisting of A_3 and associated components. The VCCS circuit supplies an output current that is linear at any level of E_y, thus extending linearity to cover very small E_y voltages. R_{1A} trims the overall circuit scale factor by setting the desired value of I_x when E_x is at a maximum. The other trim adjustments perform functions similar to those of Fig. 6-16. Optimum results with this circuit require that the

Fig. 6-17. Improved two-quadrant multiplier.

E_x	E_y	I_{o_1}	I_{o_2}
+	+	+	−
−	+	−	+
+	−	−	+
−	−	+	−
±	0	0	0
0	±	0	0

(A) Circuit structure.   (B) Input/output polarities.

Fig. 6-18. Basic operation of a monolithic four-quadrant multiplier.

four transistors be matched fairly well to track with temperature. The LM394 pairs provide for this; to a lesser extent, array types such as the CA3046 will be useful.

6.2.6 Monolithic IC Multipliers

The circuitry described so far, while useful, is intended primarily to demonstrate the general principles of variable-transconductance multiplication. This includes not only the basic premise of gain variation by control of emitter current, but also the requirements for linearization and conversion from differential to single-ended operation.

Commercial IC multipliers are typically four-quadrant extensions of the basic two-quadrant concept. These monolithic units often utilize a circuit structure similar to Fig. 6-18A.* The circuit can be viewed as a pair of cross-connected differential pairs (Q_1-Q_2 and Q_3-Q_4), fed by controlled emitter currents (from Q_5-Q_6) and having a common differential base drive (E_x). If the circuit is sectioned between Q_2-Q_3 and Q_5-Q_6, each half is a single differential pair similar to Q_1-Q_2 in Fig. 6-16. In fact, this circuit is actually a pair of two-quadrant multipliers interconnected to form one composite, four-

---

* This "gain cell" multiplier block was first described by B. Gilbert. See reference 12 at the end of the chapter.

quadrant multiplier. Operation of the circuit is best understood by examining the output current(s) of transistors Q_1 and Q_4.

Current-source transistors Q_5 and Q_6 transform one input voltage (E_y) into complementary currents $I + I_y$ and $I - I_y$. Regarding output terminal I_{o_1} first, we can see how multiplication occurs. If E_x and E_y have the polarities shown (call these positive), Q_4 will be on and receive the current $I + I_y$. When E_x is negative, Q_2 will be on and the I_{o_1} output will be $I - I_y$. This illustrates the control of polarity that E_x exercises over the $I + I_y$ currents. With E_x positive, Q_4 will be on and I_{o_1} will be the current from Q_6. If E_y is also positive at the same instant, this value of I_{o_1} will be $I + I_y$; if E_y is negative instead, the value of I_{o_1} is $I - I_y$. If both E_x and E_y are negative, I_{o_1} becomes the current from Q_5, or $I + I_y$.

When the preceding four cases are summarized, it can be seen that operation is four-quadrant—always with the correct sign for any combination of E_x and E_y. An additional feature of operation occurs when either E_x or E_y is zero. If $E_y = 0$, $I_y = 0$, and $I_{o_1} = I$. As E_x alternates polarity, Q_4 turns on as Q_2 turns off and vice versa. However, the currents in Q_5 and Q_6 remain the same and there is no net change in I_{o_1}. Likewise, if $E_x = 0$, no net change in I_{o_1} will occur as E_y is varied, because the output will contain equal proportions from Q_2 and Q_1. Due to symmetry, the currents $I + I_y$ and $I - I_y$ are equal and opposite and will, therefore, cancel each other.

The operation of the circuit for different conditions of E_x and E_y is summarized in Fig. 6-18B. The complementary output (I_{o_2}) will always receive the negative of the current appearing at I_{o_1}. Thus, the output signals at I_{o_1} and I_{o_2} are differentially multiplied *currents*. To convert them back to a voltage requires a differential current-to-voltage converter such as that used in Fig. 6-16 or 6-17.

At this point it should be noted that there is no fundamental guide to the designation of X and Y inputs. The multiplication principle is the same regardless of which input is termed "X" or "Y." This is mentioned only because there is no complete standardization of X and Y designations among manufacturers; however, this should not be a handicap if the fundamental principles are kept in mind.

To complete the multiplier, a diode linearity correction circuit is added to develop a nonlinear voltage drive for the bases of Q_1-Q_4. This linearizes the X input similar to the circuit used in Fig. 6-17. Darlington devices are used for the Q_5-Q_6 voltage-to-current converters to minimize error, with similar devices added to the X input.

The MC1495

A complete circuit that accomplishes linear four-quadrant multiplication using the Motorola MC1495 is shown in Fig. 6-19. Both

Fig. 6-19. Motorola MC1495 four-quadrant multiplier.

the X and Y inputs are fully differential and are scaled in sensitivity with an external emitter resistor. The differential- and common-mode input range is ±10 V. The flexibility of this multiplier block is maximized since virtually all circuit nodes are externally accessible, allowing operation in a variety of modes.

Due to the additional stage in the E_x input of this multiplier, a redefinition of polarities is necessary. This is shown in the functional block diagram of Fig. 6-20. Pins 4 and 8 are the differential E_x inputs, and pins 9 and 12 are the differential E_y inputs. Current scaling in both inputs is set by resistors R_x and R_y, which set currents I_x and I_y according to $I_x = E_x/R_x$ and $I_y = E_y/R_y$. In using the device, either sign may be realized by applying an input signal to the inverting or noninverting input as desired, with scaling set by R_x and R_y. A summary of input/output relations is also given in Fig. 6-20.

The AD532 and AD534

As can be appreciated from the preceding discussion, the MC1495 is in actuality a "gain-cell" chip, and requires much in the way of support circuitry to implement complete multipliers and dividers. Ready-to-use complete multiplier ICs are also available from such firms as Analog Devices and Burr-Brown. In this section, we will examine the basic applications of some of the representative units of this type.

Pin 4	Pin 9	Pin 2	Pin 14
+	+	+	−
−	+	−	+
+	−	−	+
−	−	+	−
±	0	0	0
0	±	0	0

Fig. 6-20. Functional block diagram of the Motorola MC1495 multiplier.

The Analog Devices AD532 and AD534 are complete multiplying ICs, with pretrimmed adjustments for scale factor and offset. Both devices perform the basic multiplying function of $E_o = E_x E_y/10$, but they do so with different degrees of accuracy and flexibility. Functional block diagrams of both devices are shown in Fig. 6-21.

The AD532, shown in Fig. 6-21A, consists of differential input amplifiers for the X and Y channels, a multiplier cell, and an output amplifier. This device is capable of a total error of 2.0% or less for the AD532J version, or 1.0% for the AD532K version. The dynamic range of the inputs and the output is ±10 V, and the device uses ±15-V power supplies.

The AD534, shown in Fig. 6-21B, consists of differential input amplifiers for the X and Y channels, a multiplier cell, a reference and bias circuit, an output amplifier, and differential Z inputs. This device is very accurate, with total errors of 1.0%, 0.5%, and 0.25% for the AD534J, K, and L grades, respectively.

The relative brevity of this section precludes going into all the details of the operation of these devices, and the interested reader should consult the references at the end of the chapter.

(A) The AD532.

$$V_{OUT} = \frac{(X_1 - X_2)(Y_1 - Y_2)}{10V}$$

(WITH Z TIED TO OUTPUT)

TRANSFER FUNCTION

$$V_O = A\left[\frac{(X_1 - X_2)(Y_1 - Y_2)}{SF} - (Z_1 - Z_2)\right]$$

(B) The AD534.

Courtesy Analog Devices, Inc.

Fig. 6-21. Functional block diagrams of pretrimmed IC multipliers.

6.2.7 Arithmetic Functions Using IC Multipliers

In this section, the basic arithmetic functions are illustrated, as they can be realized with pretrimmed IC multipliers.

Multipliers

Two simple, yet sufficiently complete circuits for multiplying two voltages, X and Y, using the AD532 and AD534, are shown in Fig. 6-22.

In the AD532 circuit (Fig. 6-22A), connecting the Z input to the output sets the device up for multiplication. Although it is not basically necessary, overall dc accuracy can be optimized by the optional output offset trim, using the 20-kΩ potentiometer. The input voltages, X and Y, can be either differential or single ended, as appropriate. The fully differential inputs optimize input flexibility.

The AD534 circuit (Fig. 6-22B) uses a similar differential input scheme, but also adds the flexibility of differential Z inputs. For nor-

(A) Using the AD532.

(B) Using the AD534.

Courtesy Analog Devices, Inc.

Fig. 6-22. General-purpose four-quadrant multiplier circuits using pretrimmed devices.

mal uses, Z_1 is tied to the output and Z_2 is grounded. If desired, the output can be referred to a reference voltage by applying the reference to the Z_2 input (up to ± 10 V).

Note that both devices are scaled by a $\frac{1}{10}$ factor, to allow a ± 10-V output for ± 10-V inputs (as discussed in the introduction).

Dividers

The arithmetic function of division can be accomplished as illustrated in Fig. 6-23. As can be noted, this function can be somewhat more difficult to implement, depending on which device is actually to be used.

The AD532 is set up for division as shown in Fig. 6-23A. This circuit divides an input voltage, Z, by a second voltage, X, with a scaling constant of 10. The 1.0-kΩ potentiometer trims the scale factor with the X input at -10 V, and the X_o offset potentiometer trims the offset with Z at $+10$ V; X at -1.0 V. Note that the X input is restricted to negative-range voltages only (to avoid latch-up), and the most useful dynamic range is between -0.5 V and -10 V.

(A) Using the AD532.

(B) Using the AD534.

Courtesy Analog Devices, Inc.

Fig. 6-23. Divider circuits using pretrimmed devices.

The AD534 is used as a divider as shown in Fig. 6-23B. This circuit divides a differential voltage, Z, by a second differential voltage, X, with a scaling constant of 10. If the (optional) Y input is used, a constant proportional to the Y voltage is added to the output.

Using the AD534 (K or L) with a +10-V to +1.0-V X input range, the error will be no more than 1.0% with this circuit. Greater output gain (increased scale factor) can be obtained simply by dividing down the feedback applied to the Y_2 input (a 2/1 divider will, for example, increase the scale factor by 2/1).

Square Rooters

Circuits which provide the mathematical function of square root are shown in Fig. 6-24.

The AD532 circuit, shown in Fig. 6-24A, solves for the square root of the product of the input voltage, Z, times the constant, 10, with a

Fig. 6-24. Square-root circuits using pretrimmed devices.

(A) Using the AD532.

(B) Using the AD534.

Courtesy Analog Devices, Inc.

negative range of output. The input voltage is confined to positive ranges only, and a diode must be used (a 1N914 type is adequate), as shown, to prevent latch-up. To optimize accuracy, trim the offset terminal (see Fig. 6-22A) for -1.0 V dc out with $+0.1$ V dc in, and also trim SF and X_o.

The AD534 is used in a square-root mode as shown in Fig. 6-24B. The Z input has a polarity as indicated, and a diode must be used. The output (as shown) yields positive-range voltages, but negative outputs can be obtained by making the indicated alterations. Note that a constant voltage, X, can be added (optionally) by summing in a voltage in the range of ± 10 V.

6.2.8 Communications Circuits Using Multipliers

So far, the multiplier applications discussed have involved arithmetic computation. However, even broader applications are possible using multipliers in the processing of communications signals. These functions include modulation (am and dsb), demodulation, electronic gain control, and many others. When operating at high frequencies, the output op amp becomes a limiting factor. Transconductance gain-cell multipliers such as the MC1495 are extremely fast and may be used at frequencies above 10 MHz. This factor is the single greatest advantage to using a "multiplying block" such as the MC1495.

Wideband Frequency Doubler

A common communications circuit requirement is a frequency doubler, a circuit that produces an output frequency equal to the second harmonic of the input. An ac-coupled multiplier connected in the squaring mode can perform this function with no tuned circuits, allowing operation over wide bandwidths with no adjustment. Furthermore, for a sine-wave input waveform, the output will also be a sine wave with low distortion; a THD of 1.0% or less being typically possible.

A circuit that performs the doubling function is shown in Fig. 6-25. Since the X and Y inputs in this example are identical, a common bias-setting resistor (R_8) is used. Outputs can be taken from either pin 2 or pin 14, depending on the desired phase. C_{o_1}-C_{o_2} should be chosen for negligible reactance with respect to R_{L_1} and R_{L_2}, the load impedance of the following stage. The circuit will work as shown with R_7 grounded, but an offset adjustment can be utilized for minimum distortion if desired.

* For minimum output distortion, use an offset adjustment.

Fig. 6-25. Wideband frequency doubler.

The high-frequency performance of this circuit is dependent on the RC time constant at several circuit points. R_{10}-R_{11} and/or R_L may be reduced to decrease the effects of stray capacitance at the output, and buffering with an emitter follower will also help. Similarly, reducing R_3 and R_6 will reduce the effects of stray capacitance at the input. With circuit impedances optimized for high-frequency performance, this basic configuration can operate at frequencies as high as several megahertz.

Balanced Modulation/Demodulation

A circuit very similar to the previous one is the balanced modulator/demodulator shown in Fig. 6-26. This is virtually the same circuit as Fig. 6-25, but with the X and Y inputs separated. If two separate frequencies, f_c and f_m, are applied to the two inputs, the output will contain neither of the two original inputs, only their products, in the form of $f_c \pm f_m$. There is no restriction on which input is used for the carrier or modulation, since they are symmetrical. There is also no limitation on either of the two frequencies, they may be widely separated (as in conventional modulation systems) or nearly identical, because of the untuned, wide-bandwidth method of modulation.

The circuit will work with R_4 and R_7 grounded, as shown, but for optimum suppression of the input signals both channels should be

*For greatest accuracy, use offset adjustment at pins 8 and 12. With a maximum E_{in} at one input, set the opposite input for a null at the output.

Fig. 6-26. Balanced modulator/demodulator.

nulled. This is accomplished by applying either input signal and then adjusting the offset control on the opposite channel for minimum output. With nulling, carrier suppression can approach 60 dB. If very wide bandwidth is desired, the time-constant considerations discussed for Fig. 6-25 should be applied.

The modulator/demodulator circuit can be used for am or ssb demodulation by applying a modulated carrier to one input and an unmodulated carrier of identical frequency and phase to the second input, and by adding a low-pass filter to the output. The multiplying action of the constant-level carrier and the varying-level modulated wave results in a series of rectified output pulses corresponding to the modulation envelope. The low-pass filter then removes the residual carrier components, leaving only the modulation. This form of demodulation is very linear and has a wide dynamic range, since it does not have the "diode threshold" of standard am demodulators. The low-pass filter used to recover the modulation is formed by R_{11} (or R_{10} if taken from pin 14) and C_3 plus R_{13}-C_4. C_{o_2} is a coupling capacitor chosen for low reactance in relation to R_{L_2}. The demodulator circuit, like the modulator, may be used on either output terminal. Offset adjustments are generally not necessary with the demodulator, however, since the output filter rejects any residual carrier which might leak through.

AM Modulator

Conventional amplitude modulation can also be accomplished with a multiplier as shown in Fig. 6-27. In reality, am is a variation in level of a constant carrier. In this circuit, the carrier is applied to one input of the modulator, and a fixed dc level (bias) is applied to the second input. This results in a constant-level carrier output. If modulation is then applied in addition to the bias voltage, with a p-p amplitude of twice the bias level, 100% am will result.

In Fig. 6-27, R_{14} inserts a fixed 2.5-V bias at the inverting Y input, producing a constant-level carrier at the output. A 5-V p-p signal at the modulation input will alternately double and cancel the carrier level at the output by summing with this bias. With the values shown, a 5-V p-p signal at the modulation input will result in 100% modulation. The offset adjustment for the Y channel, R_{15}, is used to suppress any direct feedthrough of the modulation signal. The circuit can be optimized for high-frequency carrier operation by reducing the values of R_{10} and R_{11} at the output, and R_3 at the input.

Electronic Gain Control

As was mentioned briefly in the introductory comments on multipliers, both two- and four-quadrant types can be used as electronic gain controls. This allows programmable or remote gain adjustments,

Fig. 6-27. Am modulator.

agc functions, and a wide variety of special electronic effects. Although either type of multiplier can be used in this manner, the two-quadrant version is more ideally suited, so this type of circuit will be emphasized in the present discussion.

To use a four-quadrant multiplier as a gain control, all that need be done is apply a signal to one input and a variable control voltage to the opposite input. Viewed as a voltage-controlled attenuator, this circuit has an attenuation of 0 dB (unity gain) when the control voltage is maximum. Below this control voltage, the output is attenuated by 20 dB for each 20-dB reduction in control voltage (linear multiplication). However, the drawback is that this relation is valid only over a dynamic range of about 60 dB, and distortion increases rapidly as the gain is reduced, with typical THD figures of 1 to 2%. Neither of these characteristics is satisfactory for a high-quality, audio-signal-processing device. They are due to the basic four-quadrant structure, which relies on a balance between two opposing two-quadrant multipliers.

Actually, an electronic gain control does not require four-quadrant capability at all, since the controlling signal can be defined as unipolar, ranging from some maximum full-scale value down to zero. The basic transconductance multiplier we have been discussing—the MC1495—can also be used in a two-quadrant mode, as illustrated in Fig. 6-28.

Conversion of the MC1495 to two-quadrant operation involves only the disabling of one of the two-quadrant multipliers shown in Fig. 6-19. In the version shown here (Fig. 6-28), Q_5 is disabled by grounding the base and emitter (pins 11 and 12), and no bias is supplied to pin 13. The remaining two-quadrant multiplier section using Q_6 is biased externally by op-amp A_2, which acts as a positive-input VCCS (see Chapter 4). Operated as shown, the circuit resembles the improved two-quadrant multiplier of Fig. 6-17. Two-quadrant multiplier operation of a differential pair is precisely controllable over an extremely wide dynamic range—100 dB or better of gain control is readily achievable. In addition, the only significant distortion mechanism is "linearization," which comes from the diodes that process the E_x signal internally. This distortion is mostly from the second harmonic; it can be controlled by scaling R_3 (R_x) appropriately, thus limiting the I_x current. For example, in the circuit shown, the THD is below 0.5% at a full-scale input of ±10 V, and it reduces to negligible values at lower input levels, where it would typically be operated in an audio circuit.

*Use an offset adjustment similar to the circuit in Fig. 6-27; null the output with $E_x = 0$, E_y maximum.
** Adjust for zero output when $E_y = 0$.
†$A_1 - A_2 = 1458$, 4558, or 4559.

Fig. 6-28. Two-quadrant multiplier using a four-quadrant device.

A further asset of the two-quadrant multiplier over the four-quadrant is in terms of noise. The two-quadrant transconductance multiplier reduces the output noise level along with the signal, whereas a four-quadrant type does not. This factor is important where good signal-to-noise ratios and wide dynamic range are important.

The circuit is otherwise similar in many regards to previous ones, with the exception of the VCCS, A_2. The accuracy of this voltage-to-current converter will determine the overall dynamic range of attenuation; it is limited at the low end by the residual offset voltage of A_2, which should be nulled for best results. Other variations of the VCCS block can also be used if they are compatible with the bias requirements of the MC1495. As shown, the current in R_5 is 2.0 mA for unity gain, and the bias voltage level at pin 10 should be +0.5 V or less.

REFERENCES

1. Analog Devices Application Note, 1970. *Evaluating, Selecting, and Using Multiplier Circuit Modules for Signal Manipulation and Function Generation.* Analog Devices, Inc., Norwood, Mass.

2. *Applications Manual for Computing Amplifiers.* Philbrick Researches, Inc., Dedham, Mass., 1966.

3. Borlase, W.; David, E. *Design of Temperature-Compensated Log Circuits Employing Transistors and Operational Amplifiers.* Analog Devices Application Note E020-10, March 1969. Analog Devices, Inc., Norwood, Mass.

4. Burwen, R. "A Complete Multiplier/Divider on a Single Chip." *Analog Dialogue,* Vol. 5, No. 1, January 1971.

5. ———; Sullivan, D. *AD530 Complete Monolithic MDSSR Technical Bulletin,* July 1971. Analog Devices, Inc., Norwood, Mass.

6. Dobkin, R. C. *Logarithmic Converters.* National Semiconductor Application Note AN-30, November 1969. National Semiconductor Corp., Santa Clara, Calif.

7. ———. *Op Amp Circuit Collection.* National Semiconductor Application Note AN-31, February 1970. National Semiconductor Corp., Santa Clara, Calif.

8. ———. *Precision AC/DC Converters.* National Semiconductor Linear Brief LB-8, August 1969. National Semiconductor Corp., Santa Clara, Calif.

9. Fullagar, D. *The 8007—A High-Performance FET-Input Operational Amplifier.* Intersil Application Bulletin A005, March 1972. Intersil, Inc., Cupertino, Calif.

10. Gilbert, B. "Accurate, Low-Cost, Easy-to-Use IC Multiplier." *Analog Dialogue,* Vol. 11, No. 1, 1977.

11. ———. "A High-Performance Monolithic Multiplier Using Active Feedback." *IEEE Journal of Solid State Circuits,* December 1974.

12. ———. "A Precise Four-Quadrant Multiplier With Sub-Nanosecond Response." *IEEE Journal of Solid State Circuits*, December 1968.

13. Giles, J. N. *Fairchild Semiconductor LIC Handbook.* Fairchild Semiconductor, Mountain View, Calif., 1967.

14. Gurski, R. J. "Logarithmic Devices." *The Lightning Empiricist*, Vol. 17, No. 1, March 1969. Philbrick/Nexus Research, Dedham, Mass.

15. Huehne, K. *The MC1556 Operational Amplifier and its Applications.* Motorola Application Note AN-522, 1970. Motorola Semiconductor Products, Inc., Phoenix, Ariz.

16. ———. *Transistor Logarithmic Conversion Using an Integrated Circuit Operational Amplifier.* Motorola Application Note AN-261A, 1971. Motorola Semiconductor Products, Inc., Phoenix, Ariz.

17. Korn, G. A.; Korn, T. M. *Electronic Analog and Hybrid Computers*, 2nd ed. McGraw-Hill Book Co., New York, 1972.

18. National Semiconductor Application Note AN-32, February 1970. *FET Circuit Applications.* National Semiconductor Corp., Santa Clara, Calif.

19. Nelson, C. T. *Super Matched Bipolar Transistor Pair Sets New Standards for Drift and Noise.* National Semiconductor Application Note AN-222, July 1979. National Semiconductor Corp., Santa Clara, Calif.

20. Paterson, W. L. "Multiplication and Logarithmic Conversion by Operational Amplifier-Transistor Circuits." *The Review of Scientific Instruments*, Vol. 34, No. 12, December 1963.

21. Renschler, E. *Analysis and Basic Operation of the MC1595.* Motorola Application Note AN-489, March 1970. Motorola Semiconductor Products, Inc., Phoenix, Ariz.

22. ———. "The Monolithic Multiplier." *Motorola Monitor*, Vol. 7, No. 3, 1969.

23. Rudin, M. *Applying Microvolt/Picoamp Instrumentation Operational Amplifiers.* Precision Monolithics Application Note. Precision Monolithics, Inc., Santa Clara, Calif.

24. Sheingold, D. H. (ed.). *Analog-Digital Conversion Handbook.* Analog Devices, Inc., Norwood, Mass., 1972.

25. ———. *Multiplier Application Guide.* Analog Devices, Inc., Norwood, Mass., 1978.

26. ———. *Nonlinear Circuits Handbook.* Analog Devices, Inc., Norwood, Mass., 1974.

27. Texas Instruments Application Bulletin CA-149, March 1970. *Logarithmic and Exponential Amplifiers With SN72709.* Texas Instruments, Inc., Dallas, Tex.

28. Tobey, G. E.; Graeme, J. G.; Huelsman, L. P. (eds.). *Operational Amplifiers—Design and Applications.* McGraw-Hill Book Co., New York, 1971.

29. Welling, B.; Kinsey, L. *Using the MC1595 Multiplier in Arithmetic Operations.* Motorola Application Note AN-490, October 1970. Motorola Semiconductor Products, Inc., Phoenix, Ariz.

30. Widlar, R. J. "Designing With Super-Beta Transistor Op-Amp ICs." *EEE,* December 1969, February and March 1970.

31. ―――. *IC Op Amp Beats FETs on Input Current.* National Semiconductor Application Note AN-29, December 1969. National Semiconductor Corp., Santa Clara, Calif.

32. ―――. *Monolithic Operational Amplifiers—The Universal Linear Component.* National Semiconductor Application Note AN-4, April 1968. National Semiconductor Corp., Santa Clara, Calif.

33. Manufacturers' Data Sheets:

Analog Devices	AD532	Multiplier
	AD534	Multiplier
	AD536	RMS Converter
	AD542	Operational Amplifier
	AD545	Operational Amplifier
	AD818	Matched Transistor Pair
National Semiconductor	LF356	Operational Amplifier
	LM11	Operational Amplifier
	LM394	Matched Transistor Pair

SEVEN

Amplifier Techniques

This chapter addresses the wide range of considerations necessary toward the optimum design of amplifiers for a variety of tasks. This includes instrumentation uses as well as general-purpose signal processing. Also included are a variety of amplifier techniques useful toward augmenting the performance characteristics of individual ICs.

7.1 INSTRUMENTATION AMPLIFIERS

One of the most useful applications of an IC op amp is the differential-input dc amplifier configuration, illustrated in Fig. 7-1. Due to the inherent rejection of common-mode noise (E_{cm}) and the linear amplification of desired signals (E_s) that it provides, this circuit and variations of it find widespread use in signal processing. Dc and low-frequency signals are commonly received from a transducer, ampli-

$$E_o = (E_a - E_b)\left(\frac{R_2}{R_1}\right)$$

$A_v = \dfrac{R_3}{R_1}$, and $R_1 = R_2$, $R_3 = R_4$;

$\therefore \dfrac{R_1}{R_3} = \dfrac{R_2}{R_4}$

Fig. 7-1. Basic differential-input instrumentation amplifier.

fied, and then transmitted in a single-ended mode. Since the desired signal may have a full-scale amplitude of typically only a few millivolts, while common-mode noise may be several volts, such factors as amplifier input drift and noise are critical to overall accuracy. Equally important is the common-mode rejection of the amplifier configuration. Several instrumentation amplifier circuits are discussed in this section, with the unique and distinguishing features of each highlighted.

7.1.1 Buffered Differential-Input Instrumentation Amplifier

One obvious disadvantage of the basic differential circuit of Fig. 7-1 is the loading effect of R_1 and R_2 on the signal source(s). If a high gain is to be realized from the stage, R_1 and R_2 must necessarily be low. However, this tends to impair common-mode rejection, as there is usually little control over the source resistances of the two inputs. Consequently, even a slight mismatch in these resistances appears as a mismatch between $R_1 + R_{s_1}$ and $R_2 + R_{s_2}$ which degrades the CMRR because the gains for both signals are no longer equal.

The positive cure for impedance mismatch between the differential inputs is a very high impedance at both inputs. This can be accomplished by a voltage follower (input buffer) arrangement as shown in Fig. 7-2. This circuit raises the input impedance to 10^{12} Ω, has a 2-nA input current, and the ability to amplify differential signals superimposed on ± 11 V of common-mode noise.

The second stage of the circuit, A_3, provides a differential voltage gain of 40 dB while further suppressing the common-mode component. The common-mode rejection properties of this configuration can be realized only when the arms of the differential "bridge" are matched. This requires that $R_2/R_4 = R_3/R_5$, as shown in the figure. The close tolerances indicated are necessary to guarantee this degree of match without "tweaking" of the circuit. If an adjustment is desired, either ratio may be trimmed for a match. It is usually preferable to trim the noninverting side (R_3-R_5) to avoid upsetting the gain relation of R_4 to R_2. Trimming allows wider tolerances on R_2-R_5. An alternate network is shown which may replace R_5 to allow the CMRR to be trimmed to 100 dB or better, the same as with the 0.1% network. Perhaps the best *practical* solution to the resistance tolerance problem is to use a very tightly *ratio*-matched and TC-tracking film network for these resistances. This way, a single part is a solution—there is no need to pay a cost penalty for overly tight *absolute*-tolerance resistors (0.01% *ratio* matches are readily available, whereas 0.01% *absolute* tolerances are very difficult to obtain!).

The output can be referred to a voltage (E_R) by disconnecting the ground at R_5 and applying E_R to R_5 from a low-impedance source.

$$E_o = (E_a - E_b) \left(\frac{R_4}{R_2}\right)$$

$$\frac{R_2}{R_4} = \frac{R_3}{R_5}$$

$$A_v = \frac{R_4}{R_2}$$

* Matching of resistor pairs R_2-R_3 and R_4-R_5 determines the overall CMRR.

** Substitute type 318 for higher speed.

† No connection for type 310; pin 2 for types 355, 356, or 312 (see text).

‡ Pin 5 for types 355 and 356 (see text).

Fig. 7-2. Buffered differential-input instrumentation amplifier.

The input offset voltage of the circuit is adjusted by R_1, which provides a differential offset to A_1 and A_2. This adustment (and R_{5B}, if used) should use high-quality components for best results, since the voltages it generates appear as equivalent input voltages. Any instability in these components will be amplified by the gain of the circuit.

For input currents lower than the 2 nA of the 310 units, FET-input amplifiers such as the 355 or 356 units can be substituted for A_1 and A_2. In such case, the offset potentiometer should be connected to pins 1 and 5 of A_1 and A_2 (as opposed to pins 1 and 8 for the 310 units) and should be a 10-kΩ value.

Improved common-mode rejection (at the expense of speed) can be obtained by using a pair of 312 units for A_1 and A_2, with pinouts the same as shown for the 310 units but with a 50-kΩ offset potentiometer.

The 307 op amp (A_3) will yield a bandwidth of 10 kHz. A type 318 may be substituted here, if desired, for a bandwidth of 150 kHz. Or, a type 301A (with reduced compensation of 5 pF) will yield a bandwidth of about 100 kHz. In general, bipolar types are preferred for the A_3 stage for best common-mode rejection, even with well-matched resistances.

7.1.2 Differential-Input Amplifier With Variable Gain

While the circuit of Fig. 7-2 is generally very useful, it has one inherent problem—an inability to adjust gain without upsetting the bridge balance and thus the CMRR. If R_4 of Fig. 7-2 is varied, for example, it will indeed adjust gain, but it will simultaneously ruin the CMRR because of the resulting bridge imbalance. What is needed is a method of varying the differential gain of the circuit with a single adjustment, while retaining a high and constant CMRR.

A modification of Fig. 7-2 allows this and is shown in Fig. 7-3. This circuit varies the gain of stage A_3 by modifying the feedback returned to R_4, in essence placing a calibrated attenuator within the feedback loop. Since feedback attenuation results in higher gain, this achieves the desired gain variation. An active attenuator (A_4) is used rather than a simple divider because A_4 presents a constant, zero-impedance source to R_4, exactly the condition needed to maintain good balance and a high CMRR. The output impedance of A_4 remains low for any setting of R_6; therefore, gain adjustments do not alter the CMRR in this circuit.

An interesting feature of this method of gain adjustment is that the gain is linearly proportional to R_6, which allows R_6 to be a calibrated rheostat for repeatable gain settings. With the values shown, gain can be varied from unity to 300. Offset adjustment R_1 operates here in the same fashion as described for Fig. 7-2, and the same

Fig. 7-3. Variable-gain instrumentation amplifier.

constraints apply. For both these circuits, good layout techniques are recommended—rf bypassing for amplifier supply leads (particularly at A_4) and short, direct signal leads. It is also recommended that the bridge resistances be low-temperature-coefficient types for best dc stability, preferably in a single array (with R_7 included also).

7.1.3 Instrumentation Amplifiers With Differential-Input Preamplifier Stages

For situations where high input impedance and the lowest offset-voltage drift are required, the configuration of Fig. 7-4 can be used. None of the circuits described previously have been optimized from the standpoint of minimum offset drift. The configuration here is unique in this regard, and a closer examination of how this is accomplished will reveal some attractive properties of the circuit. The circuit consists of two stages—the first consisting of A_1 and A_2, and the second made up by A_3 in a differential configuration. The second stage is similar to many of those already discussed.

A_1 and A_2 constitute a cross-coupled preamp stage with differential input and differential output. If A_1 and A_2 are regarded separately, they will be recognized as modified voltage followers with feedback resistances R_1-R_3 and R_4-R_3, respectively. In a conventional follower with gain, R_3 would be returned to ground. In this case, however, R_3 is shared by A_1 and A_2, and rather than being re-

$$E_o = (E_a - E_b)\left(\frac{R_3 + 2R_1}{R_3}\right)\left(\frac{R_6}{R_2}\right)$$

$R_1 = R_4$
$R_2 = R_5$
$R_6 = R_7$

$$A_v = \left(\frac{R_3 + 2R_1}{R_3}\right)\left(\frac{R_6}{R_2}\right)$$
$$= 101 \text{ as shown}$$

*Matching of ratios $\dfrac{R_2}{R_6}$ and $\dfrac{R_5}{R_7}$ determines CMRR. All gain resistors ($R_1 - R_7$) should be metal-film or wirewound types for best stability.
**$A_1 - A_2$ = OP-07 or OP-10 (see text).

Fig. 7-4. Instrumentation amplifier with differential preamp.

turned to ground, it is connected to the summing point of the opposite amplifier. This provides a return for R_3 which is at virtual ground for differential signals, but which *follows* common-mode signals. As a result, there is no current flow in R_3 (or in R_1 or R_4) for common-mode signals. This is because there is no difference in voltage across R_3, due to the theory of zero differential-input voltage of A_1 and A_2. By contrast, *differential* signals at E_a or E_b will result in a voltage drop across R_3; thus the circuit amplifies only differential signals. Common-mode voltages leave the A_1-A_2 stage with unity gain, while differential-input voltages are amplified by a factor of $(R_3 + 2R_1)/R_3$ [alternately expressed as $1 + (2R_1/R_3)$].

Several advantages may be inferred from this fact. One, the preamp stage provides an immediate gain in signal/noise ratio, because the differential signal is raised above the common-mode (noise) component by the ratio of the differential gain of the stage. Two, the gain-determining resistances (R_1, R_3, and R_4) *do not* affect the CMRR and are therefore much less critical as to tolerance. Any mismatch in R_1 and R_4 will show up as a mismatch in differential gain between the two outputs, a far less serious condition than a CMRR loss.

Another feature of this circuit is the lack of gain for common-mode input signals. This factor has a bearing not only on actual common-mode inputs, but also on the offset voltages and drifts of A_1 and A_2. If A_1 and A_2 drift at an equal rate and in the same direction, the drift appears to this stage as a common-mode signal, is not amplified by the first stage, and is rejected by the second stage. This eases the drift requirements of A_1 and A_2, as long as they match. The gain factor of the first preamp stage can be made high enough that the drift and common-mode errors of the second stage become negligible by comparison, also easing the requirements of this amplifier considerably. The total gain of both stages is again the product of the two differential gains, or generally,

$$A_v = \left(\frac{R_3 + 2R_1}{R_3}\right)\left(\frac{R_6}{R_2}\right)$$

In the circuit example of Fig. 7-4, drift can best be minimized by choosing the lowest drift devices for A_1 and A_2 (or devices with matched drifts). Single-unit OP-07 or μA714 devices, for example, have low drifts, low offset voltages, and low bias currents (as low as 1.0 μV/°C, 100 μV, and 2 nA, respectively, depending on the grade of device used). Alternatively, matched-parameter dual devices such as the OP-10, OP-04, OP-14, or 3500MP can be used. Other low-offset, low-drift devices suitable for A_1 and A_2 are the AD504, AD510, AD517, LM308A, and 725A.

Also in the circuit of Fig. 7-4 an OP-08 is used for A_3, and this device in general should have excellent CMRR characteristics if it is not to degrade the overall CMRR. For example, if A_1 and A_2 have a CMRR of 120 dB, A_3 should be of comparable quality. In short, all three amplifiers should have excellent CMRR characteristics for highest performance of this circuit.

Low-TC resistors should be used with this circuit to obtain the lowest possible drift, and consideration should be given to thermocouple effects. The circuit should also be shielded from circulating air currents to avoid thermal gradients. Offset voltages of A_1 and A_2 should not generally require nulling for the types of devices called for in this discussion (which are actively trimmed at the time of manufacture). In the event offset nulling is required, use the specific procedure recommended by the manufacturer.

As is noted in Fig. 7-4, bridge resistances R_2, R_5, R_6, and R_7 must be matched for best CMRR, and should never be trimmed for gain adjustment. If gain trim or programming is desired, resistance R_3 should be used for this purpose. Although the gain relationship is unwieldy, it nevertheless does not compromise the CMRR. The CMRR can be trimmed (if desired) by a small incremental adjustment to R_7.

Three other examples of this popular type of instrumentation amplifier stage are covered in the discussions that follow.

Gain-Programmable Instrumentation Amplifier

An instrumentation amplifier of this type that can easily be programmed for different overall gains is illustrated in Fig. 7-5. This circuit uses the LH0044 op amp, which has pretrimmed offset voltages as low as 25 μV maximum, and 10-nA typical bias currents.

In this circuit, the gain is simply selected from the table, over a range of 1 to 995 times the differential input. Pin 8 of the National Semiconductor RA201 resistor array is the output, and pin 9 is either returned to analog ground, or a variable voltage (from a low-impedance source) can be applied to offset the output to a level other than ground.

FET-Input Instrumentation Amplifier

Fig. 7-6 illustrates an amplifier of this type that uses FET-input amplifiers for the A_1 and A_2 stages. The big advantage that a circuit of this type has over those discussed previously is in the dramatic reduction in room-temperature bias currents. It will, however, be somewhat worse than the best bipolar-input stage type in terms of offset voltage drift.

Using 355 devices for A_1 and A_2 will yield a (room temperature) bias current of 200 pA or less; this becomes 50 pA or less if the 355A version is used. Offset voltage is adjustable to zero via the single potentiometer as shown. Offset voltage drift for the 355A op amp can be as high as 10 μV/°C (for two devices) referred to the input.

All resistors are part of National's RA201 resistor array.

OVERALL GAIN	INPUT STAGE GAIN	OUTPUT STAGE GAIN	JUMPER PINS ON RA201
X1	X1	X1	−
X2	X1	X2	5 to 7, 12 to 10
X5	X1	X5	6 to 7, 11 to 10
X10	X10	X1	2 to 15
X20	X10	X2	2 to 15, 5 to 7, 12 to 10
X50	X10	X5	2 to 15, 6 to 7, 11 to 10
X100	X100	X1	1 to 16
X200	X100	X2	1 to 16, 5 to 7, 12 to 10
X500	X100	X5	1 to 16, 6 to 7, 11 to 10
X995	X199	X5	1 to 14, 6 to 7, 11 to 10

Courtesy National Semiconductor Corp.

Fig. 7-5. Gain-programmable instrumentation amplifier with differential preamp.

This circuit has the unique ability to accommodate common-mode voltages to levels as high as the positive supply line (+15 V), a feature of the 355 (or 356) design. Another device that also has this feature is the 353 dual, which can include A_1 and A_2 in a single package. Best common-mode rejection is likely to be realized with a bipolar device for A_3, such as the 308 shown. However, sections of the 347 quad FET op amp can also be efficiently used in this circuit, with the 347A types giving best overall performance.

Guarded FET-Input Femtoampere Instrumentation Amplifier

The circuit of Fig. 7-7 is one optimized from the standpoint of the absolute lowest input currents. Using the AD515 op amp and appropriate construction methods, this circuit is capable of input cur-

Courtesy National Semiconductor Corp.

Fig. 7-6. FET-input instrumentation amplifier.

$$Z_{IN-CM} = 10^{15}\ \Omega \| 0.2pF$$

(ALL RESISTORS OF SAME NUMBER SHOULD BE MATCHED ±0.1%)

(BUFFER A1 BOOSTS COMMON MODE Z_{IN} BY DRIVING CABLE SHIELDS AT COMMON MODE VOLTAGE AND NEUTRALIZING CM CAPACITANCE)

Courtesy Analog Devices, Inc.

Fig. 7-7. Guarded FET-input femtoampere instrumentation amplifier.

rents of 300 fA (0.3 pA) to 75 fA (0.075 pA), depending on the grade of op amp used.

As can be noted in Fig. 7-7, complete guarding is used at the input terminals of the two input amplifiers [including driving the two cases of the devices (pin 8)], as well as circuit guards around terminals 2 and 3. Buffer A_1, an AD510 device, drives the shields of the input cables at the common-mode voltage, which is picked off from the input stage by resistors R_1. This reduces both the leakage and the effective capacitance in the cables, which should be of the highest quality dielectric, such as Teflon.

Other points that will help maintain the lowest input currents are heat sinks for the two AD515s, reduction of their supply voltages to the minimum required, and minimum output loading by maintaining R_3-R_4 values to 10 kΩ or more. With regard to the gain-determining resistances, these generally are selected as described previously, but they should, of course, be stable types.

7.1.4 Differential-Input Amplifier With High Common-Mode Range

In some situations it may be important that a circuit excel in one regard, even if another parameter is sacrificed. Such an example is the circuit of Fig. 7-8, a differential-input instrumentation amplifier with a common-mode input range of ± 100 V and a unity signal gain.

This circuit trades off input loading in return for a higher common-mode range and reduced common-mode errors. Both A_1 and A_2 are used as inverting stages; thus, both have a characteristically low input impedance, in this case the values of R_1 and R_7, or 49.9 kΩ. A virtue of the inverting configuration is the fact that there is no common-mode voltage applied to the amplifier input terminals; therefore, no error can exist due to variations in this parameter.

*Matching of ratios R_3/R_4 and R_1/R_7 determines CMRR.

Fig. 7-8. Instrumentation amplifier with common-mode range of ± 100 V.

The circuit is a combination inverting attenuator and scaling adder which rejects common-mode input components while amplifying differential ones. A_1 amplifies signal E_a by a factor of $-R_3/R_1$, or in this case $-1/10$. This signal is combined with E_b at summer A_2. E_b is passed to the output with a gain of $-R_6/R_7$, or -1, while E_a is amplified a second time by $-R_6/R_4$, or -10. The total gain for the E_a signal is then $(-1/10)(-10) = +1$. The resultant gain from both inputs to the output is therefore unity, with signs as shown. A common-mode signal, however, becomes cancelled in stage A_2; it will appear at A_2 as equal and opposite signals, summing to zero. Differential inputs are amplified by the ratio R_6/R_7.

For this circuit to work, the matching of resistor ratios is again critical and should be maintained as shown by the tolerances indicated, with resistor pairs matched as shown. Note that A_1 must scale down the common-mode input voltage linearly; therefore, the ratio of R_3/R_1 must be selected to attenuate the common-mode input voltage to ± 10 V or less at the output of A_1.

Gain can be adjusted by varying R_6, since the CMRR will not be affected as long as $R_3/R_4 = R_1/R_7$. Low TC resistors should be used for all resistances (except possibly R_2 and R_5), to maintain good thermal stability of gain and CMRR. Due to the wide bandwidth (approximately 1 MHz), rf bypassing of the power supply is also recommended. If wide bandwidth is not required, conventional inverters, such as 741s, may be used for A_1-A_2. Many duals will also work well here, and FET units will allow large values for R_1-R_7. Single-supply types, such as the 358 or 3240, can also be useful.

7.1.5 Instrumentation Amplifier With High Input Impedance

A circuit with high input impedance using only two amplifiers is illustrated in Fig. 7-9. Like the previous circuit, it uses a combination of inversion and a summation to cancel the common-mode component at the two inputs. In this case, however, a combination of follower configurations also provides an extremely high input impedance.

A_1 amplifies E_b by a factor of $(R_1 + R_2)/R_1$ (in this case, $101/100$). The signal is further amplified by A_2, which operates as an inverter for signals from A_1. The stage gain of A_2 is $-R_4/R_3$ (in this case $-100/1.0 = -100$). The overall gain to the E_b signal is, therefore, the product of both stage gains, or $(1.01)(-100) = -101$.

For signals at E_a, A_2 operates as a follower with a gain of $(R_3 + R_4)/R_3 = 101$. Therefore, the overall gain for E_a is $+101$, exactly equal and opposite that for E_b. If a common-mode signal appears at both inputs, it will be amplified by equal and opposite amounts and cancelled at the output of A_2.

Note that because of the gain relationships of this circuit, high differential gains provide the most effective common-mode rejection due

$$E_o = (E_a - E_b)\left(\frac{R_3 + R_4}{R_3}\right)$$

$$A_v = \frac{R_1 + R_1}{R_3}$$

$$R_1 = R_4$$

$$R_2 = R_3$$

* Matching of ratios R_1/R_2 and R_4/R_3 determines CMRR.

** Optional—can be used to adjust gain without altering CMRR.

Fig. 7-9. Instrumentation amplifier with high input impedance.

to the relative boost in signal/noise ratio. The circuit as shown can accommodate ± 10-V common-mode inputs while amplifying a ± 100-mV signal. The optional trim potentiometer, R_5, can be used to adjust gain, since it does not affect the CMRR.

As before, resistor ratio matching is critical to good common-mode rejection. Common-mode rejection is also dependent on the op amp used; therefore, devices with a good CMRR characteristic, such as the 308A (typically 110 dB), are desirable. The 308 amplifiers use shunt compensation (C_1 and C_2) to reduce their susceptibility to power-supply-induced noise. The circuit bandwidth is approximately 5 kHz, and can be extended by reducing the value of C_2 for stage A_2. This should be done, if possible, as it improves the ac CMRR.

Note that the offset voltage *match* between the two amplifiers is most critical to this circuit. The dc CMRR match is also critical. Amplifiers with matched input characteristics, such as the many dual bipolar-input types, will thus work very well in this type of circuit. Some examples are the OP-10, OP-04, OP-14, 3500MP, and general-purpose duals such as the 4558, 4559, and 358.

If suitable high-CMRR FET-input op amps are used, this circuit can also be an effective, very-high-input-impedance configuration, with minimal source loading. A dual AD642K device can, for example, achieve a 25-pA or less input current, with a 76-dB or better CMRR, while achieving a 0.5-mV offset. For single-supply use, a 3240 can handle 0 to +10-V ranges with a few pA of input current.

7.1.6 High-Gain, Wide-Bandwidth Instrumentation Amplifier

There are alternate methods of achieving high common-mode rejection that are worth noting. Although not based entirely on op-amp theory, the circuit of Fig. 7-10 is one such example. Q_1 and Q_2 in this circuit are matched monolithic transistors, used as an emitter-coupled pair biased by constant-current sources Q_3 and Q_4. Since the output impedance of a current source such as Q_3 or Q_4 is extremely high, it raises the common-emitter impedance of Q_1 and Q_2. As a result, neither Q_1 nor Q_2 will have significant gain for a signal applied to both bases. Therefore, this stage by itself possesses a fairly high common-mode rejection.

Differential signals applied to Q_1 and Q_2 appear across R_g and are amplified by a factor inversely proportional to the value of R_g, since the signal current flowing in R_g appears doubled in R_8. Common-mode signals are attenuated by the Q_1-Q_2 stage by a factor of 60 dB or more, and appear at the input to A_1 as a common-mode signal from Q_1-Q_2. Since this signal has already undergone a rejection in Q_1-Q_2, the balance of this bridge is not as critical—allowing 1.0% resistor tolerances. R_5 serves to null the output of A_1 when no input is present.

A unique feature is the stable, temperature-independent gain, even though Q_1 and Q_2 are not within a feedback loop. This is provided for by D_1 and Q_3-Q_4, with an output current that varies with temperature, complementing the change in transconductance of Q_1-Q_2 with temperature. The result is a gain characteristic that varies less than 1.0% over a temperature range of 0°C to +70°C.

The circuit bandwidth is limited to approximately 2 MHz by the response of A_1. The circuit can handle common-mode input voltages

*R_g varied to adjust input sensitivity and gain; can be greater than 200 kΩ if attenuation desired.

Fig. 7-10. High-gain, wide-bandwidth instrumentation amplifier.

up to ±10 V, but the differential-input range (or sensitivity) is proportional to R_g. As R_g is lowered, gain is increased and less input voltage is required for full-scale output. The range of linear gain is slightly over 40 dB—at lower values of R_g, the effect of emitter resistance in Q_1 and Q_2 begins to produce nonlinearities in the full-scale input.

7.1.7 High-Gain, Low-Drift Instrumentation Amplifier

The circuit of Fig. 7-11 is similar to that of Fig. 7-10, but uses an LM121 precision preamplifier to achieve low input currents. It also does not use overall feedback, but can still achieve a gain stability of ±2% over a temperature range of −55°C to +125°C, and 1.0% linearity for a ±10-mV range of input signals. Gain is 1000 (60 dB) and bandwidth is on the order of 5 kHz.

Courtesy National Semiconductor Corp.

Fig. 7-11. High-gain, low-drift instrumentation amplifier.

Due to the very high gain of the LM121 input-stage transistors, the input current of this amplifier will be 30 nA or less. For best results, the 3-MΩ resistors should be well matched. Gain can be trimmed by adjustment of R_4, and offset voltage nulled by R_3. When the offset is nulled, this circuit will have its minimum offset voltage drift, which will be no more than 0.2 $\mu V/°C$ using the LM121A; 1.0 $\mu V/°C$ using the LM121.

7.1.8 High-Accuracy, Gain-Programmable Instrumentation Amplifier

The circuit of Fig. 7-12 combines a number of very useful performance features in such a way as to result in an attractive, highly accurate design. Gain can be linearly programmed over a 60-dB range with one resistor, and most performance parameters are quite noteworthy.

This circuit combines the basic differential-pair principle of Fig. 7-10, but adds a twist in the form of overall feedback to the emitter. As can be noted from the table, almost all performance parameters are superior. Note that most parameters also improve with the higher gain settings, where such a circuit would most likely be necessary. Offset voltage is trimmed by R_9 in such a way that minimum offset drift occurs when the offset voltage is nulled. For lowest drift, all close-tolerance (0.1%) resistors should track to the levels indicated.

7.1.9 Simple Op-Amp Instrumentation Amplifier

The circuit of Fig. 7-13 is an example of an instrumentation amplifier with remarkable simplicity, yet good performance.

This circuit uses a FET-input amplifier in a mode that applies feedback to the internal current mirror via pin 5 and R_1. A similar value resistor, R_2, is connected from pin 1 to ground to maintain dc balance. The 10-ohm resistors used for R_3 and R_4 shunt internal resistors to provide more predictable performance (used in this manner).

Gain is set up over a range of 100 to 1000 by the expression shown. R_2 is normally connected to the output analog ground point, but may be returned to a variable dc voltage with low source impedance to reference the output to another potential. The gain coefficient from the R_2 input node to the output is unity. As shown, the gain is 700, and the circuit accepts inputs over a ±10-V common-mode range, with linearity of 0.1% or better.

7.2 COMPOSITE AMPLIFIERS

Although present day IC op-amp devices achieve superlative performance specifications in many regards, there are unique applications that can demand simultaneous high performance in different areas, which are basically incompatible with the current state of the art. An example of this is the high-speed amplifier with ultralow offset voltage and/or offset voltage drift.

Fortunately, *composite-amplifier* techniques can be used to "marry" two op amps, with each possessing notable performance in the two areas desired. Such amplifiers can be quite powerful tools, as they allow the tradeoffs that inevitably exist in circuits to be bypassed, at the expense of slightly increased parts count and complexity. This section will discuss a number of circuits of this type.

7.2.1 Fast Integrator

The fast integrator circuit of Fig. 7-14 is useful to start this discussion, as it employs a number of pertinent application details.

Performance Characteristics

	G = 10,000	G = 1,000	G = 100	G = 10	
Linearity of Gain (±10V Output)	≤ 0.01	≤ 0.01	≤ 0.02	≤ 0.05	%
Common-Mode Rejection Ratio (60 Hz)	≥ 120	≥ 120	≥ 110	≥ 90	dB
Common-Mode Rejection Ratio (1 kHz)	≥ 110	≥ 110	≥ 90	≥ 70	dB
Power Supply Rejection Ratio					
+ Supply	> 110	> 110	> 110	> 110	dB
− Supply	> 110	> 110	> 90	> 70	dB
Bandwidth (−3 dB)	50	50	50	50	kHz
Slew Rate	0.3	0.3	0.3	0.3	V/µs
Offset Voltage Drift**	≤ 0.25	≤ 0.4	≤ 2	≤ 10	µV/°C
Common-Mode Input Resistance	> 10^9	> 10^9	> 10^9	> 10^9	Ω
Differential Input Resistance	> 3×10^8	> 3×10^8	> 3×10^8	> 3×10^8	Ω
Input Referred Noise (100 Hz ≤ f ≤ 10 kHz)	5	6	12	70	$\frac{nV}{\sqrt{Hz}}$
Input Bias Current	75	75	75	75	nA
Input Offset Current	1.5	1.5	1.5	1.5	nA
Common-Mode Range	±11	±11	±11	±10	V
Output Swing (R_L = 10 kΩ)	±13	±13	±13	±13	V

**Assumes ≤ 5 ppm/°C tracking of resistors

$$*\text{Gain} = \frac{10^6}{R_S}$$

Fig. 7-12. High-accuracy, gain-programmable instrumentation amplifier.

Fig. 7-13. Simple op-amp instrumentation amplifier.

In this circuit, A_1 is operated as an integrator and A_2 as an inverter, ac-coupled to the summing point formed at R_1, R_4, R_S, and C_L. A_1 provides dc and low-frequency gain up to 500 Hz. Since A_1 is dc-connected to the (+) input of A_2, the dc gains of A_1 and A_2 are cascaded, and thus can easily be over 150 dB. Furthermore, since A_1 sees no load in dc terms, and A_2 furnishes the output load current, there can be no thermal change in offset due to output loading. Thus,

Courtesy National Semiconductor Corp.

Fig. 7-14. Fast integrator using composite amplifier.

the circuit is optimum from the standpoint of preserving the dc stability of A_1.

A_2 amplifies signals at high frequencies, in this case above 80 Hz, as set by R_3-C_3. The 101A op amp is used in this instance to achieve its feedforward-mode high speed, a 10-V/μs slew rate, and 10-MHz bandwidth. Note that the bias current of A_2 is isolated from the summing point, thus the net bias current is determined by A_1.

As a composite amplifier, this circuit has the input offset voltage, bias current, and drift of A_1, but the speed and drive capability of A_2. Note that the bias current, offset voltage, and drift of A_2 are not material to overall operation. Offset voltage adjustment is not shown in this example but can be accommodated by a small voltage at the ($+$) input of A_1, or by substituting a comparable offset-nullable device for A_1, such as the 112 (or 312).

Using the devices as shown the bias current is 2 nA or less. This can be reduced by employing an LM11 for A_1, which will lower the bias current to 50 pA maximum, with a 300-μV maximum offset voltage (adjustable to zero). The 308 (308A) and 301A commercial temperature range (0°C to +70°C) amplifiers can also be used in this circuit.

. The D_1-D_4 diode clamping network shown is not necessary for basic operation of this composite amplifier, but should be seriously considered, particularly for an integrator. Because of the very high dc gain of the loop, overload and subsequent recovery problems should be borne in mind. This is generally true of most composite amplifiers (not just this example), and serious attention should be given to preventing overload, or minimizing its consequences. Integrators such as A_1 might best be clamped with reverse-connected diodes across C_1, for example, to prevent possible latch-up modes.

7.2.2 High-Speed Inverting Amplifier

The circuit of Fig. 7-15 is a more general type of amplifier, where the feedback connection is resistive and is suitable for inverting use at high output levels and rates.

The first stage of this circuit is similar to that of Fig. 7-14, except that a low offset, low drift device is used, the 308A-1, with 1.0 μV/°C maximum drift and 500 μV maximum offset. High slew rate (70 V/μs) and GBP (15 MHz) is achieved by using a 318 device for the output stage.

7.2.3 Very-High-Speed Inverting Amplifier

The circuit of Fig. 7-16 is useful at even higher speeds, as it employs a 5195 in the output. This device has a 200 V/μs slew rate, a GBP of

Courtesy National Semiconductor Corp.

Fig. 7-15. High-speed inverting amplifier.

150 MHz, and can settle to a 0.01% level in 100 ns for a 5-V output step. The device uses ±15-V supplies as shown, but rated output is a ±5-V swing.

A_1 of this circuit is a 5105 FET-input op amp, which has a maximum offset voltage of 1.5 mV and can be optionally nulled as shown.

With R_1 and R_2 values as shown, the circuit is an inverting video amplifier with a gain of 4. It can also be used as a current-to-voltage converter for high-speed digital-to-analog output-buffer uses, with minor changes. For use as a current-to-voltage converter, the current source drive is connected directly to the summing point, R_1 is connected to ground, and the value of R_2 becomes 1.0 kΩ. With a 0- to −5-mA drive from a high-speed digital-to-analog converter, the output voltage range becomes 0 to +5 V.

7.2.4 Medium-Speed Inverter

The inverting composite amplifier of Fig. 7-17 is capable of the basic speed of the 351 amplifier, or 13 V/μs, and has a settling time of 8 μs to 0.01%, for a 10-V step change.

In this circuit, A_1 is the precision dc amplifier, an LM11C. This device will provide a bias current of less than 100 pA and an offset voltage of 600 μV or less. It drives the inverting balance pin of the 351 (pin 1) through a 47-kΩ resistor, R_5. To retain dc balance in the 351, another 47-kΩ resistor, R_6, is connected from pin 5 to ground.

For lowest bias current, particularly at high temperature, A_2 is ac-coupled to the summing node by C_1. Because of this, the 1.0-nA

Fig. 7-16. Very-high-speed inverting amplifier with low dc errors.

high-temperature bias current of the 351 is not seen by the circuit as an error. However, a tradeoff involved with this factor is a relatively long overload recovery. If this is a serious drawback, it can be eliminated by direct coupling A_2 to the summing node. Note that with low-value resistances such as R_1-R_2 (values as shown), even a 1.0-nA

Fig. 7-17. Medium-speed, high-accuracy inverter.

bias current is not a problem, as it produces only a 5-μV error in offset voltage.

7.2.5 High-Accuracy, Low-Bias-Current Follower

The circuit of Fig. 7-18 operates similarly to that of Fig. 7-17, but is arranged as a follower. It will have the low bias current and offset voltage of the LM11C and, in addition, the low-frequency CMRR will be 110 dB or more. An option shown for this circuit is the dc offset trim method for the LM11 type (which can also be adapted to the circuit of Fig. 7-17).

This circuit also ac-couples the A_2 stage to minimize bias currents. As such, it also exhibits a relatively long overload recovery time and should not be driven outside its common-mode range of ±10 V. Direct coupling of A_2 will eliminate this at the expense of an increased high temperature bias current, as mentioned previously. Settling time of the circuit is 10 μs to a 0.01% accuracy level for a 10-V step input.

Fig. 7-18. High-accuracy, low-bias-current follower.

7.2.6 Ultralow Offset High-Speed Inverter

The circuit of Fig. 7-19 is a much simplified form of composite inverting amplifier, optimized for very low offset and high speed.

As can be noted, both A_1 and A_2 in this circuit are directly coupled to the summing point. A_1 is a low-speed device, selected for its very low offset voltage—75 μV maximum for the OP-07E. A_2 is a high-speed FET-input unit, selected for its high slew rate and GBP—60

V/μs and 26 MHz, respectively, for the OP-17; slightly less if the similar 357 device is used.

A_1 drives the (+) input of A_2 through a ×1000 attenuator, R_3-R_4. This attenuator rolls off excessive ac gain from A_1, and provides an offset-null range for A_2 which will accommodate even the worst grade 357 devices, with an offset of ±10 mV.

The net offset of the circuit is that of A_1 which can be very low for the OP-07 or 714 devices—150 μV or less. Other units which may be useful for A_1 are the 308A-1 (or 308A), the 312, the LH0044, and the AD517.

Fig. 7-19. Ultralow offset high-speed inverter.

7.2.7 General-Purpose Composite Amplifier

The composite amplifier of Fig. 7-20 is a more general-purpose one and can be adapted for either inverting or noninverting modes of use over a wide range of gains.

This circuit gets its general-purpose capability by virtue of the drive method used to offset A_2. Rather than driving the (+) input of A_2, the balance input (pin 1) is driven. This allows *both* inputs of A_1 and A_2 to be directly paralleled, permitting full differential operation. The balance networks, R_1-R_3 and R_4-R_6, are chosen so that a ±10-mV offset device can be used for A_2, and A_1 will still be able to adjust the balance of the composite so that the net offset is equal to that of A_1.

As the circuit is shown, it is connected as a noninverting gain-of-11 stage by virtue of the values chosen for R_{in} and R_f. However, it can be readily rescaled for other working gains from a minimum of 4 upward. Gain-bandwidth is determined by A_2 and is 20 MHz for the 357 device, which also has a 50 V/μs slew rate. A 356 device can also be used for A_2 if gains less than 5 are required. If the 356 is used, C_1 should be increased to 4700 pF. In either case, using the 356 or the

Fig. 7-20. General-purpose composite amplifier.

357, the value of C_1 can be trimmed for best settling-time characteristics when this factor is important to the application.

7.3 PERFORMANCE ENHANCEMENT OF OP AMPS

Closely allied to composite amplifiers are methods to augment or enhance certain individual performance characteristics of op amps. Although there are not many differences between the two techniques in that they both improve performance, performance enhancement as we will describe it here encompasses a variety of useful tricks, some more complicated than others, but all useful.

7.3.1 Precision Op Amp With Low-Drift Input Stage

One of the more direct means of increasing op-amp performance with regard to offset voltage and drift is to place a preamplifier stage ahead of a more standard device. A circuit of this type is shown in Fig. 7-21.

In this circuit, an LM194 super-matched transistor pair is used as a differential preamplifier ahead of an LM112 op amp. The LM194 is loaded with a matched precision resistor pair at the two collectors, and frequency compensation is provided by C_1 and C_2 to shape the overall frequency response of the two-stage amplifier, rolling off the gain at 6 dB/octave.

As might be expected from cascading two stages, the dc gain of this op amp is very high—128 dB or more. The output stage buffers any loading effects from the input pair due to the thermal isolation between input and output.

As can be noted from the performance specifications listed, the amplifier has a very low offset voltage and offset voltage drift. To

Fig. 7-21. Precision op amp with low-drift input stage.

achieve the drift of 0.2 μV/$°$C, the LM194 pair should be nulled with potentiometer R_1 as shown, and a matched pair used for R_2 and R_3. Furthermore, the output amplifier should have a reasonably low offset drift (15 μV/$°$C or less), or it can indirectly contribute to nonideal drift. The CMRR of the circuit is very high (120 dB or more) due to the precise match of the LM194. Bias current is typically 25 nA or less, and offset current is only 0.5 nA.

The slew rate and f_t of the amplifier will be inversely proportional to C_1 and C_2 if C_C is varied for different closed-loop gains, as in the table. At unity-gain compensation ($C_C = 200$ pF), the slew rate is less than 0.1 V/μs, and f_t is about 0.25 MHz.

*See table for frequency compensation.

*Table of Typical Values for the Two Compensating
Capacitors (C_C) for Various Operating Conditions

$$C_C = \frac{8 \times 10^{-6}}{A_{cl}\, R_{SET}}†$$

A_{cl}	R_{SET}				
	120 kΩ	60 kΩ	30 kΩ	12 kΩ	6 kΩ
$A_v = 1$	68 pF	130 pF	270 pF	680 pF	1300 pF
$A_v = 5$	15 pF	27 pF	56 pF	130 pF	270 pF
$A_v = 10$	10 pF	15 pF	27 pF	68 pF	130 pF
$A_v = 50$	1.0 pF	3 pF	5 pF	15 pF	27 pF
$A_v = 100$	–	1.0 pF	3 pF	5 pF	10 pF
$A_v = 500$	–	–	1.0 pF	1.0 pF	3 pF
$A_v = 1000$	–	–	–	–	–
I_{ib}	7 nA	15 nA	30 nA	60 nA	150 nA
Gain (121)	10	20	40	100	200

† $R_{SET} \cong R_1, R_2$ (nominal)

Fig. 7-22. Precision op amp using low-drift IC preamplifier.

7.3.2 Precision Op Amp Using Low-Drift IC Preamplifier

A somewhat easier to implement approach to the precision op amp is to use a prepackaged and specified preamplifier device, such as the LM121–LM321 series. A general circuit configuration useful for this device is shown in Fig. 7-22.

In this circuit, the general rationale behind the use is similar to that of the circuit of Fig. 7-21, but the LM121 device allows somewhat easier and more predictable operation, as it is a self-contained, complete preamplifier with bias circuit and load resistors. It is simply connected ahead of a differential-input op amp as shown. The user must select the appropriate compensation capacitance and the bias-current resistance, R_{SET}.

R_{SET} is the resistance from pins 5 and 6 to V−, and should be in the range of 120 kΩ to 6 kΩ. With R_{SET} at 120 kΩ, the input bias current is less than 10 nA, while at 6 kΩ it rises to 150 nA (see the table). The operating gain of the LM121 stage varies with R_{SET} from a low of 10 to a high of 200 (again, see the table). R_{SET} is selected to provide a mutually suitable bias current and a preamplifier gain high enough to be useful (it should be high to reduce the effects of the output op amp).

With the values shown in Fig. 7-22, R_{SET} is 60 kΩ, so the bias current will be 15 nA and the preamplifier will provide a gain of 20.

With R_{SET} selected, C_C is then selected from the table in accordance with the anticipated closed-loop gain. In the circuit shown, for example, C_C should be 130 pF for unity-gain stability, or it can be removed for gains of 100 or more. The LM121A is the premium device of this series and has a drift of 0.2 μV/°C (or less) after nulling. The LM121 has a drift of 1.0 μV/°C, while the LM321A and LM321 provide similar performance over a 0°C to 70°C temperature range.

7.3.3 Precision Op Amp Using FET Preamplifier

Using techniques similar to those previously described, it is also possible to incorporate FET differential-pair preamplifiers ahead of standard op amps. Compared to bipolar-input preamplifiers, the large advantage gained by a FET preamplifier is a dramatic reduction in input currents. Furthermore, this lowering of input currents can be maintained over a broader range of temperatures since there is minimal dissipation in the FET devices, whereas in an IC op amp the dissipation effects can be serious, even at moderate ambient temperatures.

A relatively simple example of this type of circuit is shown in Fig. 7-23. Here, a monolithic n-channel JFET device is used—the

2N6483. This device is specifically designed for this type of application and features controlled offset, drift, and CMRR specifications.

In this circuit, the 2N6483 pair is loaded by a matched pair of 15-$k\Omega$ resistors and drives a standard 741 op amp as the output stage. Compensation is provided by C_1 and C_2, which results in an f_t on the order of 300 kHz with the values shown.

The 2N6483 device has the tightest specifications of its series. It has a maximum offset voltage of 5 mV, and an offset voltage drift of 5 $\mu V/°C$. The offset voltage can be adjusted to zero with the 1.0-$k\Omega$ potentiometer as shown. A constant drain current of 400 μA is provided by the LM334 current source, and R_6, R_7, and D_1.

The input bias current of the 2N6483 is dependent upon the drain to gate potential or, as used here, the common-mode voltage. Over a common-mode range to -10 V, it typically will be 10 pA or less (at room temperature). The input currents will double with each 10°C increase in temperature.

Increased CMRR in a FET preamplifier can be realized by using cascode-connected matched devices, such as the National Semicon-

Fig. 7-23. Precision op amp using FET preamplifier.

ductor NDF9406 (which will operate in the circuit shown), a device that can achieve a CMRR of 120 dB. Lower bias currents (1.0 pA or less) can be obtained by using lower input-current devices, such as the 2N5902 or 2N5906. Of course with these circuits (as well as the one of Fig. 7-23), guarding techniques must be used to screen off stray leakages. The other appropriate construction methods for low current levels should also be used (see Chapter 3).

7.3.4 Bias-Current Compensation

Although there are a large number of IC FET-input amplifiers currently available that have very low bias currents (on the order of tens of picoamperes), there are very good reasons why bias-current compensation may still be desirable. Bias-current compensation (or cancellation) is most applicable to bipolar-input op amps, which will have typical bias currents in the range of 1.0 nA to 100 nA. Two basic reasons make bias-current reduction desirable for bipolar amplifiers: one is that bipolars tend to have lower offset voltage drift (10 μV/°C or less); and FET-amplifier bias currents *increase* with temperature, whereas bipolar-amplifier bias currents *decrease* with temperature. This latter point can result in a FET-input device with a 10-nA input current at (say) 70°C, where a bipolar device can be held to below 1.0 nA. It is not at all difficult to reach 70°C *junction* temperature in ICs with moderate dissipation, even in relatively modest environments.

Some simple and effective schemes for compensating bias currents have been described by Widlar,[*] and their usefulness is illustrated in Figs. 7-24 and 7-25.

In inverting amplifiers, the bias compensation is most simple, as there is no common-mode voltage and the compensating voltage can be referred to ground. Two variations of a scheme for compensating integrators for lowest bias current (and thus lowest drift) are shown in Fig. 7-24.

In Fig. 7-24A, a medium-bias-current device, such as the 301A (80 nA), is compensated by R_1, which is returned to a variable voltage from R_2. This voltage is derived from a forward-biased diode, thus it will tend to track the bias current (which decreases as the temperature rises). R_1 is selected to provide the worst-case bias current for the IC in use (if different), and either R_2 can be adjusted, or the value of R_1 can be trimmed. For pnp-input amplifiers, the diode and supply voltage should be reversed.

Trimming is a necessary evil with these circuits since the IC bias currents are not precisely known. Compensation can be expected to

---

[*] See references 28 and 29 at the end of the chapter.

provide a 5 to 10 times reduction in bias current over a limited temperature range.

With amplifiers that have very low initial bias currents, such as the 308 types, the resistance values can easily become troublesome in the circuit of Fig. 7-24A. The variation of Fig. 7-24B divides down the diode voltage to 50 mV, which allows a more reasonable value for R_1 to be used. This division scheme effectively multiplies the value of R_1, and can be adapted to other circuits as well.

A bias-current-compensated follower is shown in Fig. 7-25A, and uses a bootstrapped pnp transistor to provide a floating current source via R_1. R_1 can be trimmed for compensation, or a potentiometer used as in Fig. 7-24A. For simplicity, a diode can be used for Q_1 also, but the pnp transistor minimizes loading on the op amp. For pnp-input op amps, use an npn transistor returned to V−.

In a noninverting amplifier, the transistor method of deriving the compensating current is very useful, as shown in Fig. 7-25B. The base of Q_1 is returned to the (−) input, which bootstraps R_1 as in Fig. 7-25A. The low base current of the pnp will not introduce large errors if the values of R_3 and R_4 are maintained relatively low. R_1 is trimmed for compensation in this circuit to avoid error currents in R_3 and R_4.

Two alternate methods of bias-current compensating a follower for high common-mode inputs are shown in Fig. 7-26. In Fig. 7-26A a scheme for providing a bias current for npn inputs is shown using a transistor array—the CA3096.

(A) Medium-bias-current types. (B) Low-bias-current types.

Fig. 7-24. Bias-current compensation—inverting amplifiers (integrators).

Here, the npn transistor of the array (Q_3) is forced to conduct a base current that will be nominally equal to the bias current to be compensated. The pnp current mirror returns this current to the (+) input of the op amp, resulting in the desired compensation. A drawback of this scheme is that it is not regulated against the supply volt-

(A) Unity-gain amplifier (follower).

(B) Gain-of-11 amplifier.

Fig. 7-25. Bias-current compensation—noninverting amplifiers.

age. (Not as shown, but it can be so adapted by using a zener connection for one of the remaining CA3096 devices.) R_1 is trimmed for compensation.

A version of this circuit useful for pnp inputs is shown in Fig. 7-26B. It works similarly, but with an npn current mirror.

Both of these circuits are really general-purpose ones, and can accommodate followers or inverters. The circuit of Fig. 7-26B can also accommodate *differential* op-amp inputs (with two compensation

(A) Npn inputs.

(B) Pnp inputs.

Fig. 7-26. Alternate bias-current compensation methods for high common-mode inputs.

currents) by adding a second npn current-source transistor to the current mirror, with an additional 1.0-kΩ emitter resistor.

7.3.5 Bias-Current Cancellation Using Matched Amplifiers

Some of the more effective methods of minimizing bias currents come about when *matched* amplifiers are used. Basically, such methods take advantage of the fact that all input bias currents in a multiple IC op amp will be matched within a few percent. The bias current of one amplifier of a dual or a quad device can then be used as a reference to develop a compensating current which effectively cancels the bias current of another amplifier on the same chip. Although the degree of compensation might be somewhat better than the more general methods described previously, the real attractiveness of this method is in the fact that it does not require trimming for good results (whereas the others do).

In Fig. 7-27A, a scheme is shown that uses one section of a 348 (or other npn-input multiple device) to cancel the bias current of a second section. In this circuit, a reference current of I_{ib} is set up in a resistor of a value 2R, which flows into the $(+)$ input of a 348 section, A_1. A resistor of value R connected to the $(-)$ input will then cause a current of $2I_{ib}$ to flow, since the inputs of A_1 will assume the same voltage.

With a high-gain pnp, such as a 2N5087 connected as shown, $1I_{ib}$ flows into the reference amplifier, A_1, and $1I_{ib}$ flows from the collector of Q_1 into the second amplifier, A_2, where its bias current is cancelled.

Although A_2 is shown here connected as a follower, it can actually be either inverting or noninverting, with the bias current fed to the appropriate input. For high common-mode range uses, the R and 2R resistances should be returned to a voltage *higher* than the greatest input expected, which will typically be more than $+10$ V. This voltage must be 1.0 V or more less than $V+$, as noted. The absolute value of the two reference resistors is not critical, but they should be selected to drop about 50 mV with the typical amplifier bias current flowing, to swamp out any differences in offset voltage.

The pnp-input scheme to cancel bias currents in Fig. 7-27B was originally developed by Frederiksen* for the 324 op amp. This device can operate with its inputs at ground potential in a single-supply mode (or at $V-$ in a dual-supply mode). Thus, the scheme of Fig. 7-27B will cancel the bias current of the A_2 section in a manner similar to that described for the 348. One should note, however, that if this cancellation technique is to operate from a single supply where the R/2R resistances are referred to ground, the input common-mode range of A_2 will no longer include ground, because of Q_1. In such an instance, the common-mode range of A_2 will start at about 0.6 V above ground (or 0.6 V above $V-$, for dual-supply uses).

It should also be noted that this scheme is adaptable to other multiple-device pnp-input amplifiers, such as the 4136, 4558, 4156, HA4741, OP-09, OP-11, etc. In the case of these amplifiers, the R/2R resistor junction should be returned to a voltage analogous to "V_{bias}"

---

* See reference 13 at the end of the chapter.

of Fig. 7-27A but more *negative* than the most negative common-mode input, yet more *positive* than the V− rail. For example, with typical ±15-V supplies and a ±10-V analog range, this would be a voltage in the range of −11 V to −12 V.

It should be noted that this scheme can be particularly attractive with multiple amplifiers with low initial bias current, such as the 158A, for example (20 nA typical bias current), as it can yield a net bias current of only 1.0 nA to 2 nA!

Fig. 7-27. Bias-current cancellation using matched amplifiers.

The scheme of Fig. 7-27C is a more general-purpose one, previously described by the author.* In this circuit, a section from a multiple device functions as a floating current inverter and provides the compensating bias current.

A_1 is the floating current source, which produces a current of $2I_{ib}$ in the resistor of R value. One bias current goes to A_1, the other goes to A_0 and cancels the bias current of A_2.

The interesting thing about this circuit is that A_1 will assume whatever voltage level to which its (+) input is referred, thus, common-mode range problems are not present. Selection criteria for the resistors are generally as outlined previously, and a small bypass capacitor for the 2R resistor will enhance stability.

Note that this scheme is applicable to *any* multiple matched amplifier, with either npn or pnp inputs. It is also obvious that it can be used with either inverting or noninverting modes of A_2 operation. It can also be used with *differential* input operation of A_2 if a second resistor of a value 2R is connected from the output of A_1 to the (−) input of A_2.

7.4 INPUT BUFFERING

A previous section has dealt with methods of designing op-amp preamplifier stages, including a FET-input type. FETs are, of course, the most direct and straightforward way by which amplifier input currents can be reduced, but often other, rather simple circuitry can be used to provide very effective buffering with minimal tradeoffs.

7.4.1 Source-Follower FET-Preamplifier Op Amp

An example of an op-amp input buffer that can be useful under certain circumstances is shown in Fig. 7-28. This circuit is an op amp with a pair of matched FET-input devices to buffer the relatively large bipolar op-amp input-stage currents. The FETs provide no voltage gain, only current gain, reducing the input currents to those of the devices employed. In the case of the NPD8301 device, the typical input current will be 50 pA.

This circuit has the principal advantage of simplicity. Also, since it has no additional voltage gain, and because FETs have little excess phase shift, stability of the op amp is not compromised and no additional compensation is usually needed.

On the minus side, however, there are two drawbacks. One of these is that common-mode rejection is relatively poor, since the FET drain currents vary with the common-mode voltage. This can be improved, however, by replacing the resistors in the source circuits with 200-μA

---

* See reference 15 at the end of the chapter.

current sources. The second disadvantage, which cannot be eliminated (only minimized), is that in this configuration, the offsets, CMRR, and drift of the FET stage and the op amp used add directly. By contrast, the drain-loaded FET preamplifier discussed earlier minimizes the contribution of the second-stage op amp to these factors by essentially reducing them by the gain factor of the preamplifier preceding it. It should be understood, therefore, that this stage may not be a good choice for an input buffer if these input parameters are critical.

Courtesy National Semiconductor Corp.

Fig. 7-28. Source-follower FET-preamplifier op amp.

There are, however, applications where it can be effectively used, which are generally those where offset voltage and drift are not highly important, but low bias current is very important. The circuit can be ·very effective with zero common-mode voltage applications, such as integrators and current-to-voltage converters. Another point is that this configuration also enjoys thermal isolation between the FET pair and the output. But loading conditions that might change the offset voltage of the *op amp* will still be seen in the net input offset.

In the example shown, an NPD8301 is used, which has a maximum offset voltage of 5 mV and a drift of 10 $\mu V/°C$. The 101A op amp adds a 2-mV offset to this, plus a 15-$\mu V/°C$ drift. Offset can be nulled to zero with the 5-kΩ potentiometer as shown. If offset is not used, the two source resistors should be a matched pair (tied to $V-$).

7.4.2 Zero-Offset FET Buffer/Follower

The circuit of Fig. 7-29 is not a general-purpose op amp, but a FET follower configured for low offset and high accuracy.

In this circuit, Q_1 and Q_2 are a well-matched FET differential pair arranged in a totem-pole follower circuit. Q_2 operates as a current source, biasing Q_1 at a constant current. With R_1 equal to R_2, and

Fig. 7-29. Zero-offset FET buffer/follower.

Q_1 and Q_2 matched, this results in nominally zero offset between the input and the bottom of R_2. The op amp preserves the linearity of the configuration by reducing the effective loading of the follower to zero.

As with the previous circuit, the offsets and drifts of the two stages of this circuit add directly. R_2 can be trimmed to adjust the offset if desired. An AD741L low-drift op amp is shown as the output buffer to minimize the offset and drift contribution of this stage.

As shown, the circuit is not a particularly fast one because of the 741. The FET follower *is* itself, however, a fast circuit and more of this speed can be made available to the output by employing a fast buffer, such as the AD509, 318, or 2500 bipolar op amps.

7.4.3 Low-Input-Current/Wide-Bandwidth Inverter

Fig. 7-30 illustrates how the positive characteristics of two different op amps can be blended to capitalize on each. This circuit circumvents the usual low input impedance associated with the inverting configuration.

Fig. 7-30. Inverter with low input current and wide bandwidth.

The circuit is an inverter with a gain of 10, as set by R_2/R_1. A high current output is provided by the 5534 (up to 20 mA), with an overall bandwidth of approximately 1.0 MHz. Very low input current is realized by using the AD544 as a follower to drive the 2-kΩ input resistor—50 pA maximum. Although the offsets and drifts of A_1 and A_2 add in this configuration, they are still low because of the devices chosen, and the offset voltage can be as low as 4 mV maximum (typically even better).

7.5 OUTPUT BUFFERING

One of the more common op-amp buffer requirements is finding means to increase the available load swing in terms of either current or voltage. This section explores various methods of achieving this goal.

Perhaps the most common requirement is to simply increase the available current from an IC op amp. The most direct way is to use a higher-current device, such as the 759, 791, 540, 541, or the 3580. However, another useful circuit is a general-purpose unity-voltage-gain *buffer,* which can be used with any IC op amp to increase its current output to, say, ±100 mA at ±10 V. Two circuits useful for this purpose are shown in Figs. 7-31 and 7-32.

In Fig. 7-31, a discrete output buffer that can be used with any op amp is shown. It is intended to be used within the feedback loop (as shown), and can deliver outputs up to ±100 mA into a 100-ohm load. Output impedance is 10 ohms.

This type of circuit is relatively simple, but it can cause problems if certain points are not considered. To provide a sufficient drive current to the output devices, Q_1 and Q_2, fixed-current-source biasing is used (Q_3 and Q_4). These transistors run at a constant 4 mA, and do not load the driving op amp as the commonly used resistors to V+ and V— would. D_1 and D_2 are thermally coupled to Q_1 and Q_2, respectively, and provide temperature-tracked forward bias for minimum crossover distortion. The idle current in Q_1 and Q_2 is set by the ratio of R_4 to R_7 (and R_5 to R_8). In this circuit, Q_1 and Q_2 idle at just over twice the current in D_1 and D_2. R_7 and R_8 also provide short-circuit protection for Q_1 and Q_2, which are 1.0-A high-speed units.

The design can either be used as shown, or tailored for individual uses. The function of R_1 may not be obvious; it is simply to prevent parasitic oscillation in Q_1 and Q_2. Good bypassing of the supplies is mandatory for this circuit, as it will deliver heavy current spikes to the supply buses. C_1 and C_2 should be solid tantalum or other low-impedance at high-frequency capacitor types.

Because of the bias-current regulation for Q_1 and Q_2, this circuit can be used over a ±10-V to ±20-V supply range with little deterioration.

An IC output buffer stage is shown in Fig. 7-32, and can employ either of the two IC types shown for A_2. These units, the Harris Semiconductor HA2635 and the National Semiconductor LH0002CN, are both wideband 100-mA devices. Furthermore, since each one is built on a common substrate, they have low sensitivity to thermal bias drift (a problem which must be considered with the circuit of Fig. 7-31). They may also be used with any op amp, in any configuration, not just the inverting one shown.

Fig. 7-31. Discrete medium-current output buffer.

C_f is a feedback capacitor that should be adjusted for best response with the IC to be used for A_1. The capacitor may have to be connected around A_1 (as optionally shown) in some cases. R_C is a bias compensation resistor, used with bipolar amplifiers.

Since so many multiple IC op amps are readily available, a logical solution to moderate increases in output current is to parallel two or more sections. However, this cannot be done indiscriminately, or disaster will result. When the appropriate precautions are taken with multiple amplifiers, quite useful (and economical) circuits can result.

| | +15 V | | C₁ | |
| Input | C_f | R_f | 1.0 μF | Output |

Fig. 7-32. IC medium-current output buffer.

*A₂ Pin Numbering

	A₂ Device	
Pin	HA2635	LH0002CN
In	3	3
Out	9	8
V +	7	2
V −	2	4
Limit +	8	1
Limit −	1	5

In Fig. 7-33, a configuration by Pease* is shown, which is actually a form of bootstrapping. It operates by combining the outputs of two like amplifiers, to enable impedance loads down to one-half that of the rating to be driven.

---

* See reference 21 at the end of the chapter.

A1, A2 = 1/2 LM747 or 1/2 LF353 or any op-amp.

Courtesy National Semiconductor Corp.

Fig. 7-33. Bootstrapping multiple amplifiers.

As can be noted, A_2 is a noninverting stage, set up for a gain of 1.1; thus, a voltage 1.1 times the output appears at the output of A_2. R_2 is set in value to be $\frac{1}{5}$ the load resistance; here, it is 120 ohms. Since V_{out} appears at one end of R_2, and 1.1 V_{out} appears at the other end, there exists 0.1 V_{out} across R_2. Since R_2 is equal to $\frac{1}{5}$ R_1, R_2 must then conduct one-half the load current, taking half the load burden from A_1.

Note that the conditions just described will exist for various other specific circuit values, as long as the key ratios are satisfied. A_1 can also be other configurations, such as inverting-gain stages. The key is that the (+) input of A_2 and the bottom of R_2 should be returned to the output of A_1 (and R_L).

Fig. 7-34. General technique for paralleling two or more amplifiers.

A more general technique for combining the outputs of two or more amplifiers is shown in Fig. 7-34. Basically, it consists of summing the outputs of a number of op amps through like, small-value resistors (to force equal current distribution).

In Fig. 7-34, A_1 is a voltage amplifier stage, and the follower-connected stages are fed from the output of A_1 and summed into a common load bus. This technique is expanded to as many sections as may be necessary. With individual amplifier ratios of ±5 mA, this will allow a ±20-mA worst-case load current from a quad IC. Typically, much more than this figure can be obtained.

For stability in the presence of difficult loads, an RC damper, such as the 15-ohm/0.047-μF combination, may be necessary for wideband op amps; low-frequency devices, such as the 324 or 348, may not need it.

Fig. 7-35. Multiple noninverting dc amplifier.

Fig. 7-36. Dual output buffer for precision op amp.

An example of this technique applied to a noninverting dc amplifier is shown in Fig. 7-35. This circuit can drive loads of 500 ohms or less to levels of ±10 V with good linearity.

The multiple-amplifier buffer technique can also be useful to increase current capacity and provide thermal isolation between a voltage amplifier and the power-dissipating output stage.

In Fig. 7-36, this idea is shown using a precision op amp, the LM11, as a voltage follower. The LM11 is buffered by a low-cost dual device—the 1458. Overall feedback is connected around A_1-A_2 and the LM11 so that the basic dc accuracy is that of the LM11. The 1458 sections serve only as low-cost current drivers at a cost and simplicity more attractive than most discrete circuits.

Some circuit subtleties to optimize the hookup for other uses are worth mentioning. D_1 and D_2 provide clamping for the output of the LM11 in the case of overdrive, and minimize recovery-time problems as well as tendencies toward latch-up.

The output buffer stage(s) should have more bandwidth and slew rate than the input stage, thus the LM11 is overcompensated by C_1. C_2 can also be used (optionally); it is preferred for stability reasons. Other devices suitable for the input stage are the 308 (and 308A) and the 312, plus other devices that can be overcompensated.

A technique that increases load voltage is to drive the load *differentially*, as shown in Fig. 7-37. Here, A_1 is a noninverting gain-of-5 stage, and A_2 inverts the output of A_1. The result is two equal but out-of-phase voltages across the output, as noted.

In this particular example the 5534 op amp is used, which can supply up to ±7 V across a differentially connected 300-ohm load, or ±20 V across a 1.0-kΩ differential load.

Fig. 7-37. Differential line driver.

With higher-voltage op amps, such as the 541, 2645, or 343, this circuit can deliver up to 100 V p-p to a floating load using ±30-V supplies. Although it is not shown, additional current output can be realized by using parallel connections for A_1 and A_2.

REFERENCES

1. *Applications Manual for Computing Amplifiers.* Philbrick Researches, Inc., Dedham, Mass., 1966.

2. Choice, L. "Drift-Matched IC Op Amps Can Save Money." *Electronics,* May 22, 1972.

3. ———. "Series-Connected Op Amps Null Offset Voltage." *Electronics,* March 27, 1972.

4. Demrow, R. *Evolution from Operational Amplifier to Data Amplifier.* Analog Devices Application Note, September 1968. Analog Devices, Inc., Norwood, Mass.

5. ———. "Op Amps as Electrometers." *Analog Dialogue,* Vol. 5, No. 2, 1971.

6. Dobkin, R. C. *Feedforward Compensation Speeds Op Amp.* National Semiconductor Linear Brief LB-2, March 1969. National Semiconductor Corp., Santa Clara, Calif.

7. ———. *IC Preamp Challenges Choppers on Drift.* National Semiconductor Application Note AN-79, February 1973. National Semiconductor Corp., Santa Clara, Calif.

8. ———. *Instrumentation Amplifier.* National Semiconductor Linear Brief LB-1, March 1969. National Semiconductor Corp., Santa Clara, Calif.

9. ———. *Op Amp Circuit Collection.* National Semiconductor Application Note AN-31, February 1970. National Semiconductor Corp., Santa Clara, Calif.

10. Erdi, G. *A Low Drift, Low Noise Monolithic Operational Amplifier for Low Level Signal Processing.* Fairchild Semiconductor Application Bulletin APP-136, July 1969. Fairchild Semiconductor, Mountain View, Calif.

11. ———. "Minimizing Offset Voltage With Temperature in Monolithic Operational Amplifiers." *Proceedings of the NEC,* Vol. 25, 1969.

12. Fairchild Semiconductor Application Bulletin APP-138, July 1969. *μA725 Instrumentation Applications.* Fairchild Semiconductor, Mountain View, Calif.

13. Frederiksen, T. M. "Multiple-Function LICs." *Proceedings of Electronic Products Magazine LIC Seminar,* March 1973.

14. Fullagar, D. *The 8007—A High-Performance FET-Input Operational Amplifier.* Intersil Application Bulletin A005, March 1972. Intersil, Inc., Cupertino, Calif.

15. Jung, W. G. "Bias-Current Cancellation Easily Implemented With Matched Op Amps." *Electronic Design,* June 21, 1977.

16. ———. *IC Converter Cookbook.* Howard W. Sams & Co., Inc., Indianapolis, 1978, pp. 150–165.

17. National Semiconductor Application Note AN-13, September 1968. *Application of the LH0002 Current Amplifier.* National Semiconductor Corp., Santa Clara, Calif.

18. Nelson, C. T. *Super Matched Bipolar Transistor Pair Sets New Standards for Drift and Noise.* National Semiconductor Application Note AN-222, July 1979. National Semiconductor Corp., Santa Clara, Calif.

19. Ott, W. E. *Combine Two Op Amps to Avoid the Speed-Accuracy Compromise.* Burr-Brown Application Note AN-64, July 1973. Burr-Brown Research Corp., Tucson, Ariz.

20. Patstone, W. "Designing Femtoampere Circuits Requires Special Considerations." *EDN,* July 1, 1972.

21. Pease, R. A. *Get More Power Out of Dual or Quad Op Amps.* National Semiconductor Linear Brief, LB-44, April 1979. National Semiconductor Corp., Santa Clara, Calif.

22. Rudin, M. *Applying Microvolt/Picoamp Instrumentation Operational Amplifiers.* Precision Monolithics Application Note. Precision Monolithics, Inc., Santa Clara, Calif.

23. Sheingold, D. H. (ed.). *Analog-Digital Conversion Handbook.* Analog Devices, Inc., Norwood, Mass., 1972.

24. Soderquist, D.; Erdi, G. *The OP-07 Ultra-Low Offset Voltage Op Amp.* Precision Monolithics Application Note AN-13, December 1975. Precision Monolithics, Inc., Santa Clara, Calif.

25. Tobey, G. E.; Graeme, J. G.; Huelsman, L. P. (eds.). *Operational Amplifiers*—Design and Applications. McGraw-Hill Book Co., New York, 1971.

26. Underwood, R. K. *New Design Techniques for FET Op Amps.* National Semiconductor Application Note AN-63, March 1972. National Semiconductor Corp., Santa Clara, Calif.

27. Widlar, R. J. "Designing With Super-Beta Transistor Op-Amp ICs." *EEE,* December 1969, February and March 1970.

28. ———. *Drift Compensation Techniques for Integrated DC Amplifiers.* National Semiconductor Application Note AN-3, November 1967. National Semiconductor Corp., Santa Clara, Calif.

29. ———. *IC Op Amp Beats FETs on Input Current.* National Semiconductor Application Note AN-29, December 1969. National Semiconductor Corp., Santa Clara, Calif.

30. ———. *Monolithic Operational Amplifiers—The Universal Linear Component.* National Semiconductor Application Note AN-4, April 1968. National Semiconductor Corp., Santa Clara, Calif.

31. Witten, S. *Designing Junction FET Input Op Amps.* Siliconix Application Note AN74-3, August 1974. Siliconix, Inc., Santa Clara, Calif.

32. Manufacturers' Data Sheets:

	AD301AC	Operational Amplifier
	AD515	Operational Amplifier
Analog	AD542	Operational Amplifier
Devices	AD544	Operational Amplifier
	AD545	Operational Amplifier
	AD642	Operational Amplifier
	AD741L	Operational Amplifier
Burr-Brown	3500MP	Operational Amplifier
Harris	2635	Buffer
Semiconductor	5105	Operational Amplifier
	5195	Operational Amplifier
	LF351	Operational Amplifier
	LF355/356/357	Operational Amplifiers
	LH0002	Buffer
	LH0044	Operational Amplifier
National	LM11	Operational Amplifier
Semiconductor	LM121	Preamplifier
	LM308/308A	Operational Amplifiers
	LM324/324A	Operational Amplifiers
	LM394	Supermatched Transistor Pair
	OP-07	Operational Amplifier
	OP-08	Operational Amplifier
Precision	OP-10	Operational Amplifier
Monolithics	OP-14	Operational Amplifier
	OP-16	Operational Amplifier
	OP-17	Operational Amplifier

EIGHT

Comparators

A comparator is a special class of op amp where the device is used to compare voltages between its two inputs. Used in this manner, the op amp operates open-loop; that is, there is no negative feedback applied to the ($-$) input as there is in the classical feedback circuits.

Circuits optimized for comparator use, therefore, need none of the phase/frequency compensation required for op-amp stabilization with feedback. In fact, these compensation components are detrimental in that they slow the response time of the comparator. Although in principle any op amp can be used as a comparator, using a compensated device, such as a 741, for example, will result in a response time in the tens of microseconds, whereas a device optimized for comparator use, such as the 311, will respond in several hundred nanoseconds.

Comparators usually interface at their outputs with digital logic; therefore, using standard op-amp outputs designed for linear ±10-V swings will require some level shifting and/or clamping in order to drive logic.

This chapter will treat the basic application considerations of comparators, how standard devices can be applied as comparators, and give representative application examples.

8.1 BASIC DIFFERENTIAL-INPUT COMPARATOR

A comparator circuit is one that provides an indication of the relative state of two input potentials. If one input is a reference potential and the other an unknown, the comparator output will indicate whether the unknown signal is above or below the reference potential. A basic op-amp comparator circuit is diagrammed in Fig. 8-1A.

In this example, V_{ref} is a positive voltage applied to the inverting input of op amp A_1. E_{in} is the unknown potential, applied to the non-inverting input. When E_{in} is lower than reference voltage V_{ref}, the output of A_1 will be at the negative saturation limit, $-E_{o(sat)}$. As soon as E_{in} rises higher than V_{ref}, the amplifier output flips to the positive saturation limit, $+E_{o(sat)}$. A graph of this transfer characteristic is shown in Fig. 8-1B.

In this circuit, the amplifier is operated in an open-loop condition; therefore, the voltage difference required to change the output from one state to the other is quite small, essentially $[+E_{o(sat)} - (-E_{o(sat)})]/A_{vo}$. Since this voltage is but a few hundred microvolts,

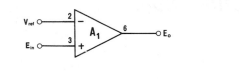

| (A) Schematic. | (B) Output voltage. |

Fig. 8-1. Basic comparator circuit.

the dominating factor that determines the exact threshold is the offset voltage of the amplifier, which may be as great as ± 10 mV in some cases. For this reason, precision comparators should be nulled so that the input-differential voltage is as close to zero as practical when the output is zero. Furthermore, any source resistances in the input path should be selected so as to minimize the offset voltage. Alternatively, a precision low-offset-voltage device with low bias currents can be employed.

It is generally desired that a comparator be capable of changing output states as rapidly as possible. Since comparator circuits normally operate without negative feedback, there is no necessity for frequency compensation, since there is no closed loop to stabilize. Frequency compensation in a comparator is usually detrimental, because it slows down the open-loop speed of the amplifier. A type 741, for example, with a slew rate of 0.5V/μs will require 40 μs to swing from -10 V to $+10$ V, due to its slew-rate limitation. By contrast, a 101 type, which has the same (0.5 V/μs) slew rate when compensated, will have a slew rate of 20 V/μs or greater with the compensation removed, so that it can accomplish the -10-V to $+10$-V swing in 1.0 μs or less.

Removal of frequency compensation also increases the high-frequency gain of the op amp as discussed in Chapter 1. This increases the frequency range over which the comparator will have maximum sensitivity, since a high open-loop gain implies that a small input voltage is required to initiate an output transition.

Comparators are subject to wide differential-input voltage swings, since both V_{ref} and E_{in} may be anywhere within the common-mode input range of ± 10 V. This requires a differential-input voltage rating of at least ± 20 V to accommodate the worst-case limits in a circuit such as Fig. 8-1A. Other comparator configurations can ease this wide voltage-swing requirement as will be seen shortly. Examples of wide differential-input capability in op amps are the 741 and the 301A (± 30 V), and many of the newer FET-input devices, such as the 357 (± 30 V).

Beyond the basic requirement of input-voltage range, speed is the next criterion in selecting op amps suitable for comparators. Speed has two meanings for comparators: response time and slew rate. Response time is simply the total time required for an output transition to occur once an input trigger has arrived. It is specified both for a positive step input (minus to plus) and a negative step input (plus to minus). Slew rate indicates how rapidly the amplifier output can change during a transition. It can also be different for positive- and negative-going slopes.

Fig. 8-2. Test circuit for using op amps as comparators.

Fig. 8-2 is a simple test circuit which can be used to evaluate different op amps, showing response times in a standard condition. It is worth noting that devices having the shortest response times and fastest slew rates are those which normally use the *most* frequency compensation—removing this compensation allows greater inherent bandwidth, or the highest GBP.

Figs. 8-1 and 8-2 are both examples of noninverting comparators; that is, the output has the same direction of polarity as the input. An inverting comparator may be required in some cases, and this configuration is obtained simply by reversing the inputs so that E_{in} is connected to the inverting ($-$) op-amp terminal. In either case, the op amp presents a high impedance to both the V_{ref} and E_{in} sources.

8.2 BASIC SINGLE-ENDED-INPUT COMPARATOR

The differential-input comparator described in the previous section is the most general configuration and the one most often used. Single-ended-input configurations are also possible, however, as illustrated in Fig. 8-3. In this example, both the signal and reference voltages are applied to a common input with the opposite input grounded. R_1 and R_2 form a voltage divider between E_{in} and V_{ref}, and V_{ref} is a voltage of polarity opposite to that of E_{in}. V_{ref} and R_1-R_2 define the threshold value of E_{in} that will cause the voltage at the junction of R_1 and R_2 to cross ground, which changes the state of the comparator. This threshold voltage is $E_{in(th)} = V_{ref}(R_1/R_2)$.

In practice, voltage V_{ref} and resistance R_2 will define a current in R_2 for $E_a = 0$ (trip point); thereafter R_1 can be selected for the desired trip level of E_{in}. Although noninverting operation of the comparator is shown, inverting operation is also possible by reversing the inputs, as in the previous example.

*May be necessary for input overvoltage protection.

(A) Schematic.

(B) Output voltage.

Fig. 8-3. Single-ended comparator.

This comparator has the advantage of being noncritical as to the specific device used for A_1 in regard to differential-input rating. The voltage between the inputs of A_1 will be smaller than E_{in} and V_{ref} by the division of R_1-R_2, and therefore a smaller input rating is tolerable for A_1. This allows use of such op amps as the 709, which is an unprotected type. E_{in} can be unrestricted in magnitude since R_1 can always be selected to scale down this voltage. It is also good practice to add a pair of back-to-back clamp diodes (D_1 and D_2) to constrain the E_a voltage. They add no error in the threshold point, because when $E_a = 0$ at the trip point, both diodes are nonconducting. The diodes can be connected as diagrammed in Fig. 8-3 or applied directly across the inputs for differential clamping. Note that many ICs, such as the 5534, for example, have such diodes built into their input stages. When using such devices, the input resistor(s) *must* be used in order to limit the maximum current when there are large voltage differentials.

8.3 COMPARATORS WITH HYSTERESIS

The comparators described thus far have been basic open-loop types, which amplify an input signal by comparison to a reference voltage. In situations where the input signal is a slowly varying potential (as with dc or very-low-frequency ac), this can be a disadvantage, for the output will also change slowly. This factor comes into play particularly when the output of the comparator is used to trigger a logic stage requiring fast trigger pulses. One solution is the introduction of positive feedback around the comparator, which alters the

(A) Schematic.

(B) Hysteresis loop.

Fig. 8-4. Differential comparator with hysteresis.

output to form a fast "snap" action. Positive feedback is introduced by feeding a portion of the output signal back to the noninverting input.

Fig. 8-4A is an inverting differential-input comparator with the reference voltage applied to the noninverting input through R_1. Without R_2, the circuit performs similar to Figs. 8-1 and 8-2. If V_{ref} is $+1.0$ V, for example, the output would switch as E_{in} goes above or below 1.0 V.

By introducing R_2, however, positive feedback is developed across R_1. If the output is high, R_2 will feed back a signal, which will be added to the reference voltage. This voltage increment will be

$$\Delta V_{ref} = (E_{o(sat)} - V_{ref})\frac{R_1}{R_1 + R_2}$$

making the new reference voltage

$$V_{ref+} = V_{ref} + \Delta V_{ref} = V_{ref} + (E_{o(sat)} - V_{ref})\frac{R_1}{R_1 + R_2}$$

Therefore, a new trip level is introduced, high by the amount of positive voltage fed back from E_o. As E_{in} crosses this voltage, the output will start to fall. Immediately, the falling condition is sensed across R_1, and the noninverting input is also driven negative. This feedback is regenerative, and the output quickly "snaps" to the opposite state. This effect is prevalent regardless of the rate of change in E_{in}, giving the circuit a constant output transition time for any speed of input variation. Since E_o is now at negative saturation, the voltage fed back to R_1 is

$$\Delta V_{ref} = (-E_{o(sat)} - V_{ref})\frac{R_1}{R_1 + R_2}$$

making a new reference voltage,

$$V_{ref-} = V_{ref} + \Delta V_{ref} = V_{ref} + (-E_{o(sat)} - V_{ref})\frac{R_1}{R_1 + R_2}$$

Positive feedback has introduced new terms, and there are now two threshold points rather than one; these are called the *upper threshold point* (UTP) and *lower threshold point* (LTP). The difference between these two thresholds is the *hysteresis*.

Graphically, the effect of hysteresis is depicted in Fig. 8-4B. For simplicity, let $V_{ref} = 0$. Assume the output is already in a high state and the input is rising, approaching the UTP. On the figure, this is line *a*. As E_{in} reaches the voltage

$$E_{in} = +E_{o(sat)} \left(\frac{R_1}{R_1 + R_2}\right)$$

the output voltage snaps from $+E_{o(sat)}$ to $-E_{o(sat)}$ (line *b*). As E_{in} decreases toward the LTP (line *c*), E_o will remain at $-E_{o(sat)}$ until

$$E_{in} = -E_{o(sat)} \left(\frac{R_1}{R_1 + R_2}\right)$$

At this point, the output voltage snaps back to $+E_{o(sat)}$ (line *d*), thus returning to the original state. The input threshold region is a voltage span determined by the amount of feedback:

$$E_{hys} = V_{ref+} - V_{ref-}$$

$$= V_{ref} + (+E_{o(sat)} - V_{ref}) \frac{R_1}{R_1 + R_2}$$

$$-V_{ref} + (-E_{o(sat)} - V_{ref}) \frac{R_1}{R_1 + R_2}$$

If $V_{ref} = 0$, this simplifies to

$$E_{hys} = \frac{R_1}{R_1 + R_2} [+E_{o(sat)} - (-E_{o(sat)})]$$

This threshold region is the hysteresis region shown on the graph as the horizontal span from the LTP to the UTP. Hysteresis is always some span about V_{ref}, although the span is not always symmetrical. Note that if V_{ref} is above or below ground, the hysteresis region will not be symmetrical as was the case for $V_{ref} = 0$. If the respective saturation voltages of the op amp are not equal, this will also make the hysteresis region asymmetrical.

Hysteresis is a useful feature in comparators for reasons other than reducing the response time. If the input signal has a low-level noise superimposed on it, an open-loop comparator will "chatter" (switch rapidly back and forth) due to noise fluctuations as the input voltage passes through the threshold region. Also, some open-loop circuits may oscillate during a transition due to stray capacitive feedback. One cure for either of these difficulties is a small amount of hysteresis, which provides a "dead zone" over which the comparator will not be responsive. Often as little as 10 mV of hysteresis, which can be negligible if the voltage being sensed is large, can eliminate these effects.

8.4 SINGLE-ENDED COMPARATOR WITH HYSTERESIS

Single-ended comparators can also be used with hysteresis; an example is shown in Fig. 8-5A. In this circuit, amplifier A_1 senses the difference between ground potential (at the inverting input) and the junction potential of R_1-R_2. In this regard it is similar to Fig. 8-3; in fact, the threshold voltage can be determined the same way by substituting the appropriate voltage representing E_o for V_{ref}. In this case,

$$E_{in(th)} = E_o \left(\frac{R_1}{R_2}\right)$$

The difference is that E_o will not be constant here, whereas previously V_{ref} was constant by definition. The circuit operates as follows: Assuming the output is in a state of negative saturation, a positive voltage applied at E_{in} will raise the potential at E_a until it reaches a potential equal to zero. This is line a in Fig. 8-5B. At this point,

$$E_{in(th+)} = -(-E_{o(sat)})\frac{R_1}{R_2}$$

the equation for the UTP. The output then snaps positive due to the feedback through R_2 (line b). The voltage at E_a is now positive due to the feedback from $+E_{o(sat)}$. When E_{in} becomes negative, it will reduce the voltage at E_a until E_a again approaches zero. This is represented by line c. When E_{in} has reached a negative value such that

$$E_{in(th-)} = -(+E_{o(sat)})\frac{R_1}{R_2}$$

the circuit has reached its LTP, and the circuit snaps negative again, tracing section d of the loop and returning it to its original state.

(A) Schematic. (B) Hysteresis loop.

Fig. 8-5. Single-ended comparator with hysteresis.

This circuit does not need a separate reference voltage, although a potential may be applied to the inverting input of A_1 as a reference if desired. Using it as in Fig. 8-5A, the output saturation voltages define the trip points in conjunction with R_1 and R_2. This configuration is generally very useful since it does not require a separate reference voltage and can use an unprotected op amp for the same reasons as in Fig. 8-3. The only drawback is the fact that the positive and negative saturation voltages are not stable potentials—they can vary from device to device and also with loading and temperature. Therefore, if the output voltage is used directly as feedback, as shown in Fig. 8-5A, the threshold voltage will vary directly with the $\pm E_{o(sat)}$ levels. With devices that have output stages that can swing "rail-to-rail," such as the 3130 or the LM10, the *supply voltage(s)* will be the saturation level(s).

Fig. 8-6. Single-ended comparator with hysteresis and clamped feedback.

8.5 COMPARATORS WITH CLAMPED FEEDBACK

A solution to the variation in threshold potential is the introduction of a zener clamping network in the positive feedback loop as in Fig. 8-6. In this circuit, back-to-back zeners D_1 and D_2 clamp the output of A_1 to $\pm V_z$, and this voltage is used as the feedback voltage. The combination of a single zener junction and two forward-biased diodes in series results in a net temperature coefficient close to zero, providing temperature-stabilized thresholds. Another low-TC alternative is to use a stabilized reference diode, such as the LM329, AD589, or LM336, within a bridge.

With the equal-value resistors shown for R_1 and R_2, the input trip level will be equal to the $\pm V_z$ reference source. Lower or higher input potentials may be realized by scaling R_1 appropriately. Two outputs are available—a direct output from pin 6, which will vary from $-E_{o(sat)}$ to $+E_{o(sat)}$, and the clamped reference $\pm V_z$ across D_1-D_2. If input voltages beyond the common-mode range of A_1 are used, a pair of input clamp diodes, such as D_3 and D_4, should also be used.

8.6 CLAMPED COMPARATORS WITH TYPE 301A AMPLIFIERS

A very useful scheme for defining the output voltage swing of a comparator is possible using type 301A amplifiers. The basic technique is shown in Fig. 8-7.

From the LM101 schematic of Chapter 2 (Fig. 2-9), the internal connection on pin 8 of a 101 or 301A is a relatively high-impedance source for either positive or negative swings. The p-p voltage swing at this point is roughly the same value as that at the output, the main difference being the dc offset of the emitter followers between pin 8 and the output. This point, then, is a convenient one to define the range of swing at the output, since it can be clamped either with zener diodes or with biased signal diodes.

Fig. 8-7A illustrates the requirements for clamping positive or negative voltages. Diode D_1 will clamp positive swings to voltage $+E_{o(clamp)} \cong +V_{clamp} + 1.2$ V, where $+V_{clamp}$ is the bias voltage applied to the cathode of D_1. The source resistance of $+V_{clamp}$ should be no greater than about 1.0 kΩ for this relationship to apply.

(A) Diode clamping.

(B) Zener clamping.

Fig. 8-7. Clamped comparators.

Similarly, diode D_2 may be used to clamp the negative swing to a negative potential, $-V_{clamp}$. The voltage at the output terminal will be $-E_{o(clamp)} \cong -V_{clamp} - 0.5$ V. The source resistance of $-V_{clamp}$ should be no more than about 200 Ω to maintain this relation.

An alternate method of accomplishing the same result uses a zener diode connected to pin 8 (Fig. 8-7B). In this case, the zener voltage and ground define the $\pm V_{clamp}$ potentials, and the output swing is the same as in Fig. 8-7A. The zener diode may, of course, be reversed for a predominately negative output swing if desired.

The advantages of voltage clamping are twofold. First, it makes available the full current output of the op amp by internally clamping at a low-current point. Second, it allows greater operating speed by avoiding saturation of the op-amp voltage-amplification stages.

To realize such speed, however, minimal capacitance should be added to the pin-8 node.

A circuit for a general-purpose comparator with a clamped 5-V logic output is shown in Fig. 8-8. R_1 and R_2 provide a +3.8-V bias for D_1, clamping the positive output to +5 V; D_2 limits the negative output excursion to −0.5 V. It should be noted that this is still an open-loop circuit, so the output voltage will change in proportion to the load current (the open loop r_o of A_1 is 75 Ω). Externally compensated FET-input devices, such as the TL070, TL080, and CA080, will also work well in this circuit.

Fig. 8-8. General-purpose comparator with 5-V logic output.

8.7 PRECISION VARIABLE CLAMPING

The circuit of Fig. 8-8 is very useful for driving DTL or TTL logic devices, which do not require great accuracy in voltage levels. It is entirely adequate for this application, although the output voltage is neither temperature-compensated nor regulated in amplitude.

More demanding applications may require a tight control of positive and negative amplitude limits, and regulation of these amplitudes with load and temperature. A circuit that accomplishes this is shown in Fig. 8-9, a comparator having both output voltage limits regulated independently without a connection to the comparison inputs.

In this circuit, A_2 and A_3 are complementary versions of precision rectifiers with independent reference voltages, $+V_{clamp}$ and $-V_{clamp}$, both operating in a closed loop through A_1. A_2 senses the positive peak of E_o and maintains it equal to $+V_{clamp}$ by adjusting the voltage applied to D_1. A_3 and D_3 perform a similar function on negative peaks, adjusting $-E_o$ equal to $-V_{clamp}$. D_2 and D_4 minimize response time by preventing saturation of A_2 and A_3.

The feedback network around the output stage of A_1 regulates the output voltage independent of the inputs to A_1. These inputs can be used in any of the previous comparator configurations, with the obvious virtues of a precisely maintained output voltage and stable $\pm V_{clamp}$ potentials. For example, the circuit can be used in a single-ended comparator such as Fig. 8-6 with improved results. Also, the threshold voltages can be made independently variable if desired by separate adjustments for $+V_{clamp}$ and $-V_{clamp}$; operating speed is determined primarily by A_2 and A_3. Note that bias-compensation resistances R_2 and R_4 are not necessary for FET amplifiers as shown, but they are appropriate for bipolar types such as the 4558.

Fig. 8-9. Precision comparator with variable clamping.

8.8 ZERO-CROSSING DETECTOR

One form of comparator finding wide use is the zero-crossing detector. Usually, it takes the form of a high-gain amplifier that changes state each time the input signal changes direction. For an ac signal, this occurs when the signal value is zero, hence the name *zero-crossing detector*. The circuit amplifies and "squares" the input signal into a series of rectangular output pulses with rising and falling slopes corresponding to the input zero crossing.

A circuit that derives the zero-crossing information of an ac signal is shown in Fig. 8-10. This is an ac logarithmic amplifier, with feedback current I_f creating a log output voltage due to diodes D_1 and D_2. Amplifier A_1 is a high-SR FET type, to optimize speed and minimize phase error at high frequencies. The output voltage is nominally $\pm V_f$, where V_f is the forward voltage drop of either diode.

This basic circuit has a dynamic range of over 70 dB, which is realized by using monolithic transistor diodes for D_1 and D_2. Should the nominal voltage drop be insufficient as an output, or if a con-

*For highest dynamic range, use a matched, monolithic
transistor pair connected as diodes — e.g., CA3086.

Fig. 8-10. Zero-crossing detector.

stant output is desired, the optional connection in the inset can be used. This is a saturated switch, delivering a 0- to +5-V output at E_{o_2}. Note that this stage can utilize components from the array.

8.9 WINDOW COMPARATORS

A window comparator, as its name implies, is a specialized form of comparator designed to detect the presence of a voltage between two prescribed voltage limits—that is, within a voltage "window." This is accomplished by logically combining the outputs of two single-ended comparators, one indicating greater than a lower limit, the other indicating less than an upper limit. If both comparators indicate a "true" condition, the output is true. If either is not true, the output is not true.

Window comparators (also referred to as *double-ended* comparators) are useful in the grading and selection of components or in the production testing of circuits to a specified output tolerance. For these purposes, a variable window voltage position and a variable window voltage width are desirable.

8.9.1 General-Purpose Window Comparator

A simple window comparator is shown in Fig. 8-11A. This circuit gives a high output (+5.0 V in this case) if E_{in} is within the voltage window set by the upper limit (UL) and lower limit (LL) voltages. For example, if UL is +4.0 V and LL is +2.0 V, E_{in} must be greater than +2.0 V and less than +4.0 V for E_o to be high. If E_{in} goes lower than +2.0 V, A_2 turns on Q_1 through D_2. If E_{in} goes higher than +4.0 V, A_1 turns on Q_1 through D_1. As long as E_{in} is within the window, both A_1 and A_2 are low, Q_1 remains off, and E_o remains true (high).

The input/output transfer characteristic of this circuit is shown in Fig. 8-11B, with the voltage examples used illustrated. Note the output is +5.0 V only when $LL \leq E_{in} \leq UL$.

A type-1458 (dual 741) op amp is convenient to use for A_1 and A_2 in this circuit if its differential-input rating is observed. The resistor-diode input clamping network is recommended here for other op amps which have lower differential ratings. For applications requiring greater speed, a FET dual such as the 3240, 353, TL072, or 772 may be substituted and the resistor-diode clamping omitted. R_3 is shown as a fixed load resistor, but may be a relay or a lamp if desired. These types of loads will be covered in a following section.

E_o high = E_{in} inside window,
E_o low = E_{in} outside window.

*A_1, A_2 = 1458 or 4558.
* *Input voltage clamp—use with unprotected types.

(A) Schematic.

(B) Input/output characteristic.

Fig. 8-11. General-purpose window comparator.

8.9.2 Internally Gated Window Comparator

The circuit of Fig. 8-11A is useful with any op amp if the maximum input voltage restrictions are observed. However, a much simpler overall circuit for a window comparator is feasible, using a pair of 301As with the clamp terminals wired together as shown in Fig. 8-12.

In this circuit, advantage is taken of the fact that the source and sink currents available at pin 8 of a 101-type op amp are unequal—the negative-going drive is the greater of the two. Therefore, the voltage at pin 8 will be low if either comparison input (A_1 or A_2) so

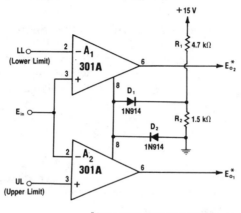

*Outputs are identical; either or both can be used.

Fig. 8-12. Internally gated window comparator.

dictates; for the voltage at pin 8 to be high, *both* A_1 and A_2 must have a high output condition. The outputs of both A_1 and A_2 will follow pin 8, since the op-amp internal circuitry thereafter has unity gain. D_1 and D_2 form a clamp network as in Fig. 8-8. The output from either A_1 or A_2 may be used, with the logic of operation being the same as in Fig. 8-11. The value of R_2 can be adjusted to accommodate other output logic levels. For example, if R_2 is 10 kΩ, the output is 10 V CMOS compatible.

8.9.3 Comparator With Variable Window

As mentioned previously, a variable-width window is very useful, allowing a single comparator to be programmed for a wide variety of tasks. Fig. 8-13 is such a circuit, generating variable UL and LL voltages for use with either of the previous comparator circuits.

This circuit combines two variable voltages, E_b (window center) and E_a (window span), such that E_b positions the window and volt-

Fig. 8-13. Comparator with variable window.

age E_a is added to E_b to set the width of the window. A_1 is a subtractor, generating a voltage of $E_b - E_a$, which is used as the LL voltage. This voltage is also added to $2E_b$ at A_2 to derive $E_b + E_a$, the UL voltage. E_b may be any voltage within the comparator common-mode range of ± 10 V. E_a is a positive voltage that is added to E_b at the input; so, the combination of $E_b + E_a$ or $E_b - E_a$ must not exceed ± 10 V for any combination of E_a and E_b. Normally this will not be a restriction, since E_a is commonly a small percentage of E_b—for example, $+5.0$ V $\pm 5\%$.

For applications where E_{in} is much greater than the common-mode range of ± 10 V, it may be scaled with a voltage divider to bring it into the comparison range, allowing window-voltage comparison of much higher voltages.

8.9.4 Staircase Window Comparator

The most basic comparator tells only one thing about an unknown voltage—whether it is above or below a reference voltage. The window comparator tells a little more about the unknown voltage—that it is between two specified voltage limits. But in certain situations, even this may not be enough. A third type of comparator, the staircase detector, tells where (within *which* window) the input voltage lies over a specified range of voltages. An output is indicated only from the comparator closest to the input voltage, generating one voltage from among a rising "staircase" of levels.

Fig. 8-14 is a staircase detector performing such a function. It is actually a series of type 301A window comparators, each similar to Fig. 8-12, but arranged for operation in a sequential fashion. E_{in} is applied in parallel to all comparators (A_1-A_6). If E_{in} is between LL_1 and UL_1, the output from A_2 will be high. When E_{in} rises above UL_1, it moves within the voltage window of the A_3-A_4 comparator (window 2, where LL_2 is the same as UL_1). Under this condition, the output of A_2 drops and A_4 switches high. Should E_{in} rise further

$$+15\,V$$

$$R_1 \gtrless 1.5\ k\Omega$$

$$R_2 \gtrless 470\ \Omega$$

A_1^* 2 3 + 8 D_1^{**}

D_2^{**}

LL₁

Window #1

E_{in}

A_2^* 2 3 + 8 6 → E_{o_1}

$\begin{cases} \text{High} \Rightarrow LL_1 < E_{in} < UL_1 \\ \text{Low} \Rightarrow LL_1 > E_{in} > UL_1 \end{cases}$

UL₁
(LL₂)

Window #2

A_3^* 2 3 + 8 D_3^{**}

D_4^{**}

A_4^* 2 3 + 8 6 → E_{o_2}

$\begin{cases} \text{High} \Rightarrow LL_2 < E_{in} < UL_2 \\ \text{Low} \Rightarrow LL_2 > E_{in} > UL_2 \end{cases}$

UL₂
(LL₃)

A_5^* 2 3 + 8 D_5^{**}

D_6^{**}

Window #3

A_6^* 2 3 + 8 6 → E_{o_3}

$\begin{cases} \text{High} \Rightarrow LL_3 < E_{in} < UL_3 \\ \text{Low} \Rightarrow LL_3 > E_{in} > UL_3 \end{cases}$

UL₃

* All amplifiers are type 301A.

** All diodes are type 1N914.

Fig. 8-14. Staircase window comparator.

(above UL_2, for instance), it moves into window 3, actuating A_6 to a high state with A_4 going low. This "staircase" of windows can be continued indefinitely using as many comparators as necessary to provide the required resolution. An output indicator (lamp, relay, etc.) added to each of the E_{o_1}, E_{o_2}, and E_{o_3} lines will indicate the presence of E_{in} within the corresponding window.

8.10 STANDARD IC COMPARATOR DEVICES

The discussion on comparators thus far has been either generalized or oriented toward how IC op amps can be used as comparators. However, as alluded to initially, it may often be undesirable to attempt to use a standard op amp as a comparator for many reasons.

Standard ICs are readily available for comparator use, in a variety of styles and performance features, and in single, dual, and quad versions.

Pinouts for two representative families of these comparators are illustrated in Fig. 8-15. Fig. 8-15A shows the type LM311 comparator, which operates from dual power supplies and has an open-collector output that is compatible with all logic families. The 311 is a workhorse device and is, perhaps, more suitable for the broadest range of applications than any other device. It can sink or source up to 50 mA and operates from power supplies from as low as 5 V up to 36 V. It can handle differential inputs of up to ±30 V and has a bias current of 100 nA and an offset voltage of 2 mV (typical figures). It is nulled (optionally) as shown in the illustration. The 311 is available in a dual version as the LH2311 and in a (single) FET-input version as the LF311.

The LM339 comparator family is illustrated in Fig. 8-15B. The basic (first introduced) device of this type is the 339 (a quad). Introduced later was the 393 (a dual). Both devices operate similarly.

The 339 is a single-supply comparator, meaning it has input and output ranges which extend to ground (or the V− supply) in operating range. The output is an npn open-collector transistor with the emitter referred to the device ground (or V−) pin. Bias current of the 339 is 25 nA and offset voltage is 2 mV (typical). The 339A device improves the offset voltage to 1.0 mV (typical). None of the devices of this family have provision for offset voltage adjustment.

In addition to the performance features just mentioned, comparators designed specifically for the voltage comparison function have features of flexibility which can be optimized unlike a standard op amp. For example, using the open-collector outputs of multiple (dual or quad) devices allows easy implementation of such functions as window comparators or other such amplitude classifiers. Two examples of this are shown in Fig. 8-16, using single-supply comparators.

(A) The LM311 single device.   (B) The LM339 quad device (single supply).

Fig. 8-15. Standard IC comparator devices.

*Input bias current flow through R_S (of V_{IN} source) can cause comparator voltage errors (for $(3\,I_{IN})(R_S) \approx V_{REF}$). This can be reduced by adding R_S and $3R_S$ as shown.

(A) Using the LM339 bipolar-input device.

WINDOW = 0.98 V WIDE.
LED ON IN WINDOW.

(B) Using the CA3290 MOSFET-input device.

Fig. 8-16. Window comparators using multiple devices (single supply).

Fig. 8-16A shows a basic window comparator which compares a voltage, V_{in}, to high- and low-limit reference voltages. When the voltage is in the window, both of the npn outputs of the 339 will be off and the 2N2222 switching transistor will be held on. When either window limit is passed, one output will then be on and the transistor and the indicator lamp will be turned off.

The MOSFET-input comparator of Fig. 8-16B uses the CA3290 dual comparator, which is a single-supply device with MOSFET input transistors. It has very low currents, on the order of only a few picoamperes, making it very useful for very-high-impedance sources. The application illustrated here is similar to the 339 in function, and turns on the LED when the input voltage is within the comparison window.

Detailed application coverage of the numerous comparator devices is simply beyond the scope of this chapter, and we only hope to make the reader aware that there are many of them to choose from. Some devices which warrant investigation (in addition to those already mentioned) are the Fairchild 710, the National 306, and the Precision Monolithics CMP-01.

8.11 PRECISION OP-AMP COMPARATOR

One application area where IC op amps *are* more useful as voltage comparators than standard comparator devices is when very high precision is required. Such a case may be when ultralow bias currents are required, very low offset voltages, and/or very high common-mode rejection. Standard comparator devices in particular fall short with regard to very low offset voltage (and drift) and CMRR.

Fig. 8-17. Precision op-amp comparator.

If an externally compensated instrumentation-grade op amp is used as the voltage comparator, it is possible to achieve voltage offsets of 500 μV or less, drifts of 1.0 μV/°C, and a CMRR of well over 100 dB. Removal of the compensation capacitance will allow maximum speed to be realized from the device. With some units, for example the SSS725,* response times of 1-2 μs can be achieved with such dc precision.

A general circuit optimized for maximum dc precision is shown in Fig. 8-17 and, as can be noted, it can generally employ any of the devices listed in the table. In actual practice, the specific device that

Fig. 8-18. Comparator output interfaces.

will be most suitable will be governed by how much speed and dc accuracy are desired.

In using this circuit, input-current-limiting resistances should be used in series with the amplifier inputs to limit the current when protection diodes are used. Note that these diodes must be used to protect bipolar input stages, either within the IC or added externally

---

* See reference 3 at the end of the chapter.

(with the 709, for example). The resistors can then be made no larger than necessary, and the 10-kΩ value indicated should be a maximum.

The output buffer serves two purposes—to minimize loading on the op amp and thus preserve its gain and drift characteristics; and also to provide a high-current TTL logic output. It will add minimal delay (compared to the op amp).

The op amps in the table that are marked with asterisks (*) are those capable of the most dc precision and are not necessarily the fastest of those shown. It is worth noting that even general-purpose units such as the 301A perform well in this circuit, as does the FET TL070 (or TL080). With some of these devices, a minimal value compensation capacitor (5 pF or so) may be found necessary to minimize the susceptibility to oscillation.

8.12 GENERAL-PURPOSE INTERFACING CIRCUITS

Fig. 8-18 illustrates a few ways in which any op-amp comparator with a bipolar output swing can be used to drive high-powered loads, other than the logic output stage shown in Fig. 8-17. All three circuits interface with an op-amp output (pin 6), with an input resistor (R_1) of 5 kΩ to 10 kΩ.

In the lamp-driver circuit, R_{surge} is added to limit the cold inrush current in Q_1. Lower-voltage lamps of up to the 150-mA current rating may be driven by reducing the lamp supply voltage appropriately. Also shown is a relay driver, using a common 24-V relay. Diode D_2 clamps the back emf of K_1 after turnoff. Again, lower-voltage relays may be driven, as long as I_{max} is 150 mA or less.

Finally, this circuit is easily adapted as an LED indicator driver, using a 2N3904 switch rather than the high-powered 2N2219. Maximum diode current is set by the supply voltage (minus approximately 1.5 V, the LED forward drop) and by R_L; in this case, I_{max} is about 20 mA.

REFERENCES

1. *Applications Manual for Computing Amplifiers.* Philbrick Researches, Inc., Dedham, Mass., 1966.

2. Dobkin, R. C. "Comparators Can Do More Than Just Compare." *EDN,* November 1, 1972.

3. Givens, S. D. *The 725 Op Amp As a Low Level Comparator.* Precision Monolithics Application Note AN-25, February 1978. Precision Monolithics, Inc., Santa Clara, Calif.

4. Korn, G. A.; Korn, T. M. *Electronic Analog and Hybrid Computers,* 2nd ed. McGraw-Hill Book Co., New York, 1972.

5. Smathers, R. T.; Frederiksen, T. M.; Howard, W. M. *LM139/LM239/ LM339 A Quad of Independently Functioning Comparators*. National Semiconductor Application Note AN-74, January 1973. National Semiconductor Corp., Santa Clara, Calif.

6. Widlar, R. J. *An IC Voltage Comparator for High Impedance Circuitry*. National Semiconductor Linear Brief LB-12, January 1970. National Semiconductor Corp., Santa Clara, Calif.

7. ———. "Designing With Super-Beta Transistor Op-Amp ICs." *EEE*, December 1969, February and March 1970.

8. ———. *IC Op Amp Beats FETs on Input Current*. National Semiconductor Application Note AN-29, December 1969. National Semiconductor Corp., Santa Clara, Calif.

9. ———. *Monolithic Operational Amplifiers—The Universal Linear Component*. National Semiconductor Application Note AN-4, April 1968. National Semiconductor Corp., Santa Clara, Calif.

10. ———. *Precision IC Comparator Runs From 5V Logic Supply*. National Semiconductor Application Note AN-41, October 1970. National Semiconductor Corp., Santa Clara, Calif.

11. Manufacturers' Data Sheets:

National Semiconductor	⌈LM139/339 ⟨LM193/393 ⌊LM311	Comparator Comparator Comparator
RCA	CA3290	Comparator

NINE

The Integrator and
The Differentiator

Previously, we have seen how modifications of the basic inverting amplifier give rise to the integrator and the differentiator. Both of these circuits are based primarily on the relationship between voltage and current in a capacitor. This chapter explores the practical points for optimum use of these two basic op-amp circuits.

9.1 THE INTEGRATOR

Fig. 9-1 illustrates the operation of an ideal integrator. If a constant current, I (amperes), is applied to capacitor C (farads), the voltage across the capacitor will rise linearly at a rate of

$$\frac{\Delta E}{\Delta t} = \frac{I}{C} \text{ volts per second}$$

Thus, a current of 1.0 μA applied to a capacitor of 1.0 μF produces a rising voltage across the capacitor, and this change occurs at the rate of 1.0 V/s.

In Fig. 9-1B, the 1.0-μA current is applied at time t = 0 and continues for a period of 4.0 seconds. At t = 4, the current is interrupted and the capacitor voltage (Fig. 9-1C) remains at the value accumulated up to that time (4.0 V). This mechanism is the basis for the op-amp integrator shown in Fig. 9-2. Capacitor C has one terminal at the summing point, the other at the output; thus, the capacitor voltage is also the output voltage. In effect, the op amp simulates an

(A) Test circuit.

(B) Applied current versus time.

(C) Resultant capacitor voltage.

Fig. 9-1. Dc current/voltage relationships for a capacitor.

ideal current source, with one important difference—the output impedance of the op amp is low. So, while it provides a constant current drive to C, it simultaneously makes the voltage across the capacitor available at a low-impedance level.

The integrator output cannot be described by a simple algebraic relation; as we have seen, for a fixed (nonzero) input the output voltage changes of a rate determined by E_{in}, R, and C. Thus, the output voltage cannot be determined without also specifying the duration of time an input has been applied. If the output rate of change is expressed in terms of the feedback current, I_f, then

$$\frac{\Delta E_o}{\Delta t} = \frac{I_f}{C}$$

$$\frac{\Delta E_o}{\Delta t} = \frac{I_f}{C},$$

$$\Delta E_o = \frac{I_f}{C} \, \Delta t.$$

Since $I_f = I_{in}$ and E_o is inverted,

$$\Delta E_o = \frac{-E_{in}}{RC} \, \Delta t.$$

Integrating,

$$E_o = \frac{-1}{RC} \int_0^t E_{in} \, \Delta t.$$

Fig. 9-2. Basic op-amp integrator.

or

$$\Delta E_o = \frac{I_f}{C} \Delta t$$

Since $I_f = I_{in}$ and, due to inversion,

$$\Delta E_o = \frac{-E_{in}}{RC} \Delta t$$

after integration from 0 to t seconds,

$$E_o = \frac{-1}{RC} \int_0^t E_{in} \Delta t$$

which is the output of the inverting integrator shown in Fig. 9-2. The 1/RC term of this expression is often called the integrator "gain," as it determines the slope of the output change. In the circuit shown,

$$\frac{1}{RC} = \frac{1}{10^6 \times 10^{-6}} = 1.0$$

so this time constant of 1.0 second produces a 1.0 V/s rate of change per volt of input. From this it can be seen that integrators make convenient circuits for the measurement of elapsed time—apply a known input to a calibrated integrator, and the voltage output can be read directly as a measure of elapsed time.

9.1.1 Realization of Practical Integrators

As may be noticed from the idealized integrator of Fig. 9-2, this configuration has an inherent drawback if E_{in} is left connected indefinitely: E_o will continue to rise until it reaches the saturation limits of A_1. This can again be appreciated by noting that the integrator is operating as an open-loop amplifier for dc inputs.

Integrators that allow operation in view of this limitation can take on various forms; for applications requiring precisely timed periods of integration, the circuits of Figs. 9-3 or 9-4 can be used. Both are sequentially operated integrators and have defined modes of operation. Since integration begins with whatever voltage is on the capacitor initially, the capacitor voltage must be reset to the desired value (usually zero) before each integration. Fig. 9-3B illustrates how this is done.

Switch S_1 is closed during the reset mode, discharging C through R_s. This leaves a residual voltage of zero. To begin the integration, S_1 is opened and S_2 is closed. During this period the circuit operates as described previously and will charge C to a potential of -4 V in 4 seconds with the values shown. At the end of this period, S_2 is opened and the circuit "holds" the voltage on the capacitor for read-out and subsequent processing.

An alternate form of the basic circuit is shown in Fig. 9-4. This circuit converts the reset cycle to an "initialize" cycle by the addition of R_1 and R_2. With S_1 closed (and S_2 open), R_1, R_2, and A_1 form an inverter, which charges C to an inverted multiple of the reference voltage. In this example the multiple is unity, thus C is initialized

Mode	Switch Positions
Reset	S_1 closed
Integrating	S_1 open, S_2 closed
Hold	S_1 open, S_2 open

(A) Test circuit.

(B) Operating sequence.

Fig. 9-3. Integrator operation.

to +4 V. The integrating and hold modes are the same as before; the only difference is that C starts the integration with a +4-V potential. For example, a +1-V input will diminish the potential on C to zero in 4 seconds.

In either circuit, switches S_1 and S_2 can be relays or (more often) solid-state switches such as FETs or analog switches. Switching is directed externally by some form of control logic. Very-low integration currents will employ ultralow-leakage switches, such as MOS-FETs or glass-enclosed reed relays.

In many applications, a simplified form of integrator can be used, as shown in Fig. 9-5. This differs from the ideal form of integrator by the addition of a dc "gain stop" resistor across C, reducing the integrator gain from the full open-loop value. The ratio of this shunt resistance to R should be as high as dc considerations allow so that

*For simplicity, it is assumed $R_1 = R_2$. Ratio can be adjusted for desired initial voltage.

(A) Test circuit.

Mode	Switch Positions
Initialize	S_1 closed, S_2 open
Integrating	S_1 open, S_2 closed
Hold	S_1 open, S_2 open

(B) Operating sequence.

Fig. 9-4. Integrator with initial voltage applied.

ideal integrator behavior is not compromised. This form of integrator can be used successfully in such applications as square-wave to triangular-wave conversion.

The use of the integrator in its unmodified form (Fig. 9-2) is generally avoided because some means of introducing dc feedback must be used to stabilize the operating point and prevent saturation. How-

Fig. 9-5. Continuous integrator.

*Ratio of shunt resistance to R will determine integrator accuracy. If possible (with dc stability), make shunt resistance 100R or even 1000R.

ever, this "classic" form of the integrator may sometimes appear as part of an overall feedback loop.

9.1.2 Error Sources in the Integrator

Fig. 9-6 illustrates the sources of error that must be considered and minimized for optimum integrator performance. Capacitor C_t must be a high-quality type with a leakage current lower than the bias current of the amplifier. Typical examples are Teflon, polystyrene, polypropylene, polycarbonate, or polyester types. The capacitor used should have very-low dielectric absorption as well as very-low leakage. Teflon, polystyrene, and polypropylene types are superior in both regards, having leakages down to the picoampere level.

*C_t should be low-leakage, low-dielectric-absorption type, such as polystyrene, polypropylene, polycarbonate, polyester, or Teflon.

**Characteristics desired of A_1:
Low I_{ib} (or compensated).
Low $I_{io}/\Delta t$.
Low V_{io} (or nulled).
Low $V_{io}/\Delta t$.
Unity-gain compensation.

† R_1-R_3 and D_1 are optional, used to compensate I_{ib} of A_1 (if bipolar-input type). See Chapter 7.

Note: adjust R_2 for minimum output drift with $E_{in} = 0$, after nulling V_{io}. If bias compensation not used, make $R_b = R_t$.
‡ Use R_d if $C_t \geq 0.1\mu F$. Use D_2-D_3 for differential protection of A_1.

Fig. 9-6. Error sources and practical problems in the integrator.

The amplifier must be compensated for unity gain and have good to excellent dc characteristics, depending on the maximum integration time. For long integration times, R_t and C_t will become large, which will reduce the integration current and make the error due to input bias current important. Any offset will be seen as an input current by the circuit and will be integrated along with the signal. Offset at the summing point can originate from either V_{io} or from $I_{ib} \times R_t$. V_{io} should be minimized by amplifier selection or nulling; I_{ib} can be minimized by choosing an op amp with high input impedance, such as a FET or super-β type. In some applications, I_{ib} can be compensated satisfactorily by using the method shown in Fig. 9-6.

Compensation of bias current is supplied by R_1, which provides a current to the summing point equal to the nominal bias current. This compensation is optimized by adjusting R_2 for minimal output drift with zero input voltage applied to R_t. The adjustment should be done after the input offset voltage has been nulled. See Chapter 7 for details of alternate bias compensation techniques.

Diode D_1 derives a voltage source for the bias current compensation and also provides some temperature tracking of the bias current. It has the further advantage of reducing sensitivity to supply-voltage changes. This compensation method works best with low-input-current bipolar amplifiers such as the type 308. (FET amplifiers do not generally require compensation.) In theory, bias current compensation can be applied to any amplifier, but it may not be necessary in many cases according to the circuit requirements. If this method is not used, it is still a good practice to include R_b, of a value nominally equal to R_t (particularly if a bipolar amplifier is being used).

Possible failure of the amplifier input stage is a problem in integrators, particularly if C_t is greater than about 0.1 μF. In such cases it is advisable to include a series resistance (R_d) to limit the discharge rate, and clamping diodes (D_2 and D_3) are recommended if the amplifier is unprotected differentially.

Integrators may also be required to operate at high speeds—for instance, in the generation of fast ramps and triangular waveforms. Such applications require a high slew rate and a high f_t for the op amp but normally with less stringent dc requirements. These applications are satisfied by such high-speed types as the 356 or OP-16.

9.1.3 Expanding Integrator Flexibility and Capability

Beyond the basic points just described, there are a number of ways in which integrator performance can be improved.

One of the most basic limitations of the integrator is the practical problem of attaining long time constants. The problems stem mainly from the very real difficulties in obtaining high-quality resistors above about 10 megohms, and capacitors above a few microfarads. If high accuracy is desired, these components should be stable types.

While film capacitors of good quality are available up to about 50 μF, they are generally undesirable from the standpoints of size, cost, and high-temperature leakage. There will also be procurement problems since they will have to be obtained through special order. On the other hand, small precision resistors are generally available up to 10 or 20 megohms (although they may not be shelf items either).

The circuit of Fig. 9-7 multiplies the time constant of an integrator circuit by replacing R_t with a T network, which raises the effective input resistance as shown, in this case to 100 megohms. A 100-second time constant can then be realized with only a 1.0-μF integrator capacitor, which is readily available in small sizes. For this technique

Fig. 9-7. Multiplying integrator time constant with T input.

For $R_3 \gg R_2$,

$$R_{effective} = R_3 \left(\frac{R_1 + R_2}{R_2} \right)$$

to be most effective, the amplifier used should have low offset voltage (and drift), such as the AD545L shown.

Note that virtually any combination of R_1, R_2, and R_3 values can be used to "multiply" R_t, but R_1 and R_2 should preferably be relatively low-value film units as shown. Since all three resistors enter into the time-constant expression, they all should be stable units. R_2 (or R_1) can be trimmed for calibration, if desired.

Bound Integrator

Fig. 9-8 illustrates a circuit that can be useful with virtually any integrator—a reliable "bound" or limit circuit.

Here, R_t, C_t, and A_1 might be any integrator, and the diodes are added across C_t to clamp A_1 before it reaches saturation. Low-leakage diodes for the bridge and for coupling to the summing point will generally be desirable, but the degree of their specification limits will depend on the individual application. The shunt bleeder resistance (R_1) will minimize diode leakage problems. The zener should, of course, be selected for a voltage higher than the greatest linear output from A_1, minus two diode voltage drops.

Fig. 9-8. Bound integrator.

Differential Integrators

Sometimes it is necessary to integrate the *difference* between two voltages (or a floating voltage). The circuits of Fig. 9-9 can accomplish this.

The circuit of Fig. 9-9A is the classic approach and requires a pair of matched resistors and capacitors. While matched resistors are readily available, capacitors are not, and the circuit tends to be impractical from this standpoint. Also, it applies common-mode voltage to the amplifier, requiring consideration of common-mode errors when high accuracy is necessary.

For: $R_t = R_t'$
$C_t = C_t'$,

$$E_0 = \frac{1}{R_t C_t} \int_0^t (E_a - E_b)\Delta t$$

(A) Using differential amplifier.

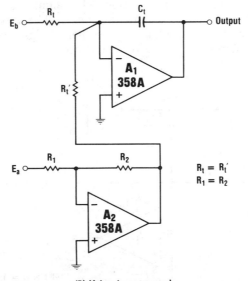

$R_t = R_t'$
$R_1 = R_2$

(B) Using inverters only.

Fig. 9-9. Differential integrators.

The alternate circuit of Fig. 9-9B uses an inverter to invert one of the differential inputs, and then combines this voltage in a combining integrator. In terms of transfer function, this yields results equivalent to the circuit of Fig. 9-9A, but requires an additional amplifier. With so many low-cost duals available, this may be a viable alternative, even though it requires an additional matched pair—R_1 and R_2. The 358A shown is a bipolar type; for lowest input currents, a FET dual, such as the AD642, will be useful.

Courtesy National Semiconductor Corp.

(A) LM11 circuit.

Courtesy Analog Devices, Inc.

(B) AD515 circuit.

Fig. 9-10. Low-bias-current integrators with reset.

Low-Bias-Current Integrator With Reset

Special problems arise when very-low-bias-current integrators must be reset to zero voltage, if the reset function is not to introduce excess leakage into the summing point. Two examples of low-bias-current integrators are shown in Fig. 9-10.

In Fig. 9-10A the LM11 op amp is shown in a low-bias-current integrator circuit, with input guarding, and guarding on the device package pins also. C_t is a high-quality Teflon, polystyrene, or polyproplyene capacitor with an insulation resistance in excess of 10^{12} ohms.

Q_1 and Q_2 are low-leakage PMOSFETs, which are used for the reset function of C_t. They are used in a T configuration, with bleeder resistance R_3 absorbing the leakage of Q_2. Reset of the integrator to zero volts out is accomplished with a negative voltage of -5 V to the RESET terminal.

The input bias current of the LM11 of 50 pA or less will allow low levels of current to be integrated. Over a temperature range of $-55°C$ to $+125°C$, the bias current of the LM11 will be no more than 150 pA, which is less than most FET amplifiers at high temperatures.

The AD515 integrator with reset shown in Fig. 9-10B is similar in basic operation, and also uses PMOSFET switches for the reset function. The AD515L used in this circuit will have a maximum (room temperature) bias current of 75 fA, which will increase to about 2 pA at its rated temperature limit of 70°C (operating).

Since this circuit is capable of such low levels of bias current, the importance of proper construction techniques and guarding, as well as the quality of the capacitor insulation, cannot be overemphasized. The PC board should also be of highest quality, such as Teflon.

9.2 THE DIFFERENTIATOR

A natural companion to the integrator circuit is the differentiator. Like the integrator, it is best understood if viewed from the standpoint of the voltage/current relationships in the capacitive element, as illustrated in Fig. 9-11.

The integrator was used to show how the voltage across a capacitor rises linearly if the current in the capacitor is maintained constant. The reverse of this concept forms the basis of the differentiator. If a linear ramp of voltage is applied across a capacitor, the current in the capacitor will remain constant as long as the rate of change (slope) of the applied voltage is constant. Fig. 9-11A is the test circuit, and Fig. 9-11B is a graph of the voltage applied to the capacitor. The voltage across the capacitor rises at the rate of 1.0 V/s for

4 seconds. During this time, the current in the capacitor (Fig. 9-11C) is constant at 1.0 μA. This is nothing more than a restatement of the basic relationship:

$$\frac{\Delta E}{\Delta t} = \frac{I}{C}$$

which may be stated as

$$I = C\left(\frac{\Delta E}{\Delta t}\right)$$

Thus, in the example shown, a 1.0 V/s rate of change across the 1.0-μF capacitor results in a 1.0-μA current in the capacitor, as shown in Fig. 9-11C.

(A) Test circuit.

(B) Applied voltage versus time.

(C) Resultant capacitor current.

Fig. 9-11. Dc voltage/current relationships for a capacitor.

When the rate of voltage change across the capacitor falls to zero, the current in the capacitor also falls to zero. This is shown on the graph as the time beyond 4 seconds where $\Delta E = 0$ and $I = 0$.

In the op-amp differentiator of Fig. 9-12, capacitor C is the input element of the configuration and resistor R is the feedback element. As in the integrator, one terminal of the capacitor is held at ground potential by the summing point.

Input current I_{in} can be expressed in terms of C and E_{in} as

$$I_{in} = C\left(\frac{\Delta E_{in}}{\Delta t}\right)$$

and since $I_f = I_{in}$, we may substitute and add the sign inversion of A_1 to write an expression for E_o:

$$E_o = -I_f R = -I_{in} R$$

which, when substituted for I_{in}, becomes

$$E_o = -RC\left(\frac{\Delta E_{in}}{\Delta t}\right)$$

Graphically, the differentiator action is illustrated by the sketches, which show the output to be an inverted product of the capacitor current (I_{in}) and R.

(A) Circuit diagram. (B) Input/output voltages.

Fig. 9-12. Basic op-amp differentiator.

Since the differentiator responds only to changes in the input voltage (a capacitor will not carry current unless the applied voltage is changing), it will yield zero output voltage for a fixed (static) input voltage. The faster the input voltage changes, the greater will be the output voltage. In terms of frequency, the differentiator gives a rising output voltage with increasing frequency, as would be expected from the decreasing input impedance due to the falling reactance of the capacitor.

In practical terms, the differentiator also has problems when applied in basic form (as in Fig. 9-12). The most apparent drawback is illustrated in Fig. 9-13. An earlier discussion of stability noted that, for stability to exist, the ideal $1/\beta$ curve must cross the open-loop

(A) Bode plot.

*For noise elimination, let $X_{C_2} = R_1$, at f_3, where
f_3 is the crossover frequency from differentiator to
integrator; i.e.,

$$C_2 = \frac{1}{2\pi f_3 R_1}.$$

(B) Practical circuit.

Fig. 9-13. Stability conditions in the differentiator.

gain curve with a net slope of less than -12 dB/octave. In Fig.
9-13A, it will be noted that the $1/\beta$ line intersects the gain curve at
f_o, with a net slope between the curves of -12 dB/octave; thus, the
characteristic is unstable. To make the $1/\beta$ line intersect the gain
curve with a net slope of -6 dB/octave (required for stability), it
must be modified to form the curve shown as $1/\beta'$. If f_o is the frequency at which the ideal $1/\beta$ curve intersected, a breakout must be
introduced in the $1/\beta$ curve at f_1, where $f_1 = f_o/3.16$. This will cause
the new curve $(1/\beta')$ to intersect the Bode plot at a frequency $f_2 =
3.16\ f_o$. The $1/\beta'$ curve, therefore, has a full decade $(f_2 = 10f_1)$ to
assume a zero phase characteristic, which ensures stability.

To accomplish the frequency breakout, a resistive "stop" (R_2) is
connected in series with C_1, as shown in Fig. 9-13B. The value of R_2

is chosen so that it is 3.16 times the reactance of C_1 at frequency f_o, or

$$R_2 = \frac{3.16}{2\pi f_o C_1}$$

This gives the minimum value of R_2 required for stability, but in practice the next higher standard value is satisfactory. From the Bode plot it can be seen that such a modification results in little sacrifice of the useful dynamic range of the differentiator.

Another problem inherent in the differentiator is the 6-dB/octave rise in gain with increasing frequency. In practice, this effect greatly increases high-frequency noise, and in some cases, the noise may mask the desired signal if the signal has a small amplitude and is low in frequency. The noise problem can be dealt with by modifying the differentiator characteristic in another fashion.

If a modified curve $(1/\beta'')$ is introduced at frequency f_3, the high-frequency gain is reduced drastically from this frequency upward, while the differentiator characteristic remains unaltered below f_3. In actuality, a $1/\beta''$ characteristic produces a combination of differentiator and integrator action, with the crossover occurring at f_3.

To realize the $1/\beta''$ curve, C_2 is added across R_1, with C_2 chosen to be equal in reactance to R_1 at the crossover frequency, f_3, or

$$C_2 = \frac{1}{2\pi f_3 R_1}$$

With this $1/\beta''$ curve, unity-gain stability is now required of A_1, whereas this was not necessarily so in the case of $1/\beta'$.

With regard to the types of devices that are best suited for differentiator use, the high-frequency amplitude-rise characteristic tends to limit the choice to devices with high slew rate and GBP. High-slew-rate FET units such as the 356 will be found useful, as will such units as the 2505, the 318, and slew-rate enhanced devices like the 535 and 530.

REFERENCES

1. *Applications Manual for Computing Amplifiers.* Philbrick Researches, Inc., Dedham, Mass., 1966.

2. Dobkin, R. C. *Op Amp Circuit Collection.* National Semiconductor Application Note AN-31, February 1970. National Semiconductor Corp., Santa Clara, Calif.

3. Giles, J. N. *Fairchild Semiconductor LIC Handbook.* Fairchild Semiconductor, Mountain View, Calif., 1967.

4. Jung, W. G. *IC Converter Cookbook.* Howard W. Sams & Co., Inc., Indianapolis, 1978, pp. 165–168.

5. Korn, G. A.; Korn, T. M. *Electronic Analog and Hybrid Computers,* 2nd ed. McGraw-Hill Book Co., New York, 1972.

6. National Semiconductor Application Note AN-32, February 1970. *FET Circuit Applications.* National Semiconductor Corp., Santa Clara, Calif.

7. Roberge, J. K. *Operational Amplifiers—Theory and Practice.* John Wiley & Sons, Inc., New York, 1975.

8. Rudin, M. *Applying Microvolt/Picoamp Instrumentation Operational Amplifiers.* Precision Monolithics Application Note. Precision Monolithics, Inc., Santa Clara, Calif.

9. Sheingold, D. H. *Analog-Digital Conversion Handbook.* Analog Devices, Inc., Norwood, Mass., 1972.

10. Tobey, G. E.; Graeme, J. G.; Huelsman, L. P. (eds.). *Operational Amplifiers—Design and Applications.* McGraw-Hill Book Co., New York, 1971.

11. Widlar, R. J. "Designing With Super-Beta Transistor Op-Amp ICs." *EEE,* December 1969, February and March 1970.

12. ———. *Drift Compensation Techniques for Integrated DC Amplifiers.* National Semiconductor Application Note AN-3, November 1967. National Semiconductor Corp., Santa Clara, Calif.

13. ———. *IC Op Amp Beats FETs on Input Current.* National Semiconductor Application Note AN-29, December 1969. National Semiconductor Corp., Santa Clara, Calif.

14. ———. *Monolithic Operational Amplifiers—The Universal Linear Component.* National Semiconductor Application Note AN-4, April 1968. National Semiconductor Corp., Santa Clara, Calif.

15. Manufacturers' Data Sheets:

Analog Devices	AD515	Operational Amplifier
	AD545	Operational Amplifier
	AD642	Operational Amplifier
National Semiconductor	LM11	Operational Amplifier

TEN

Signal-Generation Circuits

This chapter deals with the generation, shaping, and control of various kinds of signal waveforms. Discussed are signal-generation circuits such as sine-wave oscillators; multivibrators; triangle, ramp, and sawtooth generators; pulse generators; voltage-controlled oscillators; and voltage-controlled timers. These circuits will involve both new material and much of the circuit knowledge gained in previous chapters.

10.1 SINUSOIDAL OSCILLATORS

The most familiar waveform in electronics is the sine wave, and sine-wave signals of different frequencies are as fundamental to circuit work as dc supply potentials are. Generating a sine wave is not hard to do in concept, as we have already seen by the ready tendency of op amps to oscillate when amplification is really the prime intent. This section concerns itself with the controlled form of sine-wave oscillator, having a defined and predictable frequency, amplitude, and in some cases, phase.

10.1.1 Wien-Bridge Oscillators

One of the most familiar types of sine-wave generators is the Wien-bridge circuit shown in Fig. 10-1. This circuit is a classic one in electronics and has been used since the days when it was realized in vacuum-tube versions. The Wien network, composed of R_1-C_1 and R_2-C_2, provides a positive feedback path around A_1, while R_3 and L_1 provide negative feedback. At some fundamental frequency, f_o, the overall phase shift is zero and transmission at this frequency

Set $R_1 = R_2$, $C_1 = C_2$; then $f_o = \dfrac{1}{2\pi R_1 C_1}$

*Select A_1 according to operating frequency and value of R_1; see text.
* *Use R_4 to correct for lamp tolerance and set output level, or fix $R_3 + R_4$ at 750 Ω.

Fig. 10-1. Wien-bridge oscillator.

is maximum in relation to all others. Positive feedback causes the circuit to oscillate at f_o, where

$$f_o = \frac{1}{2\pi R_1 C_1}$$

and $R_1 = R_2$, $C_1 = C_2$.

The attenuation of the Wien network at the frequency of oscillation is equal to 3. If the attenuation in the negative feedback path $(R_3\text{-}L_1)$ is also 3, the bridge will be in balance and the differential input to A_1 will be small. It is this condition that must be maintained because, if the positive feedback is greater, oscillation will quickly build up until amplifier saturation is reached. On the other hand, if the negative feedback is greater, the oscillations will die out. In a practical Wien-bridge oscillator, it is therefore necessary to provide some means of automatically balancing the feedback so that the amplitude of the oscillations can be regulated. In this state the purity of the output waveform will be at a maximum, as will the frequency stability. Another requisite is that the amplifier gain be large at the frequency of oscillation—the input error will then be small, which guarantees that the Wien network operates close to its natural frequency and is stable.

Any means of stabilizing the amplitude of a Wien-bridge oscillator must involve adjustment of the negative feedback divider to maintain the attenuation at 3. Typically, this can take the form of nonlinear elements: thermal types such as lamps or thermistors, nonlinear resistors, diode clippers, zener diodes, and so on. In Fig. 10-1, the nonlinear resistance of a lamp (L_1) is used to regulate the amount of negative feedback. L_1 responds to the average (not instantaneous) output level of A_1, adjusting its terminal resistance in inverse proportion. If the output level of A_1 rises, L_1 increases resistance, counteracting the rise. Similarly, a reduction in output results in a decrease of lamp resistance, stabilizing the oscillation level.

Lamp and thermistor stabilization schemes are popular ones, due mainly to their simplicity. They have several drawbacks, however, such as an inherent thermal time constant that limits usefulness to the lower frequencies.

Resistors R_3-R_4 trim the negative feedback to accommodate lamp tolerances. If precise amplitude control or optimum stability for individual lamps is not necessary, let $R_3 + R_4 = 750$ Ω. For frequency-tunable generators, either R_1-R_2 or C_1-C_2 can be ganged as a pair (with good tracking characteristics). If C_1-C_2 are selected as the tunable elements, large values for R_1-R_2 are required to cover the lower frequencies, which raises the network impedance. In such cases, C_1-C_2 should be in a shielded enclosure and stray capacitance to ground should be minimized for best results.

The circuit of Fig. 10-1 is quite useful as a general-purpose Wien oscillator; with the appropriate amplifier, it can be used over a wide range of frequencies. Amplifiers most suitable (over the widest frequency range) are high-slew-rate FET-input units such as the TL071, AD544, 353, 3140, and 771. These devices can be useful up to 100 kHz. Lowest distortion will be realized with high-slew-rate, high-GBP types such as the 5534, 318, 2505, 2507, 2605, and 2607.

10.1.2 FET-Stabilized Wien Oscillators

Another popular method of achieving amplitude control is by using the variable channel resistance of a field-effect transistor. By sampling and rectifying the output voltage, a dc signal proportional to the output amplitude can be made to control the resistance of a FET. This technique works well within limits, but the channel resistance of the FET itself is nonlinear at high signal levels, and appreciable distortion can occur.

Fig. 10-2 is a Wien-bridge oscillator rearranged to effectively utilize the FET channel resistance as a gain control. In this circuit R_1-R_2 and C_1-C_2 again comprise the Wien network, but with the impedance of the legs scaled so that R_1-C_1 see a voltage lower than R_2-C_2. This allows the voltage level at R_1-C_1 to be of lower amplitude. The circuit uses two amplifiers in the inverting mode; gain control is accomplished by FET Q_1, which is placed at the summing point of A_2 (a point of minimum voltage). Q_1 can then operate at a level low enough to make its distortion negligible. A_2 provides a nominal gain of 2, which is trimmed by the agc and R_5 so that Q_1 is operating in the most linear portion of its characteristic.

The circuit has dual outputs available with two amplifiers; level differences are determined by the Wien network (R_1-R_2). E_{o_1} will have less residual distortion than E_{o_2} because it operates at a lower level and is filtered by the Wien network prior to being controlled by Q_1. The high output level of A_2 is sampled by R_5, which derives the bias to control Q_1. This resistor can be used as an output-level control to adjust output level linearly. Resistor R_4 can be trimmed for low distortion, which is necessary due to differences among individual FETs, if distortion is to be at the lowest level.

$$f_0 = \frac{1}{2\pi\sqrt{R_1\,R_2\,C_1\,C_2}} \quad \text{(1000 Hz as shown)}$$

$$\frac{E_{01}}{E_{02}} = \frac{R_1}{2R_2} \cong \frac{1}{2} \text{ as shown.}$$

Fig. 10-2. Wien-bridge oscillator with FET stabilization.

The amplifiers used should follow the guidelines set down for Fig. 10-1. For general-purpose use, dual devices are obviously attractive. It should be noted that the equation for operating frequency is the general form, due to the difference in R_1-R_2 and C_1-C_2. The ratio used in the bridge may be altered from that shown, if desired, but it should be appreciated that as R_2 increases above R_1, stage A_2 must supply additional gain, thus making its distortion contribution more significant, particularly at high frequencies. The ratio shown provides a good compromise between low-level operation of Q_1 and minimal gain for the A_2 stage. When properly trimmed, the oscillator has less than 0.05% distortion at both outputs with A_2 levels up to ±10 V p-p. When the oscillator is operated over a wide range of frequencies, some adjustment of C_3 may be necessary at low frequencies. Dual FET op amps, such as the TL072 or 3240, can be quite effective in this circuit. The general-purpose 4558 device shown is useful up to about 20 kHz (the values shown yield 1.0 kHz).

The FET-stabilized oscillator of Fig. 10-3 also uses a dual op amp for its implementation, but has only a single output available. In this case the second amplifier is used in a more sophisticated agc system, employing an active integrator in a comparison loop.

In this circuit, A_1 is a Wien-bridge oscillator somewhat similar to that of Fig. 10-1 except for the agc method used. Here, Q_1 is the agc element, an n-channel JFET with less than 100 ohms of "on" resistance and a relatively low cutoff voltage. Q_1 forms a variable resistance in series with R_3, with a value such that the value of $R_4 + R_5$ is twice that of $R_3 +$ the resistance of Q_1. This provides the necessary gain of 3, which is automatically stabilized by the agc loop.

The agc loop consists of D_1 to rectify the output, forming a dc voltage on R_8, which is compared (through R_9) to the -15-V supply as a reference. The output level is set by the ratio of R_9 to R_8; in this case, it results in a ± 10-V (7 V rms) output. Other levels may be realized by adjusting R_9.

A_2 forms an integrator to smooth the ripple on the rectified dc and develop an appropriate dc control level for the gate of Q_1. Resistors R_6-R_7 provide local ac feedback for Q_1, for lowest distortion.

Fig. 10-3. Low-distortion, FET-stabilized Wien-bridge oscillator.

This circuit is capable of very low distortion, on the order of 0.01% when optimized. R_5 can be trimmed for lowest distortion, if this is desired. This will likely be necessary to accommodate different FETs, due to their production spread. This adjustment is an optional "fine tweak," not necessary for the basic function, but to optimize performance in terms of distortion.

As shown, the frequency of the circuit is 5 kHz, as set by R_1-C_1 and R_2-C_2, which should, of course, be close-tolerance units. The 5532 op amp will yield very low distortion at frequencies up to about

$$f_0 = \frac{1}{2\pi R_1 C_1} \quad \text{(1.0 kHz as shown)}$$

$R_1 = R_3, R_2 \leq R_1$

$C_1 = C_2 = C_3$

*Select amplifiers according to parameters, Fig. 10-1.

**D_1-D_2 and R_5 are optional—used to limit output and adjust amplitude level. For D_1 and D_2, use back-to-back IC transistor emitter-base junctions; e.g., Q_1 and Q_2 of CA3086.

Fig. 10-4. Quadrature (sine/cosine) oscillator.

50 kHz. If the operating frequency is to be widely separated from that shown, the values of C_3 and C_4 may require proportional adjustment.

10.1.3 Quadrature (Sine/Cosine) Oscillator

In electronic systems a need often arises for two sine waves in quadrature, or with 90° of phase difference between them. This function is fulfilled by the oscillator of Fig. 10-4, which generates sine and cosine waveforms. The circuit is essentially two integrators in cascade with positive feedback. Because the phase shift of an integrator is 90°, outputs E_{o_1} and E_{o_2} differ in phase by 90°. Thus, with the loop oscillating, these outputs deliver sine and cosine waves.

In theory, all resistances and capacitances are equal in value, but in practice, one resistance (typically R_2) is slightly lowered in value to ensure starting. The remaining timing components assume close tolerance values. With R_2 slightly lowered in value, the oscillations tend to grow in amplitude; if unchecked, they will stabilize at the saturation limits of A_2. To prevent this and to exercise predictable control on output amplitude, a limiting network, consisting of D_1-D_2 and R_5, is used around A_2. With D_1-D_2 directly across A_2, the outputs will stabilize at $\pm V_Z$. R_5 is used to set the output at any level above the zener limits of D_1-D_2. Monolithic zeners are recommended in this circuit for good stability of clipping and best symmetry.

The distortion of the output waveform is reasonably small, in the vicinity of 1.0%. The sine output terminal is lower in distortion than the cosine output because additional filtering of the sine signal occurs after limiting by D_1-D_2.

This circuit is useful where fixed-frequency sine waves in quadrature are needed. Because of the number of precision components in the loop, it does not adapt well to tuned applications. For general applications, dual op amps are convenient (as shown), but diverse applications should be governed by the considerations of Fig. 10-1.

10.1.4 Three-Phase Oscillator

An interesting form of oscillator, which can generate three output signals with a phase difference of 120° and uniform amplitude, is shown in Fig. 10-5.

This circuit is actually a form of phase-shift oscillator based on three stages that have uniform phase shifts. In each stage, the phase shift is set by R_1-C_1, R_2-C_2, and R_3-C_3. Gain is nominally unity for each stage, except for the A_3 stage where the input resistor is lowered several percent in value to ensure the start of oscillations. Note that this is done by a discrete resistor shunt (R_7), which allows all of the other basic resistances (R_1–R_6) to be contained in a single array, if desired.

Oscillations are stabilized by the symmetrical zener clamp Q_1-Q_2, with the amplitude set by R_8 and R_9. The output(s) are stabilized at ± 10 V, and the frequency is set at 400 Hz. For such a relatively low frequency, the 348 or other similar op amp performs well.

A point that should be noted about this oscillator is that the limiting which takes place on output 1 unavoidably involves distortion. However, outputs 2 and 3 constitute low-pass filters for this distortion and are, therefore, cleaner. For example, 0.5% distortion at output 1 will be reduced to below 0.1% at output 2. Even more impressive results in terms of distortion are possible if an active agc scheme (such as that of Fig. 10-3) is employed, using the fourth op amp of the quad IC.

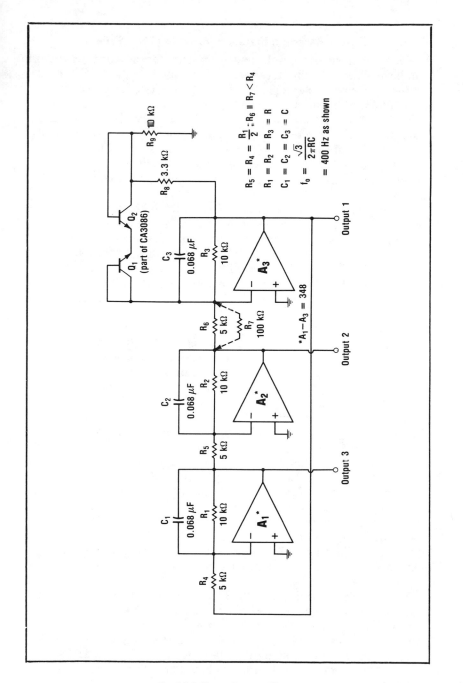

Fig. 10-5. Three-phase oscillator.

10.1.5 Oscillators Based on the State Variable Filter (SVF)

Some interesting, useful, and very-high-performance oscillators can be realized by using the state variable filter as the frequency determining element of a sine-wave oscillator. Two examples of this technique are shown in Figs. 10-6 and 10-7.

In Fig. 10-6, a state variable oscillator is shown which is amplitude stabilized by the zener diode clamping one of the integrators, A_2. This has the effect of rigidly defining the peak amplitude swing of this stage and, in turn, defines the output amplitude of all outputs. At resonance, all three outputs are of equal amplitude, but differ in phase.

Aside from the zener amplitude limiter, the other salient difference of this state variable filter is resistor R_7. This resistor provides the necessary positive feedback to initiate and sustain oscillation. The selection of R_7 is somewhat critical if maximum performance is to be realized. If it is too large, insufficient positive feedback is attained and oscillation will not start. If it is too small, the excessive positive feedback drives D_5 into hard conduction and creates excessive distortion.

Trimmer R_{7B} is selected to provide a gain of just in excess of the Q, as defined by $R_3 + R_4/2R_3$. Here, the Q is 11, which indicates that R_7 should be 10 kΩ $\times$ 11 = 110 kΩ. To guarantee self-starting, R_{7A} is purposely made several percent lower, or 90.9 kΩ.

For a given set of operating conditions, R_7 can be optimized by observing the distortion present at output 2. With D_5 being driven into a moderate degree of conduction, the total harmonic distortion will be on the order of 0.3%, and R_{7B} can be trimmed to provide this.

Due to the natural low-pass-filter action of the A_3 integrator, output 1 will be approximately 10 dB cleaner in distortion than output 2, or on the order of 0.1% (for 0.3% at output 2).

One of the advantages of a zener limiting stabilization in a scheme such as this is that it is fast and has no time constant. To optimize the limiting, a "hard" zener characteristic is utilized as provided by the LM329 (a synthesized zener). Including it in a bridge forces symmetrical limiting and minimizes even-order harmonics. The output level is fixed at 5 V rms, but can be changed by choosing other zener voltages.

This circuit, operating at 10 kHz, should best employ a high-slew-rate, high-GBP op amp, such as the indicated 347. The very best high-frequency, high-level performance will be obtained by discrete devices, such as the 5534, 318, and 2620. More-generalized applications could employ general-purpose quad devices, such as the 348, 4136, 4156, 4741, etc. All resistors should be stable film types having 1.0% tolerances.

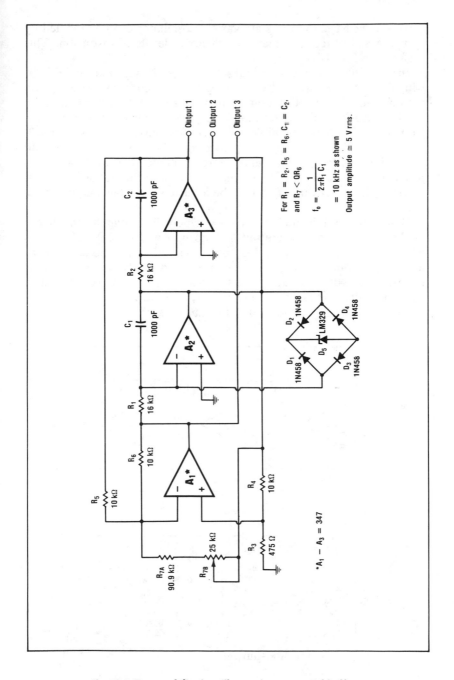

Fig. 10-6. Zener-stabilized oscillator using state variable filter.

This same basic form of state variable oscillator can be modified by applying active agc to achieve much lower levels of distortion. This is shown in Fig. 10-7.

In this circuit, gain-determining resistor R_3 is adjusted by FET Q_1 which, in turn, is driven by an integrator/rectifier consisting of op amp A_4 and D_1-D_2. The nonlinearity of the FET is minimized by local feedback, and the "infinite" dc gain of the integrator renders FET V_{GS} variations negligible. The rectifier senses outputs 1 and 3, which are 180° out of phase, providing full-wave rectification and easier filtering. Resistor R_{11} and reference diode D_5 provide a 70-μA reference current (set by R_{11}) which determines the stabilized output level. Resistor R_{11} can, of course, be adjusted for other output levels, if desired.

Distortion in this oscillator is extremely low, due to the linear method of stabilization. Output 2 distortion will be 0.005% or less when operating properly, and output 1 distortion will be 0.002% or less. Settling time for frequency changes, or at switch-on, is 5 seconds or less, and is determined by the feedback network of the integrator, C_3 and C_4-R_{13}. These components may require adjustment for frequencies largely separated from 1 kHz, as shown.

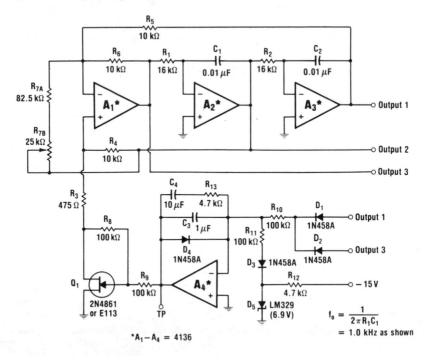

Fig. 10-7. FET-stabilized oscillator using state variable filter.

Distortion is, of course, lowest at output 1, but the extremely low levels quoted should be preserved by the use of a buffer amplifier, as described in Chapter 7. The circuit will operate with any FET as specified, but distortion can be optimized to match the exact characteristics by trimming R_7. As R_7 is increased above 82 kΩ, distortion lowers toward 0.002% (output 2). The dc bias at the test point should be −1 V to −2 V, an indication of linear operation.

All resistors in this circuit (with the exception of R_8, R_9, R_{12}, and R_{13}) should be stable, close-tolerance metalized-film units. The 4136 op amp specified is useful for frequencies up to several kilohertz; above this, one of the quad FET devices should be used. Or, discrete high-performance units could be used for A_1–A_3.

10.2 MULTIVIBRATORS

10.2.1 Astable Multivibrator

Another op-amp oscillator circuit that must be termed a classic is the astable oscillator of Fig. 10-8A. This circuit, with minor modification, can be used with virtually any op amp and is useful over a very wide range of frequencies, limited only by the devices used. The output square wave can either be taken as the full saturated swing of the device (E_{o_1}) or it can be clamped with diodes for defined limits (E_{o_2}). The operating frequency is determined by R_t-C_t and the R_1-R_2 positive feedback network, and is relatively independent of supply voltages and output swing, particularly if the clamping diodes are used.

Operation is best understood by examining the time relationships in Fig. 10-8B. The circuit uses both positive and negative feedback, with regeneration supplied by the R_1-R_2 network and integration by the R_t-C_t network. The op amp compares the voltage output from these two points and changes states as their relative states change. (Operation as described here is applicable to the use of the clamping diodes, but is also generally true if they are not used.)

Assume the R_1-R_2 junction is initially at $+\beta V_Z$, which means the output (E_{o_2}) is at $+V_Z$. The voltage across C_t (E_{C_t}) was previously at $-\beta V_Z$, but it is now charging toward $+V_Z$ through R_t (t_1). As E_{C_t} rises and reaches the potential of $+\beta V_Z$, the threshold potential of the amplifier is reached. Since E_{C_t} is applied to the ($-$) input, this positive rise causes the output to go negative. The negative-going output is immediately transmitted through R_2-R_1, and this positive feedback path causes the output to snap rapidly from positive to negative saturation. With E_{o_2} at $-V_Z$, E_{C_t} now begins to change toward this potential (t_2). The R_1-R_2 junction is now at $-\beta V_Z$, and as E_{C_t} decreases and crosses this potential, the circuit flips positive

T = oscillation period

$$T = 2R_1C_1 \log_e\left(\frac{1+\beta}{1-\beta}\right),$$

where $\beta = \dfrac{R_1}{R_1+R_2}$.

If $\beta = 0.462$, $T = 2R_1C_1$,

$$f_o = \frac{1}{T} = \frac{1}{2R_1C_1} \text{ (100 Hz as shown)}$$

* Any op amp with required differential input rating.
Suggestions:
general-purpose — 301A, TL070
vlf to medium hf — 357
hf — 709, 725, 3100

* * C_1 should be returned to V+ for polarized capacitors.

†Use R_{d_1}-R_{d_2} for differential input protection, if
necessary, or use modified values for R_1-R_2 (see text).

(A) Circuit diagram.

(B) Voltage/time relationships.

Fig. 10-8. Astable multivibrator.

by regeneration, beginning a second cycle of oscillation (t_3); t_1 and t_2 comprise one period of the oscillation cycle, which is of duration T. Since β is a fixed fraction of V_Z (or $E_{o(sat)}$ if clamping is not used) and E_{C_t} is timed against V_Z and compared to βV_Z, V_Z is eliminated from the timing expression for symmetrical values of V_Z (or $E_{o(sat)}$). If t_1 and t_2 are the half-periods, the full period T is $t_1 + t_2$, which can be shown to be

$$T = 2R_t C_t \log_e \left(\frac{1 + \beta}{1 - \beta} \right)$$

This is the *general* expression for the period of the oscillator, from which it is apparent that the period (or frequency) can be controlled by either R_t, C_t, or β (R_1 and R_2).

It can also be seen that if the natural log factor on the right of this expression is made equal to unity, the log term will disappear, which considerably simplifies time calculations. If β is made equal to 0.462, this term becomes very close to unity, which allows the use of the simplified expression. In practice, R_1 and R_2 are chosen for a β of 0.462, then R_t and C_t are chosen from the simplified equation. It should be remembered that for low offset, R_t and $R_1 \parallel R_2$ should be chosen for minimum input offset error. It is, in fact, the low input offset of the op amp that lends the circuit its innate timing precision, for as long as V_{io} is much less than βV_Z, the timing error due to amplifier offset will be negligible. With FET-input amplifiers, there is no requirement for matched source resistances due to their lower bias currents.

There are a few practical problems associated with this circuit that may or may not be significant, depending on the amplifier chosen. Since the function of the amplifier is essentially that of a comparator, performance is governed by many of the same considerations (see Chapter 8). The amplifier should *not* be frequency compensated, as compensation is not necessary for stability and it reduces high-frequency capability. The inputs to the amplifier can be subjected to large differential voltages; therefore, protection should be considered for unprotected types, and internally clamped types such as the 308 and 318 will need a series resistance (R_d) to prevent excessive differential current flow—the resistance used should be much greater than either R_t or $R_1 \parallel R_2$ for minimum degradation of timing characteristics.

At low frequencies, or when C_t becomes large, indicating use of a polarized type, two problems can occur. First, the capacitor must be polarized *properly*—this is satisfied by returning it to a supply voltage rather than ground, V+ usually being preferred. Also, C_t represents a potentially destructive element on switchoff because it looks directly into the amplifier input. For capacitance values greater than

0.1 μF, some series resistance to the $(-)$ input is desired, usually 1 kΩ or greater, to provide safety for the amplifier.

Most of the preceding problems can be dealt with by the selection of the proper device or by the judicious use of protection. For instance, either the 301A or 748 would be a good choice for general-purpose use at frequencies below 10 kHz. The 357 can be operated over an extremely wide range because of its low input current (which allows low frequencies) and wide bandwidth (which allows high frequencies). Generally, the op-amp types that are optimum for comparator use will work best in this circuit.

At the higher frequencies, stray capacitance should be minimized and resistances should be kept low. Also, transistor junction zeners work best for D_1-D_2 and are recommended for the cleanest waveforms. Op amps that can be clamped at an internal high-impedance node (such as the 301A, 2527, or 2627) allow clamping for good accuracy without excessive power dissipation.

Note that if zener clamping is used to limit E_{o_2} to approximately ± 7 V, and if β is set at less than 0.5, the differential input to A_1 will be less than the differential breakdown potential. This allows use of unprotected types without clamping, such as the 709, 725, and NE540. The NE540, for instance, is very useful because it can deliver output currents of ± 100 mA.

If desired, this astable multivibrator can be easily synchronized by injecting pulses at the $(+)$ input through C_1. The circuit can be synchronized with either positive or negative pulses.

A useful variation on the basic astable circuit of Fig. 10-8 is the high-frequency version of Fig. 10-9. This circuit is optimized for higher-frequency use, and uses a high-slew-rate and GBP device— the 3100.

It should be noted that the frequency expression for this circuit is simplified, as shown. This comes about from changing the R_2/R_1 relative resistances to a ratio of 3/1, which results in a β of 0.25. This not only results in the simplified expression, but it also reduces the maximum input differential to the amplifier to less than the zener breakdown level, even if R_2 and R_t are returned directly to the output (no clamping used). Thus, any op amp can be used, even unprotected units such as the 709 or 725, which work well in this circuit.

Another very useful version of this circuit, which uses only a single power supply, is shown in Fig. 10-10. This circuit capitalizes on the fact that the 3130 op amp has an output stage which swings rail-to-rail, delivering the full supply voltage to the load. Thus, the circuit is a useful square-wave source whose amplitude can be adjusted by varying V+ over the range of +5 V to +15 V.

This circuit also uses the simplified expression, and is arranged for oscillation at a 1.0-Hz rate. Since the 3130 has very low input

Fig. 10-9. High-frequency astable multivibrator.

currents, R_t can range up to hundreds of megohms, if desired. C_t should be a low-leakage unit, such as polypropylene.

Other single-supply op amps can also be used in this circuit, but will not swing rail-to-rail and will operate over a more narrow range of R_t. Examples are such units as the 358, 324, 3403, etc. For medium to high supply voltages, almost any op amp can be used in this circuit; they just will not have as high an output swing.

Another example of a useful astable circuit application is shown in Fig. 10-11. This circuit is arranged for single-supply operation at 5 Hz. Input clamping and current protection are provided by D_1-D_2 and R_5, and circuit values are chosen to be generally uncritical of

Fig. 10-10. Low-frequency, single-supply astable multivibrator.

*A₁ is any op amp. Use V+ equal to total supply
voltage — i.e., V+ = 30 V for ±15-V devices.

Fig. 10-11. Astable multivibrator for testing op amps (f ≅ 5 Hz).

any op amp. Thus, virtually any device can be inserted into the socket for A_1 and given a quick functional check. D_3, an LED, provides an attention-getting 5-Hz flash rate that allows the checker to be used with no equipment other than power. Even battery operation is feasible, if desired, in which case R_8 can be increased to prolong battery life.

10.2.2 Monostable (One-Shot) Multivibrator

A modification of Fig. 10-8A yields a circuit that is stable in only one output state (monostable); this circuit is shown in Fig. 10-12.

The addition of D_1 across C_t clamps the $(-)$ input of the op amp at $+0.6$ V, which forces the amplifier to assume a defined output state. Since the positive feedback from R_1-R_2 can rise above this level, the output latches to the "high" state, or $+E_{o(sat)}$. Triggering is accomplished through D_2, which passes the differentiated negative input pulse at C_1-R_3 to the $(+)$ input. A negative input pulse that pulls the $(+)$ input below $+0.6$ V causes the output to flip to the negative output state, $-E_{o(sat)}$. This action is regenerative, and the output stays in the negative state because the $(-)$ input cannot immediately follow due to R_t-C_t. C_t then starts charging toward $-E_{o(sat)}$ through R_t.

The voltage at the $(+)$ input at this time is $-\beta E_{o(sat)}$. As the voltage across C_t reaches this voltage, the amplifier flips positive once again, due to regeneration. The circuit does not completely recover, however, until C_t charges back up to $+0.6$ V, where D_1 clamps it in a static state. Because of this relatively long recharge cycle, the recovery time is poor, but it can be improved if desired by adding

Fig. 10-12. Monostable multivibrator.

R_4-D_3, which provides a shorter time constant for recovery. The time of the output pulse width is determined by the initial capacitor voltage ($+0.6$ V) and by $-E_{o(sat)}$:

$$T = R_tC_t\log_e\left(\frac{-E_{o(sat)} - (V_{f(D_1)})}{-E_{o(sat)} - (\beta E_{o(sat)})}\right)$$

This is the complete, precise form of the equation, which in many situations can be simplified further. If $E_{o(sat)} \gg 0.6$ V, the initial capacitor charge can be assumed to be zero with slight error (about 5% for silicon diodes, half this figure for germanium). This yields a new equation,

$$T \cong R_tC_t\log_e\left(\frac{1}{1-\beta}\right)$$

To simplify further: if β is made 0.632, the log term becomes equal to unity, or

$$T \cong R_tC_t$$

The presence of D_1 also introduces a temperature coefficient of about $0.017\%/°C$, which should be considered in precise applications.

The triggering network of C_1-R_3 may need some alteration to suit different triggering requirements. R_3 should be greater than R_1 so that timing is not upset. Note that β determines the trigger sensitivity since it sets the voltage at the ($+$) input.

In the example shown, R_t and C_t are chosen for a 1.0-ms pulse width, and β is set at 0.632 by R_1-R_2. As with the astable multivibrator on which this circuit is based, the timing period is independent of supplies, and zener clamping may be used at the output. Speed is not a prime feature of this circuit, so an uncompensated op amp should be used to optimize this factor. The 301A and 748 are good for pulse widths down to approximately 100 μs; below this, one of the faster types mentioned previously should be used. Input protection is a consideration in this circuit as in the astable circuit. The circuit can also be rearranged to deliver positive-going output pulses, if desired, by reversing D_1 and D_2 (and D_3 if used). Note that D_1 and D_3 (if used) should be low-leakage types if high R_t values are used. If a FET-input device such as the 357 or 351 is used, very long times are possible. This circuit can also be arranged for single-supply use.

10.2.3 Bistable Multivibrator

The third general form of multivibrator, the bistable, is shown in Fig. 10-13. This circuit is essentially a comparator with ac input coupling through C_1-R_3 (see Chapter 8). Input sensitivity can be adjusted by altering β, since $\pm\beta E_{o(sat)}$ is the voltage required for triggering at the ($-$) input.

Although a dual-supply circuit using a 301A is shown in Fig. 10-13, a single-supply version can be arranged simply by applying a $V+/2$ voltage to the bottom of R_3 and making R_1 a pair of 100-kΩ resistors—one connected to ground, the other connected to $V+$. A_1 should then be a single-supply device, such as the 358, 324, 3140, etc.

*Adjust $\beta \left(\dfrac{R_1}{R_1+R_2} \right)$ for desired trigger sensitivity.

Fig. 10-13. Bistable multivibrator.

10.3 FUNCTION GENERATORS

As will soon be noted, many of the following circuits use voltage comparators in combination with integrators to generate time-dependent functions. To a large degree, many of these circuits will be limited primarily by the device used as a comparator. The response time and slew rate define the upper limit of usable speed; therefore, nearly all the devices recommended will be uncompensated types to take advantage of the greater potential speed. An optimum selection for a given application must be based on the performance of the op amp as a comparator. It is recommended that the performance of various devices as comparators (Chapter 8) be reviewed to keep the pertinent considerations in mind when making the choice between an op amp and a true comparator device.

10.0.1 Basic Circuit

One of the most useful op-amp oscillator circuits is the triangle/square-wave function generator of Fig. 10-14A. This circuit, comprised of an "ideal" integrator (A_2) and a comparator with hysteresis (A_1), simultaneously generates ultralinear triangle waveforms and symmetrical square waves. Operation over an extremely wide range of frequencies is possible using appropriate devices, from ultralow frequencies with periods measured in hours, up to hundreds of kilohertz.

The circuit is best understood by regarding the timing diagram in Fig. 10-14B. Assume that the output of comparator A_1 has just switched to the high state and that E_{o_2} is at $+V_Z$ (breakdown voltage of D_1-D_2). The input to the integrator is then $+V_Z$, which means output E_{o_1} will integrate at a rate

$$\frac{E_{in}}{RC} = \frac{V_Z}{R_tC_t}V/s$$

A_1 compares the sum of the voltages E_{o_1} and E_{o_2} against the ground reference on its ($-$) input. As E_{o_1} ramps negative, the junction of R_1-R_2 decreases toward zero (t_1). When E_{o_1} crosses $-V_Z$ (or when E_{o_1} is equal and opposite to E_{o_2}), the voltage at the ($+$) input of A_1 crosses zero and A_1 changes state rapidly, aided by positive feedback. E_{o_2} is now at $-V_Z$, and A_2 begins to integrate positive toward $+V_Z$ (t_2). When E_{o_1} crosses $+V_Z$, A_1 changes back to the high state and the cycle repeats.

The output voltage of A_1 is clamped at $\pm V_Z$, which determines the output amplitudes. The positive and negative ramp slopes are determined by $\pm V_Z$, R_t, and C_t, and are equal if the zener voltages are symmetrical (usually the case).

The unclamped direct output from A_1 (E_{o_3}) is available for external use. This output can be used to feed A_2 (in lieu of the clamping network), but it will introduce side effects. First, the frequency will vary as the saturation voltages or supply voltages of A_1 change. Second, if A_1 is used to feed A_2 directly, R_1 must always be greater than R_2 to set $E_{o_1} < E_{o_3}$. A_2 cannot be allowed to saturate, which would happen if $R_2 = R_1$ (or $E_{o_1} = E_{o_3}$). This modification may be useful

E_{o_1} = p-p output from A_2
$= \pm V_z \left(\dfrac{R_2}{R_1} \right)$

$E_{o_2} = \pm V_z$

$E_{o_3} = \pm E_{o(sat)}$

$t_1 = t_2$ and $T = t_1 + t_2 = \dfrac{2\,E_{o_1}R_1C_1}{V_z}$ (4.0 ms as shown)

$D_1 - D_4 = $ 1N458A
$D_5 = $ LM329

* Input overvoltage protection, for A_2 if required.

(A) Circuit diagram.

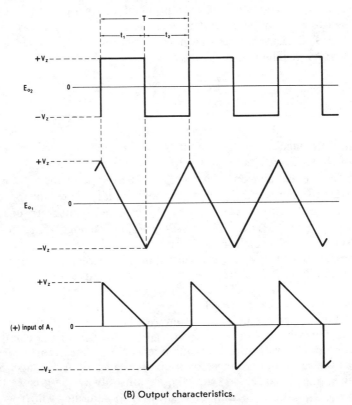

(B) Output characteristics.

Fig. 10-14. Function generator.

for noncritical applications, however, as it does eliminate R_3 and D_1-D_2.

Since the circuit is actually a linear ramp generator made to oscillate between two voltage limits, an expression for the operating period (or frequency) must include both slopes of the ramp and the voltage limits. The pertinent timing data is shown in Fig. 10-14B, where t_1 and t_2 are the half-periods and T is the period of a single cycle.

The time for the first half-cycle is

$$t_1 = \frac{E_o t}{\Delta E_o}$$

Since

$$\frac{\Delta E_o}{t} = \frac{E_{in}}{RC}$$

then

$$t_1 = \frac{E_o RC}{E_{in}}$$

or

$$t_1 = \frac{E_{o_1} R_t C_t}{V_z}$$

where E_{o_1} is the desired peak-to-peak amplitude from A_2. Similarly, for the second half-cycle,

$$t_2 = \frac{E_{o_1} R_t C_t}{V_z}$$

Since the zener voltages (hence the times) are symmetrical, the period T is then

$$T = \frac{2E_{o_1} R_t C_t}{V_z}$$

This equation can be used in designing the circuit for specific times or specific output voltages. The output voltage (E_{o_1}) is scaled to V_z by a factor of 2:1; therefore, the relationship used to select R_1 and R_2 is

$$E_{o_1} = \frac{R_2}{R_1} 2 V_z$$

These points may be further illustrated in the example shown, which uses a 6.9-V zener, the LM329. In Fig. 10-14A, $R_1 = R_2$, so the output is 16 volts peak-to-peak. The frequency is then $1/4R_t C_t$, or approximately 250 Hz.

Frequency can be varied without amplitude change by varying either R_t or C_t. Variation of R_t allows frequency change over many decades—limited at the low end by the bias current of A_2 and at the high end by the output current of A_2 or by its slew rate. C_t is most conveniently changed in decade steps, with low maximum values for reasons of economy. Obviously, as the stability of the frequency is directly proportional to R_t and C_t, they should be low-TC, close-tolerance types. Similarly, R_1-R_2 should be stable types for frequency and amplitude stability. D_1–D_5 provide low TC due to the low TC of the 329.

As always, amplifier selection plays an important role in performance. Since A_1 operates as a comparator, it should be an uncompensated or high-slew-rate type. Two good choices for A_1 are the 357 and the TL080, as shown. Op amp A_2 must be internally compensated and have a high slew rate for high-frequency operation; thus, the 356 or the AD544 are good choices here. At ultralow frequencies where the integration current becomes very small, the low bias current of FET-input types is quite attractive. If extension of the low-frequency range is achieved by large C_t values, input protection precautions should be taken for A_2, if the amplifier is unprotected. Dual and quad FET types are excellent general-purpose choices, but will sacrifice some speed in the A_1 stage, compared to the units shown.

10.3.2 Modifications to the Basic Function Generator

The function generator of Fig. 10-14A not only is a versatile circuit in its own right, but it adapts readily to many extremely useful variations.

As discussed previously, the frequency of the function generator is controllable by varying either R_t or C_t. Variation of R_t is the simplest means of frequency change, but there is an alternate method that is attractive for other reasons. This circuit (Fig. 10-15) introduces a divider network, β, composed of R_5 and R_6, and placed between the clamping diodes and R_t. R_5 and R_6 vary the fraction of $\pm V_z$ that is fed to R_t; thus, the input to the integrator in this circuit is $\pm \beta V_z$. If the term βV_z is substituted in the expression for t_1 and t_2, the new timing equation for T is

$$t_1 = t_2 = \frac{E_{o_1} R_t C_t}{\beta V_z}$$

and

$$T = t_1 + t_2 = \frac{2E_{o_1} R_t C_t}{\beta V_z}$$

The use of R_5-R_6 represents a reduction in input current to A_2, the fraction being equal to β. Thus, similar to large values of R_t, it

Fig. 10-15. Variable-frequency function generator (20 Hz to 20 kHz).

383

places a limitation on A_2 (in terms of input current) for very low frequencies. Dynamic range of frequency is optimized by selecting R_t such that when β is minimum the input current is still much greater than the bias current of A_2. Frequency variations of 1000:1 are relatively easy to achieve, and ratios of 10,000:1 are possible.

The reason behind the β voltage divider may already be obvious —the control of gain from unity to some fraction of the input can next be provided by an analog multiplier, as discussed in Chapter 6. Thus, if β (R_5 plus R_6) is replaced by a two-quadrant multiplier, the frequency may be made electronically variable, with a dynamic range proportional to the range of the multiplier.

In the example shown, the dynamic range is 3 decades or more; R_t and C_t are chosen for an upper frequency limit of 20 kHz, and the oscillator can be adjusted from 20 Hz to 20 kHz using R_5. FET-input devices, such as the AD544 shown, are recommended for best high-frequency operation and low input current. This will yield the best overall frequency capability and widest dynamic range.

A point that should be appreciated is that the offset voltage of A_2 *must* be low for a wide dynamic range of operation. This can be accomplished by specifying a low offset device, such as the AD544 or the OP-16, or by careful trimming. As an alternative, a composite ultralow offset voltage connection can be employed for the A_2 function.

10.3.3 Function Generator With Independently Variable Slopes

Another modification to the basic function generator allows independent control of positive and negative slopes, both of which have a dynamic range of control limited only by the integrating op amp. With individual ramp control, the basic triangular output wave can be modified into a sawtooth waveform, either positive-going or negative-going.

The circuit shown in Fig. 10-16 uses a diode bridge at the summing point of integrator A_2, which acts as a current-mode gate under control of A_1. If the output of A_1 is high, D_1 and D_4 are switched on, causing R_{t_1} to inject current into the summing point from V+ through D_1. When the output of A_1 is low, D_2 and D_3 switch on and R_{t_2} conducts current from V− to the summing point of A_2, thus controlling positive ramp slopes. If these currents are termed I_{i_1} and I_{i_2}, respectively, new expressions for the output slopes of A_2 can be written. If the negative slope has duration t_1 (Fig. 10-16) and the positive slope has duration t_2; then, for the negative slope,

$$\frac{\Delta E_o}{\Delta t} = \frac{I_{i_1}}{C_t}$$

or

Fig. 10-16. Function generator with independently variable slopes.

$$t_1 = \frac{E_{o_1} C_t}{I_{i_1}}$$

where E_{o_1} is the desired peak-to-peak output swing from A_2. For the positive slope,

$$\frac{\Delta E_o}{\Delta t} = \frac{I_{i_2}}{C_t}$$

or

$$t_2 = \frac{E_{o_1} C_t}{I_{i_2}}$$

and

$$T = t_1 + t_2$$

In practice, the control of I_{i_1} and I_{i_2} to vary ramp slopes can involve any of several methods: potentiometers for R_{t_1} and R_{t_2}, fixed resistors returned to variable voltages, or current sources. If R_{t_1} and R_{t_2} are potentiometers, the most stable method of control is a variable resistance to $V+$ or $V-$ because diodes D_1 and D_3 introduce some temperature dependence into I_{i_1} and I_{i_2}, and this variance is minimized when the voltage is high. Ideally, I_{i_1} and I_{i_2} are generated by constant-current sources such as those described in Chapter 4. If the current source is made voltage-controlled, it allows voltage control of either the wave period or, in the case of dual (complementary) current sources, the frequency at a constant duty cycle.

This circuit can also be used as a variable-period pulse generator with precise control of pulse width and frequency. A wide dynamic range of operation is available (many decades). C_t can be switch-selected for decade ranges, and R_{t_1} and R_{t_2} can be made calibrated potentiometers.

The considerations in this circuit differ little from the previous one. D_1-D_4 are ideally a matched diode bridge as shown. This has the bonus of allowing the use of "extra" diodes (D_5-D_6) as clamps for the input from A_1. R_5 is chosen so that it can supply adequate current to absorb I_{i_1} or I_{i_2} at their highest levels. Any excess current provided by R_5 is absorbed in the clamps, D_5-D_6. Amplifier selection is governed by the previous restrictions—the devices shown are for medium-speed use. R_{t_1}, R_{t_2}, and C_t in this circuit example are chosen to yield a minimum total period of 1.0 ms. R_{t_1} and R_{t_2} allow the period to be lengthened to a total of 100 ms. This circuit can serve as a useful source of adjustable ramp, triangular, pulse, and square waveforms.

10.3.4 Triangle to Sine-Wave Converter

The formation of sine waves in a function generator is normally a conversion process, one that synthesizes approximate sine curves from a triangular input wave. Many sine-wave generators use biased diodes to "round" and shape the peaks of triangle waves. The circuit of Fig. 10-17 is much simpler in concept, yet produces excellent results. It can be used with any triangle wave having constant amplitude and a 50% duty cycle, such as those just described.

The circuit uses a differential amplifier (A_1) and a matched transistor pair (Q_1-Q_2) with a controlled amount of emitter coupling. As has been previously described in the section on multipliers and instrumentation amplifiers (Chapters 6 and 7), an undegenerated, emitter-coupled amplifier is linear only for small signal levels. However, if operation is held to a region of controlled nonlinearity, an emitter-coupled pair can convert a linear input voltage such as a triangle wave into a good approximation of a sine-wave output. This is what Q_1-Q_2 of Fig. 10-17 accomplish, and A_1 converts the sinusoidal output current of Q_1-Q_2 to a buffered sine-wave output voltage.

Since this scheme involves precise control over the conduction of Q_1 and Q_2, it is critically dependent upon both the input amplitude

Fig. 10-17. Triangle to sine-wave converter.

and the degree of emitter coupling. R_1 and R_2 are chosen for approximately 300 to 400 mV p-p drive at Q_1. With levels in this range, R_3 can be set for a point of minimum output distortion. This is best done with a distortion analyzer, but an oscilloscope can also be used. Once R_3 is set, the input level must not change, or the distortion in the output will climb rapidly. For this reason, high-stability components are preferred for R_1–R_4; R_3 should preferably be a high-resolution trimmer, such as a 10-turn potentiometer.

Distortion is also affected to a smaller degree by the match of Q_1-Q_2. A matched transistor pair can be used without nulling and distortion will still be reasonably low ($\leqslant 1.0\%$). However, optimum performance (total harmonic distortion $\cong 0.3\%$) is obtained by offset nulling or selection of a tightly controlled offset-voltage pair ($V_{io} < 0.5$ mV). Resistors R_{10} and R_{11} may be used to scale the sine-wave output level. The values used in this example yield levels comparable to those of the triangular input waveforms; they should be ratio matched as indicated. The op amp (A_1) should be consistent with required speeds—a type 357 yields optimum performance in this regard. Note that this amplifier could also be from a quad device, such as the TL074, 347, 774, 3471, etc. The LM394 is a tightly controlled (50 μV) offset device, eliminating the null requirement. More loosely matched pairs can be used, such as the MAT-01, AD818, or CA3046, in which case nulling at the base of Q_2 may be helpful.

10.3.5 Gain-Controlled Buffer Amplifier

Function generators can be very useful as laboratory tools, and the gain-controlled stage of Fig. 10-18 is a handy addition. The circuit gain is variable from zero to a maximum of R_2/R_1. Most of the function generators discussed have an output voltage of $E_o = \pm V_Z$, which is about ± 7-8 V. The ratio of R_2/R_1 shown scales this value continuously from zero to ± 10 V or so, and allows linear calibration of the output. Minimum rise and fall times are governed by the amplifier—

$E_o = \pm 10$ V maximum, reducible to zero by adjusting R_2.

*Select for required bandwidth and slew rate. A_1 must be stable at unity gain.

**Trim if necessary for exact full-scale output desired.

Fig. 10-18. Buffer with feedback gain control.

a type 318 or 2520 is recommended here. The output impedance remains low for any setting of R_2. For greater output current (up to ± 50 mA), use an inside-the-loop unity-gain buffer (such as the LH0002) between A_7 and E_o (see Chapter 7).

10.4 SAWTOOTH GENERATORS

One common circuit requirement is the sawtooth generator, frequently used to generate ramp voltages for timing purposes. The previous function generator with independent slope adjustments can be used to generate sawtooth waveforms, but circuit requirements often dictate a more specialized type of generator. The waveform itself can have either a linear or an exponential slope, depending on the application. Other variations are in the form of control: driven, triggered, free-running, or synchronized.

10.4.1 Basic Low-Frequency Sweep Generator

The sawtooth generator of Fig. 10-19 may be recognized as an integrator with clamping transistor Q_1 added, to reset the capacitor to zero at the end of each timing cycle. The circuit requires an external control voltage (E_c) to command the state of the ramp generator. If E_c is high, the circuit is in the hold mode. In this state, D_1 is reverse biased and Q_1 is in saturation in parallel with C_t. This makes the output voltage essentially zero, which establishes the output dc base line. The circuit will remain in this state indefinitely as long as E_c is high. When E_c is taken low, D_1 pulls the gate of Q_1 low; this turns Q_1 off.

With Q_1 off, the circuit begins to integrate and the output voltage rises at the rate of I_t/C_t volts per second. This rise continues until E_c again goes high, turning on Q_1 and discharging C_t. From this it may be seen that although R_t and C_t set the slope of the output waveform, the timing of the input control will determine the final end-point voltage. In designing this circuit for a specific application, the E_c timing characteristic must be known beforehand.

In the example shown, the values are chosen to be compatible with one typical requirement, a 60-Hz sweep generator for tv-raster vertical scan. Assuming a typical hold (retrace) interval of approximately 1.5 ms, R_t and C_t provide a slope of 10 V in 15 ms, the active portion of the vertical scan.

This sweep generator is best confined to low-frequency use as shown, generally below 1.0 kHz. For these applications, the 741 types are adequate. The circuit can be used at higher frequencies with a high-speed FET-input type, such as the 356. A subsequent circuit shows an alternate form of sweep that allows the use of a low-frequency device for timing. Modification of this circuit for negative-going output waveforms is accomplished by substituting a p-channel

Fig. 10-19. Low-frequency sweep generator.

FET, such as a 2N5116, for Q_1 and returning R_t to V+. Also, D_1 is reversed, as is the sense of the logic control. For the basic ramp circuit of Fig. 10-19, the controlling voltage, E_c, can easily be generated by the one-shot multivibrator shown in the inset. This circuit senses voltage E_o from A_1 and produces a 1.5-ms positive pulse when E_o reaches +10 V (adjustable by R_3). A_1 and A_2 can be dual 741s for slow speeds; dual FET types for higher speeds.

10.4.2 Fast Precision Sweep Generator

Due to slew-rate and bandwidth limitations, the sweep generator of Fig. 10-19 must use a high-speed op amp above about 1.0 kHz. The circuit of Fig. 10-20, however, produces fast sweeps of over 10 V/μs using a low-frequency op amp. A_1 and Q_1 form a precision current source, I_t (Chapter 4), and Q_2 is a saturated switch that holds C_t near zero volts when E_c is high. When E_c falls low, Q_2 switches off and C_t begins to charge toward +15 V, forming a linear ramp with a slope of I_t/C_t (V/s). This voltage rise across C_t is buffered by A_2, a low-input-current, high-speed follower. The voltage E_o from A_2 represents the output from the generator, with timing according to E_c and slope set by I_t and C_t.

The key to higher speed is that A_1 does not see the high rate of voltage change—it is isolated by the collector of Q_1. Since Q_2 is a high-speed device, the real limitation on sweep speed is buffer A_2,

$$I_t = \frac{V+}{R_3}\left(\frac{R_1}{R_1+R_2}\right) = \frac{15}{R_3}\left(\frac{R_1}{R_1+R_2}\right)$$

Sweep slope $= \dfrac{\Delta E_o}{\Delta t} = \dfrac{I_t}{C_1}$

Maximum slope is approximately 13 V/μs due to A_2.

*$A_1 - A_2$ = TL072

**The function of Q_2 can also be realized by open-collector logic gates—e.g., 7406, 7407.

†Trim R_3 if a wide-tolerance capacitor (5.0%) is used for C_1.

Fig. 10-20. Fast precision sweep generator.

which must be faster than the fastest trace (or retrace) of the saw-tooth voltage across C_t. Thus, if single devices are used for A_1 and A_2, A_1 can be a general-purpose type but A_2 should be a fast device.

As shown, the circuit does not tax the speed capability of A_2 to any great extent, except during the retrace interval. Retrace time is set by C_t and the R_{on} of Q_2. The selection of a low-R_{on} device for Q_2 will minimize the baseline offset; as shown, the offset will be 16 mV or less with the 80-Ω R_{on} of the 2N4093.

The values in this example are chosen as typical of a tv raster—a period of 63.5 μs, with approximately 50 μs active. Thus, E_o has a 0.2-V/μs rate of rise, or 10 V in 50 μs. The indicated values are precise, but R_3 may be trimmed to set the output slope. If independence of slope from the +15-V line is desired, R_1 may be changed to a 2.5-V zener reference, in which case R_3 should be 12.5 kΩ.

10.4.3 Long-Period Timers

The two previous circuits are variations of the same type—i.e., driven sawtooth generators. The next circuit type differs in that it responds to input triggers; after triggering it generates a single saw-tooth of prescribed duration, then returns to the standby state. It is similar to the monostable multivibrator, but in this case the timing ramp is buffered for external use. The circuit is also capable of extremely short recovery times, thus allowing immediate retriggering.

A dual-supply version of this timer is shown in Fig. 10-21. It consists basically of a transistor switch (Q_1), a timing network (R_t-C_t), a buffer (A_1), and a comparator (A_2). The state of switch Q_1 is controlled by the comparator, which receives trigger pulses from an external source.

In the standby state, output E_{o_2} is high, clamped at $+V_Z$ by D_1-D_2. This voltage holds Q_1 in the on state via D_5 and R_6, and output E_{o_1} remains near zero volts. In this condition, the feedback path through R_1-R_2 scales the $+V_Z$ voltage at E_{o_2} to $+V_Z R_2 (R_1 + R_2)$ at the (+) input of A_2; for this example, the input voltage of A_2 is $+V_Z/2$. Thus, a trigger pulse of $+(V_Z/2 + V_f)$ volts at D_3 (or D_4) is required to overcome the bias on A_2, where V_f is the diode voltage drop. This positive pulse switches A_2 to the low state, which disables clamp Q_1. C_t then begins timing toward +15 V with a time constant of $R_t C_t$. The voltage at E_{o_1} required to reset A_2 will be $-(-V_Z R_2/R_1)$; in this case, simply $+V_Z$. When E_{o_1} reaches $+V_Z$, A_2 switches to the high state, shorting C_t and resetting the circuit to its standby state. The action is extremely fast due to the small time constant formed by $R_5 C_t$ and the fact that there is some regeneration for the reset mode (whereas none exists for the trigger mode). The circuit will thus respond almost instantly to a second trigger pulse after reset.

Fig. 10-21. Dual-supply timer circuit.

The timing equation for this circuit is dependent upon V+, zener voltage V_z, and R_tC_t according to

$$t = R_tC_t\log_e\left(\frac{V+}{(V+) - (R_2/R_1)V_z}\right)$$

In the present example, V+ = 15 V, V_z = 7.5 V, and $R_1 = R_2$, so the timing expression becomes

$$t = 0.7 R_tC_t$$

As shown, the circuit is suitable for timing periods of up to 10 seconds with R_t maximum, but larger values of C_t can be used for longer periods. R_t can also be increased, but there is an upper limit of about 5 MΩ in standard potentiometer values. C_t can be switch-selected for decade timing changes—good-quality capacitors should be used, such as plastic-film types. The 356 is a good choice for A_1 in general-purpose applications, but A_2 should be uncompensated to optimize its triggering capability. The push-button trigger circuit shown is designed to minimize the effects of switch bounce; S_1 triggers only on actuation, not on release.

The three circuit outputs consist of two timing gates from A_2, which are negative during the timing interval, and the sawtooth output, which rises exponentially toward $+V_z$. Generally, for a timer the gate is the working output, but the sawtooth output may also be useful.

For single-supply uses, the timer shown in Fig. 10-22 will be found useful. This circuit uses a 555 timer as the monostable,* and a 3140 single-supply FET-input op amp to buffer the timing ramp across C_t. A low-leakage CMOS switch (A_3, a 4016) is used across C_t.

In this circuit, the timing range is extended without using large resistances or capacitances. As can be noted, the V+ voltage is divided by R_1 and R_2 prior to being applied to R_t. In this case, R_1 and R_2 yield a division ratio of 90:1. This, when multiplied by the basic 555 timing period of $1.1R_tC_t$, achieves a new timing period of T = $100R_tC_t$.

This circuit is most useful with single supplies in the range of +10 V to +15 V. Timing can be trimmed with R_2, or with optional control R_6. Although a timing interval of 20 minutes is shown, it can range much longer if desired. The circuit is flexible since it has two outputs, pin 7 of the 555 having been made available as an uncommitted second output. It also has an enable input, if one is desired. If the long timing feature is not necessary, R_1 and R_2 can be eliminated and R_t returned directly to V+.

---

* See reference 8 at the end of the chapter.

Fig. 10-22. Single-supply timer circuit.

10.4.4 Synchronized Sawtooth Oscillator

The sawtooth generators described thus far have been either driven or triggered types, both of which require an external oscillator for excitation. Drive sources for these circuits can be made from any of the astable oscillators described previously, but it is sometimes advantageous to make the sweep-generating functions part of the same circuit. An example of this is the sawtooth oscillator of Fig. 10-23, which is a source of both sawtooth and pulse waveforms, capable of being externally synchronized.

This circuit may be recognized as similar to the function generator of Fig. 10-14A, with suitable modifications for the sawtooth asymmetry, tunability, and synchronization. The use of D_3 and D_4 in series with R_{t_1} and R_{t_2} allows the negative and positive slopes to be set simply and independently. Tuning of the circuit is set by the variable-β network, R_5-R_6. If the negative output slope has duration t_1 and the positive slope has duration t_2, the design equations for these periods are

$$t_1 = \frac{E_{o_1} R_{t_1} C_t}{\beta V_Z - V_{f_3}}$$

and

$$t_2 = \frac{E_{o_1} R_{t_2} C_t}{\beta V_Z - V_{f_4}}$$

where V_{f_3} and V_{f_4} are the forward voltage drops of D_3 and D_4, respectively.

The circuit components here are chosen to be compatible with a 60-Hz sweep generator. R_{t_1} is set at $R_{t_2}/15$, yielding a trace/retrace ratio of 15 ($t_2 = 15$ ms and $t_1 = 1.0$ ms). R_5 provides a variation of 0.5:1 to allow tuning over a 2:1 range. In practice, frequency control R_5 is set for a natural frequency slightly lower than the incoming sync pulses. R_{t_1} and R_{t_2} may be altered to yield virtually any desired degree of asymmetry for various other applications.

The sync input, E_s, may be applied to either the $(-)$ or $(+)$ input of A_1, depending on the type of pulse available. Synchronization for either input occurs at the beginning of the t_1 interval.

Since this design example chosen is one of low frequency, an internally compensated amplifier may be used for A_1, such as the 4558. As previously, three outputs are available: the sawtooth, E_{o_1}, and the two rectangular outputs, E_{o_2} and E_{o_3}. This circuit is a very useful one, and the substitution of high-speed op amps will allow its application over a wide range of frequencies.

Fig. 10-23. Synchronized sawtooth oscillator.

10.5 VOLTAGE-CONTROLLED SIGNAL GENERATION AND MODULATION

An extension of basic op-amp circuit design is the adaptation to voltage control. Voltage-controlled functions and modulation techniques are extremely useful in instrumentation and control systems. By making some function of a periodic waveform vary according to another voltage, it is possible to transmit dc or low-frequency information as a modulated carrier, often with greater accuracy and greater convenience. This section examines basic op-amp techniques used to produce amplitude modulation, pulse-width modulation, and frequency modulation.

Fig. 10-24. Pulse-amplitude modulator.

10.5.1 Pulse-Amplitude Modulator

A simple form of encoding a low-frequency signal on a carrier is by pulse-amplitude modulation, as in Fig. 10-24. This circuit processes a bipolar pulse carrier, E_c, by clamping its positive and negative excursions with diodes D_1 and D_2. D_2 clamps the negative peak of E_o to a voltage -0.6 V lower than the bias voltage of D_3 or zero volts, since the forward drops of D_2 and D_3 cancel. D_1 and D_4 perform a similar function for the positive peaks, clamping them to the voltage at the anode of D_4, which is E_m, provided by voltage follower A_1. The connection of D_1 and D_4 is arranged to cancel their forward drops and temperature coefficients, and to clamp E_o to E_m. Thus, as E_m varies from 0 to +10 V, the positive peaks of E_o vary in accordance, accomplishing amplitude modulation of the E_o pulses.

This circuit by nature has a high output impedance, essentially the value of R_1. A buffer may be required for low-impedance loads. The input voltage, E_c, should always be greater than the most positive peak of E_m for effective clamping. If E_c is small, some amplification may be necessary. This can be provided by a comparator such as A_2, which regenerates the input pulses to full amplitude with uniform rise and fall times.

As shown, the circuit responds to positive modulating voltages and delivers positive output pulses. For negative-going outputs, reverse all diodes, change the bias to −15 V, and let E_m vary from 0 V to −10 V. If minimum temperature drift of the clamping voltages is not required, the circuit can be simplified by wiring A_1 as a standard follower, with D_1 connected to its output and D_2 connected directly to ground.

10.5.2 Voltage-Controlled Monostable Circuit (Voltage to Pulse-Width Converter)

A monostable multivibrator that delivers an output pulse width proportional to an input voltage can be used as a pulse-width modulator (or voltage to pulse-width converter); Fig. 10-25 is such a circuit. The highly linear and precisely controlled ramp used to time the output pulse width is made available as an output. Hence, this circuit can also be used as a triggered voltage-controlled sweep generator. The circuit consists of two basic parts: a voltage-controlled integrator (A_1) and a threshold comparator (A_2). A_1 generates a voltage ramp with slope controlled by E_{in}, R_t, and C_t. A_2 controls the ramp-limit voltage. Pulse width t_c is determined by

$$t_c = \frac{E_{o_1} R_t C_t}{E_{in}}$$

In the quiescent state, A_2 is high, holding Q_1 on and clamping the output of A_1 at a voltage near ground. The circuit is stable in this state, since positive feedback from E_{o_2} holds the (+) input of A_2 at $+V_Z R_1/R_2$, a voltage greater than the ground level on its (−) input.

A negative trigger pulse at E_t greater than this bias will flip the comparator to the negative output state, which turns off Q_1 and starts a negative ramp of voltage from A_1. The output from A_1 decreases linearly with a slope of $R_t C_t/E_{in}$ volts per second. This voltage appears at the (−) input of A_2, attenuated by a factor of $R_4/(R_4 + R_5)$. Furthermore, the negative threshold of A_2 is at $-V_Z R_1/(R_1 + R_2)$. Thus, if the ratios R_2/R_1 and R_5/R_4 are made equal, the comparator threshold voltage is simply $-V_z$. When E_{o_1} crosses $-V_z$, then, A_2 flips back to the positive (stable) state, which turns Q_1 on, discharging C_t. This returns the circuit to its original state, ready for a second trigger pulse. The circuit has three outputs: the ramp output from A_1 (or E_{o_1}), and the two comparator outputs, E_{o_2} and E_{o_3}. As may be noted from the timing of E_{o_1}, the recovery time (t_r) of the ramp makes the total cycle time slightly in excess of t_c (the time duration of E_{o_2} and E_{o_3}). Controlling the recovery time of A_1 involves adjusting the simple RC time constant of t_r, as shown.

$$t_c = \frac{E_{0_1} R_1 C_t}{E_{in}}$$

$t_r = R_{on(Q_1)} C_t$ where,

t_c is the output period (pulse width),
t_r is the recovery period,
E_{0_1} is the p-p output of A_1.

*A_1-A_2 best suited for medium-long pulse widths ($t_c \geq 1.0$ ms). Substitute faster types for shorter pulse widths.

Fig. 10-25. Voltage-controlled monostable circuit (voltage to pulse-width converter).

The circuit responds to positive input voltages at E_{in}. With $E_{in} = +1.0$ V, t_c is 10 ms, decreasing to 1.0 ms at $E_{in} = +10$ V. Longer times are possible by scaling R_t or C_t. For shorter pulse widths, a faster integrator should be used for A_1, such as a 356 type. Also, A_2 should be speed-optimized for microsecond pulse widths; this can take the form of a higher-speed op amp and high-speed (transistor) diodes for D_1-D_2.

Another use for this circuit would be as a resistance-measuring device. By making E_{in} a reference voltage, the output pulse width will be proportional to R_t (which would be the unknown resistance).

With a FET-input op amp for A_1, the circuit could easily measure resistances of up to 100 MΩ or more.

10.5.3 Voltage-to-Frequency Converters

Using op amps as integrators, comparators, and monostables in a circuit topology like that of Fig. 10-26 allows a special class of A/D converter to be implemented—the voltage-to-frequency converter.

*Basic V/F Relationships:

$$t_1 = \frac{\Delta V C_1}{I_2 - I_1}, \quad t_2 = \frac{\Delta V C_1}{I_1}$$

Thus,

$$\Delta V C_1 = t_1 (I_2 - I_1)$$

and

$$\Delta V C_1 = t_2 I_1$$

so

$$t_1 (I_2 - I_1) = t_2 I_1$$

Then in terms of t_1,

$$t_2 = \frac{t_1 (I_2 - I_1)}{I_1}$$

Solving for total period, T :

$$T = t_1 + t_2 = t_1 + \left(\frac{t_1 (I_2 - I_1)}{I_1} \right)$$

Simplifying,

$$T = t_1 \left(\frac{I_2}{I_1} \right)$$

In terms of frequency,

$$f = \frac{1}{T} = \frac{I_1}{t_1 I_2}$$

In terms of V_{in},

$$f = \frac{V_{in}}{R_{in} t_1 I_2}$$

Fig. 10-26. Block diagram of voltage-to-frequency (V/F) converter.

The voltage-to-frequency, or V/F, converter is capable of extremely high accuracies over a very wide dynamic range—on the order of 0.01% and 10,000/1 (80 dB), respectively. These figures would equate to 12 bits of conversion (or more).

All of the functional blocks depicted in Fig. 10-26 can be implemented by using op amps as they have been described in this book. However, it is most likely not efficient or practical to do so, since there already exist IC V/F devices* which achieve this function economically and efficiently with very high accuracy. Accordingly, two representative V/F converter circuits using IC V/F devices will be presented here.

A good example of the high performance that can be realized with V/F techniques is the precision V/F converter circuit of Fig. 10-27. Here, a 356 op amp is used as an integrator, driving either an RC4151 (Raytheon) or an LM331 (National Semiconductor) V/F

$$*t_1 = 1.1R_oC_o, \quad I_2 = \frac{1.9}{R_s}, \quad I_1 = \frac{V_{in}}{R_{in}}$$

Note: $I_1 < I_2$

$$f_o = \frac{1}{T} = \frac{I_1}{I_2 t_1} = \frac{V_{in}}{R_{in} I_2 t_1}$$

$$**C_1 \geq 2.7 \times 10^{-5} t_1$$

$$\text{Choose } A_2 \text{ SR} \geq \frac{2.5 \times 10^{-5}}{t_1}$$

Fig. 10-27. Wide-range precision V/F converter (0 to −10 V; 0 to 100 kHz).

IC, A_1. The V/F IC provides the block functions (shown in Fig. 10-26) of the comparator, the monostable, and the gated current source. To set up the V/F for a given input voltage range, which is to be made to correspond to an output frequency range, the relationships shown in the illustration are used.

I_1 is the full-scale input, which should be 100 μA, thus the desired full-scale voltage will define R_{in}. Here, R_{in} is 100 kΩ with $V_{in \, (max)}$ equal to −10 V. I_2 is the V/F reference current, which is set to 135 μA by virtue of the 1.9-V V/F reference voltage and R_s. Time period t_1 is the monostable pulse width, set by R_o and C_o as shown. By making R_o variable, overall calibration can be accomplished.

Output from this circuit is a train of TTL-compatible pulses, and calibration is achieved by adjusting R_o for 100 kHz with a −10-V

* See reference 7 at the end of the chapter.

(exact) input. The low-frequency end of the range is calibrated by trimming the op-amp offset for an output frequency of 100 Hz with a −10-mV input voltage.

Due to the very high dynamic range and high slew rate of the FET-input op amp, this circuit is capable of a linearity error of less than 0.1% of full scale, with errors appreciably smaller at lower full-scale

$$*\, f_o = \frac{I_1}{I_2 t_1} \text{ (general)}$$

In terms of V_{in}, with $\dfrac{R_5}{R_4 + R_5} = \dfrac{1}{10}$,

$$f_o = \frac{V_{in}}{10 R_{in} I_2 t_1}$$

Fig. 10-28. Single-supply V/F converter (0 to +10 V; 0 to 10 kHz).

portions of the range. Useful dynamic range of the circuit will be 10,000/1, or more, if offset trim is used for A_2 and a 331A device for the V/F.

A single-supply V/F circuit useful for 0- to +10-V inputs and a 0- to 10-kHz output is shown in Fig. 10-28. This circuit is set up very similar to that of Fig. 10-27, but op amp A_2 is used as a noninverting integrator in this case. Time period t_1 of the V/F is lowered for the 10-kHz range.

In this circuit, R_4 and R_5 reduce the 10-V maximum input to 1.0 V, as applied to A_2, a FET-input, single-supply op amp. Calibration is for a 10-kHz output with a +10-V input by means of R_s. The offset of A_2 is trimmed also, for a 10-Hz output with a 10-mV input. Linearity error of this circuit is 0.05%, or less, over the 10-kHz range.

REFERENCES

1. *Applications Manual for Computing Amplifiers.* Philbrick Researches, Inc., Dedham, Mass., 1966.

2. Burwen, R. "Ultra Low Distortion Oscillator." *EDN/EEE,* June 1, 1971.

3. Dobkin, R. C. *Op Amp Circuit Collection.* National Semiconductor Application Note AN-31, February 1970. National Semiconductor Corp., Santa Clara, Calif.

4. Giles, J. N. *Fairchild Semiconductor LIC Handbook.* Fairchild Semiconductor, Mountain View, Calif., 1967.

5. Grebene, A. B. "Monolithic Waveform Generation." *IEEE Spectrum,* April 1972.

6. Jung, W. G. *Audio IC Op-Amp Applications,* 2nd ed. Howard W. Sams & Co., Inc., Indianapolis, 1978.

7. ———. *IC Converter Cookbook.* Howard W. Sams & Co., Inc., Indianapolis, 1978.

8. ———. *IC Timer Cookbook.* Howard W. Sams & Co., Inc., Indianapolis, 1977.

9. ———. "LEDs Do Dual Duty in Sine Wave Oscillator." *EDN,* August 20, 1976.

10. ———. "Low Distortion Oscillator Uses State Variable Filter." *Electronics,* February 5, 1976.

11. ———. "The Signal Path: Function Generators." *db, The Sound Engineering Magazine,* December 1975.

12. ———. "The Signal Path: Sine Wave Oscillators." *db, The Sound Engineering Magazine,* July 1976.

13. Korn, G. A.; Korn, T. M. *Electronic Analog and Hybrid Computers,* 2nd ed. McGraw-Hill Book Co., New York, 1972.

14. Miler, G. G. *A Simple Square-Triangle Waveform Generator.* Harris Semiconductor Application Note 510/A, October 1970. Harris Semiconductor, Melbourne, Fla.

15. Olson, H. "Use Diodes for Amplitude Control in 0.001 Hz Wien Bridge Oscillator." *Electronic Design,* April 1, 1972.

16. Routh, W. S. *An Applications Guide for Operational Amplifiers.* National Semiconductor Application Note AN-20, February 1969. National Semiconductor Corp., Santa Clara, Calif.

17. Smith, J. I. *Modern Operational Circuit Design.* John Wiley & Sons, Inc., New York, 1971.

18. Tobey, G. E.; Graeme, J. G.; Huelsman, L. P. (eds.). *Operational Amplifiers —Design and Applications.* McGraw-Hill Book Co., New York, 1971.

19. Widlar, R. J. *Drift Compensation Techniques for Integrated DC Amplifiers.* National Semiconductor Application Note AN-3, November 1967. National Semiconductor Corp., Santa Clara, Calif.

20. ———. *IC Op Amp Beats FETs on Input Current.* National Smiconductor Application Note AN-29, December 1969. National Semiconductor Corp., Santa Clara, Calif.

21. ———. *Monolithic Operational Amplifiers—The Universal Linear Component.* National Semiconductor Application Note AN-4, April 1968. National Semiconductor Corp., Santa Clara, Calif.

III

Appendix

Manufacturers' Data Sheets
For General-Purpose Op Amps

This appendix includes catalog specification sheets for selected general-purpose op amps that will be useful in a large percentage of applications. These devices are well accepted as industry standards, and the data sheets reproduced here are those of the original manufacturers.

Space does not permit the inclusion of data sheets for the more-specialized devices; thus, it is suggested that the reader assemble catalog information for these types by writing the various manufacturers listed in Table A-1. These manufacturers are the original sources of the respective devices listed.

Inasmuch as a number of device types are featured in this section, the data sheets are presented in abbreviated form to conserve space. Complete performance information is included, but (in some cases) specific application examples are omitted. The reader is encouraged to assemble complete (and most current) catalog information by writing the manufacturer in question.

In some cases, the data sheet presented is an example of the forerunner of a generic type of op amp. Related and similarly performing amplifiers (such as duals or quads) are listed in Table A-2.

For simplicity, the device numbers used in most of the circuits in this book are presented in *generic form,* as listed in the right-hand column of Table A-1. Thus, for example, a "301A" op amp implies a National Semiconductor LM301A device. Since each generic type listed may actually fan-out to as many as five different specific devices (excluding package options), it is easy to appreciate why this must be done (see OP-07 for an example).

Table A-1. Original Source Manufacturers and Their Respective Devices

Manufacturer	Prefix	Part No. Example(s)	Devices (Generic Form)
Analog Devices, Inc. Route One Industrial Park P.O. Box 280 Norwood, MA 02062 (617) 329-4700	"AD"	AD542J AD542K AD542L	504, 509, 510, 515, 517, 518, 540, 542, 544, 545
Burr-Brown International Airport Industrial Park P.O. Box 11400 Tucson, AZ 85734 (602) 746-1111	None	3500A 3500B 3500C	3500, 3500MP, 3521, 3528, 3580, 3581
Fairchild Semiconductor 464 Ellis Street Mountain View, CA 94042 (415) 962-5011	"μA"	μA741 μA741C	702, 709, 714, 715, 725, 740, 741, 747, 748, 759, 771, 772, 774, 776, 791, 798
Harris Semiconductor P.O. Box 883 Melbourne, FL 32901 (305) 727-5430	"HA"	HA2600 HA2602 HA2605	2500, 2510, 2520, 2600, 2620, 2640, 2900, 4622, 4741, 5100, 5130, 5160, 5190
Intersil, Inc. 10710 North Tantau Avenue Cupertino, CA 95014 (408) 996-5000	"ICL"	ICL7611	7611, 7612, 7613, 7614, 7621, 7622, 7631, 7641, 8007, 8008, 8043, 8500
Motorola Semiconductor Products, Inc. P.O. Box 20912 Phoenix, AZ 85036 (602) 244-6900	"MC"	MC3303 MC3403 MC3503	1436, 1437, 1456, 1458, 1741S, 3403, 3458, 3471, 4741, 34001, 34002
National Semiconductor Corp. 2900 Semiconductor Drive Santa Clara, CA 95051 (408) 737-5000	"LF" "LH" "LM"	LF356 LF256 LF156 LH0002 LH0002C LM301A LM201A LM101A	301A, 307, 308, 308A, 310, 312, 316, 318, 321, 324, 343, 344, 347, 348, 349, 351, 353, 354, 355, 356, 357, 358, 2902, 2904, 0002, 0044, LM10, LM11
Precision Monolithics, Inc. 1500 Space Park Drive Santa Clara, CA 95050 (408) 246-9222	"OP"	OP-07 OP-07A OP-07C OP-07D OP-07E	OP-01, OP-02, OP-04, OP-05, OP-07, OP-08, OP-09, OP-10, OP-11, OP-12, OP-14, OP-15, OP-16, OP-17, OP-20
Raytheon Semiconductor 350 Ellis Street Mountain View, CA 94042 (415) 968-9211	"RC" "RM"	RC4558 RM4558	4131, 4132, 4136, 4156, 4558, 4559

Table A-1. Original Source Manufacturers and Their Respective Devices (cont)

Manufacturer	Prefix	Part No. Example(s)	Devices (Generic Form)
RCA Solid State Division Route 202 Somerville, NJ 08876 (201) 685-6000	"CA"	CA3140 CA3140A CA3140B	3100, 3130, 3140, 3160, 3193, 3240
Signetics Corp. 811 East Arques Avenue Sunnyvale, CA 94086 (408) 739-7700	"NE" "SE"	NE535 SE535	530, 531, 532, 535, 538, 540, 541, 5530, 5532, 5533, 5534, 5535, 5538
Texas Instruments, Inc. P.O. Box 225012 Dallas, TX 75265 (214) 238-2011	"TL"	TL071 TL071A TL071B	TL060, TL061, TL062, TL064, TL070, TL071, TL072, TL074, TL075, TL080, TL081, TL082, TL084, TL087, TL088, TL287, TL288

Table A-2. Basic Device Types and Their Generic Relations*

Basic Type	Generic Relation*	Manufacturer
741	μA748 (single) μA747 (dual) MC1458 (dual) MC4741 (quad) LM348 (quad)	Fairchild Fairchild Motorola Motorola National
301A	LM307 (single) LH2301 (dual)	National National
4558	RC4559 (dual) RC4136 (quad)	Raytheon Raytheon
324	LM358 (dual) MC3403 (quad)	National Motorola
3140	CA3130 (single) CA3160 (single) CA3240 (dual)	RCA RCA RCA
TL070 Series	TL060 Series TL080 Series	Texas Instruments Texas Instruments
351	LF353 (dual) LF347 (quad)	National National
355/356/357	LFT355/356/357 OP-15/OP-16/OP-17	National Precision Monolithics

*This table lists devices that are generically related to the standard types, the data sheets of which are reproduced in this appendix. Complete information on these devices may be obtained by writing the manufacturer in question.

In some cases, it is not appropriate (and may actually cause confusion) to delete the prefix used by a manufacturer. For example, both Signetics and Analog Devices use a "500" series generic device number system, with many identically appearing generic numbers for *different* devices. Thus, an Analog Devices AD540 op amp should be understood to be entirely different than a Signetics NE540, but *both* are actual devices that are available. Further confusion can arise when a prefix preceding a part number beginning in zero is dropped; an OP-07 would then be an 07 (which is ambiguous). Even worse, an OP-10 and an LM10 without prefixes would appear identical (which they are not, of course). In such cases, we have endeavored to use complete part numbers, such as TL071, OP-02, LM10, etc., as well as AD540 versus NE540.

As noted at the beginning of this appendix, the manufacturers of the devices listed in Table A-1 are the original sources of those devices. In addition, most manufacturers supply, or "second-source," standard devices that are not of their own origin. A second-source cross-reference listing, available from most manufacturers, will be helpful in identifying alternate sources of the various devices. However, some caution should be extended to the reader as to what constitutes a *true* alternate-source device. Generally, if a device is listed as a "direct" or "pin-for-pin" replacement, it is an electrical and mechanical duplicate of the original. If, however, a device is listed as a "functional" equivalent, it is not necessarily a direct substitute mechanically or electrically in all details. In these cases, consult the manufacturer's data sheets in order to be assured of suitability. In all cases, alternate-source types should be qualified by in-circuit testing as a final verification of suitability.

µA741
FREQUENCY-COMPENSATED OPERATIONAL AMPLIFIER
FAIRCHILD LINEAR INTEGRATED CIRCUITS

GENERAL DESCRIPTION — The µA741 is a high performance monolithic Operational Amplifier constructed using the Fairchild Planar* epitaxial process. It is intended for a wide range of analog applications. High common mode voltage range and absence of latch-up tendencies make the µA741 ideal for use as a voltage follower. The high gain and wide range of operating voltage provides superior performance in integrator, summing amplifier, and general feedback applications.

- NO FREQUENCY COMPENSATION REQUIRED
- SHORT CIRCUIT PROTECTION
- OFFSET VOLTAGE NULL CAPABILITY
- LARGE COMMON MODE AND DIFFERENTIAL VOLTAGE RANGES
- LOW POWER CONSUMPTION
- NO LATCH-UP

ABSOLUTE MAXIMUM RATINGS

Supply Voltage	
µA741A, µA741, µA741E	±22 V
µA741C	±18 V
Internal Power Dissipation (Note 1)	
Metal Can	500 mW
Molded and Hermetic DIP	670 mW
Mini DIP	310 mW
Flatpak	570 mW
Differential Input Voltage	±30 V
Input Voltage (Note 2)	±15 V
Storage Temperature Range	
Metal Can, Hermetic DIP, and Flatpak	−65°C to +150°C
Mini DIP, Molded DIP	−55°C to +125°C
Operating Temperature Range	
Military (µA741A, µA741)	−55°C to +125°C
Commercial (µA741E, µA741C)	0°C to +70°C
Pin Temperature (Soldering)	
Metal Can, Hermetic DIPs, and Flatpak (60 s)	300°C
Molded DIPs (10 s)	260°C
Output Short Circuit Duration (Note 3)	Indefinite

CONNECTION DIAGRAMS

8-PIN METAL CAN
(TOP VIEW)
PACKAGE OUTLINE 5B
PACKAGE CODE H

Note: Pin 4 connected to case

ORDER INFORMATION

TYPE	PART NO.
µA741A	µA741AHM
µA741	µA741HM
µA741E	µA741EHC
µA741C	µA741HC

14-PIN DIP
(TOP VIEW)
PACKAGE OUTLINES 6A, 9A
PACKAGE CODES D   P

ORDER INFORMATION

TYPE	PART NO.
µA741A	µA741ADM
µA741	µA741DM
µA741E	µA741EDC
µA741C	µA741DC
µA741C	µA741PC

8-PIN MINI DIP
(TOP VIEW)
PACKAGE OUTLINES 6T 9T
PACKAGE CODES R   T

ORDER INFORMATION

TYPE	PART NO.
µA741C	µA741TC
µA741C	µA741RC

10-PIN FLATPAK
(TOP VIEW)
PACKAGE OUTLINE 3F
PACKAGE CODE F

ORDER INFORMATION

TYPE	PART NO.
µA741A	µA741AFM
µA741	µA741FM

Notes on following pages.

*Planar is a patented Fairchild process.

Courtesy Fairchild Semiconductor

μA741A

ELECTRICAL CHARACTERISTICS: V_S = ±15 V, T_A = 25°C unless otherwise specified.

CHARACTERISTICS (see definitions)	CONDITIONS		MIN	TYP	MAX	UNITS
Input Offset Voltage	$R_S \leq 50\Omega$			0.8	3.0	mV
Average Input Offset Voltage Drift					15	μV/°C
Input Offset Current				3.0	30	nA
Average Input Offset Current Drift					0.5	nA/°C
Input Bias Current				30	80	nA
Power Supply Rejection Ratio	V_S = +20, −20; V_S = −20, +10V, R_S = 50Ω			15	50	μV/V
Output Short Circuit Current			10	25	40	mA
Power Dissipation	V_S = ±20V			80	150	mW
Input Impedance	V_S = ±20V		1.0	6.0		MΩ
Large Signal Voltage Gain	V_S = ±20V, R_L = 2kΩ, V_{OUT} = ±15V		50			V/mV
Transient Response	Rise Time			0.25	0.8	μs
(Unity Gain)	Overshoot			6.0	20	%
Bandwidth (Note 4)			.437	1.5		MHz
Slew Rate (Unity Gain)	V_{IN} = ±10V		0.3	0.7		V/μs
The following specifications apply for −55°C ≤ T_A ≤ +125°C						
Input Offset Voltage					4.0	mV
Input Offset Current					70	nA
Input Bias Current					210	nA
Common Mode Rejection Ratio	V_S = ±20V, V_{IN} = ±15V, R_S = 50Ω		80	95		dB
Adjustment For Input Offset Voltage	V_S = ±20V		10			mV
Output Short Circuit Current			10		40	mA
Power Dissipation	V_S = ±20V	−55°C			165	mW
		+125°C			135	mW
Input Impedance	V_S = ±20V		0.5			MΩ
Output Voltage Swing	V_S = ±20V,	R_L = 10kΩ	±16			V
		R_L = 2kΩ	±15			V
Large Signal Voltage Gain	V_S = ±20V, R_L = 2kΩ, V_{OUT} = ±15V		32			V/mV
	V_S = ±5V, R_L = 2kΩ, V_{OUT} = ±2 V		10			V/mV

NOTES
1. Rating applies to ambient temperatures up to 70°C. Above 70°C ambient derate linearly at 6.3mW/°C for the metal can, 8.3mW/°C for the DIP and 7.1mW/°C for the Flatpak.
2. For supply voltages less than ±15V, the absolute maximum input voltage is equal to the supply voltage.
3. Short circuit may be to ground or either supply. Rating applies to +125°C case temperature or 75°C ambient temperature.
4. Calculated value from: $BW(MHz) = \dfrac{0.35}{\text{Rise Time } (\mu s)}$

μA741

ELECTRICAL CHARACTERISTICS: $V_S = \pm 15$ V, $T_A = 25°C$ unless otherwise specified.

CHARACTERISTICS (see definitions)	CONDITIONS	MIN	TYP	MAX	UNITS
Input Offset Voltage	$R_S \leqslant 10$ kΩ		1.0	5.0	mV
Input Offset Current			20	200	nA
Input Bias Current			80	500	nA
Input Resistance		0.3	2.0		MΩ
Input Capacitance			1.4		pF
Offset Voltage Adjustment Range			±15		mV
Large Signal Voltage Gain	$R_L \geqslant 2$ kΩ, $V_{OUT} = \pm 10$ V	50,000	200,000		
Output Resistance			75		Ω
Output Short Circuit Current			25		mA
Supply Current			1.7	2.8	mA
Power Consumption			50	85	mW
Transient Response (Unity Gain) — Rise time	$V_{IN} = 20$ mV, $R_L = 2$ kΩ, $C_L \leqslant 100$ pF		0.3		μs
Transient Response (Unity Gain) — Overshoot			5.0		%
Slew Rate	$R_L \geqslant 2$ kΩ		0.5		V/μs

The following specifications apply for $-55°C \leqslant T_A \leqslant +125°C$:

		MIN	TYP	MAX	UNITS
Input Offset Voltage	$R_S \leqslant 10$ kΩ		1.0	6.0	mV
Input Offset Current	$T_A = +125°C$		7.0	200	nA
Input Offset Current	$T_A = -55°C$		85	500	nA
Input Bias Current	$T_A = +125°C$		0.03	0.5	μA
Input Bias Current	$T_A = -55°C$		0.3	1.5	μA
Input Voltage Range		±12	±13		V
Common Mode Rejection Ratio	$R_S \leqslant 10$ kΩ	70	90		dB
Supply Voltage Rejection Ratio	$R_S \leqslant 10$ kΩ		30	150	μV/V
Large Signal Voltage Gain	$R_L \geqslant 2$ kΩ, $V_{OUT} = \pm 10$ V	25,000			
Output Voltage Swing	$R_L \geqslant 10$ kΩ	±12	±14		V
Output Voltage Swing	$R_L \geqslant 2$ kΩ	±10	±13		V
Supply Current	$T_A = +125°C$		1.5	2.5	mA
Supply Current	$T_A = -55°C$		2.0	3.3	mA
Power Consumption	$T_A = +125°C$		45	75	mW
Power Consumption	$T_A = -55°C$		60	100	mW

TYPICAL PERFORMANCE CURVES FOR μA741A AND μA741

OPEN LOOP VOLTAGE GAIN
AS A FUNCTION OF
SUPPLY VOLTAGE

OUTPUT VOLTAGE SWING
AS A FUNCTION OF
SUPPLY VOLTAGE

INPUT COMMON MODE
VOLTAGE RANGE AS A
FUNCTION OF SUPPLY VOLTAGE

μA741E

ELECTRICAL CHARACTERISTICS: V_S = ±15 V, T_A = 25°C unless otherwise specified.

CHARACTERISTICS (see definitions)	CONDITIONS	MIN	TYP	MAX	UNITS
Input Offset Voltage	R_S ≤ 50Ω		0.8	3.0	mV
Average Input Offset Voltage Drift				15	μV/°C
Input Offset Current			3.0	30	nA
Average Input Offset Current Drift				0.5	nA/°C
Input Bias Current			30	80	nA
Power Supply Rejection Ratio	V_S = +10, −20; V_S = +20, −10V; R_S = 50Ω		15	50	μV/V
Output Short Circuit Current		10	25	40	mA
Power Dissipation	V_S = ±20V		80	150	mW
Input Impedance	V_S = ±20V	1.0	6.0		MΩ
Large Signal Voltage Gain	V_S = ±20V, R_L = 2kΩ, V_{OUT} = ±15V	50			V/mV
Transient Response — Rise Time			0.25	0.8	μs
(Unity Gain) — Overshoot			6.0	20	%
Bandwidth (Note 4)		.437	1.5		MHz
Slew Rate (Unity Gain)	V_{IN} = ±10V	0.3	0.7		V/μs
The following specifications apply for 0°C ≤ T_A ≤ 70°C					
Input Offset Voltage				4.0	mV
Input Offset Current				70	nA
Input Bias Current				210	nA
Common Mode Rejection Ratio	V_S = ±20V, V_{IN} = ±15V, R_S = 50Ω	80	95		dB
Adjustment For Input Offset Voltage	V_S = ±20V	10			mV
Output Short Circuit Current		10		40	mA
Power Dissipation	V_S = ±20V			150	mW
Input Impedance	V_S = ±20V	0.5			MΩ
Output Voltage Swing	V_S = ±20V, R_L = 10kΩ	±16			V
	R_L = 2kΩ	±15			V
Large Signal Voltage Gain	V_S = ±20V, R_L = 2kΩ, V_{OUT} = ±15V	32			V/mV
	V_S = ±5V, R_L = 2kΩ, V_{OUT} = ±2 V	10			V/mV

EQUIVALENT CIRCUIT

Courtesy Fairchild Semiconductor

µA741C

ELECTRICAL CHARACTERISTICS: $V_S = \pm 15$ V, $T_A = 25°C$ unless otherwise specified.

CHARACTERISTICS (see definitions)	CONDITIONS	MIN	TYP	MAX	UNITS
Input Offset Voltage	$R_S \leqslant 10$ kΩ		2.0	6.0	mV
Input Offset Current			20	200	nA
Input Bias Current			80	500	nA
Input Resistance		0.3	2.0		MΩ
Input Capacitance			1.4		pF
Offset Voltage Adjustment Range			± 15		mV
Input Voltage Range		± 12	± 13		V
Common Mode Rejection Ratio	$R_S \leqslant 10$ kΩ	70	90		dB
Supply Voltage Rejection Ratio	$R_S \leqslant 10$ kΩ		30	150	μV/V
Large Signal Voltage Gain	$R_L \geqslant 2$ kΩ, $V_{OUT} = \pm 10$ V	20,000	200,000		
Output Voltage Swing	$R_L \geqslant 10$ kΩ	± 12	± 14		V
	$R_L \geqslant 2$ kΩ	± 10	± 13		V
Output Resistance			75		Ω
Output Short Circuit Current			25		mA
Supply Current			1.7	2.8	mA
Power Consumption			50	85	mW
Transient Response (Unity Gain) Rise time	$V_{IN} = 20$ mV, $R_L = 2$ kΩ, $C_L \leqslant 100$ pF		0.3		μs
Overshoot			5.0		%
Slew Rate	$R_L \geqslant 2$ kΩ		0.5		V/μs

The following specifications apply for $0°C \leqslant T_A \leqslant +70°C$:

Input Offset Voltage				7.5	mV
Input Offset Current				300	nA
Input Bias Current				800	nA
Large Signal Voltage Gain	$R_L \geqslant 2$ kΩ, $V_{OUT} = \pm 10$ V	15,000			
Output Voltage Swing	$R_L \geqslant 2$ kΩ	± 10	± 13		V

TYPICAL PERFORMANCE CURVES FOR µA741E AND µA741C

OPEN LOOP VOLTAGE GAIN AS A FUNCTION OF SUPPLY VOLTAGE

OUTPUT VOLTAGE SWING AS A FUNCTION OF SUPPLY VOLTAGE

INPUT COMMON MODE VOLTAGE RANGE AS A FUNCTION OF SUPPLY VOLTAGE

TYPICAL PERFORMANCE CURVES FOR μA741A, μA741, μA741E AND μA741C

Courtesy Fairchild Semiconductor

TYPICAL APPLICATIONS

UNITY-GAIN VOLTAGE FOLLOWER

$R_{IN} = 400 M\Omega$
$C_{IN} = 1 pF$
$R_{OUT} << 1 \Omega$
B.W. = 1 MHz

NON-INVERTING AMPLIFIER

GAIN	R1	R2	B W	R_{IN}
10	1 kΩ	9 kΩ	100 kHz	400 MΩ
100	100 Ω	9.9 kΩ	10 kHz	280 MΩ
1000	100 Ω	99.9 kΩ	1 kHz	80 MΩ

INVERTING AMPLIFIER

GAIN	R1	R2	B W	R_{IN}
1	10 kΩ	10 kΩ	1 MHz	10 kΩ
10	1 kΩ	10 kΩ	100 kHz	1 kΩ
100	1 kΩ	100 kΩ	10 kHz	1 kΩ
1000	100 Ω	100 kΩ	1 kHz	100 Ω

CLIPPING AMPLIFIER

$$\frac{E_{OUT}}{E_{IN}} = \frac{R2}{R1} \text{ if } |E_{OUT}| \leqslant V_Z + 0.7 \text{ V}$$

where V_Z = Zener breakdown voltage

419

National Semiconductor

Operational Amplifiers/Buffers

LM101A/LM201A/LM301A Operational Amplifiers

General Description

The LM101A series are general purpose operational amplifiers which feature improved performance over industry standards like the LM709. Advanced processing techniques make possible an order of magnitude reduction in input currents, and a redesign of the biasing circuitry reduces the temperature drift of input current. Improved specifications include:

- Offset voltage 3 mV maximum over temperature (LM101A/LM201A)
- Input current 100 nA maximum over temperature (LM101A/LM201A)
- Offset current 20 nA maximum over temperature (LM101A/LM201A)
- Guaranteed drift characteristics
- Offsets guaranteed over entire common mode and supply voltage ranges
- Slew rate of 10V/µs as a summing amplifier

This amplifier offers many features which make its application nearly foolproof: overload protection on the input and output, no latch-up when the common mode range is exceeded, freedom from oscillations and compensation with a single 30 pF

capacitor. It has advantages over internally compensated amplifiers in that the frequency compensation can be tailored to the particular application. For example, in low frequency circuits it can be overcompensated for increased stability margin. Or the compensation can be optimized to give more than a factor of ten improvement in high frequency performance for most applications.

In addition, the device provides better accuracy and lower noise in that high impedance circuitry. The low input currents also make it particularly well suited for long interval integrators or timers, sample and hold circuits and low frequency waveform generators. Further, replacing circuits where matched transistor pairs buffer the inputs of conventional IC op amps, it can give lower offset voltage and drift at a lower cost.

The LM101A is guaranteed over a temperature range of −55°C to +125°C, the LM201A from −25°C to +85°C, and the LM301A from 0°C to 70°C.

Schematic** and Connection Diagrams (Top Views)

Metal Can Package

Note: Pin 4 connected to case.
Order Number LM101AH, LM201AH or LM301AH
See NS Package H08C

Dual-In-Line Package

Order Number LM301AJ
See NS Package J08A

Order Number LM301AN
See NS Package N08A

Dual-In-Line Package

Note: Pin 6 connected to bottom of package.
Order Number LM101AJ-14, LM201AJ-14 or LM301AJ
See NS Package J14A

**Pin connections shown are for metal can.

Courtesy National Semiconductor Corp.

Absolute Maximum Ratings

	LM101A/LM201A	LM301A
Supply Voltage	±22V	±18V
Power Dissipation (Note 1)	500 mW	500 mW
Differential Input Voltage	±30V	±30V
Input Voltage (Note 2)	±15V	±15V
Output Short Circuit Duration (Note 3)	Indefinite	Indefinite
Operating Temperature Range	−55°C to +125°C (LM101A) −25°C to +85°C (LM201A)	0°C to +70°C
Storage Temperature Range	65°C to +150°C	−65°C to +150°C
Lead Temperature (Soldering, 10 seconds)	300°C	300°C

Electrical Characteristics (Note 4)

PARAMETER	CONDITIONS	LM101A/LM201A			LM301A			UNITS
		MIN	TYP	MAX	MIN	TYP	MAX	
Input Offset Voltage LM101A, LM201A, LM301A	$T_A = 25°C$ $R_S \leq 50 \text{ k}\Omega$		0.7	2.0		2.0	7.5	mV
Input Offset Current	$T_A = 25°C$		1.5	10		3.0	50	nA
Input Bias Current	$T_A = 25°C$		30	75		70	250	nA
Input Resistance	$T_A = 25°C$	1.5	4.0		0.5	2.0		MΩ
Supply Current	$T_A = 25°C$ $V_S = \pm 20V$ $V_S = \pm 15V$		1.8	3.0		1.8	3.0	mA mA
Large Signal Voltage Gain	$T_A = 25°C, V_S = \pm 15V$ $V_{OUT} = \pm 10V, R_L \geq 2 \text{ k}\Omega$	50	160		25	160		V/mV
Input Offset Voltage	$R_S \leq 50 \text{ k}\Omega$ $R_S \leq 10 \text{ k}\Omega$			3.0			10	mV mV
Average Temperature Coefficient of Input Offset Voltage	$R_S \leq 50 \text{ k}\Omega$ $R_S \leq 10 \text{ k}\Omega$		3.0	15		6.0	30	μV/°C μV/°C
Input Offset Current	$T_A = T_{MAX}$ $T_A = T_{MIN}$			20			70	nA nA nA
Average Temperature Coefficient of Input Offset Current	$25°C \leq T_A \leq T_{MAX}$ $T_{MIN} \leq T_A \leq 25°C$		0.01 0.02	0.1 0.2		0.01 0.02	0.3 0.6	nA/°C nA/°C
Input Bias Current				0.1			0.3	μA
Supply Current	$T_A = T_{MAX}, V_S = \pm 20V$		1.2	2.5				mA
Large Signal Voltage Gain	$V_S = \pm 15V, V_{OUT} = \pm 10V,$ $R_L \geq 2k$	25			15			V/mV
Output Voltage Swing	$V_S = \pm 15V$ $R_L = 10 \text{ k}\Omega$ $R_L = 2 \text{ k}\Omega$	±12 ±10	±14 ±13		±12 ±10	±14 ±13		V V
Input Voltage Range	$V_S = \pm 20V$ $V_S = \pm 15V$	±15	+15, −13		±12	+15, 13		V V
Common-Mode Rejection Ratio	$R_S \leq 50 \text{ k}\Omega$ $R_S \leq 10 \text{ k}\Omega$	80	96		70	90		dB dB
Supply Voltage Rejection Ratio	$R_S \leq 50 \text{ k}\Omega$ $R_S \leq 10 \text{ k}\Omega$	80	96		70	96		dB dB

Note 1: The maximum junction temperature of the LM101A is 150°C, and that of the LM201A/LM301A is 100°C. For operating at elevated temperatures, devices in the TO-5 package must be derated based on a thermal resistance of 150°C/W, junction to ambient, or 45°C/W, junction to case. For the flat package, the derating is based on a thermal resistance of 185°C/W when mounted on a 1/16 inch thick epoxy glass board with ten, 0.03 inch wide, 2 ounce copper conductors. The thermal resistance of the dual-in-line package is 187°C/W, junction to ambient.

Note 2: For supply voltages less than ±15V, the absolute maximum input voltage is equal to the supply voltage.

Note 3: Continuous short circuit is allowed for case temperatures to 125°C and ambient temperatures to 75°C for LM101A/LM201A, and 70°C and 55°C respectively for LM301A.

Note 4: Unless otherwise specified, these specifications apply for C1 = 30 pF, ±5V ≤ V_S ≤ ±20V and −55°C ≤ T_A ≤ +125°C (LM101A), ±5V ≤ V_S ≤ ±20V and −25°C ≤ T_A ≤ +85°C (LM201A), ±5V ≤ V_S ≤ ±15V and 0°C ≤ T_A ≤ +70°C (LM301A).

Courtesy National Semiconductor Corp.

Guaranteed Performance Characteristics LM101A/LM201A

Guaranteed Performance Characteristics LM301A

Typical Performance Characteristics

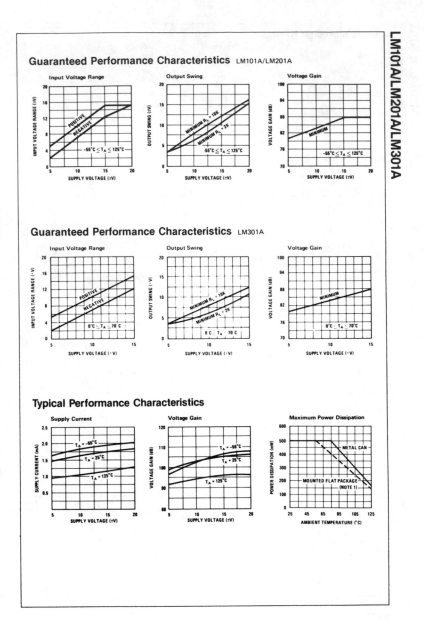

Courtesy National Semiconductor Corp.

422

Typical Performance Characteristics (Continued)

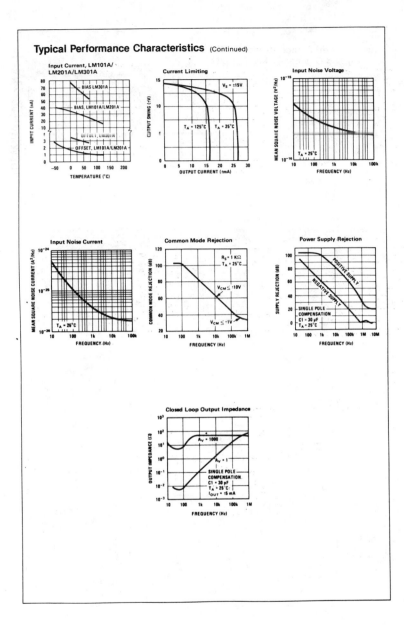

Courtesy National Semiconductor Corp.

Typical Performance Characteristics
for Various Compensation Circuits**

**Pin connections shown are for metal can.

Typical Applications **

Variable Capacitance Multiplier

$$C = 1 + \frac{R_4}{R_5} \, C1$$

Simulated Inductor

$L = R1\ R2\ C1$
$R_s = R2$
$R_p = R1$

Fast Inverting Amplifier With High Input Impedance

Inverting Amplifier with Balancing Circuit

†May be zero or equal to parallel combination of R1 and R2 for minimum offset.

Sine Wave Oscillator

$f_0 = 10\ kHz$

Integrator with Bias Current Compensation

*Adjust for zero integrator drift. Current drift typically 0.1 nA/°C over −55°C to +125°C temperature range.

Application Hints **

Protecting Against Gross Fault Conditions

*Protects input
†Protects output
Protects output—not needed when R4 is used.

Compensating For Stray Input Capacitances Or Large Feedback Resistor

$$C2 = \frac{R1\ C_s}{R2}$$

Isolating Large Capacitive Loads

Although the LM101A is designed for trouble free operation, experience has indicated that it is wise to observe certain precautions given below to protect the devices from abnormal operating conditions. It might be pointed out that the advice given here is applicable to practically any IC op amp, although the exact reason why may differ with different devices.

When driving either input from a low-impedance source, a limiting resistor should be placed in series with the input lead to limit the peak instantaneous output current of the source to something less than 100 mA. This is especially important when the inputs go outside a piece of equipment where they could accidentally be connected to high voltage sources. Large capacitors on the input (greater than 0.1 μF) should be treated as a low source impedance and isolated with a resistor. Low impedance sources do not cause a problem unless their output voltage exceeds the supply voltage. However, the supplies go to zero when they are turned off, so the isolation is usually needed.

The output circuitry is protected against damage from shorts to ground. However, when the amplifier output is connected to a test point, it should be isolated by a limiting resistor, as test points frequently get shorted to bad places. Further, when the amplifier drives a load external to the equipment, it is also advisable to use some sort of limiting resistance to preclude mishaps.

Precautions should be taken to insure that the power supplies for the integrated circuit never become reversed—even under transient conditions. With reverse voltages greater than 1V, the IC will conduct excessive current, fuzing internal aluminum interconnects. If there is a possibility of this happening, clamp diodes with a high peak current rating should be installed on the supply lines. Reversal of the voltage between V⁺ and V⁻ will always cause a problem, although reversals with respect to ground may also give difficulties in many circuits.

The minimum values given for the frequency compensation capacitor are stable only for source resistances less than 10 kΩ, stray capacitances on the summing junction less than 5 pF and capacitive loads smaller than 100 pF. If any of these conditions are not met, it becomes necessary to overcompensate the amplifier with a larger compensation capacitor. Alternately, lead capacitors can be used in the feedback network to negate the effect of stray capacitance and large feedback resistors or an RC network can be added to isolate capacitive loads.

Although the LM101A is relatively unaffected by supply bypassing, this cannot be ignored altogether. Generally it is necessary to bypass the supplies to ground at least once on every circuit card, and more bypass points may be required if more than five amplifiers are used. When feed-forward compensation is employed, however, it is advisable to bypass the supply leads of each amplifier with low inductance capacitors because of the higher frequencies involved.

**Pin connections shown are for metal can.

GENERAL DESCRIPTION

The 4558 integrated circuit is a dual high gain operational amplifier internally compensated and constructed on a single silicon chip using the planar epitaxial process.

Combining the features of the 741 with the close parameter matching and tracking of a dual device on a monolithic chip results in unique performance characteristics. Excellent channel separation allows the use of the dual device in single 741 operational amplifier applications providing the highest possible packaging density. It is especially well suited for applications in differential-in, differential-out as well as in potentiometric amplifiers and where gain and phase matched channels are mandatory.

DESIGN FEATURES

- 2.5 MHz Unity Gain Bandwidth Guaranteed
- Supply Voltage ±22V for RM4558 and ±15V for RC4558
- Short-Circuit Protection
- No Frequency Compensation Required
- No Latch-Up
- Large Common-Mode and Differential Voltage Ranges
- Low Power Consumption
- Parameter Tracking Over Temperature Range
- Gain and Phase Match Between Amplifiers

SCHEMATIC DIAGRAM (1/2 Shown)

CONNECTION INFORMATION

TE (TO-99)
Metal Can Package
(Top View)

Order Part Nos.:
RC4558T, RM4558T

DE and NB
Dual In-line Packages
(Top View)

Order Part Nos.:
RC4558NB, RV4558NB
RC4558DE, RV4558DE
RM4558DE

PIN	FUNCTION
1	A OUTPUT
2	A –INPUT
3	A +INPUT
4	V$^-$
5	B +INPUT
6	B –INPUT
7	B OUTPUT
8	V$^+$

RAYTHEON

Courtesy Raytheon Semiconductor

ABSOLUTE MAXIMUM RATINGS

Supply Voltage .... RM4558: ±22V / RC4558: ±18V
Internal Power Dissipation (Note 1) 500mW
Differential Input Voltage .... ±30V
Input Voltage (Note 2) .... ±15V
Storage Temperature Range .... -65°C to +150°C

Operating Temperature Range .. RM4558: -55°C to +125°C / RV4558: -40°C to +85°C / RC4558: 0°C to +70°C
Lead Temperature (Soldering, 10s) .... 300°C
Output Short-Circuit Duration (Note 3) .... Indefinite

ELECTRICAL CHARACTERISTICS (V_CC = ±15V, T_A = 25°C unless otherwise specified)

PARAMETER	CONDITIONS	RM4558			RV/RC4558			UNITS
		MIN	TYP	MAX	MIN	TYP	MAX	
Input Offset Voltage	$R_S \leq 10k\Omega$		1.0	5.0		2.0	6.0	mV
Input Offset Current			5.0	200		30	200	nA
Input Bias Current			40	500		200	500	nA
Input Resistance		0.3	1.0		0.3	1.0		MΩ
Large-Signal Voltage Gain	$R_L \geq 2k\Omega$ $V_{out} = \pm 10V$	50,000	300,000		20,000	300,000		
Output Voltage Swing	$R_L \geq 10k\Omega$	±12	±14		±12	±14		V
	$R_L \geq 2k\Omega$	±10	±13		±10	±13		V
Input Voltage Range		±12	±13		±12	±13		V
Common Mode Rejection Ratio	$R_S \leq 10k\Omega$	70	100		70	100		dB
Supply Voltage Rejection Ratio	$R_S \leq 10k\Omega$		10	150		10	150	μV/V
Power Consumption (All Amplifiers)	$R_L = \infty$		100	170		100	170	mW
Transient Response (unity gain)	V_{IN} 20mV R_L 2kΩ $C_L \leq 100pF$							
Risetime			0.3			0.3		μs
Overshoot			15.0			15.0		%
Slew Rate (unity gain)	$R_L \geq 2k\Omega$		1.3			1.3		V/μs
Channel Separation (Gain = 100)	f = 10kHz $R_S = 1k\Omega$		90			90		dB
Unity Gain Bandwidth (Gain = 1)		2.5	3.0		2.0	3.0		MHz

The following specifications apply for -55°C ≤ T_A ≤ +125°C for RM4558; 0°C ≤ T_A ≤ +70°C for RC4558; -40°C ≤ T_A ≤ +85°C for RV4558

PARAMETER	CONDITIONS	RM4558 MIN	RM4558 MAX	RC MIN	RC MAX	UNITS
Input Offset Voltage	$R_S \leq 10k\Omega$		6.0		7.5	mV
Input Offset Current			500		300/500*	nA
Input Bias Current			1500		800/1500	nA
Large-Signal Voltage Gain	$R_L \geq 2k\Omega$ $V_{out} = \pm 10V$	25,000		15,000		
Output Voltage Swing	$R_L \geq 2k\Omega$	±10		±10		V

| Power Consumption | $V_S = \pm 15V$ $T_A = +125°C$ / $T_A = -55°C$ | 90 (TYP) / 120 | 150 (MAX) / 200 | 90 / 120 | 150 / 200 | mW |

*RV4558

MATCHING CHARACTERISTICS (V_CC = ±15V, T_A = 25°C unless otherwise specified)

PARAMETER	CONDITIONS	RM4558 TYP	RC4558 TYP	UNITS
Voltage Gain	$R_L \geq 2k\Omega$	±.5	±1.0	dB
Input Bias Current		±15	±15	nA
Input Offset Current		±7.5	±7.5	nA
Input Offset Voltage	$R_S \geq 10k\Omega$	±.1	±.2	mV

NOTE 1: Rating applies for case temperatures to 125°C; derate linearly at 6.5mW/°C for ambient temperatures above +75°C for RM4558.
NOTE 2: For supply voltages less than ±15V, the absolute maximum input voltage is equal to the supply voltage.
NOTE 3: Short circuit may be to ground on one amp only. Rating applies to +125°C case temperature or +75°C ambient temperature for RC4558 and to +85°C ambient temperature for RV4558.

RAYTHEON

Courtesy Raytheon Semiconductor

TYPICAL ELECTRICAL DATA

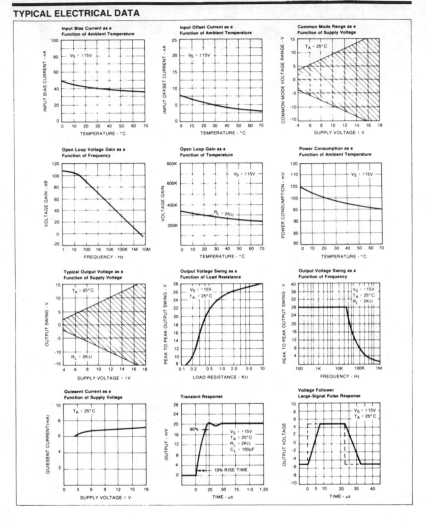

RAYTHEON

Courtesy Raytheon Semiconductor

TYPICAL ELECTRICAL DATA

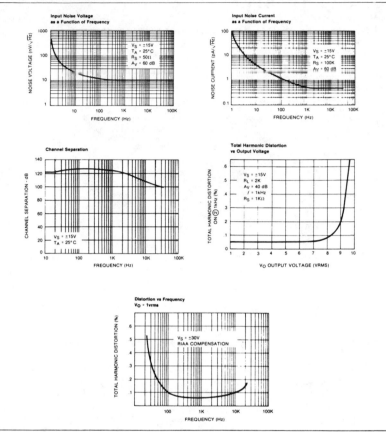

Courtesy Raytheon Semiconductor

![National Semiconductor]

Operational Amplifiers/Buffers

LM124/LM224/LM324, LM124A/LM224A/LM324A, LM2902
low power quad operational amplifiers

general description

The LM124 series consists of four independent, high gain, internally frequency compensated operational amplifiers which were designed specifically to operate from a single power supply over a wide range of voltages. Operation from split power supplies is also possible and the low power supply current drain is independent of the magnitude of the power supply voltage.

Application areas include transducer amplifiers, dc gain blocks and all the conventional op amp circuits which now can be more easily implemented in single power supply systems. For example, the LM124 series can be directly operated off of the standard +5 V_{DC} power supply voltage which is used in digital systems and will easily provide the required interface electronics without requiring the additional ±15 V_{DC} power supplies.

unique characteristics

- In the linear mode the input common-mode voltage range includes ground and the output voltage can also swing to ground, even though operated from only a single power supply voltage.

- The unity gain cross frequency is temperature compensated.

- The input bias current is also temperature compensated.

advantages

- Eliminates need for dual supplies
- Four internally compensated op amps in a single package
- Allows directly sensing near GND and V_{OUT} also goes to GND
- Compatible with all forms of logic
- Power drain suitable for battery operation

features

- Internally frequency compensated for unity gain
- Large dc voltage gain   100 dB
- Wide bandwidth (unity gain)   1 MHz
  (temperature compensated)
- Wide power supply range:
  Single supply   3 V_{DC} to 30 V_{DC}
  or dual supplies   ±1.5 V_{DC} to ±15 V_{DC}
- Very low supply current drain (800μA) — essentially independent of supply voltage (1 mW/op amp at +5 V_{DC})
- Low input biasing current   45 nA_{DC}
  (temperature compensated)
- Low input offset voltage   2 mV_{DC}
  and offset current   5 nA_{DC}
- Input common-mode voltage range includes ground
- Differential input voltage range equal to the power supply voltage
- Large output voltage   0 V_{DC} to V^+ − 1.5 V_{DC}
  swing

connection diagram

Dual-In-Line and Flat Package

schematic diagram (Each Amplifier)

Order Number LM124D, LM124AD, LM224D or LM224AD
See NS Package D14E

Order Number LM124F, LM124AF, LM224F or LM224AF
See NS Package F14A

Order Number LM124J, LM124AJ, LM224J, LM224AJ, LM324J, LM324AJ or LM2902J
See NS Package J14A

Order Number LM324N, LM324AN or LM2902N
See NS Package N14A

Courtesy National Semiconductor Corp.

absolute maximum ratings

	LM124/LM224/LM324, LM124A/LM224A/LM324A	LM2902
Supply Voltage, V+	32 VDC or ±16 VDC	26 VDC or ±13 VDC
Differential Input Voltage	32 VDC	26 VDC
Input Voltage	–0.3 VDC to +26 VDC	–0.3 VDC to +26 VDC
Power Dissipation (Note 1)		
Molded DIP	570 mW	570 mW
Cavity DIP	900 mW	
Flat Pack	800 mW	
Output Short-Circuit to GND (One Amplifier) (Note 2) V+ ≤ 15 VDC and TA = 25 C	Continuous	Continuous
Input Current (VIN < –0.3 VDC) (Note 3)	50 mA	50 mA
Operating Temperature Range		–40°C to +85°C
LM324/LM324A	0°C to +70°C	
LM224/LM224A	–25°C to +85°C	
LM124/LM124A	–55°C to +125°C	
Storage Temperature Range	–65°C to +150°C	–65°C to +150°C
Lead Temperature (Soldering, 10 seconds)	300°C	300°C

electrical characteristics (V+ = +5.0 VDC, Note 4)

PARAMETER	CONDITIONS	LM124A			LM224A			LM324A			LM124/LM224			LM324			LM2902			UNITS
		MIN	TYP	MAX	MIN	TYP	MAX	MIN	TYP	MAX	MIN	TYP	MAX	MIN	TYP	MAX	MIN	TYP	MAX	
Input Offset Voltage	TA = 25 C, (Note 5)		1	2		1	3		2	3		±2	±5		±2	±7		±2	±7	mVDC
Input Bias Current (Note 6)	IIN(+) or IIN(–), TA = 25 C		20	50		40	80		45	100		45	150		45	250		45	250	nADC
Input Offset Current	IIN(+) – IIN(–), TA = 25 C		2	10		2	15		5	30		3	30		5	50		5	50	nADC
Input Common-Mode Voltage Range (Note 7)	V+ = 30 VDC, TA = 25 C	0		V+ –1.5	0		V+ –1.5	0		V+ –1.5	0		V+ –1.5	0		V+ –1.5	0		V+ –1.5	VDC
Supply Current	RL = ∞, VCC = 30V, (LM2902 VCC = 26V)		1.5	3		1.5	3		1.5	3		1.5	3		1.5	3		1.5	3	mADC
	RL = ∞ On All Op Amps. Over Full Temperature Range		0.7	1.2		0.7	1.2		0.7	1.2		0.7	1.2		0.7	1.2		0.7	1.2	mADC
Large Signal Voltage Gain	V+ = 15 VDC (For Large VO Swing) RL ≥ 2 kΩ, TA = 25 C	50	100		50	100		25	100		50	100		25	100		25	100		V/mV
Output Voltage Swing	RL ≥ 2 kΩ, TA = 25 C	0		V+ –1.5	0		V+ –1.5	0		V+ –1.5	0		V+ –1.5	0		V+ –1.5	0		V+ –1.5	VDC
Common-Mode Rejection Ratio	DC, TA = 25 C	70	85		70	85		65	85		70	85		65	85		50	70		dB
Power Supply Rejection Ratio	DC, TA = 25 C	65	100		65	100		65	100		65	100		65	100		50	100		dB
Amplifier to Amplifier Coupling (Note 8)	f = 1 kHz to 20 kHz, TA = 25 C (Input Referred)		–120			–120			–120			–120			–120			–120		dB
Output Current Source	VIN+ = 1 VDC, VIN– = 0 VDC, V+ = 15 VDC, TA = 25 C	20	40		20	40		20	40		20	40		20	40		20	40		mADC
Sink	VIN– = 1 VDC, VIN+ = 0 VDC, V+ = 15 VDC, TA = 25 C	10	20		10	20		10	20		10	20		10	20		10	20		mADC
	VIN– = 1 VDC, VIN+ = 0 VDC, TA = 25 C, VO = 200 mVDC	12	50		12	50		12	50		12	50		12	50		12	50		µADC
Short Circuit to Ground	TA = 25 C, (Note 2)		40	60		40	60		40	60		40	60		40	60		40	60	mADC

electrical characteristics (con't)

PARAMETER	CONDITIONS	LM124A MIN	TYP	MAX	LM224A MIN	TYP	MAX	LM324A MIN	TYP	MAX	LM124/LM224 MIN	TYP	MAX	LM324 MIN	TYP	MAX	LM2902 MIN	TYP	MAX	UNITS
Input Offset Voltage	(Note 5)			4			4			5			±7			±9			±10	mVDC
Input Offset Voltage Drift	$R_S = 0\,\Omega$		7	20		7	20		7	30		7			7			7		μV/°C
Input Offset Current	$I_{IN(+)} - I_{IN(-)}$			30			30			75			100			±150		45	±200	nADC
Input Offset Current Drift			10	200		10	200		10	300		10	300		10			10		pADC/°C
Input Bias Current	$I_{IN(+)}$ or $I_{IN(-)}$		40	100		40	100		40	200		40	300		40	500		40	500	nADC
Input Common-Mode Voltage Range (Note 7)	$V^+ = 30\ V_{DC}$	0		V^+-2	0		V^+-2	0		V^+-2	0		V^+-2	0		V^+-2	0		V^+-2	VDC
Large Signal Voltage Gain	$V^+ = +15\ V_{DC}$ (For Large V_O Swing) $R_L \geq 2\ k\Omega$	25			25			15			25			15			15			V/mV
Output Voltage Swing V_{OH}	$V^+ = +30\ V_{DC}$, $R_L = 2\ k\Omega$	26	28		26	28		26	28		26	28		26	28		22	24		VDC
	$R_L \geq 10\ k\Omega$	27	28		27	28		27	28		27	28		27	28		23	24		VDC
V_{OL}	$V^+ = 5\ V_{DC}$, $R_L \leq 10\ k\Omega$		5	20		5	20		5	20		5	20		5	20		5	100	mVDC
Output Current Source	$V_{IN}{}^+ = +1\ V_{DC}$, $V_{IN}{}^- = 0\ V_{DC}$, $V^+ = 15\ V_{DC}$	10	20		10	20		10	20		10	20		10	20		10	20		mADC
Sink	$V_{IN}{}^- = +1\ V_{DC}$, $V_{IN}{}^+ = 0\ V_{DC}$, $V^+ = 15\ V_{DC}$	10	15		5	8		5	8		5	8		5	8		5	8		mADC
Differential Input Voltage	(Note 7)			V^+			V^+			V^+			V^+			V^+			V^+	VDC

Note 1: For operating at high temperatures, the LM324/LM324A, LM2902 must be derated based on a +125°C maximum junction temperature and a thermal resistance of 175°C/W which applies for the device soldered in a printed circuit board, operating in a still air ambient. The LM224/LM224A and LM124/LM124A can be derated based on a +150°C maximum junction temperature. The dissipation is the total of all four amplifiers—use the external resistors, where possible, to allow the amplifier to saturate or to reduce the power which is dissipated in the integrated circuit.

Note 2: Short circuits from the output to V^+ can cause excessive heating and eventual destruction. The maximum output current is approximately 40 mA independent of the magnitude of V^+. At values of supply voltage in excess of +15 V_{DC}, continuous short-circuits can exceed the power dissipation ratings and cause eventual destruction. Destructive dissipation can result from simultaneous shorts on all amplifiers.

Note 3: This input current will only exist when the voltage at any of the input leads is driven negative. It is due to the collector-base junction of the input PNP transistors becoming forward biased and thereby acting as input diode clamps. In addition to this diode action, there is also lateral NPN parasitic transistor action on the IC chip. This transistor action can cause the output voltages of the op amps to go to the V^+ voltage level (or to ground for a large overdrive) for the time duration that an input is driven negative. This is not destructive and normal output states will re-establish when the input voltage, which was negative, again returns to a value greater than −0.3 V_{DC}.

Note 4: These specifications apply for $V^+ = +5\ V_{DC}$ and 55°C ≤ T_A ≤ +125°C, unless otherwise stated. With the LM224/LM224A, all temperature specifications are limited to −25°C ≤ T_A ≤ +85°C, the LM324/LM324A temperature specifications are limited to 0°C ≤ T_A ≤ +70°C, and the LM2902 specifications are limited to −40°C ≤ T_A ≤ +85°C.

Note 5: $V_O = 1.4\ V_{DC}$, $R_S = 0\,\Omega$ with V^+ from 5 V_{DC} to 30 V_{DC} and over the full input common-mode range (0 V_{DC} to $V^+ - 1.5\ V_{DC}$).

Note 6: The direction of the input current is out of the IC due to the PNP input stage. This current is essentially constant, independent of the state of the output so no loading change exists on the input lines.

Note 7: The input common-mode voltage of either input signal voltage should not be allowed to go negative by more than 0.3V. The upper end of the common-mode voltage range is $V^+ - 1.5V$, but either or both inputs can go to +32 V_{DC} without damage (+26 V_{DC} for LM2902).

Note 8: Due to proximity of external components, insure that coupling is not originating via stray capacitance between these external parts. This typically can be detected as this type of capacitive increases at higher frequencies.

typical performance characteristics

LM124/LM224/LM324,
LM124A/LM224A/LM324A, LM2902

typical performance characteristics (LM2902 only)

Input Current

Voltage Gain

application hints

The LM124 series are op amps which operate with only a single power supply voltage, have true-differential inputs, and remain in the linear mode with an input common-mode voltage of 0 V_{DC}. These amplifiers operate over a wide range of power supply voltage with little change in performance characteristics. At 25°C amplifier operation is possible down to a minimum supply voltage of 2.3 V_{DC}.

The pinouts of the package have been designed to simplify PC board layouts. Inverting inputs are adjacent to outputs for all of the amplifiers and the outputs have also been placed at the corners of the package (pins 1, 7, 8, and 14).

Precautions should be taken to insure that the power supply for the integrated circuit never becomes reversed in polarity or that the unit is not inadvertently installed backwards in a test socket as an unlimited current surge through the resulting forward diode within the IC could cause fusing of the internal conductors and result in a destroyed unit.

Large differential input voltages can be easily accommodated and, as input differential voltage protection diodes are not needed, no large input currents result from large differential input voltages. The differential input voltage may be larger than V^+ without damaging the device. Protection should be provided to prevent the input voltages from going negative more than $-0.3 V_{DC}$ (at 25°C). An input clamp diode with a resistor to the IC input terminal can be used.

To reduce the power supply current drain, the amplifiers have a class A output stage for small signal levels which converts to class B in a large signal mode. This allows the amplifiers to both source and sink large output currents. Therefore both NPN and PNP external current boost transistors can be used to extend the power capability of the basic amplifiers. The output voltage needs to raise approximately 1 diode drop above ground to bias the on-chip vertical PNP transistor for output current sinking applications.

For ac applications, where the load is capacitively coupled to the output of the amplifier, a resistor should be used, from the output of the amplifier to ground to increase the class A bias current and prevent crossover distortion. Where the load is directly coupled, as in dc applications, there is no crossover distortion.

Capacitive loads which are applied directly to the output of the amplifier reduce the loop stability margin. Values of 50 pF can be accommodated using the worst-case non-inverting unity gain connection. Large closed loop gains or resistive isolation should be used if larger load capacitance must be driven by the amplifier.

The bias network of the LM124 establishes a drain current which is independent of the magnitude of the power supply voltage over the range of from 3 V_{DC} to 30 V_{DC}.

Output short circuits either to ground or to the positive power supply should be of short time duration. Units can be destroyed, not as a result of the short circuit current causing metal fusing, but rather due to the large increase in IC chip dissipation which will cause eventual failure due to excessive junction temperatures. Putting direct short-circuits on more than one amplifier at a time will increase the total IC power dissipation to destructive levels, if not properly protected with external dissipation limiting resistors in series with the output leads of the amplifiers. The larger value of output source current which is available at 25°C provides a larger output current capability at elevated temperatures (see typical performance characteristics) than a standard IC op amp.

The circuits presented in the section on typical applications emphasize operation on only a single power supply voltage. If complementary power supplies are available, all of the standard op amp circuits can be used. In general, introducing a pseudo-ground (a bias voltage reference of $V^+/2$) will allow operation above and below this value in single power supply systems. Many application circuits are shown which take advantage of the wide input common-mode voltage range which includes ground. In most cases, input biasing is not required and input voltages which range to ground can easily be accommodated.

Courtesy National Semiconductor Corp.

Solid State Division

Mini-DIP
CA3140E
CA3140AE

H-1817

All Types
8-Lead TO-5
With Dual-In-Line
Formed Leads
"DIL-CAN"
(S Suffix)

All Types
8-Lead TO-5
(T Suffix)

H-1787   H-1528

BiMOS Operational Amplifiers
With MOS/FET Input, Bipolar Output

Features:

- MOS/FET Input Stage
  (a) Very high input impedance (Z_{IN}) — 1.5 TΩ typ.
  (b) Very low input current (I_I) — 10 pA typ. at ± 15 V
  (c) Low input-offset voltage (V_{IO}) — to 2 mV max.
  (d) Wide common-mode input-voltage range (V_{ICR}) — can be swung 0.5 volt below negative supply-voltage rail
  (e) Output swing complements input common-mode range
  (f) Rugged input stage — bipolar diode protected
- Directly replaces industry type 741 in most applications

The CA3140B, CA3140A, and CA3140 are integrated-circuit operational amplifiers that combine the advantages of high-voltage PMOS transistors with high-voltage bipolar transistors on a single monolithic chip. Because of this unique combination of technologies, this device can now provide designers, for the first time, with the special performance features of the CA3130 COS/MOS operational amplifiers and the versatility of the 741 series of industry-standard operational amplifiers.

The CA3140, CA3140A, and CA3140 BiMOS operational amplifiers feature gate-protected MOS/FET (PMOS) transistors in the input circuit to provide very-high-input impedance, very-low-input current, and high-speed performance. The CA3140B operates at supply voltages from 4 to 44 volts; the CA3140A and CA3140 from 4 to 36 volts (either single or dual supply). These operational amplifiers are internally phase-compensated to achieve stable operation in unity-gain follower operation, and, additionally, have access terminals for a supplementary external capacitor if additional frequency roll-off is desired. Terminals are also provided for use in applications requiring input offset-voltage nulling.

The use of PMOS field-effect transistors in the input stage results in common-mode input-voltage capability down to 0.5 volt below the negative-supply terminal, an important attribute for single-supply applications. The output stage uses bipolar transistors and includes built-in protection against damage from load-terminal short-circuiting to either supply-rail or to ground.

The CA3140 Series has the same 8-lead terminal pin-out used for the "741" and other

- Includes numerous industry operational amplifier categories such as general-purpose, FET input, wideband (high slew rate)
- Operation from 4-to-44 volts Single or Dual supplies
- Internally compensated
- Characterized for ± 15-volt operation and for TTL supply systems with operation down to 4 volts
- Wide bandwidth — 4.5 MHz unity gain at ± 15 V or 30 V; 3.7 MHz at 5 V
- High voltage-follower slew rate — 9 V/μs
- Fast settling time — 1.4 μs typ. to 10 mV with a 10-V_{p-p} signal
- Output swings to within 0.2 volt of negative supply
- Strobable output stage

Applications:

- Ground-referenced single-supply amplifiers in automobile and portable instrumentation
- Sample and hold amplifiers
- Long-duration timers/multivibrators (microseconds—minutes—hours)
- Photocurrent instrumentation
- Peak detectors   ▪ Active filters
- Comparators
- Interface in 5 V TTL systems & other low-supply voltage systems
- All standard operational amplifier applications
- Function generators   ▪ Tone controls
- Power supplies   ▪ Portable instruments
- Intrusion alarm systems

CA3140B, CA3140A, CA3140   BiMOS Operational Amplifiers

Printed in USA/3-77

Supersedes issue dated 5-76

Courtesy RCA Solid State Division

industry-standard operational amplifiers. They are supplied in either the standard 8-lead TO-5 style package (T suffix), or in the 8-lead dual-in-line formed-lead TO-5 style package "DIL-CAN" (S suffix). The CA3140 is available in chip form (H suffix). The CA3140A and CA3140 are also available in an 8-lead dual-in-line plastic package (Mini-DIP-E suffix). The CA3140B is intended for operation at supply voltages ranging from 4 to 44 volts, for applications requiring premium-grade specifications and with electrical limits established for operations over the range from −55°C to +125°C. The CA3140A and CA3140 are for operation at supply voltages up to 36 volts (±18 volts). The CA3140 ages up to 36 volts (±18 volts). All types can be operated safely over the temperature range from −55°C to +125°C.

TYPICAL ELECTRICAL CHARACTERISTICS

CHARACTERISTIC	TEST CONDITIONS $V^+ = +15$ V $V^- = -15$ V $T_A = 25°C$		CA3140B (T,S)	CA3140A (T,S,E)	CA3140 (T,S,E)	UNITS
Input Offset Voltage Adjustment Resistor	Typ. Value of Resistor Between Term. 4 and 5 or 4 and 1 to Adjust Max. V_{IO}		43	18	4.7	kΩ
Input Resistance R_1			1.5	1.5	1.5	TΩ
Input Capacitance C_I			4	4	4	pF
Output Resistance R_O			60	60	60	Ω
Equivalent Wideband Input Noise Voltage e_n (See Fig. 39)	BW = 140 kHz R_S = 1 MΩ		48	48	48	μV
Equivalent Input Noise Voltage e_n (See Fig.10)	$f = 1$ kHz	$R_S =$ 100 Ω	40	40	40	nV/$\sqrt{Hz}$
	$f = 10$ kHz		12	12	12	
Short-Circuit Current to Opposite Supply Source I_{OM}^+			40	40	40	mA
Sink I_{OM}^-			18	18	18	mA
Gain-Bandwidth Product, (See Figs. 5 &18) f_T			4.5	4.5	4.5	MHz
Slew Rate, (See Fig.6) SR			9	9	9	V/μs
Sink Current From Terminal 8 To Terminal 4 to Swing Output Low			220	220	220	μA
Transient Response: Rise Time t_r	$R_L = 2$ kΩ $C_L = 100$ pF		0.08	0.08	0.08	μs
Overshoot (See Fig. 37)			10	10	10	%
Settling Time at 10 V_{p-p}, (See Fig.17) t_s	$R_L = 2$ kΩ $C_L = 100$ pF Voltage Follower	1 mV	4.5	4.5	4.5	μs
		10 mV	1.4	1.4	1.4	

Courtesy RCA Solid State Division

ELECTRICAL CHARACTERISTICS FOR EQUIPMENT DESIGN

At V^+ = 15 V, V^- = 15 V, T_A = 25°C Unless Otherwise Specified

CHARACTERISTIC	LIMITS									UNITS
	CA3140B			CA3140A			CA3140			
	Min.	Typ.	Max.	Min.	Typ.	Max.	Min.	Typ.	Max.	
Input Offset Voltage, $|V_{IO}|$	—	0.8	2	—	2	5	—	5	15	mV
Input Offset Current, $|I_{IO}|$	—	0.5	10	—	0.5	20	—	0.5	30	pA
Input Current, I_I	—	10	30	—	10	40	—	10	50	pA
Large-Signal Voltage Gain, A_{OL} ● (See Figs. 4,18)	50 k	100 k	—	20 k	100 k	—	20 k	100 k	—	V/V
	94	100	—	86	100	—	86	100	—	dB
Common-Mode Rejection Ratio, CMRR (See Fig.9)	—	20	50	—	32	320	—	32	320	μV/V
	86	94	—	70	90	—	70	90	—	dB
Common-Mode Input-Voltage Range, V_{ICR} (See Fig.20)	−15	−15.5 to +12.5	12	−15	−15.5 to +12.5	12	−15	−15.5 to +12.5	11	V
Power-Supply Rejection Ratio, PSRR $\Delta V_{IO}/\Delta V$ (See Fig.11)	—	32	100	—	100	150	—	100	150	μV/V
	80	90	—	76	80	—	76	80	—	dB
Max. Output Voltage■ V_{OM}^+ (See Figs.13,20) V_{OM}^-	+12	13	—	+12	13	—	+12	13	—	V
	−14	−14.4	—	−14	−14.4	—	−14	−14.4	—	
Supply Current, I^+ (See Fig.7)	—	4	6	—	4	6	—	4	6	mA
Device Dissipation, P_D	—	120	180	—	120	180	—	120	180	mW
Input Current, I_I ▲ (See Fig.19)	—	10	30	—	10	—	—	10	—	nA
Input Offset Voltage $|V_{IO}|$ ▲	—	1.3	3	—	3	—	—	10	—	mV
Input Offset Voltage Temp. Drift, $\Delta V_{IO}/\Delta T$	—	5	—	—	6	—	—	8	—	μV/°C
Large-Signal Voltage Gain, A_{OL} ▲ (See Figs.4,18)	20 k	100 k	—	—	100 k	—	—	100 k	—	V/V
	86	100	—	—	100	—	—	100	—	dB
Max. Output Voltage,★ V_{OM}^+ V_{OM}^-	+19	+19.5	—	—	—	—	—	—	—	V
	−21	−21.4	—	—	—	—	—	—	—	
Large-Signal Voltage Gain, A_{OL} ♦★	20 k	50 k	—	—	—	—	—	—	—	V/V
	86	94	—	—	—	—	—	—	—	dB

● At V_O = 26V_{p-p}, +12V, −14V and R_L = 2 kΩ. ■ At R_L = 2 kΩ.

▲ At T_A = −55°C to +125°C, V^+ = 15 V, V^- = 15 V, V_O = 26V_{p-p}, R_L = 2 kΩ.

♦ At V_O = +19 V, −21 V, and R_L = 2 kΩ. ★ At V^+ = 22 V, V^- = 22 V.

TOP VIEW
S and T Suffixes

Fig. 1 — Functional diagrams of the CA3140 series.

TOP VIEW
E Suffix

Courtesy RCA Solid State Division

MAXIMUM RATINGS, *Absolute-Maximum Values:*

	CA3140, CA3140A	CA3140B
DC SUPPLY VOLTAGE		
(BETWEEN V+ AND V− TERMINALS)	36 V	44 V
DIFFERENTIAL-MODE INPUT VOLTAGE	±8 V	±8 V
COMMON-MODE DC INPUT VOLTAGE	(V+ +8 V) to (V− −0.5 V)	
INPUT-TERMINAL CURRENT		1 mA
DEVICE DISSIPATION:		
WITHOUT HEAT SINK −		
UP TO 55°C		630 mW
ABOVE 55°C	Derate linearly 6.67 mW/°C	
WITH HEAT SINK −		
Up to 55°C		1 W
Above 55°C	Derate linearly 16.7 mW/°C	
TEMPERATURE RANGE:		
OPERATING (ALL TYPES)		−55 to + 125°C
STORAGE (ALL TYPES)		−65 to +150°C
OUTPUT SHORT-CIRCUIT DURATION*		INDEFINITE
LEAD TEMPERATURE (DURING SOLDERING):		
AT DISTANCE 1/16 ± 1/32 INCH (1.59 ± 0.79 MM)		
FROM CASE FOR 10 SECONDS MAX.		+265°C

* Short circuit may be applied to ground or to either supply.

TYPICAL ELECTRICAL CHARACTERISTICS FOR DESIGN GUIDANCE
At V^+ = 5 V, V^- = 0 V, T_A = 25°C

CHARACTERISTIC		CA3140B (T,S)	CA3140A (T,S,E)	CA3140 (T,S,E)	UNITS
Input Offset Voltage	$|V_{IO}|$	0.8	2	5	mV
Input Offset Current	$|I_{IO}|$	0.1	0.1	0.1	pA
Input Current	I_I	2	2	2	pA
Input Resistance		1	1	1	TΩ
Large-Signal Voltage Gain	A_{OL}	100 k	100 k	100 k	V/V
(See Figs.4,18)		100	100	100	dB
Common-Mode Rejection Ratio,	CMRR	20	32	32	µV/V
		94	90	90	dB
Common-Mode Input-Voltage Range	V_{ICR}	−0.5	−0.5	−0.5	V
(See Fig.20)		2.6	2.6	2.6	
Power-Supply Rejection Ratio	$\Delta V_{IO}/\Delta V^+$	32	100	100	µV/V
		90	80	80	dB
Maximum Output Voltage	V_{OM}^+	3	3	3	V
(See Figs.13,20)	V_{OM}^-	0.13	0.13	0.13	
Maximum Output Current:					
Source	I_{OM}^+	10	10	10	mA
Sink	I_{OM}^-	1	1	1	
Slew Rate (See Fig.6)		7	7	7	V/µs
Gain-Bandwidth Product (See Fig.5)	f_T	3.7	3.7	3.7	MHz
Supply Current (See Fig.7)	I^+	1.6	1.6	1.6	mA
Device Dissipation	P_D	8	8	8	mW
Sink Current from Term. 8 to Term. 4 to Swing Output Low		200	200	200	µA

Courtesy RCA Solid State Division

Fig.2 — Block diagram of CA3140 series.

Fig.3 — Schematic diagram of CA3140 series.

CIRCUIT DESCRIPTION

Fig.2 is a block diagram of the CA3140 Series PMOS Operational Amplifiers. The input terminals may be operated down to 0.5 V below the negative supply rail. Two class A amplifier stages provide the voltage gain, and a unique class AB amplifier stage provides the current gain necessary to drive low-impedance loads.

A biasing circuit provides control of cascoded constant-current flow circuits in the first and second stages. The CA3140 includes an on-chip phase-compensating capacitor that is sufficient for the unity gain voltage-follower configuration.

Input Stages — The schematic circuit diagram of the CA3140 is shown in Fig.3. It consists of a differential-input stage using PMOS field-effect transistors (Q9, Q10) working into a mirror pair of bipolar transistors (Q11, Q12) functioning as load resistors together with resistors R2 through R5. The mirror-pair transistors also function as a differen-

Courtesy RCA Solid State Division

tial-to-single-ended converter to provide base-current drive to the second-stage bipolar transistor (Q13). Offset nulling, when desired, can be effected with a 10-kΩ potentiometer connected across terminals 1 and 5 and with its slider arm connected to terminal 4. Cascode-connected bipolar transistors Q2, Q5 are the constant-current source for the input stage. The base-biasing circuit for the constant-current source is described subsequently. The small diodes D3, D4, D5 provide gate-oxide protection against high-voltage transients, e.g., static electricity.

Second Stage — Most of the voltage gain in the CA3140 is provided by the second amplifier stage, consisting of bipolar transistor Q13 and its cascode-connected load resistance provided by bipolar transistors Q3, Q4. On-chip phase compensation, sufficient for a majority of the applications is provided by C1. Additional Miller-Effect compensation (roll-off) can be accomplished, when desired, by simply connecting a small capacitor between terminals 1 and 8. Terminal 8 is also used to strobe the output stage into quiescence. When terminal 8 is tied to the negative supply rail (terminal 4) by mechanical or electrical means, the output terminal 6 swings low, i.e., approximately to terminal 4 potential.

Output Stage — The CA3140 Series circuits employ a broadband output stage that can sink loads to the negative supply to complement the capability of the PMOS input stage when operating near the negative rail. Quiescent current in the emitter-follower cascade circuit (Q17, Q18) is established by transistors (Q14, Q15) whose base-currents are "mirrored" to current flowing through diode D2 in the bias circuit section. When the CA3140 is operating such that output terminal 6 is sourcing current, transistor Q18 functions as an emitter-follower to source current from the V+ bus (terminal 7), via D7, R9, and R11. Under these conditions, the collector potential of Q13 is sufficiently high to permit the necessary flow of base current to emitter follower Q17 which, in turn, drives Q18.

When the CA3140 is operating such that output terminal 6 is sinking current to the V− bus, transistor Q16 is the current-sinking

element. Transistor Q16 is mirror-connected to D6, R7, with current fed by way of Q21, R12, and Q20. Transistor Q20, in turn, is biased by current-flow through R13, zener D8, and R14. The dynamic current-sink is controlled by voltage-level sensing. For purposes of explanation, it is assumed that output terminal 6 is quiescently established at the potential mid-point between the V+ and V− supply rails. When output-current sinking-mode operation is required, the collector potential of transistor Q13 is driven below its quiescent level, thereby causing Q17, Q18 to decrease the output voltage at terminal 6. Thus, the gate terminal of PMOS transistor Q21 is displaced toward the V− bus, thereby reducing the channel resistance of Q21. As a consequence, there is an incremental increase in current flow through Q20, R12, Q21, D6, R7, and the base of Q16. As a result, Q16 sinks current from terminal 6 in direct response to the incremental change in output voltage caused by Q18. This sink current flows regardless of load; any excess current is internally supplied by the emitter-follower Q18. Short-circuit protection of the output circuit is provided by Q19, which is driven into conduction by the high voltage drop developed across R11 under output short-circuit conditions. Under these conditions, the collector of Q19 diverts current from Q4 so as to reduce the base-current drive from Q17, thereby limiting current flow in Q18 to the short-circuited load terminal.

Bias Circuit — Quiescent current in all stages (except the dynamic current sink) of the CA3140 is dependent upon bias current flow in R1. The function of the bias circuit is to establish and maintain constant-current flow through D1, Q6, Q8 and D2. D1 is a diode-connected transistor mirror-connected in parallel with the base-emitter junctions of Q1, Q2, and Q3. D1 may be considered as a current-sampling diode that senses the emitter current of Q6 and automatically adjusts the base current of Q6 (via Q1) to maintain a constant current through Q6, Q8, D2. The base-currents in Q2, Q3 are also determined by constant-current flow D1. Furthermore, current in diode-connected transistor D2 establishes the currents in transistors Q14 and Q15.

Courtesy RCA Solid State Division

Fig.4 — Open-loop voltage gain vs supply voltage and temperature.

Fig.5 — Gain-bandwidth product vs supply voltage and temperature.

Fig.6 — Slew rate vs supply voltage and temperature.

Fig.7 — Quiescent supply current vs supply voltage and temperature.

Fig.8 — Maximum output voltage swing vs frequency.

Fig.9 — Common-mode rejection ratio vs frequency.

Fig.10 — Equivalent input noise voltage vs frequency.

Fig.11 — Power supply rejection ratio vs frequency.

Courtesy RCA Solid State Division

APPLICATIONS CONSIDERATIONS

Wide dynamic range of input and output characteristics with the most desirable high input-impedance characteristic is achieved in the CA3140 by the use of an unique design based upon the PMOS-Bipolar process. Input-common-mode voltage range and output-swing capabilities are complementary, allowing operation with the single supply down to four volts.

The wide dynamic range of these parameters also means that this device is suitable for many single-supply applications, such as, for example, where one input is driven below the potential of terminal 4 and the phase sense of the output signal must be maintained — a most important consideration in comparator applications.

OUTPUT CIRCUIT CONSIDERATIONS

Excellent interfacing with TTL circuitry is easily achieved with a single 6.2-volt zener diode connected to terminal 8 as shown in Fig.12. This connection assures that the maximum output signal swing will not go more positive than the zener voltage minus two base-to-emitter voltage drops within the CA3140. These voltages are independent of the operating supply voltage.

Fig.12 — Zener clamping diode connected to terminals 8 and 4 to limit CA3140 output swing to TTL levels.

Fig.13 shows output current-sinking capabilities of the CA3140 at various supply voltages. Output voltage swing to the negative supply rail permits this device to oper-

ate both power transistors and thyristors directly without the need for level-shifting circuitry usually associated with the 741 series of operational amplifiers.

Fig.16 show some typical configurations. Note that a series resistor, R_L, is used in both cases to limit the drive available to the driven device. Moreover, it is recommended that a series diode and shunt diode be used at the thyristor input to prevent large negative transient surges that can appear at the gate of thyristors, from damaging the integrated circuit.

Fig.14 — Typical incremental offset-voltage shift vs operating life.

OFFSET-VOLTAGE NULLING

The input-offset voltage can be nulled by connecting a 10-kΩ potentiometer between terminals 1 and 5 and returning its wiper arm to terminal 4, see Fig.15a. This technique, however, gives more adjustment range than required and therefore, a considerable portion of the potentiometer rotation is not fully utilized. Typical values of series resistors that may be placed at either end of the potentiometer, see Fig.15b, to optimize its utilization range are given in the table "Electrical Characteristics For Design Guidance" shown in this bulletin.

An alternate system is shown in Fig.15c. This circuit uses only one additional resistor of approximately the value shown in the table. For potentiometers, in which the resistance does not drop to zero ohms at either end of rotation, a value of resistance 10% lower than the values shown in the table should be used.

LOW-VOLTAGE OPERATION

Operation at total supply voltages as low as 4 volts is possible with the CA3140. A current regulator based upon the PMOS threshold voltage maintains reasonable constant operating current and hence consistent performance down to these lower voltages.

The low-voltage limitation occurs when the upper extreme of the input common-mode voltage range extends down to the voltage at terminal 4. This limit is reached at a total

Fig.13 — Voltage across output transistors Q15 and Q16 vs load current.

Fig.15 — Three offset-voltage nulling methods.

supply voltage just below 4 volts. The output voltage range also begins to extend down to the negative supply rail, but is slightly higher than that of the input. Fig.20 shows these characteristics and shows that with 2-volt dual supplies, the lower extreme of the input common-mode voltage range is below ground potential.

Fig.16 — Methods of utilizing the $V_{CE}(sat)$ sinking-current capability of the CA3140 series.

BANDWIDTH AND SLEW RATE

For those cases where bandwidth reduction is desired, for example, broadband noise reduction, an external capacitor connected between terminals 1 and 8 can reduce the open-loop −3 dB bandwidth. The slew rate will, however, also be proportionally reduced by using this additional capacitor. Thus, a 20% reduction in bandwidth by this technique will also reduce the slew rate by about 20%.

Fig.17 shows the typical settling time required to reach 1 mV or 10 mV of the final value for various levels of large signal inputs for the voltage-follower and inverting unity-gain amplifiers. The exceptionally fast settling time characteristics shown in Fig.18 are largely due to the high combination of high gain and wide bandwidth of the CA3140.

Fig.17 — Input voltage vs settling time.

INPUT CIRCUIT CONSIDERATIONS

As mentioned previously, the amplifier inputs can be driven below the terminal 4 potential, but a series current-limiting re-

Courtesy RCA Solid State Division

Fig. 18 — Open-loop voltage gain and phase lag
vs frequency.

Fig. 19 — Input current vs ambient
temperature.

sistor is recommended to limit the maximum input terminal current to less than 1 mA to prevent damage to the input protection circuitry.

Moreover, some current-limiting resistance should be provided between the inverting input and the output when the CA3140 is used as a unity-gain voltage follower. This resistance prevents the possibility of extremely large input-signal transients from forcing a signal through the input-protection network and directly driving the internal constant-current source which could result in positive feedback via the output terminal. A 3.9-kΩ resistor is sufficient.

The typical input current is in the order of 10 pA when the inputs are centered at nominal device dissipation. As the output supplies load current, device dissipation will increase, raising the chip temperature and resulting in increased input current. Fig.19 shows typical input-terminal current versus ambient temperature for the CA3140.

It is well known that MOS/FET devices can exhibit slight changes in characteristics (for example, small changes in input offset voltage) due to the application of large differential input voltages that are sustained over long periods at elevated temperatures.

Both applied voltage and temperature accelerate these changes. The process is reversible and offset voltage shifts of the opposite polarity reverse the offset. Fig.14 shows the typical offset voltage change as a function of various stress voltages at the maximum rating of 125°C (for TO-5); at lower temperatures (TO-5 and plastic), for example, at 85°C, this change in voltage is considerably less. In typical linear applications, where the differential voltage is small and symmetrical, these incremental changes are of about the same magnitude as those encountered in an operational amplifier employing a bipolar a transistor input stage.

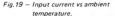

Fig. 20 — Output-voltage-swing capability and
common-mode input-voltage range
vs supply voltage and temperature.

LINEAR
INTEGRATED
CIRCUITS

TYPES TL070, TL070A, TL071, TL071A, TL071B, TL072, TL072A, TL072B, TL074, TL074A, TL074B, TL075
LOW-NOISE JFET-INPUT OPERATIONAL AMPLIFIERS

BULLETIN NO. DL-S 12640, SEPTEMBER 1978—REVISED OCTOBER 1979

20 DEVICES COVER COMMERCIAL, INDUSTRIAL, AND MILITARY TEMPERATURE RANGES

- Low Noise . . . V_n = 18 nV/$\sqrt{Hz}$ Typ
- Low Harmonic Distortion . . . 0.01% Typ
- Wide Common Mode and Differential Voltage Ranges
- Low Input Bias and Offset Currents
- Output Short-Circuit Protection

- High Input Impedance . . . JFET-Input Stage
- Internal Frequency Compensation
- Low Power Consumption
- Latch-Up-Free Operation
- High Slew Rate . . . 13 V/μs Typ

description

The JFET-input operational amplifiers of the TL071 series are designed as low-noise versions of the TL081 series amplifiers with low input bias and offset currents and fast slew rate. The low harmonic distortion and low noise make the TL071 series ideally suited as amplifiers for high-fidelity and audio preamplifier applications. Each amplifier features JFET-inputs (for high input impedance) coupled with bipolar output stages all integrated on a single monolithic chip.

Device types with an "M" suffix are characterized for operation over the full military temperature range of -55°C to 125°C, those with an "I" suffix are characterized for operation from -25°C to 85°C, and those with a "C" suffix are characterized for operation from 0°C to 70°C.

TEXAS INSTRUMENTS
INCORPORATED
POST OFFICE BOX 225012 • DALLAS, TEXAS 75265

Courtesy Texas Instruments, Inc.

TYPES TL070, TL070A, TL071, TL071A, TL071B, TL072, TL072A, TL072B, TL074, TL074A, TL074B, TL075 LOW-NOISE JFET-INPUT OPERATIONAL AMPLIFIERS

schematic (each amplifier)

absolute maximum ratings over operating free-air temperature range (unless otherwise noted)

		TL07_C	TL07_I	TL07_C TL07_AC TL07_BC	UNIT
Supply voltage, V_{CC+} (see Note 1)		18	18	18	V
Supply voltage, V_{CC-} (see Note 1)		−18	−18	−18	V
Differential input voltage (see Note 2)		±30	±30	±30	V
Input voltage (see Notes 1 and 3)		±15	±15	±15	V
Duration of output short circuit (see Note 4)		Unlimited	Unlimited	Unlimited	
Continuous total dissipation at (or below) 25°C free-air temperature (see Note 5)		680	680	680	mW
Operating free-air temperature range		−55 to 125	−25 to 85	0 to 70	°C
Storage temperature range		−65 to 150	−65 to 150	−65 to 150	°C
Lead temperature 1/16 inch (1,6 mm) from case for 60 seconds	J, JG or W package	300	300	300	°C
Lead temperature 1/16 inch (1,6 mm) from case for 10 seconds	N or P package		260	260	°C

NOTES: 1. All voltage values, except differential voltages, are with respect to the midpoint between V_{CC+} and V_{CC-}.
2. Differential voltages are at the noninverting input terminal with respect to the inverting input terminal.
3. The magnitude of the input voltage must never exceed the magnitude of the supply voltage or 15 volts, whichever is less.
4. The output may be shorted to ground or to either supply. Temperature and/or supply voltages must be limited to ensure that the dissipation rating is not exceeded.
5. For operation above 25°C, free-air temperature, refer to Dissipation Derating Table. In the J and JG packages, TL07_M chips are alloy-mounted; TL07_I, TL07_C, TL07_AC, and TL07_BC chips are glass-mounted.

DISSIPATION DERATING TABLE

PACKAGE	POWER RATING	DERATING FACTOR	ABOVE T_A
J (Alloy-Mounted Chip)	680 mW	11.0 mW/°C	88°C
J (Glass-Mounted Chip)	680 mW	8.2 mW/°C	67°C
JG (Alloy-Mounted Chip)	680 mW	8.4 mW/°C	69°C
JG (Glass-Mounted Chip)	680 mW	6.6 mW/°C	47°C
N	680 mW	9.2 mW/°C	76°C
P	680 mW	8.0 mW/°C	65°C
W	680 mW	8.0 mW/°C	65°C

Also see Dissipation Derating Curves, Section 2.

DEVICE TYPES, SUFFIX VERSIONS, AND PACKAGES

	TL070	TL071	TL072	TL074	TL075
TL07_M	JG,	JG,	JG,	J, W	*
TL07_I	JG, P	JG, P	JG, P	J, N	*
TL07_C	JG, P	JG, P	JG, P	J, N	N
TL07_AC	JG, P	JG, P	JG, P	J, N	*
TL07_BC	*	JG, P	JG, P	J, N	*

*These combinations are not defined by this data sheet.

TEXAS INSTRUMENTS
INCORPORATED

POST OFFICE BOX 225012 • DALLAS, TEXAS 75265

Courtesy Texas Instruments, Inc.

TYPES TL070, TL070A, TL071, TL071A, TL071B, TL072, TL072A, TL072B, TL074, TL074A, TL074B, TL075
LOW-NOISE JFET-INPUT OPERATIONAL AMPLIFIERS

electrical characteristics, $V_{CC\pm} = \pm 15$ V

PARAMETER	TEST CONDITIONS†	Types	TL07_M MIN	TYP	MAX	TL07_I MIN	TYP	MAX	TL07_C TL07_AC TL07_BC MIN	TYP	MAX	UNIT
V_{IO} Input offset voltage	$R_S = 50\ \Omega$, $T_A = 25°C$	'70, '71, '72, '75‡		3	6		3	6		3	10	mV
		'74		3	9		3	6		3	10	
		'70A, '71A, '72A, '74A								3	6	
		'71B, '72B, '74B								2	3	
	$R_S = 50\ \Omega$, $T_A = $ full range	'70, '71, '72, '75‡			9			9			13	
		'74			15			9			13	
		'70A, '71A, '72A, '74A									7.5	
		'71B, '72B, '74B									5	
α_{VIO} Temperature coefficient of input offset voltage	$R_S = 50\ \Omega$, $T_A = $ full range			10			10			10		$\mu V/°C$
I_{IO} Input offset current§	$T_A = 25°C$	'70, '71, '72, '74, '75‡		5	50		5	50		5	50	pA
		'70A, '71A, '72A, '74A								5	50	
		'71B, '72B, '74B								5	50	
	$T_A = $ full range	'70, '71, '72, '74, '75‡			20			10			2	nA
		'70A, '71A, '72A, '74A									2	
		'71B, '72B, '74B									2	
I_{IB} Input bias current§	$T_A = 25°C$	'70, '71, '72, '74, '75‡		30	200		30	200		30	200	pA
		'70A, '71A, '72A, '74A								30	200	
		'71B, '72B, '74B								30	200	
	$T_A = $ full range	'70, '71, '72, '74, '75‡			50			20			7	nA
		'70A, '71A, '72A, '74A									7	
		'71B, '72B, '74B									7	
V_{ICR} Common-mode input voltage range	$T_A = 25°C$	'70, '71, '72, '74, '75‡	±11	±12		±11	±12		±10	±11		V
		'70A, '71A, '72A, '74A							±11	±12		
		'71B, '72B, '74B							±11	±12		
V_{OPP} Maximum peak-to-peak output voltage swing	$T_A = 25°C$, $R_L = 10\ k\Omega$		24	27		24	27		24	27		V
	$T_A = $ full range, $R_L \geqslant 10\ k\Omega$		24			24			24			
	$R_L \geqslant 2\ k\Omega$		20	24		20	24		20	24		
A_{VD} Large-signal differential voltage amplification	$R_L \geqslant 2\ k\Omega$, $V_O = \pm 10$ V, $T_A = 25°C$	'70, '71, '72, '74, '75‡	35	200		50	200		25	200		V/mV
		'70A, '71A, '72A, '74A							50	200		
		'71B, '72B, '74B							50	200		
	$R_L \geqslant 2\ k\Omega$, $V_O = \pm 10$ V, $T_A = $ full range	'70, '71, '72, '74, '75‡	20			25			15			
		'70A, '71A, '72A, '74A							25			
		'71B, '72B, '74B							25			
B_1 Unity-gain bandwidth	$T_A = 25°C$, $R_L = 10\ k\Omega$			3			3			3		MHz
r_i Input resistance	$T_A = 25°C$			10^{12}			10^{12}			10^{12}		Ω
CMRR Common-mode rejection ratio	$R_S \leqslant 10\ k\Omega$, $T_A = 25°C$	'70, '71, '72, '74, '75‡	80	86		80	86		70	76		dB
		'70A, '71A, '72A, '74A							80	86		
		'71B, '72B, '74B							80	86		
k_{SVR} Supply voltage rejection ratio ($\Delta V_{CC\pm}/\Delta V_{IO}$)	$R_S \leqslant 10\ k\Omega$, $T_A = 25°C$	'70, '71, '72, '74, '75‡	80	86		80	86		70	76		dB
		'70A, '71A, '72A, '74A							80	86		
		'71B, '72B, '74B							80	86		
I_{CC} Supply current (per amplifier)	No load, No signal, $T_A = 25°C$			1.4	2.5		1.4	2.5		1.4	2.5	mA
V_{O1}/V_{O2} Channel separation	$A_{VD} = 100$, $T_A = 25°C$			120			120			120		dB

†All characteristics are specified under open-loop conditions unless otherwise noted. Full range for T_A is $-55°C$ to $125°C$ for TL07_M; $-25°C$ to $85°C$ for TL07_I; and $0°C$ to $70°C$ for TL07_C, TL07_AC, and TL07_BC.
‡Types TL075I and TL075M are not defined by this data sheet.
§Input bias currents of a FET-input operational amplifier are normal junction reverse currents, which are temperature sensitive as shown in Figure 18. Pulse techniques must be used that will maintain the junction temperatures as close to the ambient temperature as is possible.

TEXAS INSTRUMENTS
INCORPORATED

POST OFFICE BOX 225012 • DALLAS, TEXAS 75265

Courtesy Texas Instruments, Inc.

TYPES TL070, TL070A, TL071, TL071A, TL071B, TL072, TL072A, TL072B, TL074, TL074A, TL074B, TL075
LOW-NOISE JFET-INPUT OPERATIONAL AMPLIFIERS

operating characteristics, $V_{CC\pm} = \pm15$ V, $T_A = 25°C$

	PARAMETER	TEST CONDITIONS		TL07_M			ALL OTHERS			UNIT
				MIN	TYP	MAX	MIN	TYP	MAX	
SR	Slew rate at unit gain	$V_I = 10$ V, $C_L = 100$ pF,	$R_L = 2$ kΩ, See Figure 1	10	13			13		V/µs
t_r	Rise time	$V_I = 20$ mV,	$R_L = 2$ kΩ,		0.1			0.1		µs
	Overshoot factor	$C_L = 100$ pF,	See Figure 1		10			10		%
V_n	Equivalent input noise	$R_S = 100$ Ω	$f = 1$ kHz		18			18		nV/$\sqrt{Hz}$
	voltage		$f = 10$ Hz to 10 kHz		4			4		µV
I_n	Equivalent input noise current	$R_S = 100$ Ω,	$f = 1$ kHz		0.01			0.01		pA/$\sqrt{Hz}$
THD	Total harmonic distortion	$V_{O(rms)} = 10$ V, $R_L \geq 2$ kΩ,	$R_S \leq 1$ kΩ, $f = 1$ kHz		0.01			0.01		%

PARAMETER MEASUREMENT INFORMATION

FIGURE 1—UNITY-GAIN AMPLIFIER

FIGURE 2—GAIN-OF-10 INVERTING AMPLIFIER

FIGURE 3—FEED-FORWARD COMPENSATION

INPUT OFFSET VOLTAGE NULL CIRCUITS

FIGURE 4   FIGURE 5

TEXAS INSTRUMENTS
INCORPORATED

POST OFFICE BOX 225012 • DALLAS, TEXAS 75265

Courtesy Texas Instruments, Inc.

TYPICAL CHARACTERISTICS†

FIGURE 6   FIGURE 7   FIGURE 8

FIGURE 9   FIGURE 10   FIGURE 11

FIGURE 12   FIGURE 13   FIGURE 14

†Data at high and low temperatures are applicable only within the rated operating free-air temperature ranges of the various devices. A 18-pF compensation capacitor is used with TL070 and TL070A.

TEXAS INSTRUMENTS
INCORPORATED

POST OFFICE BOX 225012 ● DALLAS, TEXAS 75265

TYPICAL CHARACTERISTICS†

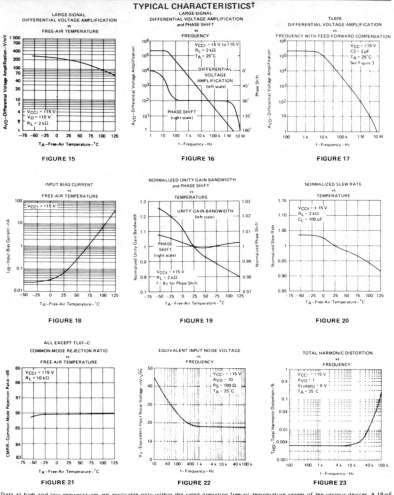

FIGURE 15

FIGURE 16

FIGURE 17

FIGURE 18

FIGURE 19

FIGURE 20

FIGURE 21

FIGURE 22

FIGURE 23

†Data at high and low temperatures are applicable only within the rated operating free-air temperature ranges of the various devices. A 18-pF compensation capacitor is used with TL070 and TL070A.

TEXAS INSTRUMENTS
INCORPORATED
POST OFFICE BOX 225012 • DALLAS, TEXAS 75265

Courtesy Texas Instruments, Inc.

TYPICAL CHARACTERISTICS†

FIGURE 24

FIGURE 25

†Data at high and low temperatures are applicable only within the rated operating free-air temperature ranges of the various devices. A 18-pF compensation capacitor is used with TL070 and TL070A.

Courtesy Texas Instruments, Inc.

National Semiconductor

SEPTEMBER 1977

LF351 Wide Bandwidth JFET Input Operational Amplifiers

BI-FET II™ Technology

General Description

The LF351 is a low cost high speed JFET input operational amplifier with an internally trimmed input offset voltage (BI-FET II™ technology). The device requires a low supply current and yet maintains a large gain bandwidth product and a fast slew rate. In addition, well matched high voltage JFET input devices provide very low input bias and offset currents. The LF351 is pin compatible with the standard LM741 and uses the same offset voltage adjustment circuitry. This feature allows designers to immediately upgrade the overall performance of existing LM741 designs.

The LF351 may be used in applications such as high speed integrators, fast D/A converters, sample-and-hold circuits and many other circuits requiring low input offset voltage, low input bias current, high input impedance, high slew rate and wide bandwidth. The device has low noise and offset voltage drift, but for applications where these requirements are critical, the LF356 is recommended. If maximum supply current is important, however, the LF351 is the better choice.

Features

- Internally trimmed offset voltage   2 mV
- Low input bias current   50 pA
- Low input noise voltage $16 \text{ nV}/\sqrt{\text{Hz}}$
- Low input noise current $0.01 \text{ pA}/\sqrt{\text{Hz}}$
- Wide gain bandwidth   4 MHz
- High slew rate   13 V/µs
- Low supply current   1.8 mA
- High input impedance $10^{12}\Omega$
- Low total harmonic distortion $A_V = 10$,   <0.02%
  $R_L = 10\text{k}$, $V_O = 20$ Vp-p, BW = 20 Hz–20 kHz
- Low 1/f noise corner   50 Hz
- Fast settling time to 0.01%   2 µs

Typical Connection

Simplified Schematic

Connection Diagrams

Metal Can Package

NC 8

BALANCE 1

INVERTING INPUT 2

NON-INVERTING INPUT 3

V⁻

V⁺

6 OUTPUT

5 BALANCE

TOP VIEW

Note. Pin 4 connected to case.

Dual-In-Line Package

BALANCE 1   8 NC

INPUT 2   7 V⁺

INPUT 3   6 OUTPUT

V⁻ 4   5 BALANCE

TOP VIEW

IM-B20M97/Printed in U.S.A.

Courtesy National Semiconductor Corp.

Absolute Maximum Ratings

Supply Voltage	±18V
Power Dissipation (Note 1)	500 mW
Operating Temperature Range	0°C to +70°C
T_j(MAX)	115°C
Differential Input Voltage	±30V
Input Voltage Range (Note 2)	±15V
Output Short Circuit Duration	Continuous
Storage Temperature Range	−65°C to +150°C
Lead Temperature (Soldering, 10 seconds)	300°C

DC Electrical Characteristics (Note 3)

SYMBOL	PARAMETER	CONDITIONS	LF351A			LF351B			LF351			UNITS
			MIN	TYP	MAX	MIN	TYP	MAX	MIN	TYP	MAX	
V_{OS}	Input Offset Voltage	$R_S = 10\,k\Omega$, $T_A = 25°C$		1	2		3	5		5	10	mV
		Over Temperature			4			7			13	mV
$\Delta V_{OS}/\Delta T$	Average TC of Input Offset Voltage	$R_S = 10\,k\Omega$		10			10			10		$\mu V/°C$
I_{OS}	Input Offset Current	$T_j = 25°C$, (Notes 3, 4)		25	50		25	100		25	100	pA
		$T_j < 70°C$			2			4			4	nA
I_B	Input Bias Current	$T_j = 25°C$, (Notes 3, 4)		50	100		50	200		50	200	pA
		$T_j \leq 70°C$			4			8			8	nA
R_{IN}	Input Resistance	$T_j = 25°C$		10^{12}			10^{12}			10^{12}		Ω
A_{VOL}	Large Signal Voltage Gain	$V_S = ±15V$, $T_A = 25°C$ $V_O = ±10V$, $R_L = 2\,k\Omega$	50	100		50	100		25	100		V/mV
		Over Temperature	25				25		15			V/mV
V_O	Output Voltage Swing	$V_S = ±15V$, $R_L = 10\,k\Omega$	±12	±13.5		±12	±13.5		±12	±13.5		V
V_{CM}	Input Common-Mode Voltage Range	$V_S = ±15V$	±11	+15 12		±11	+15 −12		±11	+15 −12		V. V
CMRR	Common-Mode Rejection Ratio	$R_S \leq 10\,k\Omega$	80	100		80	100		70	100		dB
PSRR	Supply Voltage Rejection Ratio	(Note 5)	80	100		80	100		70	100		dB
I_S	Supply Current			1.8	2.8		1.8	2.8		1.8	3.4	mA

AC Electrical Characteristics (Note 3)

SYMBOL	PARAMETER	CONDITIONS	LF351A			LF351B			LF351			UNITS
			MIN	TYP	MAX	MIN	TYP	MAX	MIN	TYP	MAX	
SR	Slew Rate	$V_S = ±15V$, $T_A = 25°C$		13			13			13		V/μs
GBW	Gain Bandwidth Product	$V_S = ±15V$, $T_A = 25°C$		4			4			4		MHz
e_n	Equivalent Input Noise Voltage	$T_A = 25°C$, $R_S = 100\Omega$, $f = 1000$ Hz		16			16			16		$nV/\sqrt{Hz}$
i_n	Equivalent Input Noise Current	$T_j = 25°C$, $f = 1000$ Hz		0.01			0.01			0.01		$pA/\sqrt{Hz}$

Note 1: For operating at elevated temperature, the device must be derated based on a thermal resistance of 150°C/W junction to ambient or 45°C/W junction to case.

Note 2: Unless otherwise specified the absolute maximum negative input voltage is equal to the negative power supply voltage.

Note 3: These specifications apply for $V_S = ±15V$ and $0°C \leq T_A \leq +70°C$. V_{OS}, I_B and I_{OS} are measured at $V_{CM} = 0$.

Note 4: The input bias currents are junction leakage currents which approximately double for every 10°C increase in the junction temperature, T_j. Due to limited production test time, the input bias currents measured are correlated to junction temperature. In normal operation the junction temperature rises above the ambient temperature as a result of internal power dissipation, P_D. $T_j = T_A + \Theta_{jA} P_D$ where Θ_{jA} is the thermal resistance from junction to ambient. Use of a heat sink is recommended if input bias current is to be kept to a minimum.

Note 5: Supply voltage rejection ratio is measured for both supply magnitudes increasing or decreasing simultaneously in accordance with common practice.

Typical Performance Characteristics

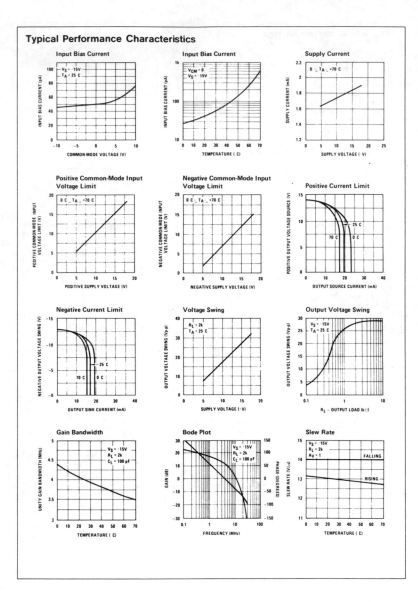

Typical Performance Characteristics (Continued)

Pulse Response

Small Signal Inverting

Small Signal Non-Inverting

Large Signal Inverting

Large Signal Non-Inverting

Current Limit ($R_L = 100\Omega$)

Application Hints

The LF351 is an op amp with an internally trimmed input offset voltage and JFET input devices (BI-FET II™). These JFETs have large reverse breakdown voltages from gate to source and drain eliminating the need for clamps across the inputs. Therefore, large differential input voltages can easily be accommodated without a large increase in input current. The maximum differential input voltage is independent of the supply voltages. However, neither of the input voltages should be allowed to exceed the negative supply as this will cause large currents to flow which can result in a destroyed unit.

Exceeding the negative common-mode limit on either input will cause a reversal of the phase to the output and force the amplifier output to the corresponding high or low state. Exceeding the negative common-mode limit on both inputs will force the amplifier output to a

Courtesy National Semiconductor Corp.

Application Hints (Continued)

high state. In neither case does a latch occur since raising the input back within the common-mode range again puts the input stage and thus the amplifier in a normal operating mode.

Exceeding the positive common-mode limit on a single input will not change the phase of the output; however, if both inputs exceed the limit, the output of the amplifier will be forced to a high state.

The amplifier will operate with a common-mode input voltage equal to the positive supply; however, the gain bandwidth and slew rate may be decreased in this condition. When the negative common-mode voltage swings to within 3V of the negative supply, an increase in input offset voltage may occur.

The LF351 is biased by a zener reference which allows normal circuit operation on ±4V power supplies. Supply voltages less than these may result in lower gain bandwidth and slew rate.

The LF351 will drive a 2 kΩ load resistance to ±10V over the full temperature range of 0°C to +70°C. If the amplifier is forced to drive heavier load currents, however, an increase in input offset voltage may occur on the negative voltage swing and finally reach an active current limit on both positive and negative swings.

Precautions should be taken to ensure that the power supply for the integrated circuit never becomes reversed in polarity or that the unit is not inadvertently installed

backwards in a socket as an unlimited current surge through the resulting forward diode within the IC could cause fusing of the internal conductors and result in a destroyed unit.

Because these amplifiers are JFET rather than MOSFET input op amps they do not require special handling.

As with most amplifiers, care should be taken with lead dress, component placement and supply decoupling in order to ensure stability. For example, resistors from the output to an input should be placed with the body close to the input to minimize "pick-up" and maximize the frequency of the feedback pole by minimizing the capacitance from the input to ground.

A feedback pole is created when the feedback around any amplifier is resistive. The parallel resistance and capacitance from the input of the device (usually the inverting input) to AC ground set the frequency of the pole. In many instances the frequency of this pole is much greater than the expected 3 dB frequency of the closed loop gain and consequently there is negligible effect on stability margin. However, if the feedback pole is less than approximately 6 times the expected 3 dB frequency a lead capacitor should be placed from the output to the input of the op amp. The value of the added capacitor should be such that the RC time constant of this capacitor and the resistance it parallels is greater than or equal to the original feedback pole time constant.

Detailed Schematic

National Semiconductor

JUNE 1977

BI-FET Technology

LF155/LF156/LF157 Monolithic JFET Input Operational Amplifiers

LF155, LF155A, LF255, LF355, LF355A, LF355B **low supply current**
LF156, LF156A, LF256, LF356, LF356A, LF356B **wide band**
LF157, LF157A, LF257, LF357, LF357A, LF357B **wide band decompensated** (AV_{MIN} = 5)

General Description

These are the first monolithic JFET input operational amplifiers to incorporate well matched, high voltage JFETs on the same chip with standard bipolar transistors (BI-FET Technology). These amplifiers feature low input bias and offset currents, low offset voltage and offset voltage drift, coupled with offset adjust which does not degrade drift or common-mode rejection. The devices are also designed for high slew rate, wide bandwidth, extremely fast settling time, low voltage and current noise and a low 1/f noise corner.

Advantages

- Replace expensive hybrid and module FET op amps
- Rugged JFETs allow blow-out free handling compared with MOSFET input devices
- Excellent for low noise applications using either high or low source impedance—very low 1/f corner
- Offset adjust does not degrade drift or common-mode rejection as in most monolithic amplifiers
- New output stage allows use of large capacitive loads (10,000 pF) without stability problems
- Internal compensation and large differential input voltage capability

Applications

- Precision high speed integrators
- Fast D/A and A/D converters
- High impedance buffers
- Wideband, low noise, low drift amplifiers
- Logarithmic amplifiers

- Photocell amplifiers
- Sample and Hold circuits

Common Features

(LF155A, LF156A, LF157A)

■ Low input bias current	30 pA
■ Low Input Offset Current	3 pA
■ High input impedance	$10^{12}\Omega$
■ Low input offset voltage	1 mV
■ Low input offset voltage temperature drift	$3\mu V/^\circ C$
■ Low input noise current	0.01 pA/$\sqrt{Hz}$
■ High common-mode rejection ratio	100 dB
■ Large dc voltage gain	106 dB

Uncommon Features

	LF155A	LF156A	LF157A (A_V = 5)*	UNITS
■ Extremely fast settling time to 0.01%	4	1.5	1.5	μs
■ Fast slew rate	5	12	50	V/μs
■ Wide gain bandwidth	2.5	5	20	MHz
■ Low input noise voltage	20	12	12	nV/$\sqrt{Hz}$

Simplified Schematic

*C = 2 pF on LF157

© 1977 National Semiconductor Corp.

IM B20M67/Printed in U.S.A.

Courtesy National Semiconductor Corp.

Absolute Maximum Ratings

	LF155A/6A/7A	LF155/6/7	LF355B/6B/7B LF255/6/7 LF355B/6B/7B	LF355A/6A/7A LF355/6/7
Supply Voltage	±22V	±22V	±22V	±18V
Power Dissipation (P_d at 25°C) and Thermal Resistance (θ_{jA}) (Note 1)				
T_{jMAX}				
(H and J Package)	150°C	150°C	115°C	115°C
(N Package)			100°C	100°C
(H Package) P_d	670 mW	670 mW	570 mW	570 mW
θ_{jA}	150°C/W	150°C/W	150°C/W	150°C/W
(J Package) P_d	670 mW	670 mW	570 mW	570 mW
θ_{jA}	140°C/W	140°C/W	140°C/W	140°C/W
(N Package) P_d			500 mW	500 mW
θ_{jA}			155°C/W	155°C/W
Differential Input Voltage	±40V	±40V	±40V	±30V
Input Voltage Range (Note 2)	±20V	±20V	±20V	±16V
Output Short Circuit Duration	Continuous	Continuous	Continuous	Continuous
Storage Temperature Range	−65°C to +150°C	−65°C to +150°C	−65°C to +150°C	−65°C to +150°C
Lead Temperature (Soldering, 10 seconds)	300°C	300°C	300°C	300°C

DC Electrical Characteristics (Note 3)

SYMBOL	PARAMETER	CONDITIONS	LF155A/6A/7A MIN	TYP	MAX	LF355A/6A/7A MIN	TYP	MAX	UNITS
V_{OS}	Input Offset Voltage	$R_S = 50\Omega$, $T_A = 25°C$		1	2		1	2	mV
		Over Temperature			2.5			2.3	mV
$\Delta V_{OS}/\Delta T$	Average TC of Input Offset Voltage	$R_S = 50\Omega$		3	5		3	5	$\mu V/°C$
$\Delta TC/\Delta V_{OS}$	Change in Average TC with V_{OS} Adjust	$R_S = 50\Omega$, (Note 4)		0.5			0.5		$\mu V/°C$ per mV
I_{OS}	Input Offset Current	$T_j = 25°C$, (Notes 3, 5)		3	10		3	10	pA
		$T_j \leq T_{HIGH}$			10			1	nA
I_B	Input Bias Current	$T_J = 25°C$, (Notes 3, 5)		30	50		30	50	pA
		$T_J \leq T_{HIGH}$			25			5	nA
R_{IN}	Input Resistance	$T_J = 25°C$		10^{12}			10^{12}		Ω
A_{VOL}	Large Signal Voltage Gain	$V_S = \pm15V$, $T_A = 25°C$ $V_O = \pm10V$, $R_L = 2k$	50	200		50	200		V/mV
		Over Temperature	25			25			V/mV
V_O	Output Voltage Swing	$V_S = \pm15V$, $R_L = 10k$	±12	±13		±12	±13		V
		$V_S = \pm15V$, $R_L = 2k$	±10	±12		±10	±12		V
V_{CM}	Input Common-Mode Voltage Range	$V_S = \pm15V$	±11	+15.1 −12		±11	+15.1 −12		V V
CMRR	Common-Mode Rejection Ratio		85	100		85	100		dB
PSRR	Supply Voltage Rejection Ratio	(Note 6)	85	100		85	100		dB

AC Electrical Characteristics $T_A = 25°C$, $V_S = \pm15V$

SYMBOL	PARAMETER	CONDITIONS	LF155A/355A MIN	TYP	MAX	LF156A/356A MIN	TYP	MAX	LF157A/357A MIN	TYP	MAX	UNITS
SR	Slew Rate	LF155A·6A; $A_V = 1$,	3	5		10	12					V/μs
		LF157A; $A_V = 5$							40	50		V/μs
GBW	Gain Bandwidth Product			2.5		4	4.5		15	20		MHz
t_s	Settling Time to 0.01%	(Note 7)		4			1.5			1.5		μs
e_n	Equivalent Input Noise Voltage	$R_S = 100\Omega$ f = 100 Hz		25			15			15		nV/$\sqrt{Hz}$
		f = 1000 Hz		25			12			12		nV/$\sqrt{Hz}$
i_n	Equivalent Input Noise Current	f = 100 Hz		0.01			0.01			0.01		pA/$\sqrt{Hz}$
		f = 1000 Hz		0.01			0.01			0.01		pA/$\sqrt{Hz}$
C_{IN}	Input Capacitance			3			3			3		pF

Courtesy National Semiconductor Corp.

DC Electrical Characteristics (Note 3)

SYMBOL	PARAMETER	CONDITIONS	LF155/6/7			LF255/6/7 LF355B/6B/7B			LF355/6/7			UNITS
			MIN	TYP	MAX	MIN	TYP	MAX	MIN	TYP	MAX	
V_{OS}	Input Offset Voltage	$R_S = 50\Omega$, $T_A = 25°C$		3	5		3	5		3	10	mV
		Over Temperature			7			6.5			13	mV
$\Delta V_{OS}/\Delta T$	Average TC of Input Offset Voltage	$R_S = 50\Omega$		5			5			5		µV/°C
$\Delta TC/\Delta V_{OS}$	Change in Average TC with V_{OS} Adjust	$R_S = 50\Omega$, (Note 4)		0.5			0.5			0.5		µV/°C per mV
I_{OS}	Input Offset Current	$T_j = 25°C$, (Notes 3, 5)		3	20		3	20		3	50	pA
		$T_j \leq T_{HIGH}$			20			1			2	nA
I_B	Input Bias Current	$T_J = 25°C$, (Notes 3, 5)		30	100		30	100		30	200	pA
		$T_J \leq T_{HIGH}$			50			5			8	nA
R_{IN}	Input Resistance	$T_J = 25°C$		10^{12}			10^{12}			10^{12}		Ω
A_{VOL}	Large Signal Voltage Gain	$V_S = \pm15V$, $T_A = 25°C$ $V_O = \pm10V$, $R_L = 2k$	50	200		50	200		25	200		V/mV
		Over Temperature	25			25			15			V/mV
V_O	Output Voltage Swing	$V_S = \pm15V$, $R_L = 10k$	±12	±13		±12	±13		±12	±13		V
		$V_S = \pm15V$, $R_L = 2k$	±10	±12		±10	±12		±10	±12		V
V_{CM}	Input Common-Mode Voltage Range	$V_S = \pm15V$	±11	+15.1 −12		±11	+15.1 −12		±10	+15.1 −12		V
CMRR	Common-Mode Rejection Ratio		85	100		85	100		80	100		dB
PSRR	Supply Voltage Rejection Ratio	(Note 6)	85	100		85	100		80	100		dB

DC Electrical Characteristics $T_A = 25°C$, $V_S = \pm15V$

PARAMETER	LF155A/155, LF255, LF355A/355B		LF355		LF156A/156, LF256/356B		LF356A/356		LF157A/157 LF257/357B		LF357A/357		UNITS
	TYP	MAX	TYP	MAX	TYP	MAX	TYP	MAX	TYP	MAX	TYP	MAX	
Supply Current	2	4	2	4	5	7	5	10	5	7	5	10	mA

AC Electrical Characteristics $T_A = 25°C$, $V_S = \pm15V$

SYMBOL	PARAMETER	CONDITIONS	LF155/255/ 355/355B	LF156/256, LF356B	LF156/256/ 356/356B	LF157/257, LF357B	LF157/257/ 357/357B	UNITS
			TYP	MIN	TYP	MIN	TYP	
SR	Slew Rate	LF155/6: $A_V = 1$, LF157: $A_V = 5$	5	7.5	12	30	50	V/µs V/µs
GBW	Gain Bandwidth Product		2.5		5		20	MHz
t_s	Settling Time to 0.01%	(Note 7)	4		1.5		1.5	µs
e_n	Equivalent Input Noise Voltage	$R_S = 100\Omega$ f = 100 Hz	25		15		15	nV/$\sqrt{Hz}$
		f = 1000 Hz	20		12		12	nV/$\sqrt{Hz}$
i_n	Equivalent Input Current Noise	f = 100 Hz	0.01		0.01		0.01	pA/$\sqrt{Hz}$
		f = 1000 Hz	0.01		0.01		0.01	pA/$\sqrt{Hz}$
C_{IN}	Input Capacitance		3		3		3	pF

Notes for Electrical Characteristics

Note 1: The maximum power dissipation for these devices must be derated at elevated temperatures and is dictated by T_{jMAX}, θ_{jA}, and the ambient temperature, T_A. The maximum available power dissipation at any temperature is $P_d = (T_{jMAX} - T_A)/\theta_{jA}$ or the 25°C P_{dMAX}, whichever is less.

Note 2: Unless otherwise specified the absolute maximum negative input voltage is equal to the negative power supply voltage.

Note 3: Unless otherwise stated, these test conditions apply:

	LF155A/6A/7A LF155/6/7	LF255/6/7	LF355A/6A/7A	LF355B/6B/7B	LF355/6/7
Supply Voltage, V_S	$\pm15V \leq V_S \leq \pm20V$	$\pm15V \leq V_S \leq \pm20V$	$\pm15V \leq V_S \leq \pm18V$	$\pm15V \leq V_S \pm20V$	$V_S = \pm15V$
T_A	$-55°C \leq T_A \leq +125°C$	$-25°C \leq T_A \leq +85°C$	$0°C \leq T_A \leq +70°C$	$0°C \leq T_A \leq +70°C$	$0°C \leq T_A \leq +70°C$
T_{HIGH}	$+125°C$	$+85°C$	$+70°C$	$+70°C$	$+70°C$

and V_{OS}, I_B and I_{OS} are measured at $V_{CM} = 0$.

Note 4: The Temperature Coefficient of the adjusted input offset voltage changes only a small amount (0.5μV/°C typically) for each mV of adjustment from its original unadjusted value. Common-mode rejection and open loop voltage gain are also unaffected by offset adjustment.

Note 5: The input bias currents are junction leakage currents which approximately double for every 10 C increase in the junction temperature, T_J. Due to limited production test time, the input bias currents measured are correlated to junction temperature. In normal operation the junction temperature rises above the ambient temperature as a result of internal power dissipation, Pd. $T_J = T_A + \theta_{jA}$ Pd where θ_{jA} is the thermal resistance from junction to ambient. Use of a heat sink is recommended if input bias current is to be kept to a minimum.

Note 6: Supply Voltage Rejection is measured for both supply magnitudes increasing or decreasing simultaneously, in accordance with common practice.

Note 7: Settling time is defined here, for a unity gain inverter connection using 2 kΩ resistors for the LF155/6. It is the time required for the error voltage (the voltage at the inverting input pin on the amplifier) to settle to within 0.01% of its final value from the time a 10V step input is applied to the inverter. For the LF157, $A_V = -5$, the feedback resistor from output to input is 2 kΩ and the output step is 10V (See Settling Time Test Circuit, page 9).

Typical DC Performance Characteristics

Curves are for LF155, LF156 and LF157 unless otherwise specified.

Typical DC Performance Characteristics (Continued)

Negative Common-Mode Input Voltage Limit

Open Loop Voltage Gain

Output Voltage Swing

Typical AC Performance Characteristics

Gain Bandwidth

Gain Bandwidth

Normalized Slew Rate

LF155 Small Signal Pulse Response, $A_V = +1$

LF156 Small Signal Pulse Response, $A_V = +1$

LF157 Small Signal Pulse Response, $A_V = +5$

LF155 Large Signal Pulse Response, $A_V = +1$

LF156 Large Signal Pulse Response, $A_V = +1$

LF157 Large Signal Pulse Response, $A_V = +5$

Courtesy National Semiconductor Corp.

Typical AC Performance Characteristics (Continued)

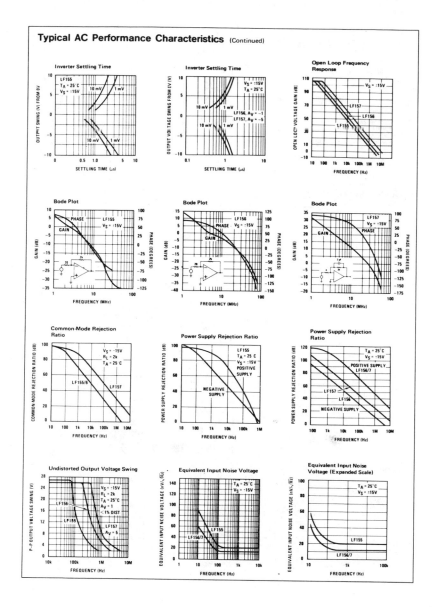

Typical AC Performance Characteristics (Continued)

Detailed Schematic

*C = 2 pF on LF157

Connection Diagrams

Metal Can Package (H)

NC
BALANCE 1
INPUT 2
INPUT 3
4
V⁻
8
7 V⁺
6 OUTPUT
5 BALANCE

Note 4: Pin 4 connected to case.
TOP VIEW

Dual-In-Line Package (N or J)

BALANCE 1
INPUT 2
INPUT 3
V⁻ 4
8 NC
7 V⁺
6 OUTPUT
5 BALANCE

TOP VIEW

Courtesy National Semiconductor Corp.

Application Hints

The LF155/6/7 series are op amps with JFET input devices. These JFETs have large reverse breakdown voltages from gate to source and drain eliminating the need for clamps across the inputs. Therefore large differential input voltages can easily be accomodated without a large increase in input current. The maximum differential input voltage is independent of the supply voltages. However, neither of the input voltages should be allowed to exceed the negative supply as this will cause large currents to flow which can result in a destroyed unit.

Exceeding the negative common-mode limit on either input will cause a reversal of the phase to the output and force the amplifier output to the corresponding high or low state. Exceeding the negative common-mode limit on both inputs will force the amplifier output to a high state. In neither case does a latch occur since raising the input back within the common-mode range again puts the input stage and thus the amplifier in a normal operating mode.

Exceeding the positive common-mode limit on a single input will not change the phase of the output however, if both inputs exceed the limit, the output of the amplifier will be forced to a high state.

These amplifiers will operate with the common-mode input voltage equal to the positive supply. In fact, the common-mode voltage can exceed the positive supply by approximately 100 mV independent of supply voltage and over the full operating temperature range. The positive supply can therefore be used as a reference on an input as, for example, in a supply current monitor and/or limiter.

Precautions should be taken to ensure that the power supply for the integrated circuit never becomes reversed

in polarity or that the unit is not inadvertently installed backwards in a socket as an unlimited current surge through the resulting forward diode within the IC could cause fusing of the internal conductors and result in a destroyed unit.

Because these amplifiers are JFET rather than MOSFET input op amps they do not require special handling.

All of the bias currents in these amplifiers are set by FET current sources. The drain currents for the amplifiers are therefore essentially independent of supply voltage.

As with most amplifiers, care should be taken with lead dress, component placement and supply decoupling in order to ensure stability. For example, resistors from the output to an input should be placed with the body close to the input to minimize "pickup" and maximize the frequency of the feedback pole by minimizing the capacitance from the input to ground.

A feedback pole is created when the feedback around any amplifier is resistive. The parallel resistance and capacitance from the input of the device (usually the inverting input) to ac ground set the frequency of the pole. In many instances the frequency of this pole is much greater than the expected 3 dB frequency of the closed loop gain and consequently there is negligible effect on stability margin. However, if the feedback pole is less than approximately six times the expected 3 dB frequency a lead capacitor should be placed from the output to the input of the op amp. The value of the added capacitor should be such that the RC time constant of this capacitor and the resistance it parallels is greater than or equal to the original feedback pole time constant.

Typical Circuit Connections

V_{OS} Adjustment

- V_{OS} is adjusted with a 25k potentiometer
- The potentiometer wiper is connected to V^+
- For potentiometers with temperature coefficient of 100 ppm/°C or less the additional drift with adjust is ≈ 0.5 μV/°C/mV of adjustment
- Typical overall drift: 5 μV/°C ±(0.5 μV/°C/mV of adj.)

Driving Capacitive Loads

*LF155/6 R = 5k
LF157 R = 1.25k

Due to a unique output stage design, these amplifiers have the ability to drive large capacitive loads and still maintain stability. $C_{L(MAX)} \cong 0.01 \ \mu F$.

Overshoot ≤ 20%

Settling time (t_s) ≅ 5 μs

LF157. A Large Power BW Amplifier

For distortion ≤ 1% and a 20 Vp-p V_{OUT} swing, power bandwidth is: 500 kHz.

Courtesy National Semiconductor Corp.

Typical Applications

Settling Time Test Circuit

- Settling time is tested with the LF155/6 connected as unity gain inverter and LF157 connected for $A_V = -5$
- FET used to isolate the probe capacitance
- Output = 10V step
- $A_V = -5$ for LF157

Large Signal Inverter Output, V_{OUT} (from Settling Time Circuit)

LF355	LF356	LF357
5V/DIV	5V/DIV	5V/DIV
2 μs/DIV	1 μs/DIV	1 μs/DIV

Low Drift Adjustable Voltage Reference

- $\Delta V_{OUT}/\Delta T = \pm 0.002\%/°C$
- All resistors and potentiometers should be wire-wound
- P1: drift adjust
- P2: V_{OUT} adjust
- Use LF155 for
  - ▲ Low I_B
  - ▲ Low drift
  - ▲ Low supply current

Courtesy National Semiconductor Corp.

Typical Applications (Continued)

Fast Logarithmic Converter

- Dynamic range: $100 \ \mu A \leq I_i \leq 1 \ mA$ (5 decades), $|V_O| = 1V/\text{decade}$
- Transient response: $3 \ \mu s$ for $\Delta I_i = 1$ decade
- C1, C2, R2, R3: added dynamic compensation
- V_{OS} adjust the LF156 to minimize quiescent error
- R_T: Tel Labs type Q81 + 0.3%/°C

$$|V_{OUT}| = \left[1 + \frac{R2}{R_T}\right] \frac{kT}{q} \ \ln V_i \left[\frac{R_r}{V_{REF} \ R_i}\right] = \log V_i \ \frac{1}{R_i \ I_r} \quad R2 = 15.7k, \ R_T = 1k, \ 0.3\%/°C \ \text{(for temperature compensation)}$$

Precision Current Monitor

- $V_O = 5 \ R1/R2 \ (V/mA \ of \ I_S)$
- R1, R2, R3: 0.1% resistors
- Use LF155 for
  - ▲ Common-mode range to supply range
  - ▲ Low I_B
  - ▲ Low V_{OS}
  - ▲ Low supply current

8-Bit D/A Converter with Symmetrical Offset Binary Operation

- R1, R2 should be matched within ±0.05%
- Full-scale response time: $3 \ \mu s$

E_O	B1	B2	B3	B4	B5	B6	B7	B8	COMMENTS
+9.920	1	1	1	1	1	1	1	1	Positive Full-Scale
+0.040	1	0	0	0	0	0	0	0	(+) Zero-Scale
−0.040	0	1	1	1	1	1	1	1	(−) Zero-Scale
−9.920	0	0	0	0	0	0	0	0	Negative Full-Scale

Index